CADRES, BUREAUCRACY, AND POLITICAL POWER IN COMMUNIST CHINA

Studies of the East Asian Institute
Columbia University

CADRES, BUREAUCRACY, AND POLITICAL POWER IN COMMUNIST CHINA

A. DOAK BARNETT

With a Contribution by
EZRA VOGEL

COLUMBIA UNIVERSITY PRESS

NEW YORK AND LONDON 1967

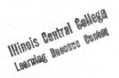

A. Doak Barnett is Professor of Government in the Department of Public Law
and Government at Columbia University.

Copyright © 1967 Columbia University Press
Library of Congress Catalog Card Number: 67-15895
Printed in the United States of America

THE EAST ASIAN INSTITUTE OF COLUMBIA UNIVERSITY

The East Asian Institute of Columbia University was established in 1949 to prepare graduate students for careers dealing with East Asia, and to aid research and publication on East Asia during the modern period. The faculty of the Institute are grateful to the Ford Foundation and the Rockefeller Foundation for their financial assistance.

This volume is sponsored by the Contemporary China Studies Program, which was organized in 1959 under the aegis of the Institute to support advanced graduate work, individual research by faculty and visiting scholars, research projects and conferences, and the publication of scholarly works on contemporary China.

The Studies of the East Asian Institute were inaugurated in 1962 to bring to a wider public the results of significant new research on modern and contemporary East Asia.

TO

J.B.B.

Preface

THE TASK of understanding how the political system in Communist China operates today is a challenging one. The sheer size of the burcaucratic structure of power, and the enormity of the problems of governing more than 700 million people, pose many questions that demand study. Moreover, in China a revolutionary totalitarian system has been superimposed on a society which already possessed a highly developed authoritarian and bureaucratic government, evolved over many centuries. The present leaders are determined not merely to maintain their power and control over the population, but also to modernize and develop the country, restructure its society, transform the nation's system of values, and in general carry out a drastic and complete revolution. What kind of political system has resulted from the amalgam of centuries-old bureaucratic traditions and the totalitarian political structures and modes of operation introduced by the Communists?

The task of understanding the political system in China today poses a special challenge, also, because of its difficulty: The leaders in Peking have attempted, with some success, to maintain strict control not only over Chinese society itself but also over the information about it which reaches the outside world. As a consequence, even though now, seventeen years after the Communists' assumption of power in China, we do know a good deal about the broad outlines of the political system—the over-all structure of political institutions, the general distribution of power, and so on—there is much that we do not know, or understand only dimly, about the actual operation of the political system—how particular institutions are organized and function; how the various elements in the system interrelate; and how the complex structures of Party and government perform day-to-day tasks, particularly at the local level where the political system comes into closest contact with the mass of the people.

Our present knowledge of government and politics in Communist China comes from a variety of sources. The bulk of what we know has been derived from painstaking analysis of material published on the China mainland. Much can be learned from such material despite the tight political control exercised over the written word, because the Chinese Communist leaders must openly publish many of their communications with both the rank-and-file members of the ruling bureaucratic elite and the mass of the Chinese population. Decisions and instructions must be disseminated and pressing problems must be widely discussed; accomplishments are publicized and the population is subjected to unrelenting exhortation and instruction. Even though the official publications used for these purposes select and slant the information they present, and even though there is a substantial margin for error in the analysis and understanding of the data they provide, a great deal can be learned through careful study of what the Chinese print for their own purposes. But there are serious limits to what can be learned in this fashion. Apart from the fact that it is difficult to interpret the information which is available, on many aspects of the political system virtually no information at all is contained in the official publications of the regime.

Visitors to Communist China are another source of some information. Although very few Americans have been allowed to visit the China mainland since 1949, there has been a substantial flow of diplomats, politicians, businessmen, newsmen, and even tourists from other non-Communist countries—European as well as Asian, African, and Latin American—who have gone to China for varying purposes and for varying periods of time. What they have seen and heard has added to the available information about Communist China, but in many respects their reports have been disappointing as a source of new knowledge and understanding. Even those well qualified both to observe and to understand what they have observed—and they constitute only a small minority of the total—have found it extremely difficult to penetrate the restrictions and barriers which make the study of a totalitarian society such as that in China extraordinarily difficult.

Emigrees from Communist China, in Hong Kong and elsewhere,

provide another important source of information about the Chinese Communist political system, a source which has been only partially utilized in any systematic fashion over the past seventeen years. Despite the great problems and pitfalls in gathering information about a society from people who, for varying motives, have cut their ties with that society, emigrees are clearly one of the most important sources—and, in some instances, the only source—of information about many of those aspects of the political system which cannot be adequately understood on the basis of the available Chinese publications. They are the principal source for the information and analyses in this book.

The aims of this book are modest, a fact which should be made clear at the start. My principal purpose is not to present general theories or a broad analysis of government and politics, but rather to provide detailed information on the organization and operation of the political system in Communist China, especially at the local level. that I, and Professor Ezra Vogel of Harvard, gathered during extended periods of intensive interviewing of Chinese emigrees in Hong Kong. The bulk of the book consists of three case studies, dealing with a ministry, a county, and a commune.

I have had a long-standing interest in Chinese government and politics, which I have attempted to study systematically and continuously for almost twenty years, first on the China mainland immediately before and during Communist takeover, then in Hong Kong for several years, and most recently through research based on the published Chinese Communist materials available in the United States. Naturally, what I have learned in the past is reflected in this book, since it helped me both to formulate the questions I asked and to evaluate the data I gathered; but the detailed information contained in this volume is derived primarily from interviews with emigrees from Communist China, conducted in 1964–1965.

Although there are hundreds of thousands of Chinese now in Hong Kong who have lived under Communist rule on the China mainland, there are many obstacles to systematic and scientific study of China based on interviews with them. For one thing, they do not by any means constitute a representative cross-section of the population in China. Even though there are emigrees from virtually every major area of the country, the majority have come from coastal areas of south China near Hong Kong. The emigrees include persons with a variety of social and occupational backgrounds, but the greatest number of them are ordinary farmers and workers who know relatively little about the political system under which they lived. There are strikingly few who have occupied high-level positions in the Chinese Communist regime—a fact that in itself is very significant—and even those who have held low-level positions in the Party or government are few and difficult to locate. Moreover, most of the emigrees from the mainland to Hong Kong have simply melded into the resident population, a fact which makes it extremely difficult for any interviewer to be systematic in selecting exactly the kind of persons he would like to interview. The sensitive political atmosphere in Hong Kong also inhibits any attempt to organize large-scale, systematic interviewing projects. Of necessity, therefore, most interviewing must be based on a sample which is extremely limited.

Soon after I started research for this book in Hong Kong in mid-1964, I decided that I would concentrate my efforts on intensive interviewing of one particular group of persons: ex-cadres[1] who had worked within either the Communist Party apparatus or the government bureaucracy in China. My aim was to interview a few such persons in great depth and then to try to piece together, as "case studies," their reconstructions of the organization and operation of the particular institutions within which they had worked.

During the course of the year I was able to locate and interview twenty ex-cadres who had worked in a variety of positions and jobs in the Chinese Communist regime. They included both former Party and Young Communist League members and non-Party cadres. Among them were persons who had worked in central, provincial, county, and commune organizations, although those who had worked at the county level and below predominated; in general they had held fairly low-level jobs. The careers of the majority had been in the coastal provinces of south China, particularly Kwangtung and

---

[1] The term "cadre," which is normally used in reference to a group of people, has been adopted, in Western writing on Communist China, as the accepted translation for the Chinese term *kan pu* and like the Chinese term it is now generally used in writing about China to refer to a single person as well as to a group. For a discussion of the meaning of the term in the context of the Chinese political system, see pp. 39ff., 188ff.

Fukien, but some had lived and worked in northeast, north, central, and south China as well.

I interviewed all these ex-cadres in Mandarin—which they all were able to use, even when it was not their native dialect. I spent many hours with each of them. The longest and most useful interviews were with the three men whose case studies form the bulk of this volume. The interviews with these three men alone took several months, during which I spent three hours a day in actual interviewing; the rest of the time was spent on ancillary research, to maximize the usefulness of the interviews, and on writing up the results. Most of the remainder of my stay in Hong Kong was devoted to similar interviewing of other ex-cadres.

Parts I, II, and III of this book describe a ministry, a county, and a commune, respectively. Although each section is based primarily on the data provided by one man about the institutions or the area in which he worked, each also reflects the totality of my interviewing, as well as a great deal of supplementary research in documentary materials, which was required to carry out the interviews and to check, to the extent possible, the reliability or plausibility of the data obtained through interviewing. It would have been reassuring to find detailed published material about these same institutions and areas, or to be able to interview other ex-cadres who had personal knowledge about them, in order to obtain direct corroboration of the information provided by my primary sources, but such concrete corroborating evidence has simply not been available. All that can be said is that for the most part the information contained in these three case studies is not only plausible but is also consistent with comparable information about other institutions and areas obtained from other ex-cadre emigrees and with the data that is obtainable from Chinese Communist written sources.

Part II, on a county, was written jointly by Professor Ezra Vogel of Harvard and myself, on the basis of interviews that we had conducted, independently, with the same man. When we discovered that we had both gathered a great deal of information about the same county, we decided that we should cross-check and combine our data. We concluded, to our satisfaction, that the material which we had separately obtained was, in general, mutually consistent and reinforcing. Professor Vogel—who has done a great deal of other interviewing of ex-cadres in Hong Kong and is currently writing a book on the government and politics of the city of Canton which should make a major contribution to our understanding of the political system in Communist China—also read and commented on the other sections of this book, and the entire book has been improved by his criticisms and suggestions, even though he obviously does not assume responsibility for any parts except the one which he wrote jointly with me.

There are many sorts of questions that can and should be raised about the reliability of information obtained in interviews with emigrees in Hong Kong. One, of course, is the question of political biases. To what extent do Chinese emigrees interviewed by Western researchers distort reality, either consciously or unconsciously, because of their political biases? The undeniable answer is that political biases do affect what emigrees report. However, after months of interviewing I became convinced that the distortion of reality was less than I had anticipated, and that there were ways of minimizing it. Only two of the ex-cadres I interviewed seemed to display the extreme biases of "professional anti-Communists." The majority of the men interviewed seemed capable of considerable objectivity in judging different aspects of the Chinese Communist regime. Actually, a number of them had broken with the regime, not primarily because they were opposed to it on philosophical or ideological grounds, but rather because they had gotten into personal difficulties of one sort or another and felt either that they had no promising future under it or, in some cases, that they were likely personally to suffer severely under it. Their decisions to come to Hong Kong appeared in many instances, therefore, to be more personal than political. With only one exception, they had had friends or relatives in Hong Kong to whom they could turn—which, of course, is not the case for most people in China.

In my interviews with them, I made clear at the start that I was not primarily interested in hearing them express their general judgments and personal feelings about the regime as a whole, but that I wanted them simply to report how organizations they had known were structured and functioned so that I could then form my own judgments. It was usually not until the final interviews with an emigree that I would question him about his own general feelings and attitudes.

Political bias is by no means the only problem that one has to face in such interviewing. It sometimes takes a considerable period of time to form any sort of judgment about the degree of reliability of information obtained from particular informants. There are in Hong Kong not a few emigrees who, for a variety of motives, are willing and even eager to fabricate information for Western interviewers, and I encountered some of them. Others are clearly well informed and reliable on some subjects, but not on others. It was essential, therefore, to design questions so that there would be numerous opportunities to cross-check the emigree's answers for internal consistency and plausibility. Such tests can help to expose unreliable data, or even fabricated information, even though they cannot fully guarantee accuracy or reliability.

Another basic problem derived from the fact that the emigrees interviewed had to rely almost wholly on their own memories, and even when they seemed to be essentially sincere in their attempt to reconstruct their past knowledge and experience, it was not always easy to judge how good their memories actually were. Here again, careful cross-checking, plus tests of internal consistency and plausibility, were essential to evaluate what they reported.

At times even the most reliable informants made errors which I discovered by cross-checking. Perhaps even more important, there seemed to be a tendency on the part of some of them first to report facts which they knew from personal experience and then to fill in additional details which seemed plausible, logical, or likely to them from their general knowledge and experience, because they were reluctant to admit that they did not know or remember certain things. It was sometimes possible to differentiate between what they knew definitely and what they thought was likely, but it would be difficult to claim that this was always possible. I became convinced in certain instances, also, that an emigree in reconstructing the organization and functioning of a particular institution was, consciously or unwittingly, drawing upon his experience in more than one place, and that what I received, therefore, was a composite picture which in a fundamental sense was based on reality but may not have been a wholly reliable and accurate picture of the single institution being discussed.

In general, though, I was impressed not only by the memories of those I interviewed, but also by the knowledge and grasp of organizational detail exhibited by the best-informed of them. Their excellent memories reflected, I believe, both the tremendous stress placed on memory of detail in the educational system in China and the desirability for any ambitious cadre working in the political hierarchy in China today to acquire detailed knowledge about the organization and operation of political instructions. I was also impressed by the fact that in some respects virtually all of these ex-cadres were amateur political sociologists, of the Marxist-Leninist variety of course, and I concluded that they had found it essential to think in such terms to operate with any hope of success in the political system.

Obviously, however, memories are fallible, particularly about details such as numbers. As the reader will discover, this study contains a great many details and numbers provided by the ex-cadres interviewed; one cannot assume they are all absolutely reliable and exact, but the figures used in this volume appear to be within the general range of what one might expect on the basis of available documentary evidence, and I believe that they do accurately reflect the general order of magnitude of the organizations described.

The three ex-cadres who served as the primary sources for Parts I, II, and III of this volume shared a highly developed awareness of organizational and political problems, but their backgrounds and experiences were varied.

The primary informant on a ministry was a man in his thirties who had been a non-Party state cadre. A native of coastal south China who came from a landlord family background and had relatives overseas, he received a university-level education under the Communist regime and then worked as a state cadre in various jobs connected with economic administration. He graduated from a specialized college in Manchuria in the mid-1950s, worked briefly in that region in a provincial department concerned with domestic economic matters, and then was transferred to work in the research institute of a ministry in Peking. In the latter 1950s he spent a period "transferred downward" [2] to a rural area in north China, where he worked both in county-level organizations and in an agricultural producers' cooperative; then he was posted to south China, where he worked in a special district and later as a teacher in a school run by a provincial department. In the early 1960s he was again "transferred downward," this time to work in a commune. He came to Hong Kong in 1962, a year in which the Communists temporarily allowed large numbers of persons to leave south China. His main reasons for leaving were first, that he felt he did not have a real future in his career in China (at one point he had applied for Communist Party membership but was turned down; at another time he was publicly criticized by the Party, in part because of his landlord family background), and second, because he wished to reestablish contact with his relatives overseas.

The primary informant on a county was a man in his late twenties who had been a Party member and had spent virtually his entire career in public security work. Born in a coastal south China province, of "middle peasant" parents, he eventually acquired a "lower middle school" education (equivalent, roughly, to junior high school). He joined the Communist guerrillas in the mountain areas of his home province just before Communist takeover, when he was still in his early teens, then spent three years in the regular People's Liberation Army, where he first joined the Communist youth organization (then called the New Democratic Youth League). Immediately after demobilization he attended a public security training school in east China, and soon thereafter he joined the Party. His entire subsequent career was in public security work in either his home province or the province adjacent to it. Although he worked briefly in a provincial department and in special district organizations, and twice attended special training schools, most of his work was in organizations at the county level, where he held a variety of posts in public security bureaus (his top bureau position was that of a section chief) and in the Party apparatus. He held a fairly wide variety of Party posts, and at different times he worked for the County Party Committee's Political and Legal Department, for several of the committee's special campaign staff offices, and in special investigatory groups; at one time

[2] See pp. 6ff. and 174ff. for a discussion of the "transfer downward" policy of the regime.

he was deputy secretary of a rural Party committee. In the early 1960s his work involved him in contacts with Macao and Hong Kong, and when he got into difficulties with his home organization he decided in 1962 to make a break and settle in Hong Kong.

The primary informant on a commune was a man in his twenties who was a Young Communist League member. He too had come from a coastal south China province. Although of "middle peasant" background, his family was fairly well off because of overseas Chinese connections. Consequently, he was able to complete higher middle school. Immediately thereafter, in the late 1950s, he became a cadre in a newly formed commune, and worked as an accountant both in the commune headquarters and in one of its brigades. Gradually he became disillusioned with the regime, largely because of the harshness of life and the general economic conditions in his home area; partly influenced by some older men in his father's generation, he decided to escape to Hong Kong. In 1964, after obtaining permission to leave his commune to visit a relative in east China, he arranged instead to go secretly by boat to Macao, from where he later moved to Hong Kong.

In the case of each of these three men, I became convinced that their experiences had enabled them to become genuinely knowledgeable about the particular institutions or areas which they discussed with me in great detail. However, I believe that even in these cases, the informants' memories were not always infallible, and that there may have been a tendency at times, in reconstructing a particular situation, to draw on a variety of past experiences—to produce what in fact may be, to some extent at least, a composite picture rather than a wholly accurate reconstruction of a particular situation. And I cannot be absolutely certain that the informants have not on occasion added to facts that they knew from personal knowledge others that they felt were plausible on the basis of their general knowledge. Moreover, since there has been no way to obtain proof of many of the details they reported to me, it has not been possible to test the accuracy and exactness of all the information that they provided. It is for this reason, as well as because of the necessity of disguising the identity of the informants, that I have presented the case studies in this volume without specifically identifying the areas or institutions that are described. Although it is impossible to vouch for every detail presented in this volume, I am confident that these studies do closely reflect reality and that they provide a great deal of important information about the political system in Communist China that is not available from other sources. In my judgment, they provide, at the very least, an extremely useful schematic picture, based on concrete reality, of the structure and functioning of the types of Party and government institutions described.

In each case study the descriptions apply essentially to a particular point in time—the period just before the informant left the institution or area involved. Although some data on earlier developments are included, no attempt is made to give a complete account, since the ex-cadres interviewed could not trace accurately and in detail all the many organizational changes that had taken place over time. Because the situation in China since 1949 has been extremely dynamic and changes have occurred almost constantly, the picture presented is inevitably incomplete.

The case studies are full of organizational details, largely because this was the kind of information that the ex-cadres were best able to report—and in research of this sort one is peculiarly the captive of one's sources; one can pose an infinite number of questions, but the answers one can obtain are limited by the mental processes as well as the memories of one's informants. I fear that some readers will feel that there is an excess of such details, and that at times the trees may be more visible than the forest. I have included the details, neverthe less, because I believe that many readers will find them interesting as well as useful, and because, to the best of my knowledge, a great many of them have not been published elsewhere. There is also some deliberate repetition in this volume; that is, certain aspects of political organization and operations are described in each of the case studies. This was felt to be desirable in order to give as complete a picture as possible in each of the case studies and also to indicate how certain aspects of the system apply at different levels.

Among the many questions I tried to explore in my discussions with all the ex-cadres I interviewed were the following: What was the structure of the organizations in which they worked? What special patterns of organization existed? What sorts of people staffed the organizations? What sorts of careers did they have? What kinds of personnel management techniques prevailed? What sorts of lives did cadres lead? What were the relations between Party and non-Party organizations and between Party and non-Party cadres? Who made decisions and where did real authority and power reside? What were the characteristics of the dominant leaders? And what sorts of relations did they have with their subordinates? What were the functions of the organizations? What sorts of relations did they have with other organizations? How did they fit into the hierarchy, or hierarchies, of power in China? What sorts of links existed with both higher and lower levels of authority? What was the pattern of communication, upward and downward? To what extent did the organizations operate on the basis of policies formulated at higher levels and to what extent did they formulate policies themselves? Did centralized authority flow downward effectively? Did lower-level bodies have any significant authority to adapt policies to local situations? What methods were used to implement policies once they had been defined? What were the strengths and weaknesses of these methods? What forms of persuasion or coercion were involved? What problems existed within the bureaucratic structure? In general, what was the pattern of relationships between the Party and government and the mass of ordinary people? What were the systems of political control and social mobilization? How great was the impact of the regime on the population?

The information obtained in my interviews throws considerable light, I believe, on these and many other questions. I also obtained information on many specific policies pursued by the regime, but such information tended to be fragmentary. I have therefore focused on the data about the structure and operation of the political system rather than on the specific policies that the regime has pursued.

Information obtained from emigree sources alone is not an adequate basis for broad generalizations about the Chinese Communist regime and political system as a whole. But I believe that the information I have gathered throws light on many aspects of the regime. This has stimulated me to reexamine some prevailing assumptions about the Chinese political system, and I cannot refrain from making some general observations on the subject. These ideas are briefly put forward, as tentative hypotheses, in Part IV.

I am deeply grateful to the organizations and individuals who have assisted me in a variety of ways as I have done the research for and writing of this book. The year in Hong Kong would not have been possible without generous grants from The Rockefeller Foundation and the United States Office of Education, as well as from Columbia University's Council for Research in the Social Sciences and Contemporary China Studies Committee. In addition to the invaluable assistance of Professor Ezra Vogel, who, as I have already stated, is co-author of Part II of the book, I have been assisted in my research by a number of people who can share credit for whatever usefulness this volume possesses, without bearing any responsibility for its faults; I would like particularly to express my appreciation to the following persons: P. J. Chang, Ch'en Chung-wen, Szu-t'u Hsiang, Eva and Richard Tiao, Wu Ling-tzu, Michel Oksenberg, Thomas Bernstein, Parris Chang, Jerome Cohen, Richard Sorich, and the staff members of the Universities Service Centre and the Union Research Institute in Hong Kong. I am also indebted to Mrs. Mary Schoch for her preparation of the manuscript and to Mrs. Michelle Kamhi for her editorial assistance.

My wife Jeanne and our three children, Katherine, Stewart, and Martha, shared the time in Hong Kong with me, and as always Jeanne assisted me in essential ways, so numerous that I will not attempt to list them.

Finally, I am indebted, of course, to the men whom I interviewed. Without their willingness to pass on their knowledge about the organization and operation of the political system in Communist China this book could not have been written.

A. Doak Barnett

March, 1966

Contents

Note on Terminology   xxx

PART I: A Central Ministry   1

Position of Ministries in the Bureaucracy   3

Central Committee Departments and Committees
and State Council Staff Offices / 4 Functional
"Systems" / 6 "General Systems" / 8 The
Ministries / 9

Organization of Ministry M   11

Top Leaders and Offices / 11 Ministry Staff Office and Staff Office for Soviet Experts / 13 Major Subdivisions of the Ministry / 14 Administrative Affairs and Business Affairs / 15 Ministry
Bureaus / 16

Party Leadership and Control   18

Central Committee and State Council in Relation
to Ministry M / 21 Party Monopoly of Leader-
ship Posts: Party Organization in the Ministry / 23
"Party Life" / 25 Recruitment and Selection of
New Party Members / 27 Party Subsidiaries:
Young Communist League, Labor Union, and
Women's Association / 29 Indoctrination: The
"Study" System / 30 Political Campaigns / 32
Party Dominance at All Levels of the Government
Bureaucracy / 35

Stratification of Status in the Bureaucracy   38

> Types of Cadres / 39   Salary and Job Grades /
> 41   Seniority: "Old Cadres" and "New Cadres"
> / 43   Other Categories of Cadres / 45

Personnel Management   48

> Personnel Bureau / 48   Personnel Dossiers / 49
> Annual and Special "Assessments" / 50   Sources
> of Personnel / 52   Advancement Opportunities
> / 54   Impersonal and Personal Factors / 56
> Raises, Promotions, and Transfers / 57   Mobility
> of Personnel / 58   "Transfer Downward" / 60
> Bureau of Supervision / 61

Patterns of Work   64

> Meetings / 64   Secrecy and Security–Conscious-
> ness / 65   Rhythm of Work: Daily and Weekly
> Patterns / 68   Plan Periods and Political Cam-
> paigns: Tension and Relaxation / 69

Channels of Authority and Patterns of Communication   71

> Downward Flow of Authority / 72   Central Au-
> thority and Local Flexibility / 74   Official Busi-
> ness Visits to and from the Ministry / 75   The
> Planning Bureau / 78   The Planning Process /
> 79   Roles of the Ministry and the Provincial De-
> partments in Planning / 82   Draft and Final Plans
> / 83   Bureau of Statistics / 85   Bureau of Fi-
> nance and Accounting / 87   In-Service Training
> and Education / 88   Research / 90   Publishing
> / 93

"Administrative Support"   95

> General Affairs Division / 96   Routine Adminis-
> trative Services / 97   Building Security and
> Ministry Transport / 98   Collective Living: Mess
> Halls and Guest Houses / 99   Collective Living:

Apartment Buildings, or Dormitories / 100   Decline of Personal Life / 102

PART II: A County   105

Position of the County in the Administrative System   107

Administrative Divisions from the Central Government to the Counties / 107   Great Administrative Regions / 111   Provinces and Equivalent
Bodies / 113   Intermediate Units Between Provinces and Counties / 115   Counties and Equivalent Bodies / 117   Characteristics of County X
/ 120   Administrative Divisions of County X
(1962) / 121   Representativeness of County X /
121

The Party in County X: Organization and Operation   123

Party Primacy / 123   Over-All Growth of the
Party / 124   Party Organization: The Party Congress / 125   Top Party Leaders: Party Committee and Standing Committee / 127   Social
Characteristics of Party Leadership / 129   Outsiders Versus Local Leaders / 133   Party Secretaries / 134   Party Committee Staff Office / 135
Special Work Group / 139   Temporary Campaign Staff Offices / 140   Campaign Approach
to Policy Implementation / 141   Total Staff of
County Party Apparatus / 143   Party Control
Committee / 144   Administrative Punishments
/ 145   Party Departments / 147   Party Organization Department / 151   Party Membership in
the County / 153   Party Committees and Branches
/ 157   "Organization Branches" / 158   Personnel Management and Control / 161   "Party Life"
/ 161   Political Study / 164   Personnel Dossiers
/ 165   Personnel Assessments / 166   Training:
Party School / 168   "Rectification" Campaigns
/ 169   Manual Labor by Cadres / 172   "Trans-

fer Downward" of Cadres / 174 Geographical Mobility of Cadres / 176 Mobility in the Bureaucracy / 177 Recruitment of New Party Members / 179 Prospects for Advancement / 181 Young Communist League / 183 Young Pioneers / 184 Mass Organizations: General Labor Union and Women's Association / 185 State Cadres on Party and Government Tables of Organization / 187 Social Stratification of the Elite / 188 Other Cadre Ranking Systems / 189 Official Ranking System: Salaries and Benefits / 190 Work Schedules / 193 Party Political and Legal Department / 194 Party Seacoast Department / 197 Party United Front Department / 198 Party Propaganda and Education Department / 200 Party Rural Work Department / 202 Party Industry and Communications Department, Finance and Trade Department / 203

The Government in County X:
Organization and Operation   205

County People's Congress / 205 County People's Council / 207 People's Political Consultative Conference / 208 County Magistrate and Deputies / 210 People's Council Staff Office / 211 Personnel Section / 213 Committee on Planning and Statistics / 214 Civil Affairs Section / 216 Labor Bureau / 217 Market Management Committee / 218 Political Control: The Political and Legal "System" / 219 Public Security Bureau / 221 Policemen / 224 Characteristics of Public Security Personnel / 227 Weapons Control / 228 Use of Violence / 228 Methods of Political Control / 229 Control over the "Five [Bad] Elements" / 231 Control over Population Movement / 233 "Social Surveys" / 234 Public Security Reports / 235 People's Procuracy /

237 People's Court / 239 Military Service Bureau / 241 Conscription / 242 Militia Forces / 244 Relations with the Regular Army / 249 United Front Work / 250 Overseas Chinese Section and Association / 251 Association of Industry and Commerce, and Office for the Reform of Private Entrepreneurs / 254 Minorities, Religious Groups, Societies, and Clans / 256 Mass Persuasion, Education, and a "New Culture" / 258 Education Bureau and School System / 260 State–Operated Middle Schools / 260 State–Operated Primary Schools / 262 "People–Operated" Middle Schools / 263 "People–Operated" Primary Schools / 264 Office for the Elimination of Illiteracy / 265 Association for the Dissemination of Science / 267 Bureau of Culture / 268 New China Bookstore and County Broadcasting Station / 269 Bureau of Health / 271 Committee for Physical Education and Sports / 274 Expansion of Economic Functions: Three Economic "Systems" / 275 Agriculture, Forestry, and Water Conservancy "System" / 276 Bureau of Agriculture / 277 Water Conservancy Bureau / 280 Bureau of Agriculture and Land Reclamation / 283 Forestry Bureau and Meteorological Station / 283 Finance and Trade "System" / 284 Food Control: Grain Bureau / 285 Finance and Tax Bureau / 290 People's Bank / 293 Management of Commerce: Bureau of Commerce / 294 Commercial Companies / 295 Supply and Marketing Cooperatives and Free Markets / 296 Industry and Communications "System" / 298 Bureau of Industry / 299 Industrial Factories / 300 Handicraft Cooperative / 304 Construction Bureau / 304 Postal and Telecommunications Bureau / 305 Communications Bureau / 306 Transportation and Navigation

Management Stations / 307   Importance of
County-Level Agencies / 308

PART III: A Commune and a Brigade   311

Recent Administrative Changes Below the County Level   313

General Trends / 314   Communes: Large Units
and Merger of Government and Collectives / 316
Evolution from the pre–1949 Period Onward /
318 Administrative Village Level / 321 Bottom
Levels / 322 Changes in One County's Initial
Communist Takeover and Reorganization / 325
Leadership at Lower Levels / 328 Beginnings of
Collectivization / 331 Big Push to Collectivi-
zation / 334 Establishment of Communes / 336

Commune C   339

General Characteristics and Evolution / 339 The
Party: Roles and Organization / 343 Top Leadership / 346 Commune Organization / 349
Functions of Various Departments / 352 Economic Functions of the Commune / 357

Production Brigade B   363

General Characteristics and Organization / 363
The Party / 367 Top Leadership / 370 Economic Functions / 372 Mass Communication and
Mass Persuasion / 379 Education and Health /
386 Political Control: The Apparatus for Coercion / 389 Control of Travel and Food / 394
Sanctions in the Control System / 399 Manipulation of Social Tensions and Conflicts / 403 The
Family and Other Social Institutions / 412

Production Teams   418

PART IV: Conclusions   425

Some Generalizations and Hypotheses / 427

Appendix 447

FIGURE 1 (Ministry M and Its Subordinate Bodies in Relation to Party and Government Hierarchies) / 449   FIGURE 2 (Organization of Ministry M) / 450   FIGURE 3 (Party Organization in Ministry M) / 451   FIGURE 4 (Major Administrative Divisions to the County Level) / 452   FIGURE 5 (Major Administrative and Collective Subunits under County A) / 453   FIGURE 6 (Structure of Leadership Organizations in Commune C) / 454   FIGURE 7 (Structure of Leadership Organizations in Brigade B) / 455   TABLE I (Functional "Systems" and Their Central Supervisory Bodies in Party and Government) / 456   TABLE II (Organization of County X) / 458

Glossary 461
Index 555

NOTE ON TERMINOLOGY USED IN THE TEXT

Political terminology in present-day China is a mixture of old and new terms. In times of revolution, the vocabulary of politics generally undergoes great change, and not surprisingly this has taken place in China during the past seventeen years. At the same time, the imprint of two thousand years of bureaucratic tradition remains strong, and not a few terms now used are inherited from the past. Because of the mixture of old and new, I decided to include in this volume, particularly for the benefit of specialists, a glossary giving the current Chinese forms for many terms, especially organizational and institutional titles. This glossary, which uses the Wade-Giles romanization system, is not intended to be a dictionary of political terminology; it includes only those Chinese terms that actually appear in the text of the book. It is hoped that the glossary will be of interest and use to readers who know the Chinese language; other readers can simply ignore the Chinese terms, both in the text and in the glossary.

Part I
A CENTRAL MINISTRY

Position of Ministries in the Bureaucracy

SEVERAL important organizational hierarchies reach from the center of national power to the local level in Communist China. All play significant roles in the political system. However, the one with ultimate authority and undisputed primacy is the Communist Party, which monopolizes the processes of policy-making. Next in importance is the government bureaucracy, which, in implementing Party-defined policies, carries the major load of administration. Knowledge of the way in which these parallel hierarchies function and interrelate is essential to any understanding of how the political system in Communist China operates today.

Under the principles of "democratic centralism," final decision-making authority is highly centralized in both the Communist Party and the government. In the Party, the Central Committee, elected by the Party Congress, is theoretically the ultimate repository of power between congress sessions. The Central Committee meets infrequently, however, and is not the most important body operationally. In practice, the Politburo and its Standing Committee, together with the Party Secretariat, run the Party organization, and the Party in turn directs all the other organizational hierarchies in the country, including the government bureaucracy.

In the government, the National People's Congress—or its Standing Committee, which functions in its name between annual sessions—is theoretically the "highest organ of state power." Operationally, however, the State Council (cabinet) and its "inner cabinet" (consisting of the premier and the deputy premiers) are in charge of the government and are immediately responsible for directing all the ministries and other administrative agencies of the central government, as well as all local governments and administrative agencies.

Central Committee Departments and Committees and State Council Staff Offices

Beneath the top-level bodies in the Party and the government there are important, though relatively little-known, subsidiary organizations that supervise the work of the vast bureaucracy which administers China. In the Party, these are—in addition to the Secretariat —the Central Committee departments and committees. In the government, they are the State Council's staff offices. Each of these departments, committees, or staff offices oversees one broad functional field of Party and/or government activities involving numerous agencies with related sorts of work.

The number of Central Committee departments and committees has varied over time. At present there are known to be ten (eight departments and two committees):[1] the Organization Department, Propaganda Department, United Front Department, Agriculture and Forestry Political Department, Industry and Communications Political Department, Finance and Trade Political Department, International Liaison Department, Higher Education Department, Women's Work Committee, and Military Affairs Committee.[2]

[1] The Party Control Committee, or Commission, is not included in this listing of functional departments and committees under the Central Committee.

[2] The Military Affairs Committee differs from the others in many respects and is a particularly powerful leadership group, but like the others it bears responsibility for activities in only one area of Party and government operations.

The Party's organs concerned with the military establishment include, in addition to the Military Affairs Committee, the powerful General Political Department, which directs the Party apparatus within military units.

In 1964–1965, the former Rural Work Department, Finance and Trade Work Department, Industrial Work Department, and Communications Work Department were converted into the three above-named political departments, ostensibly modeled on the Political Department of the People's Liberation Army.

The number of State Council staff offices, or equivalent bodies, in the government has also varied at different periods. From 1949 to 1954, there were four top-level committees comparable to the present staff offices; they covered the following fields: culture and education; finance and economics; political and legal affairs; and people's supervision. When the government was reorganized in 1954, eight staff offices were established. Although they were at first simply numbered one to eight and had no titles indicating their fields of responsibility, they were known to be in charge of political and legal affairs; culture and education; heavy industry; light industry; finance and trade; communications; agriculture, forestry, and water conservancy; and "state capitalism" (i.e., united front work, particularly as related to private entrepreneurs).[3] By the end of 1959, following a further reorganization, some of these had been merged and a new one had been added, so that six staff offices remained; they covered political and legal affairs, culture and education, industry and communications, finance and trade, agriculture and forestry, and foreign affairs. These six are still in existence today but the Staff Office for Political and Legal Affairs is now called the Staff Office for Internal Affairs.

No personnel in the Women's Work Committee have been identified since 1957, but the organization is presumed still to exist.

The Central Committee's Higher Education Department was first mentioned in 1965 and was probably newly established at that time.

Some years ago there was also a Social Affairs Department, engaged in political security work, but it is believed to have gone out of existence.

There is some basis for speculation as to whether there may now be at the Central Committee level a Political and Legal Department. None has been mentioned publicly, but a department with this label was established in the late 1950s under many, if not all, county and provincial Party Committees, whose organization in general follows that of the Central Committee; and some ex-Party cadres believe that a department with that title also exists under the Central Committee.

In a sense, one might consider the headquarters organization of the Young Communist League, the Party's subsidiary organization for youth, as comparable to a Central Committee organ such as the Women's Work Committee. At local levels, in fact, Party Committees often include a Youth Work Committee as well as a Women's Work Committee. However, the League has its own constitution and is considered to be a separate organization from the Party.

[3] Foreign Affairs were then handled directly by the Premier's Secretariat.

Only limited information is available concerning the precise roles played in the political system by the Central Committee departments and committees or the State Council staff offices. Yet to understand the organization and operation of Party and government in Communist China it is essential to examine the broad functional areas for which these top-level bodies are responsible, the chains of command of which they are a part, and the close interrelationships of Party and government in relation to these functional groupings and hierarchies.

Functional "Systems"

Politics and administration in China are conventionally analyzed primarily in terms of the principal regional layers of authority in the Party and/or government hierarchies, starting from the national level and working downward through the great administrative regions (now with Party organs only), provinces, special districts, counties, districts (now existing only in some areas), and communes (plus the component units of the communes). However, the operation of the political system as a whole can also be usefully analyzed in terms of functional "systems," each of which constitutes a distinct chain of command organized on a nationwide basis and reaching from the central authorities to the local level. In fact, there are two, and in some instances three, different types of vertical, functional chains of command which are called *hsi t'ung*, which literally means "system" (it can also be translated as "network" or "organizational sector"), by members of the bureaucracy in China.

With few exceptions, each ministry, as well as many other ministry-level organs in the central government in Peking, operates as the command headquarters for a nationwide functional "system" which includes equivalent bodies performing similar work at each level of government, from the center down to the local level. These are grouped together into what might for convenience be labeled "general systems," which include at the national level several (sometimes many) ministries, and often other agencies as well, whose work is closely related. (Occasionally, although less frequently, members of the bureaucracy use the term *hsi t'ung* to refer even to functional hierarchies whose apexes are subministry bureaus. Under some ministries there are, in fact, bureaus which head distinguishable chains of command and directly supervise, to some extent at least, equivalent bodies performing similar functions at lower levels; these might, for convenience, be called "subsystems.")

When cadres working in the Party and government bureaucracies (or at least emigree ex-cadres who have worked in them) use the term *hsi t'ung*, as they constantly do, they appear to have in mind "systems" which have the following characteristics: a distinct function or line of work; a vertical nationwide organizational structure with specialized institutions and personnel (or groupings of institutions and personnel on the basis of functional interrelationships) at each level of the administrative hierarchy into which China is divided; and distinct, centralized, special channels of authority and communication (in addition to the principal channels that go through the leading Party and government bodies at each geographical-administrative level) through which there is a direct flow of instructions from top to bottom as well as of reports from bottom to top.

These vertical functional systems are extremely important in many ways. They are important, for example, in the planning process. The annual plan of a county grain bureau normally is based more on preliminary targets passed down from the Ministry of Grain through a provincial grain department than it is on decisions emanating from the local County People's Council. (The role of the central authorities in planning has varied over time and varies a great deal from one functional field to another, however; at some periods, central ministries dealing with certain economic fields such as industry have delegated a great deal of planning authority to equivalent bodies at the provincial level.) The functional "systems" also have a significant influence on personnel policies and individual careers. For example, it appears that a cadre working in the field of education and culture, if transferred or promoted, is generally more likely to be given a new job in some agency in the same general field than in one of the others, such as political and legal affairs or industry and communications. The boundaries between systems are in no sense rigid, but they have enough reality so that cadres in both Party and government bureaucracies are constantly aware of them and in many respects think in terms of them.

"General Systems"

While there is some basis for difference of opinion as to which groupings of institutions and functions in China today are or should be regarded as "general systems," in the sense that the term is used here, it is possible to identify ten major functional areas—all supervised by specialized Central Committee and/or State Council organs —which show at least some, if not all of the characteristics noted above.[4] (See Table 1 in Appendix.)

Five of these fields—"political and legal affairs" (or "internal affairs"), "propaganda and education" (or "culture and education"), "rural work" (or "agriculture and forestry," or "agriculture, forestry, and water conservancy"), "industry and communications," and "finance and trade"—are not only referred to as "systems" by cadres, but each is supervised jointly at the national level by both Central Committee departments and State Council staff offices[5] and usually by comparable bodies at lower levels in the Party and government hierarchies.

Each of the other five fields is unique in some respects, and only one of them is regularly called a *hsi t'ung*, but all five can nevertheless be regarded as distinct functional "systems" in at least some respects. "United front work," or "Party mass work," involves many activities that consist primarily of Party work; at the same time it does involve a number of government bodies, and at one time there was a State Council staff office as well as a Central Committee department concerned with it. Cadres always refer to "united front work," or "Party mass work," as a "system." [6] "Foreign affairs," is different from the others because it operates almost entirely at the national level and is concerned basically with external rather than internal matters. Two others, "women's work" and "youth work," are atypical because they relate almost exclusively to Party work; there are

[4] As noted below, however, only six of the ten appear to be regularly referred to as *hsi t'ung* by Chinese Communist cadres.

[5] See pp. 21ff. for ex-cadres' impressions of the relationships between these bodies, and between them and the ministries.

[6] The available evidence does not make wholly clear whether "Party mass work" and "united front work" are identical in meaning, but on the basis of present information it is presumed that they are.

specialized organs and personnel dealing with these fields at all levels in the Party, but no comparable organs exist in the government. The field of "military affairs" is unique because of its special importance; in the government it is directly supervised by the highest Party and government authorities rather than through a State Council staff office, and in the Party the Military Affairs Committee is obviously different from and more important than most Central Committee departments. Nevertheless, this, too, can in some respects be regarded as a distinct functional "system."

The Ministries

The majority of government ministries (and some other central government agencies as well) fit into one or another of these "general systems," and, as stated earlier, each also constitutes the apex of a vertical "system" of its own. It is the ministries which carry the main burden of day-to-day administration at the national level.

Over the years there has been roughly a doubling of the number of central ministries and other organs of equivalent status, such as national commissions, in the Peking regime. In 1949, there were only twenty-four central organs of ministry rank; by the start of 1965 there were forty-six. Altogether, there have been over seventy different ministry-level bodies in existence at one time or other during the past seventeen years. Some of these have been totally abolished, while others are recent creations. Most are still functioning. Many changes have resulted from mergers and splits due to the growth or decline of particular functions in the political system as a whole and from the regime's continuing search for rational patterns of administrative organization. Major reorganizations have occurred periodically—in 1952, 1954, 1955, 1956, 1958, 1959, and 1965. On the surface, because of the frequency of changes, there appears to have been a fairly high degree of administrative instability at the national level, but in actuality the continuity of both functions and institutions may have been greater than it might appear, since bureaus and other sub-ministry bodies have often remained essentially intact, still performing many of their basic tasks, despite mergers or splits at the ministry level.

Since the bulk of government work at the national level is done by the ministries, a detailed examination of one ministry can reveal much of how the bureaucracy is organized and operates at the center of the Chinese Communist regime. The ministry that will be analyzed below—which will be called Ministry M—is one of roughly fifty that have existed at one time or another during the past seventeen years in the three broad functional fields, or "general systems," concerned with economic affairs. Its existence, during the second half of the 1950s, was relatively brief. But its functions did not disappear when the ministry was abolished; they were simply absorbed, together with most of the bureaus and personnel performing them, by one of the other economic ministries.

It would be difficult to argue that any single ministry in Peking is typical of the seventy-odd ministry-level bodies that have existed since 1949. No such claim is made for Ministry M. Nevertheless, Ministry M can be legitimately regarded as representative of top-level bodies in the central government, since many of its basic characteristics are shared by other organs in the central government bureaucracy.

Organization of Ministry M

Top Leaders and Offices

THE TOP LEADERS of Ministry (*pu*) M, the men who occupied the pinnacle of its bureaucratic hierarchy, were the minister (*pu chang*), two deputy ministers (*fu pu chang*), and four assistants to the minister (*pu chang chu li*). Directly under them were three special offices. One was the minister's own small, private office (*pu chang pan kung shih*), run by three personal staff secretaries (*mi shu*). Another was the Ministry Staff Office (*pan kung t'ing*), a fairly large unit and one of key importance to the functioning of the organization as a whole. Finally, there was a small, specialized Staff Office for Soviet Experts (*su lien chuan chia pan kung shih*).[7]

Also at this same level in the power hierarchy, and in close physical proximity to both the minister's office and the staff offices, were central offices of four organizations which were not, strictly speaking, part of the ministry's bureaucratic structure but were nevertheless of crucial importance in the direction and control of the ministry's personnel and work. The most important of these was the Party and League Staff Office (*tang t'uan pan kung shih*), which housed the ministry's Party Committee (*tang wei hui*, or *tang wei*, for short) and Young Communist League (YCL) Committee (*t'uan wei hui*, or *t'uan wei*, for short). Adjacent to that office were the offices of the ministry's Labor Union (*kung hui*) and Women's Association (*fu*

---

[7] Such offices existed at one time in a great many ministries; since the Sino-Soviet split they have been closed down.

nü lien ho hui, or *fu nü hui,* for short), both of which were Party-controlled and -directed mass organizations.

Ministers in Peking are obviously persons with broad responsibilities and high rank and status in the bureaucracy. Each is responsible for supervising the entire work not only of his ministry but also of its subordinate regional counterparts throughout the country; in short, as already stated, each minister heads one of the basic functional "systems" into which government work in China is divided on a nationwide basis. Except for the few who are non-Party figure-heads, most ministers possess the power and perquisites to go with such responsibility and status. In Ministry M, the minister reportedly held grade six in the twenty-four–grade salary system according to which all state cadres were paid (see pp. 40 ff. and 190 ff. for descriptions of this ranking system).

The work of the two deputy ministers in Ministry M was divided on a functional basis. One supervised all the ministry units dealing with "administrative affairs," while the other was responsible for overseeing the work of the substantive or "business" units.[8] The salary grades of the deputy ministers were seven and eight, only slightly below that of the minister. When the minister went on extended business trips (*ch'u ch'ai*), one of the deputies was normally designated to act for him (*tai li*) during his absence.

Each of the four assistants to the minister in Ministry M was responsible for over-all management (*kuan li*) of certain specific bureaus or other important subunits. They were generally regarded as able, enterprising bureaucrats who were not yet fully qualified in experience to have the status (*ti wei*) of ministers or deputy ministers but doubtless would be in time. In salary grade, there was not much difference between them (seven to nine) and the deputy ministers, and on occasion, in fact, an assistant to the minister might outrank a deputy minister in salary. In Ministry M one assistant to the minister held grade seven while one of the deputy ministers held grade eight.

[8] See below, p. 15, for clarification of this distinction; this functional division of responsibility applies to most deputy chiefs of units throughout the bureaucracy in China.

Ministry Staff Office and Staff Office for Soviet Experts

The Ministry Staff Office in Ministry M was an important service unit responsible not only for helping the minister, deputy ministers, and assistants to the minister in their work but also for performing a variety of administrative functions for the ministry as a whole. It carried a heavy work load. The director (*chu jen*) of this office was a highly experienced administrator who previously had headed several ministry bureaus and was therefore competent to handle a wide range of the routine administrative aspects of the ministry's work. Under him there were three deputy directors (*fu chu jen*) and a staff of between ten and twenty cadres—not including office boys or "general service employees" (*ch'in tsa jen yüan*). With occasional exceptions the entire staff consisted of Party members; although the work of the Ministry Staff Office was not as politically sensitive as that of certain ministry organs, such as the Personnel Bureau, it was sufficiently so that few non-Party cadres were assigned to it.

The director of the Ministry Staff Office was the custodian of the ministry's chop, or seal, and the minister's own personal chop. These chops are important, since in China all official communications must bear some sort of chop to be valid. The director and his staff also drafted many of the reports and speeches made by top ministry personnel. Incoming ministry correspondence was channeled through the staff office, where it was given a classification number and was then distributed to the appropriate bureau or other unit for action. Some of the most important ministry files—particularly those containing correspondence with higher authorities—were maintained in the staff office, although the bureaus kept much of the less important material in their own files. The staff office organized the periodic ministry staff meetings (*pu wu hui yi*) convened by the minister and his deputies, and it frequently played a major role in setting up other important meetings, such as the conferences of representatives from provincial bodies convened by the ministry's bureaus. The staff office director and his deputies were involved in much of the top-level liaison work carried out between Ministry M and other ministries. The office was also responsible for supervision of the myriad administrative activities related to housekeeping and "livelihood" (*sheng huo*) in the ministry, including building maintenance, as well as operation of the ministry's dormitories, dining halls, guest houses, schools, nurseries, sports field, laundry, and shops.

The Staff Office for Soviet Experts was a small unit, with a director, a deputy, and two other staff members. It operated under the direct supervision of the minister. It, in turn, supervised the ministry's Translation Office for Soviet Experts (*su lien chuan chia fan yi shih*), which had a staff of five interpreters and translators competent to translate either from Russian into Chinese or vice versa. These two offices were less important in Ministry M than in many other central government organs, since Ministry M had relatively few Soviet experts assigned to it. At one point, in fact, there were only three Soviet experts working in the ministry—one adviser on general policies and organizational matters and two technicians providing advice in specialized fields—and the persons assigned to help the experts outnumbered them three to one.[9]

Major Subdivisions of the Ministry

Over the years, there have been periodic changes in the pattern of subdivisions in the central ministries. At times there have been three levels: bureaus (*chü* or *szu*), divisions (*ch'u*), and sections (*k'o*). However, during periods of organizational retrenchment and simplification, these have sometimes been reduced to two: either bureaus and divisions or bureaus and sections. Even when retrenchment has resulted in a reduction of levels, however, there has generally been a tendency to reestablish a three-level system, if only in a *de facto* sense. In some cases where sections have been eliminated, moves have gradually been made to split the divisions once again into units equivalent to sections. In other cases, where divisions have been eliminated, a feeling has soon developed that the sections, because of their low

---

[9] Ministry personnel considered the Soviet experts—whose role was purely advisory, rather than operational—to be useful, but there was some resentment about their high salaries and special treatment. Reportedly, their salaries were much higher than that of the minister, and each of them was assigned a car for his individual use.

status, have been unable to perform their functions effectively; thus they have again been upgraded to division status, and then eventually redivided into subunits equivalent to sections.

There have also been changes in the labels and powers assigned to the bureau-level units. For example, these units have sometimes been called *chü* and sometimes *szu*. The distinction is not entirely clear, but the *chü* appear to have had somewhat greater independent authority. (Some ex-cadres assert that the *chü* had greater authority to issue instructions in their own name to subordinate organizations outside the ministry; others say that they had greater financial autonomy and authority.)

In addition to having a number of bureaus, most ministries have also had several other types of important subunits; these have included "independent" (i.e., not under any bureau) divisions (*ch'u*) and offices (*shih*), and special units, such as research institutes (*yen chiu so*), of roughly the same status as the bureaus.

Ministry M was divided in eighteen major units (not counting subunits) below the executive superstructure. These included fourteen bureaus, two independent divisions, one office (*shih*), and one research institute.

Administrative Affairs and Business Affairs

As mentioned earlier, the work of Ministry M was divided into two general categories: "administrative affairs (*hsing cheng shih wu*), sometimes referred to simply as "administration" (*hsing cheng*) or, most frequently, as "affairs" (*shih wu*); and "business affairs," or simply "business" (*yeh wu*). In Ministry M the former included units which dealt with matters of political control, planning, personnel, fiscal affairs, and general administration (matters concerning the operation and organization of the ministry as a whole), while the "business" units were specialized bodies which conducted the actual substantive work of the ministry. Whenever the regime has attempted, as it periodically has, to fight bureaucratism and cut down on "unessential" personnel, the tendency—or at least the aim—has been to reduce the size and functions of units dealing with "affairs" while emphasizing and strengthening those responsible for "business."

But in practice, the former are of crucial importance in the system, since they are the ones which concern themselves with the staffing, organization, and control of the bureaucracy as a whole; and attempts to cut them back appear to have had only limited success.

Ministry Bureaus

For the bulk of the work of Ministry M, the key operating organs were the bureau-level units. The bureaus, like the ministry itself, possessed organizational chops or seals (*yin chang*) which empowered them to communicate directly, in their own name, with organizations other than those under their own parent body, and they were the lowest units in the central government hierarchy which did have this authority. This meant that they could and did issue direct instructions to subordinate bodies—to equivalent units in provincial governments, for example—and while the most important communications were cleared with the Minister's office and issued in the ministry's name, many of lesser importance went out directly from the bureaus in their own name.

In Ministry M the size of the bureaus varied considerably, from a minimum of about ten persons to a maximum of sixty or seventy or more. In rough terms, bureaus in this particular ministry could be considered "small" if they had a staff of less than twenty persons, "medium-sized" if they had twenty to forty persons, and "large" if they had over forty. (In the descriptions of specific bureaus which follow, these terms will be used to indicate the approximate size of the bureaus. Figures used are estimates of actual personnel, not "tables of organization" figures.)

Every bureau-level unit was headed by a chief (*chü chang*) of relatively high rank, and in Ministry M, all except one of these chiefs were Party members. Bureau chiefs normally held grade ten, eleven, or twelve. Under them there were usually one to three deputy chiefs (*fu chü chang*), generally men holding grade twelve, thirteen, or fourteen. When the post of chief was temporarily vacant, one of the deputies might serve as acting chief, sometimes for a fairly long period, if no one was available with rank and experience sufficient to warrant his appointment as permanent chief.

Except for some very small bureaus, the bureaus in Ministry M were usually subdivided into divisions. Each of these also was headed by a chief (*ch'u chang*), usually of grade thirteen, fourteen or fifteen. Normally there was one deputy (*fu ch'u chang*), of grade fourteen, fifteen, or sixteen. Some, but not all, divisions in Ministry M were further subdivided into sections; these were headed by chiefs (*k'o chang*) of grade fifteen, sixteen or seventeen, with one deputy of grade sixteen, seventeen, or eighteen.

As the above indicates, salary grade levels for different job levels often overlapped (*chiao t'i chi*); for example, a man of grade thirteen might be either a deputy bureau-chief or a division chief.

The bulk of a bureau's staff, other than the various unit chiefs noted above, were called simply "section members" or bureau "staff members" (*k'o yüan* or *pan shih yüan*), or "ordinary cadres" (*p'u t'ung kan pu* or *yi pan kan pu*). (*Pan shih yüan* was usually applied to only the lowest-ranking cadres in a bureau, holding grades twenty-one through twenty-four.)

Party Leadership
and Control

ALL GOVERNMENT organizations in Communist China, including the
central ministries, function under very close Party direction; in fact
they operate essentially as administrative agencies performing assigned tasks on behalf of the Communist Party. The Party acts as
the primary policy-making body, while government units—containing non-Party as well as Party personnel—are responsible for implementing Party-defined policies.

Party control and leadership of government organizations are exercised in a variety of ways. First of all, the Central Committee's
departments and committees within the Party's own hierarchy in
reality form a kind of "shadow government"; as already indicated,
each department or committee is responsible for one of the broad
functional fields—or "general systems"—into which most government work falls, and it provides continuous policy guidance to all
the government agencies within that field.

Secondly, Party members monopolize the key leadership posts in
government bodies at all levels, and they are directly subject to instructions from higher Party officials as well as from government authorities. Party instructions always have primacy, since the Party is
universally recognized as the ultimate authority on policy. Large
numbers of non-Party cadres still work in the government, but the
number occupying leadership posts, in ministries or any other major
government agencies, has steadily declined. In the relatively few
cases where a non-Party cadre still holds a leading position, there is
invariably a powerful Party man directly under him, usually as dep-

uty head of the organization, who exercises—and is generally recognized as exercising—real power and authority. In many instances non-Party cadres occupying high posts are purely figureheads; there have even been cases where they were denied access to important documents and were excluded from important meetings within their own organizations. In other instances, they do perform some functions of administrative leadership but can be overruled on policy matters by Party men, even on occasion by those who are ostensibly their subordinates.

In all major central government bodies, including the ministries, another important device to ensure Party control is the "Party Fraction" (*tang tsu*, sometimes translated as "leading Party members group").[10] Each Party Fraction in a central ministry is composed of the top Party leaders within the organization (generally three to five men in a ministry); ostensibly they are elected by the regular Party hierarchy in the organization, but in Ministry M they were said to be designated by the Party's Central Committee departments (in all probability the Organization Department [*tsu chih pu*] acting jointly with the relevant functional department supervising the "general system" to which Ministry M belonged). The defined responsibility of all such fractions is to ensure that Party policies are implemented. In reality, their responsibilities are much greater than this; generally they act as the ultimate decision-making group within the ministry or other government agency in which they operate.

Another major element in the system of Party control over government agencies consists of the Party's basic committees (*tang wei*) and branches (*chih pu*), which are established within all government organizations, as within all other institutions in society where there are sufficient Party members to form Party branches. Under the Party's committee system, every Party member working for a government agency must belong to a Party branch within that agency, and these are led by Party committees especially created for government bodies. Within these Party organizations, all members live a disciplined "Party life" (*tang ti sheng huo*) which, among other things, subjects them to a chain of command different from that of

10 These "fractions" also exist in provincial governments and in some special district governmental agencies.

non-Party cadres and ensures that they maintain their separateness and integrity as an elite group distinct from ordinary cadres. Major policies often are transmitted to Party members in the government through the Party chain of command before they are disseminated to non-Party cadres through the regular channels of the government.

Party control is reinforced, also, by the Party-directed mass organizations that exist within all government agencies, from the central government to the county level. These mass organizations—the Young Communist League (*ch'ing nien t'uan*), the Labor Union (*kung hui*), and the Women's Association (*fu nü lien ho hui*)—act as "transmission belts" between the Party and non-Party cadres in government agencies. The YCL, composed of young cadres who are potential recruits for the Party, is particularly important; in fact its members are for all practical purposes directly subject to Party discipline.

The Party also exercises continuous political influence on all cadres in the government through the political "study" (*hsüeh hsi*) sessions which non-Party as well as Party cadres must attend. All government employees are organized into small groups which meet regularly for study within their government units. These indoctrination groups are directly managed by the Party hierarchy, which determines the subjects and materials to be studied.

The Party's control is further enhanced by its monopoly of posts in certain key control and "watchdog" units within government organizations. These include the personnel (*jen shih*) units, major staff offices (*pan kung shih*), and, when they existed, the supervision (*chien ch'a*) units—all of which operate with a relatively high degree of secrecy and wield great power. In many respects the most important of these, in terms of Party control, are doubtless the personnel units. Control over personnel policies and assignments are obviously crucial in any large bureaucratic hierarchy. In the government in China virtually all personnel units are staffed entirely by Party men, and in effect they act as extensions into the government structure of the Party's organization departments, which have the power of ultimate decision about government personnel, including both non-Party and Party cadres.

In Ministry M all these mechanisms were present and ensured effective Party leadership and control.

Central Committee and State Council
in Relation to Ministry M

Two organizations—one government unit and one Party organ—provided over-all leadership, guidance, and coordination for the "general system" to which Ministry M, along with five other central ministries, belonged. One was a State Council staff office (*pan kung shih*), which was one of the eight such offices existing at that time; the other was a department (*pu*) of the Party's Central Committee, one of the eight known Central Committee departments operating at the time. As already stated, very little has been publicly revealed about the operation of these bodies, and almost no emigree ex-cadres are persons of sufficient rank to have had very much direct, personal knowledge of their operations. However, some ex-cadres have had at least minimal contact with them, and, at present, the impressions and opinions of these men provide virtually the only basis for judgments about them.

The State Council staff office giving guidance to Ministry M was headed by a member of the Party Politburo who was also a deputy premier (*fu tsung li*) and concurrently headed one of the ministries within the "general system" coordinated by his staff office. This man was clearly the most influential single person in both the Party and government hierarchies dealing with this general field of government operations. He was said to spend the majority of his time in the staff office rather than in his ministry office. The role of his staff office was that of providing general supervision, guidance, and leadership to all the ministries within its jurisdiction, but apparently—according to ex-cadres who worked in the ministries—it did not exercise direct "line control" over them. This kind of control reportedly rested with the State Council itself, in theory (although, in practice, often with the Party Central Committee). However, the ministries are said to have sent regular and frequent reports to the State Council staff office concerning all of their normal day-to-day operations.

The Party department that concerned itself with the same government bodies as those supervised by this State Council staff office was headed by a Central Committee member. Another Central Committee member was one of his deputies. This deputy also headed one of the government ministries and was concurrently a member of the State Council staff office. Thus an interlocking directorship was created which linked government and Party in a way that is common in the Chinese system.

An ex-cadre who had opportunities to visit this department estimates that it had a staff of between one and two hundred persons— which was said to be larger than the size of the corresponding State Council staff office—and was divided into at least three main units: one for general affairs (*tsung wu*), which dealt with a wide range of administrative matters; one for personnel (*jen shih*), which reportedly had final control over assignments of both Party and non-Party cadres in all organizations within the "general system" under its jurisdiction; and one for "business" (*yeh wu*), which was responsible for providing guidance to the ministries on major substantive policy matters. While some persons working in these divisions, especially in the one concerned with "business," had specialized or technical experience and competence relevant to their work (a number had been drawn, for example, from the ministries and the provincial departments), others were said to be simply dependable Party "organization men."

While in theory the department's main responsibility was to ensure that Party policies were implemented by the government ministries, in practice it was apparently an important policy-making body—at least it was so regarded by cadres in the ministries. In fact, even though its top man was clearly of lower rank in the Party hierarchy than the head of the State Council staff office, the department, rightly or wrongly, was viewed by at least some cadres in the ministries as more important than the staff office in providing policy direction to the ministries.

The ministries had frequent contact with, and regularly reported to, the department as well as the staff office. The department was said to convene frequent meetings of ministers and/or their deputies to discuss plans and policies; and direct contacts were also maintained between ministry bureaus and the department's divisions (whose chiefs, incidentally, outranked the ministry bureau chiefs). Personnel matters were a major concern of the department, which, in collaboration with the Party's Organization Department, was said to make the decisions regarding all assignments to government posts of the level of bureau chief and above—although personnel actions for government posts were formally processed through the government's own channels and were publicly announced by the government. Along with many other government bodies, including government planning agencies, the department apparently participated actively in the process of formulating annual plans; and reportedly its approval was necessary before the ministries' plans could be finally adopted. Once plans had been adopted, the department continuously checked on their implementation and on the general performance of the ministries. It was also said that the department played a significant role in mediating interagency complaints and disputes.

It is not wholly clear what sorts of relationships or division of responsibilities and functions existed between the State Council staff office and the Central Committee department. Obviously, both were very powerful bodies. Both, moreover, ensured close Party direction of the government ministries, since high-ranking Party leaders headed the staff office as well as the Party department. Neither, of course, made the most important policy decisions; these were made either in the Party's Politburo (*cheng chih chü*) or its Standing Committee (*ch'ang wu wei yüan hui*),[11] or in the State Council (*kuo wu yüan*) or its "inner cabinet," which was composed entirely of Party Central Committee men. However, both the staff office and the Party department obviously kept in close touch with the ministries and through continuous supervision ensured that the Party's major policies were effectively implemented.

Party Monopoly of Leadership Posts: Party Organization in the Ministry

The monopoly of leadership posts by Party members was virtually complete in Ministry M. Not only were the minister, the deputy ministers, and the assistants to the minister all Party men, but, as already stated, every bureau except one was headed by a Party mem-

---

[11] In practice the Party Secretariat doubtless also plays an important role in policy-making, even though it is not considered to be, strictly speaking, a policy-making body.

ber, as were the overwhelming majority of subordinate divisions and sections.

The Party Fraction in Ministry M consisted of five men, all of whom were also, as would be expected, leading members of the ministry's Party Committee. The minister headed the Party Fraction; and the other four members were the two deputy ministers and two of the four assistants to the minister. One of the assistants to the minister, rather than the minister himself, was secretary (*shu chi*) of the Party Committee. The Party Fraction was said to be the real center of power and authority in the ministry, more important even than the Party Committee, and it was believed to meet very frequently. Low-ranking members of the ministry knew little about how it actually operated, but they were fully aware of its existence, its membership, and its power.

Of the personnel working in Ministry M—who totaled slightly over one thousand cadres—roughly a third were Party members (*tang yüan*). All of them belonged to basic Party branches (*tang chih pu*), which were grouped into general branches (*tsung chih pu*), and were under the leadership of the Party Committee (*tang wei*), organized for the ministry as a whole. This committee, elected by its constituent units, was headed by a secretary (*shu chi*) and several deputies (*fu shu chi*); in addition, it had a number of committeemen (*wei yüan*) with special functions, of which those for organization (*tsu chih*), propaganda (*hsüan ch'uan*), united front (*t'ung chan*) work, youth (*ch'ing nien*) and women (*fu nü*) were most important. At each level the general membership elected a secretary and other functionaries, and from the branches upward, representatives were elected by each unit to the next higher level. The choice of secretaries had to be approved at the next higher level, however, and in practice higher-level units frequently designated the persons whom they wished to be selected as secretaries of subordinate units.

There was a Party branch in every bureau or other unit of equivalent rank in the ministry, and each general branch covered several bureaus. Each of the Party branches and general branches was, like the Party Committee, headed by a secretary plus one or more deputies, and also had certain designated committeemen responsible for particular aspects of its work. Although the branches were considered to be the "basic" units in the hierarchy, most of them were subdivided into "cells," or small groups (*hsiao tsu*), corresponding to the subunits under bureaus.

The Party Committee's office was located next to the ministry's Personnel Bureau, and these two organizations, both of whose work was generally highly classified, worked closely together. There was, in fact, an important overlap of personnel between them, and one of the deputy Party secretaries headed the Personnel Bureau.

Party organizations in the ministry had a variety of important functions and responsibilities. First of all, they were responsible for the thought and behavior of all Party members—for ensuring their loyalty and discipline, supervising their participation in regular "Party life," disseminating Party instructions to them, punishing those who deviated from Party-defined norms, and recruiting, screening, and indoctrinating new recruits. They were also responsible for organizing, leading, and indoctrinating all non-Party cadres, through the mass organizations and study groups directed by the Party. At all times, the Party organizations were expected to guarantee that the ministry effectively implemented the basic policies and programs defined by higher authorities; and within the ministry, Party leaders dominated all important decision-making. During major political campaigns, moreover, the Party organs in effect took over direct control of the activities of all ministry personnel. Generally, during such campaigns the ministry's Party Committee, in collaboration with the Personnel Bureau, established a Party campaign staff office (called X *yün tung pan kung shih*) to manage the campaign. Since, during these campaigns, study meetings, "struggle meetings," and various other types of propaganda, indoctrination, and mobilizational activity took precedence over the routine activities of ministry personnel, the Party Committee temporarily became the real command headquarters within the ministry.

"Party Life"

All Party members within the ministry were required to participate actively in collective "Party life" or "organizational life" (*tang ti sheng huo* or *tsu chih sheng huo*) within the basic Party branches to which they belonged. This included regular payment of dues and attendance at weekly branch meetings. Dues amounting to about 1 percent of one's salary were collected monthly by the heads of Party "cells" or by the branch secretaries and were forwarded to the Party Committee. Those who failed to pay on time were subjected to group criticism and pressure; and delinquency for six months resulted in expulsion from the Party. Attendance at Party branch meetings was equally important. All Party branches in the ministry met every Friday evening, normally from 7:00 to 9:00 P.M. Absence from these meetings, like failure to pay dues, was severely criticized and, if continued for six months, resulted in expulsion from the Party. Periodic "Party classes" (*tang k'o*) were also organized by the Party Committee; in Ministry M these were usually open to non-Party members, and one of their functions was to indoctrinate persons aspiring to Party membership.

"Party life" meetings served a variety of purposes. In them instructions and information from higher Party authorities were periodically disseminated to all rank-and-file members; and there was regular discussion of current policies and programs. There was also regular criticism (*p'i p'ing*) and self-criticism (*chien t'ao*) of all Party members' work. A portion of time during each meeting was also generally devoted to systematic indoctrination, including political "study" (*hsüeh hsi*). Directives and materials for study in these Party meetings came from higher Party authorities. Basic directives were believed to originate in the Central Committee's Propaganda Department; from there they came down through the hierarchy to the propaganda committeeman of the ministry's Party Committee, who in turn disseminated them to the Party branches. Some of the material for study consisted simply of specified editorials or articles in major Party journals, such as the *People's Daily* (*jen min jih pao*) or the *Red Flag* (*hung ch'i*). Some, however, was specially prepared, classified material. Party members were expected to maintain strict secrecy about what took place in their branch meetings, and they therefore avoided discussing them with non-Party cadres. This fact tended to highlight the distinction between, and maintain a certain separation of, Party and non-Party personnel in the ministry.

Recruitment and Selection
of New Party Members

Although over the years there was a steady increase in the percentage of Party members in the central ministries, the Party Committee in Ministry M, as in most ministries, maintained tight control over recruitment policies. It was by no means easy to join the Party. There were always, however, a substantial number of ambitious activists, especially young people belonging to the YCL, who were eager to join, some because of genuine idealism and others because of the rewards in terms of prestige, power, and advancement opportunities which Party membership almost automatically conferred. These young activists were among the most energetic and enthusiastic cadres in the entire ministry, often outperforming established Party members in their attempt to prove their eligibility for Party membership. The Party consciously encouraged their activism, but in finally deciding whom to admit to the Party, it was extremely selective and restrictive, so much so, in fact, that some ambitious young non-Party cadres privately grumbled and accused Party members of being preoccupied mainly with a desire to protect their power and privileges as the dominant in-group.

A person wishing to join the Party first applied to the Party Branch within his bureau, submitting a lengthy application (*ju tang shen ch'ing shu*), with two endorsements by Party members, which summarized his personal history and his reasons for desiring to join the Party. If, after a preliminary investigation of the applicant's personnel dossier (*tang an*), filed in the ministry's Personnel Bureau, the Party concluded that the application might be seriously considered, the branch secretly assigned a Party member to "cultivate" (*p'ei yang*) him. This investigator attempted unobtrusively to get to know the applicant as well as possible and to learn all about his attitudes and work as well as his personal history, patterns of friendship, and way of life. If the investigator's report was favorable, the Party Branch then discussed the applicant and decided tentatively to approve or disapprove. Those tentatively approved by the branch were then discussed by both a general branch and the Party Committee. If both these groups also tentatively approved, the branch then convened a special meeting in the bureau, at which the applicant was asked to present his case for Party membership orally, and then his qualifications were discussed by all those present. In Ministry M, interestingly, non-Party activists were sometimes invited to attend these meetings, perhaps because they might add to knowledge about the applicant, perhaps to be educated about the Party. If the consensus at such a meeting favored admission, the applicant then became a candidate member. If, however, he was extensively criticized in the meeting, he was told to improve himself and try again later; sometimes persons tried two or three times before finally being accepted.

A few applicants were said to be admitted under a somewhat simplified procedure that was referred to as "secret admission" (*mi mi ju tang*). Reportedly, children or other relatives of ranking Party members, and persons who had developed a close relationship with key Party leaders in the ministry, such as the Party secretary, were virtually the only persons so admitted.

The Party hierarchy in the ministry was responsible for disciplining its own members; and branches, with Committee approval, could inflict a range of administrative punishments on errant members. One of the most dreaded punishments was expulsion from the Party, since in a society totally dominated by the Party this meant, in effect, ostracism by the power elite, and it condemned a person to suspicion and lowly status throughout his subsequent career.

As already indicated, all Party members in Ministry M were in effect set apart from non-Party cadres as a special elite and really operated in a dual capacity—both as Party members *and* as ministry staff members. The authority and primacy of Party members were acknowledged at every level in the ministry. Non-Party cadres in every bureau, division, and section normally deferred to Party members because they all realized that in the final analysis the Party's will would prevail and that Party members had a special pipeline from and to higher authorities through their Party meetings. Non-Party cadres also realized that their own lives and careers depended, fundamentally, upon their relations with Party members in their own units, since the views of higher authorities (including the Personnel Bureau) about them would depend largely on the reports made by Party members concerning their attitudes and behavior. In many basic units—i.e. the divisions and sections—the subordination of non-

Party cadres was underlined by the requirement that they make periodic oral reports on their "ideological state of mind" (*szu hsiang hui pao*, literally, "report on one's thought") to the head of the head of the Party organization within their unit.

Party Subsidiaries: Young Communist League, Labor Union, and Women's Association

Party direction of non-Party cadres in the ministry was exercised to a degree, as already stated, through three subsidiary mass organizations. The most important of these was the Young Communist League (YCL), a youth organization that was mainly for persons between the ages of fourteen or fifteen[12] and twenty-five, although it contained a good many members who were overage, including its top leaders. In Ministry M, the secretary of the YCL was a member of the Party Committee (its youth committeeman) who concurrently worked in the ministry's Personnel Bureau; the deputy secretaries, however, were younger men. Formally elected by the YCL's membership in the ministry, the top leaders in the YCL Committee were actually designated by the Party Committee. The hierarchy under them paralleled that of the Party, with YCL general branches, branches, and small groups reaching down to the lowest units in the ministry.

All YCL units, like Party units, held "League life" (*t'uan ti sheng huo*) meetings every Friday evening; there were also periodic "League classes" (*t'uan k'o*). And YCL members paid the same dues (about 1 percent of salary) as Party members. The YCL operated simply as an extension of the Party, concentrating on young people in the ministry, and it was responsible for assisting the Party in all of its work. It also served as a preliminary screening organization for potential Party recruits, and a high percentage of new Party members were drawn from its ranks.

The Labor Union (*kung hui*) in Ministry M was also a Party-created and -directed organization, but it was more loosely organized and less important. It was headed by a chairman (*chu hsi*), a deputy

[12] Before 1957, the lower age limit was fourteen; in 1957, it was changed to fifteen.

chairman (*fu chu hsi*), and several committeemen responsible for special fields such as welfare (*fu li*) and culture and sports (*wen t'i*). These were part-time positions held by persons with regular ministry jobs. All the union's leadership and functionary posts were held by Party members.[13] The union was not particularly active in Ministry M, however (or reputedly, in some other ministries either). Membership, which was open to both Party and non-Party members, was voluntary. Most employees of the ministry joined, even though this involved payment of dues (1 percent of salary), because the union administered certain important welfare programs, including labor insurance, and provided some recreational facilities and educational programs. It organized biweekly film showings, for example, as well as special annual outings. Every Wednesday evening, normally from 7:00 to 9:00 P.M., there was a union "life and self-criticism meeting" (*sheng huo chien t'ao hui*), but attendance was fairly irregular; many Party members, in particular, missed a great many of these meetings. In short, the labor union was not a center of power or influence in any way comparable to the Party, although it did perform some useful functions under Party direction.

The third Party-directed mass organization, the Women's Association (*fu nü lien ho hui*), was even more loosely organized. In some respects, actually, it was little more than a paper organization in Ministry M. Like the Labor Union it was led by Party members employed in the ministry. Its special responsibility was to implement programs specifically relating to women, but like all mass organizations it was also expected to give general support to the Party in carrying out all policies. In this particular ministry, however, its activities were not extensive and it was relatively unimportant.

Indoctrination: The "Study" System

One of the most important instruments for Party leadership and control over all personnel in Ministry M—as in virtually all institutions in Communist China today—was a system of regular indoctrination labeled "theoretical study" (*li lun hsüeh hsi*). One half-day every

[13] At times labor unions in government agencies have been headed by non-Party members.

week, Saturday afternoon, was set aside for this directed study, in which all Party and non-Party cadres had to participate. The aim was both to educate all cadres in a positive sense and to exercise tight ideological control over them.

The ministry's Party Committee, and most particularly its propaganda committeeman, was responsible for directing the program of study; but it obtained the collaboration of the Personnel Bureau in organizing the entire staff of the ministry into small groups, and instructions and materials for study were issued through the bureau. The study groups, each with a designated head, generally consisted of ten to twenty persons, and they contained both Party and non-Party cadres. Sometimes they were established on the basis of the sections and divisions in which the cadres worked. At other times, however, persons were specially assigned to study groups by the Personnel Bureau on the basis of their educational level and ideological sophistication. In Ministry M, there were three levels of groups—referred to simply as higher, middle, and lower—with different study programs for each. The higher-level groups, composed almost entirely of college graduates, dealt with fairly advanced questions of Marxist-Leninist theory; the middle-level ones placed more stress on specific political and economic policies and problems; and the lower-level groups concentrated on subjects such as the history of the Communist movement in China. In Ministry M, some special groups were also established for cadres of the rank of division chief and above, regardless of their educational or ideological level; one explanation given for this by ex-cadres was the belief that some of the poorly educated "old cadres," who held many leading posts in the ministry, might have been embarrassed if they had been mixed with ordinary cadres whose grasp of ideological problems exceeded theirs. However, section chiefs apparently were always assigned to regular study groups along with ordinary cadres.

As was true in the case of political study in the Party branches, materials for these general study groups included both designated Party publications and other specially prepared and mimeographed materials provided by the Party Committee and the Personnel Bureau. Periodic lectures were organized, but small group discussion, including criticism and self-criticism, was considered to be the most important element in the study process, and Party and YCL members, as well as activists hoping to join the Party, invariably played leading roles in it. Active participation was expected of everyone, though, and persons showing lack of interest risked exposure to organized group criticism. Over time, however, this group indoctrination process tended, perhaps not surprisingly, to become routinized. During certain periods group discussion was irregular, and a substantial amount of time was allotted to self-study, during which individuals could simply read designated materials at their own desks. The process became routinized, also, in the sense that many ordinary cadres who had participated for years in such study found it increasingly dull and boring, and in periods of comparative political relaxation, when the general level of tension in China dropped, they sometimes simply went through the proper motions, without devoting serious attention to it. However, although political study could become somewhat routinized during periods of relaxation, such periods never lasted for long, and when the regime promoted one of its major political campaigns, as it did at fairly regular intervals, the indoctrination of cadres in the entire bureaucracy was greatly intensified and had to be taken seriously by all cadres.

The Party Committee, as part of its general propaganda program within the ministry, also ran a regular "wall newspaper," focusing on internal news and information. It was a handwritten paper, posted periodically on a large board near the ministry's main entrance. And during campaigns the walls of the ministry were plastered with posters and "large-character newspapers" (ta tzu pao) written by ministry personnel.

Political Campaigns

The importance of major political campaigns in China can hardly be overstated, in terms of their effects on the bureaucracy as well as on relations between the regime and the population as a whole. Both the cumulative effects of past campaigns and the conscious or unconscious anticipation of future campaigns have helped to create the special psychological milieu in which members of the bureaucracy operate.

Over the years, national political campaigns have occurred at frequent intervals. Some "rectification" (*cheng feng*) campaigns have been aimed primarily at cadres in the Party and government bureaucracies, and have been designed to tighten discipline as well as to combat bureaucratization and various sorts of "bourgeois" or other undesirable influences which the regime's top leaders regard as corrosive and subversive. Other campaigns have been massive, nationwide, Party-directed struggles against designated class enemies (e.g. landlords, capitalists, counterrevolutionaries). Even though the major targets of these campaigns have been groups outside the bureaucracy, the cadres have been affected in many ways. Not only have the cadres been fully mobilized to participate in these campaigns, but, because many, if not most, have themselves had connections with the target groups, they have been affected by actual or potential "guilt by association." Consequently each campaign has been a period in which the cadres' loyalty to the regime has been tested, and all cadres have been pressured to cleanse and purify themselves of subversive "feudal" or "bourgeois" influences of the past.

Every major campaign has involved enormous organizational activity, and has introduced a period of apprehension, anxiety, and tension within the bureaucracy as well as throughout society as a whole. Generally, within the bureaucracy, political study has been dramatically increased until, at the peak of such a campaign, normal work has come virtually to a halt while everyone has devoted almost full time for weeks—and sometimes months—to endless group discussion, usually culminating in tense, emotional "struggle meetings" (*tou cheng hui*).

In Ministry M, special *ad hoc* leadership organizations were established by both the Party Committee and the Personnel Bureau to manage each major campaign. In one major campaign, for example, the Party unit responsible for organizing all campaign activities consisted of five men and was popularly referred to as the "Five-Man Small Group" (*wu jen hsiao tsu*). Under its direction, the Personnel Bureau set up a special campaign staff office (X *yün tung pan kung shih*) which was also composed wholly of Party members. Both of these organizations devoted full time to organizing and directing propaganda meetings, large lectures, small group sessions, and "struggle meetings."

In many campaigns, special campaign indoctrination meetings

slowly increased until they occupied about half time, and finally full time for perhaps a month or two. As a campaign progressed, emphasis shifted from fairly generalized propaganda and indoctrination to increasingly emotional discussions in which everyone had to engage in criticism and self-criticism. Finally, a climax was reached when a number of specific cadres were singled out and made the targets of mass public denunciation within the ministry in huge "struggle meetings." In major political campaigns there had to be specific human targets to "struggle" against; errors and evils, as well as virtues, had to be personified.

These "struggle meetings," as described by ex-cadres from central ministries who have participated in them, are psychologically unnerving, even terrifying, experiences for all who take part, whether as targets of abuse or simply as observers. They are carefully planned and directed by Party personnel, and the hapless victims are pilloried with torrents of abuse in a succession of public meetings that may last several days. The victims must stand with bowed heads while accusations are shouted at them; and in contrast to some other types of criticism meetings, such as "debate meetings" (*pien lun hui*), they cannot speak in self-defense except when specifically instructed to do so by the Party leaders directing the meetings. The charges made in these accusation meetings generally include ones to which large numbers of cadres in the audience may feel vulnerable—e.g. charges of having a politically tainted past or of holding wrong general attitudes—and consequently it is fairly easy for many cadres to identify themselves secretly with the victims. Those who do so often feel under the greatest compulsion to join publicly in the denunciations, fearing that failure to do so might suggest that they secretly sympathize with the persons under attack.

The effects of these campaigns within the bureaucracy are subtle and far-reaching. By dramatically demonstrating the Party's power to determine the fate of every cadre, and by clearly defining attitudes and behavior that are unacceptable to the Party, they create strong incentives for all cadres to submit to the Party's authority in order to minimize the risks of being singled out for punishment. Ex-cadres assert that even in periods of relaxation, all cadres consciously or unconsciously anticipate the recurrence of political campaigns in the future. Non-Party cadres, in particular, feel that they are under continuous scrutiny by the Party members in their organization and that any tendency to challenge the Party's authority, or even any clash of personality with ordinary Party members, may make them vulnerable to political attack in some future campaign. This strongly reinforces the tendencies of most non-Party cadres to be deferential and responsive to the opinions of Party members and clearly strengthens the authority of the Party.

Party Dominance at All Levels of the Government Bureaucracy

Party dominance of the government bureaucracy operates not only at the upper levels of leadership in the hierarchy; it also reaches effectively to the lowest levels of the bureaucracy. The situation in one relatively small division of a ministry may serve as an illustration of this fact.

The division in question had a staff of ten. Three of the staff members, including the division chief, were Party members; and two others belonged to the YCL. The chief, a woman, was the wife of a high-ranking Party leader, and while she had some training relevant to the work of the division, her principal qualification for the job was political experience and reliability.[14] All the Party and YCL members in this particular division had at least limited experience which qualified them for work in this particular division—which was definitely not the case in all divisions in the ministry—but the most highly qualified specialists in the unit were non-Party cadres, and the general level of expertise was considerably higher among this group than among the Party personnel.

According to a former non-Party cadre who worked in this division, a clear "psychic distance" was consistently maintained between the Party members and non-Party cadres. Non-Party cadres were fully conscious of the power and authority conferred by Party membership, whatever the salary rank of an individual. The regular closed Party meetings and the Party members' special access to certain

[14] Many wives of top Party leaders work in government organs, and frequently they hold positions which they might well not have obtained without the help of their husband's prestige.

classified Party materials were constant reminders of their special position. Non-Party cadres felt, moreover, that Party members were continuously judging them. Party members were wary about forming close personal relationships, even within the office, with non-Party cadres, perhaps partly because of the Party's suspicion that such relationships might contribute to the formation of undesirable groups or cliques (*chi t'uan*). Outside the office there was relatively little social contact between Party members and non-Party cadres, even though they often lived in close proximity in government-run apartments.

Despite the reserve that characterized both sides of this relationship, however, in "normal times" (i.e. except during political campaigns, when all relationships became unusually tense) working relations between the Party and non-Party cadres were fairly harmonious and smooth on questions that did not involve ideological or political issues. In staff meetings, both Party members and non-Party cadres expressed their views quite freely on technical questions, and frequently the opinions of qualified non-Party cadres prevailed. However, on any matter that involved controversial ideological or political matters, or on which a definite Party policy had been adopted, the opinions of the Party members were unchallengeable. Non-Party cadres were sensitive, moreover, to the possibility that some seemingly nonpolitical matter might have significant political implications; and if it became clear that this was the case, they would normally simply submit to the views of the Party members even if it was against their best judgment on purely technical grounds. As a former cadre describing this unit put it, "In staff meetings, whenever politics were involved, Party members almost always took the lead in the discussion. We non-Party cadres would listen, and if all the Party and YCL members obviously agreed, we generally concluded that this was a question which they had already discussed, and perhaps had received concrete instructions about, in a previous Party meeting. So we would just go along, whatever our personal opinions. In short, if the Party had a definite position on a question, the Party members simply decided the issue."

At every level in the Chinese government bureaucracy, therefore, Party members now dominate most of the leading posts; and in most organizations this was true by the middle or latter 1950s. At top levels the few non-Party men in leadership positions are mainly "democratic personages," kept on as symbols of the supposed "united front" character of the regime; and, as already stated, they invariably have Party subordinates who hold real power. At lower levels, a highly qualified non-Party cadre may head a unit within a ministry, such as a section, but even in these cases there is usually at least one key Party man on his staff who has special political authority. In short, Party membership in itself confers great prestige and authority, and special political status (*cheng chih ti wei*); and, not infrequently, relatively low-ranking Party members are recognized as having greater political authority on many matters than higher-ranking non-Party cadres.

Stratification of Status in the Bureaucracy

WHILE THE distinction between Party and non-Party cadres is one of the crucial ways of differentiating members of the Chinese government bureaucracy, it is only one of many. Within a few years after the Communists had assumed power, the bureaucracy had already become highly stratified and notably rank- and status-conscious.

As dedicated revolutionaries, the top Chinese Communist leaders have fought a continuing battle against "bureaucratism" in all its forms and have placed great stress on the need for promoting a "mass line style of work" that demands close contacts between the ruling elite and those ruled, and between different levels within the bureaucracy. But in many respects it appears to have been a losing battle. However disturbing this may be to the Chinese leaders—and there is much evidence that they do find it disturbing—it is really not very surprising. In fact, it has probably been inevitable. For centuries China has been ruled by the largest and one of the most highly organized bureaucracies that has ever existed anywhere, and it has not been possible to eradicate fully the influence of the country's deep-rooted bureaucratic traditions. The bureaucrats in China today, therefore, are inheritors of these long traditions, as well as of the Communists' brief tradition of revolutionary antibureaucratism. Perhaps even more important, the sheer size of the bureaucracy required to rule China, the enormity of its tasks, and the Communists' totalitarian concepts of power, all reinforce the tendency toward a highly organized, stratified bureaucratic structure of authority, in fact if not in theory. In short, the problems of administering a huge totalitarian nation have been very different from the Party's earlier problems of organizing a revolutionary movement, and it has simply not been possible to create an enormous ruling bureaucracy and still preserve the purity of revolutionary values and outlook that were the ideal of the Chinese Communists' leaders during their revolutionary struggle for power. (The regime's operational methods are still significantly influenced, however, by the leaders' revolutionary background and outlook; this will be discussed on pp. 65 ff. and 141 ff.)

The distinction between cadres (*kan pu*) and the masses (*ch'ün chung*) is a basic one in China today. All cadres, including non-Party cadres as well as Party members, belong to the ruling elite, and despite the impressive "mass line" policies promoted by the regime, the gap between cadres and noncadres, i.e. between the elite and the ordinary people, the rulers and the ruled, is very real indeed. As one goes up in the Chinese bureaucracy, the gap between cadres and ordinary people steadily widens, as one might expect, but even at the lowest levels the cadres tend to regard themselves, and are clearly regarded by the Chinese masses, as a group apart because of their power and authority.

To understand the hierarchy of authority in China, however, it is necessary to analyze not only the gap between the elite and the masses but also the complex stratification of rank, status, and prestige among the ruling bureaucrats themselves; that is, among the cadres.

Types of Cadres

One must start by analyzing the term "cadre" (*kan pu*), for as used in Communist China today the term has a variety of meanings. In its broadest usage, it includes all those, both Party members and non-Party cadres, who hold any post as a functionary in the bureaucratic hierarchies in China, from top to bottom. The term implies roles of leadership and authority, but over the years it has been applied to an increasingly large number of people, so that now even those in low-level functionary posts are labeled "cadres."

There are a great many different types of cadres in Communist China today, however. One important distinction is between state cadres (*kuo chia kan pu*) and local cadres (*ti fang kan pu*). The term "state cadre" is used to describe persons in the bureaucratic hierarchies of Party and government (and some in the mass organizations) who receive their salary from the state; as will be explained below, however, in general usage it does not necessarily include all such people. "Local cadres" are those at the commune level and below who receive their income not from the state but from their collective institutions, and they are often referred to as "commune," "brigade," or "team" cadres, as well as "local" cadres.[15] (As will be explained later, however, communes also generally have some state cadres, paid by the state.)

Although, as already stated, the term "state cadre" is used only for those on the state payroll in the government, Party, or mass organization hierarchies,[16] it does not include all such persons. Generally, a state cadre is an administrative cadre (*hsing cheng kan pu*) in a government or Party office who is paid on the basis of a nationwide ranking system with twenty-four salary grades in urban areas and twenty-six in rural areas (or at least in those areas from which information is currently available). In at least some areas, however, it apparently is also applied to nonadministrative teaching personnel, and sometimes to medical and technical personnel as well, even though each of these groups has a separate national system of salary and rank gradations. The term is not generally used, however, for certain other groups who do receive their salaries from the state. For example, it is not usually applied to active military personnel; officers (*chün kuan*) above a certain rank (reportedly second lieutenant, or *shao wei*) in the military services are generally referred to as "army cadres" (*chün tui kan pu*) rather than as "state cadres," while rank-and-file troops are merely referred to as "ordinary soldiers" (*p'u t'ung ping*). Certain commercial cadres, such as salesmen (*ying yeh yüan*), for whom there is also a separate ranking system, may in some cases be referred to as "state cadres" and in others not. Ordinary workers in nonadministrative posts in factories are not considered to be state cadres. Even in administrative work, the lowest levels of employees in government or Party organizations—i.e. general service

[15] Sometimes the term "local cadre" is used, however, with other meanings; for example, it may be used to refer to all cadres who work at governmental levels below the central government.

[16] According to ex-cadres, Party cadres normally receive their pay from the state, regardless of whether they hold Party or government posts.

personnel (*ch'in tsa jen yüan*)—whose salary grade is below twenty-four in urban areas or twenty-six in rural areas, are generally not considered to be state cadres, even though they are paid by the state.

In Ministry M all the members of the staff of the ministry were considered to be state cadres (except general service personnel below grade twenty-four).

Salary and Job Grades

Prior to the mid-1950s, salary systems in China were relatively confused and unstandardized. Even though an official ranking system for cadres was introduced in the early 1950s, the rapid growth and constant changes in the bureaucracy in that period led to the development of many irrational ratings and inequities, and there were numerous instances where work, rank, and pay levels were not reasonably linked. This situation gave rise to a good many cadre complaints. (Some who complained were later subjected to criticism during the "antirightist campaign" of 1957.)

Then in 1956, the regime readjusted grades and salaries and attempted to regularize the system. Since that time all administrative state cadres throughout the country have been ranked and paid according to the standardized national system. To compensate for regional variations in living costs, however, the country has been divided into eleven major categories of areas, and salaries are adjusted by area.

Average salaries paid to most administrative cadres in the central ministries have not been exceptionally high, even by comparison with workers' wages, but there have been striking differentials between the highest and lowest levels of cadre pay. In Ministry M, for example, the minister, grade six, reportedly received close to Y400 a month; bureau chiefs, grades nine to twelve, roughly Y200–250; division chiefs, grades thirteen to fifteen, roughly Y150–200; and section chiefs, grades fifteen to seventeen, roughly Y100–135.[17] The lowest-ranking state cadres in the ministry, grade twenty-four, re-

[17] These figures, based on the memory of an ex-cadre, are estimates and may not, therefore, be precisely correct, but they provide a useful indication of the general range of salaries.

ceived about Y45 a month. In short, those at the bottom of the hierarchy received roughly one-ninth the salary of the head of the ministry.

As in most hierarchical bureaucratic systems, rankings were not only important because they were the basis for salary payments; they were also significant measures of status and prestige, as well as determinants of job opportunities. Persons tended to receive deference and respect according to their salary grades, which were generally known by others in their organization. The correlation between salary grades and job ranks was not exact, however. Cadres could be and sometimes were given job promotions without automatic salary raises (*t'i chi pu t'i hsin*), one reason being that the regime strongly felt the necessity to keep government costs down. But even if there was often a lag, salary raises eventually tended to follow job promotions.

Normally, the tables of organization (*pien chih*) of government units specified a range of salary grades for a particular job level. Commonly, a particular job might be open to cadres of three salary levels. In Ministry M, for example, the specifications for salary levels of cadres at various job levels were reported to be as follows: minister, six to four; deputy ministers, eight to six; assistants to the minister, nine to seven; director of the staff office, eleven to nine; bureau chiefs, twelve to ten; division chiefs, fifteen to thirteen; section chiefs, seventeen to fifteen; and ordinary cadres, twenty-four to eighteen (persons in this last category were referred to either as *k'o yüan* or as *pan shih yüan*, the latter label generally being used for those having the lowest ranks). General service personnel, including office boys, messengers, cleaning personnel, and so on, had salary grades lower than twenty-four and, as already stated, were not considered state cadres.

Although cadres were often categorized by these salary grades (e.g. a person would be called a "grade fifteen cadre," *shih wu chi kan pu*), they were referred to even more frequently by job level. These rankings, which in Ministry M tended even more than the salary ratings to reflect a person's real status in the stratified hierarchy, were obviously basic determinants of the character of all relationships among cadres. In the ministry, people were called "minister-level cadres" (*pu chang chi kan pu*); "bureau-chief–level cadres" (*chü chang chi kan pu*); "division-chief–level cadres" (*ch'u chang chi kan pu*); "section-chief–level cadres" (*k'o chang chi kan pu*); or simply "ordinary cadres" (*yi pan kan pu* or *p'u t'ung kan pu*). All cadres were highly sensitive to the differences in authority and prestige which these ranks denoted.

In earlier years, distinctions were commonly made between high-ranking cadres (*kao chi kan pu*), middle-rank cadres (*chung chi kan pu*), and lower-ranking cadres (*hsia chi kan pu*), but over time these labels were used less and less, at least in Ministry M, perhaps because they were not as precise as the job-rank labels listed above.

One of the most notable aspects of all these formal ranking systems was the great and real gap between those at the top and those at the bottom. The relative equalitarianism of earlier years rapidly declined after the Communists' assumption of power, and was replaced by a system in which ratings indicated very great differentials in power, prestige, salaries, and other prerogatives—and also involved great psychological distance between those at the top and those at the bottom.

Seniority: "Old Cadres" and "New Cadres"

These formal systems of ranking, basic as they are, do not by any means reveal the entire picture of stratification within the bureaucracy in China. The gap between Party and non-Party cadres has already been discussed. But even among Party cadres[18] there has de-

[18] The term "Party cadre" is itself a complex one which can have several meanings or usages. Actually, three different Chinese terms are in use, each with a somewhat different meaning, and one could translate these terms differently as follows: (1) *tang kan pu*—"Party cadre," (2) *tang yüan kan pu*—"Party-member cadres," and (3) *tang ti kan pu*—"Party's cadre." When these distinctions are made, the differences in meanings appear to be as follows: (1) *tang kan pu* is applied to Party members who are cadres or functionaries in the Party organization itself —as contrasted with ordinary Party members; (2) *tang yüan kan pu* is applied to all Party members who hold any cadre positions, whether in the Party, government, mass organizations, or other institutions—as contrasted with non-Party cadres (*fei tang kan pu*); and (3) *tang ti kan pu*, the most variable term of the three, is at times used to mean the same as either (1) or (2) above, or even as a synonym for "state cadres," but at

veloped an extremely important pattern of stratification based primarily on seniority, or length of service since one either "joined the Party" (*ts'an chia tang*) or "joined the revolution" (*ts'an chia ko ming*).

The broadest division of Party cadres in Ministry M was between "old cadres" (*lao kan pu*) and "new cadres" (*hsin kan pu*). Although this distinction was a very important one—all "old cadres" enjoyed great prestige—it was not very precise; the date separating the two could vary. As used by cadres in Ministry M, however, the year of "liberation," 1949, was generally felt to be the most important dividing line.

"Old cadres" were further differentiated into numerous subgroups, on the basis of seniority. The terms most used in the ministry included "long march cadres" (*ch'ang cheng kan pu*), "Yenan cadres" (*yen an kan pu*), "1938 cadres" (*san pa kan pu*),[19] "anti-Japanese war cadres" (*k'ang jih chan cheng kan pu*), and "liberation war cadres" (*chieh fang chan cheng kan pu*).

The "long march cadres," who participated in the Communists' epic retreat from Kiangsi to Shensi in the mid-1930s, had the greatest prestige, and many occupied the highest Party and government posts. In Ministry M, even those with limited qualifications were often given secondary positions of leadership, such as chiefs of subordinate units within the ministry; and, if necessary, able deputies were assigned to them to carry the real work load. Very few were "ordinary cadres."

Only slightly less prestigious were the "Yenan cadres," and "anti-Japanese war cadres," who joined the Party in the 1930s and early 1940s. More numerous and slightly younger than "long march cadres," these groups occupied a high percentage of politically important or sensitive posts in Ministry M. When necessary, they too

times is used in a more restricted sense to mean all cadres, whether Party members or not, who work for Party administrative organs.

In the text of this discussion, no attempt will be made to use these three different terms, however, and the term "Party cadres" will be used to mean all Party members who hold any cadre positions, whether in the sense of (1) or (2) above.

[19] A variation of this term was "1938 line Cadres" (*san pa hsien kan pu*).

were assigned more qualified younger men to assist them in their work.

The term "1938 cadres" included all those who joined the Party prior to that year. A large majority of ministers in the central government, including the head of Ministry M, have belonged to this category.

"Liberation war cadres," who joined the Party in the post–World War II struggle against the Nationalists, were the largest group of prestigious "old cadres," and, in Ministry M, as in many other ministries, they occupied a wide range of leadership jobs, especially at middle levels.

Still another category consisted of "uprising cadres" (*ch'i yi kan pu*),[20] who switched sides from the Nationalists to the Communists in the last days of the civil war. These might be either Party or non-Party men but were generally the latter. Their prestige was not particularly high, in Ministry M or elsewhere.

The significance of these seniority rankings was not simply that they indicated important gradations of status and prestige. To a considerable degree (although not, of course, invariably) high seniority ratings opened the door to positions of power and authority in the bureaucracy, whether or not the cadres involved possessed special technical competence or experience qualifying them for such posts. One explanation for this, apparently, was the tendency of the top leaders to equate seniority with political reliability, and perhaps also with general organizational skills, which were rated as more important than special technical competence for many leadership posts in the bureaucracy.

Other Categories of Cadres

In addition to these seniority ratings there were still further categories used to define different groups of cadres. Frequently a broad distinction was made between "leadership cadres" (*ling tao kan pu*) and "ordinary cadres" (*yi pan kan pu*). Use of the former term in

[20] Also used were the terms "uprising generals" (*ch'i yi chiang ling*) and "uprising personages" (*ch'i yi jen shih*).

Ministry M was elastic to a degree. Sometimes it was used to differentiate the top leaders in the ministry from all other, lower-ranking personnel, but at other times it was applied to all chiefs and deputy chiefs of ministry subunits down to and including the sections.

Rankings according to education or "cultural standard" (*wen hua ch'eng tu*) were also often used to describe cadres. Sometimes these indicated the level of schooling completed by a cadre, but at other times they were simply estimates of self-achieved levels of literacy or general education. For example, if a cadre was considered to have achieved the general literacy and educational level of a middle school graduate, he might be described as having a *chung hsüeh wen hua ch'eng tu* even if he had not completed formal education at that level. These achievement labels generally did not have very significant status implications to the Communists themselves; leading cadres could, and many did, have relatively low "cultural achievement" levels. However, they probably were somewhat more important in the eyes of most non-Party cadres, a large number of whom were fairly well educated, and tended, privately at least, to look down on Party cadres with limited education.

The term "intellectual" (*chih shih fen tzu*) was applied more often to non-Party cadres than to Party members. This, too, was a term that was somewhat variable in its usages. At times, it could be used to include all those with the equivalent of a lower middle school education—and in the countryside it sometimes included virtually all literate persons. University graduates were often set apart and described as "higher" (*kao chi*) intellectuals.[21] Only rarely were these labels applied to Party members, however. Despite the regime's conscious policy of fostering its own "proletarian" (*wu ch'an chieh chi*) and "red and expert" (*yu hung yu chuan*) intellectuals, the term still tended to imply, in the minds of many Party members, a taint of undesirable bourgeois influence, since the majority of intellectuals were still inherited from the old regime.

A complete catalogue of terms defining cadre groupings would have to include additional ones, such as "demobilized army men"

---

[21] When employed in a more restricted sense, "intellectual" referred to graduates of college or the equivalent, and "higher intellectuals" to such people as university teachers above the level of lecturer, doctors, engineers, editors, and the like.

(*fu yüan chün jen*) and "transferred (or reassigned) army men" (*chuan yeh chün jen*). The former were persons released from military service, generally to return to their home towns or villages, while the latter were persons released and sent from military service to definite civilian job assignments in the Party or government hierarchies, including jobs in the central ministries. While they might be Party members or not, former army men in general, because of the political, organizational, and technical training provided in the military services, were regarded as an important source of recruitment for new members of the elite. Consequently these labels carried at least a degree of prestige.

As the above suggests, while all cadres were considered to be part of the ruling elite, positions within the elite were carefully graded on the basis of job, salary, seniority in the Party, and other criteria. All cadres were labeled with commonly used terms that described their status; and, not surprisingly, the majority of cadres in this highly stratified hierarchy were notably rank-conscious.

While the stratification of status was most important in terms of power, authority, and prestige, it was reflected, also, in the perquisites and privileges accorded to different ranks of cadres. This was especially true in the central ministries, and less so in local administrations at lower levels of the bureaucracy. In Ministry M, housing, transportation, dining facilities, and even office furniture depended on one's rank, in a fashion suggestive of a New York corporation's organization rather than of a revolutionary and ostensibly egalitarian leadership. These perquisites of rank in the ministry will be described later; see pp. 99–101.

Personnel Management

Personnel Bureau

THE PERSONNEL BUREAU (*jen shih chü*) in Ministry M was one of the most powerful units in the organization. Staffed entirely by Party members, located adjacent to the Party Committee office, and having an overlap of personnel with that committee, its influence derived not only from its responsibility for personnel management but also from the fact that it served as a key "watchdog" or control organ. Like the Party Committee, it operated in an atmosphere of great secrecy and security-consciousness. Since the Party itself retained ultimate control over personnel management, including decisions on appointments, transfers, promotions, demotions, and punishments of all cadres, whether Party members or not, the bureau served in effect as a special extension of the Party apparatus into the government bureaucracy.

In Ministry M the Personnel Bureau was a medium-size one, with three divisions, labeled Cadres Divisions No. 1, No. 2, and No. 3 (*ti yi kan pu ch'u*, etc.). The largest of these handled the affairs of most of the ministry's personnel and maintained the dossiers of some of them; it was also responsible, in collaboration with the Party Committee, for organizing the weekly "study" meetings for all cadres in the ministry. Another division handled wage problems and disbursements. The smallest bore special responsibility for investigation and clearance of personnel sent abroad, either for training or on other missions.[22]

As stated earlier, personnel actions affecting all ministry staff members of bureau-chief rank or above were reportedly handled di-

[22] Final investigation and clearance was done, however, by the Public Security authorities.

rectly by higher authorities—i.e. by departments of the Party Central Committee and/or by the State Council's Personnel Bureau (which was later absorbed by the Ministry of Interior). The bureau in the ministry handled actions affecting lower-ranking cadres, but in some cases transfers to other ministries or to provincial departments (*t'ing*) required approval from the Central Committee departments, and in at least a few cases, it was apparently the Central Committee which provided the transferred cadres with the necessary official "letters of introduction" (*chieh shao hsin*) to their new posts.

To cite a specific case, one cadre from Ministry M, a non-Party man, who was being transferred to a provincial government department, went through the following procedure: He was sent with transfer papers by the ministry's Personnel Bureau to the Central Committee department supervising the ministry. After receiving its endorsement on his transfer papers, he then went to the Central Committee's Organization Department, which gave him a letter of introduction to the Party Organization Department in the province. At the provincial level, the sequence was reversed; after first going to the Party Organization Department, he then went to the Party department supervising his line of work, and only thereafter reported to the personnel unit of the government department to which he had been transferred. It was unusual for an individual, especially a non-Party cadre, to visit all these offices in person, as this man did. The explanation in his case was probably the fact that his transfer was urgent and his visits to the Party offices doubtless speeded up the process. But apparently this was the routing for the paper work involved in many transfers.

Personnel Dossiers

Individual personnel dossiers (*tang an*) were maintained on all cadres working for the ministry. Although the dossiers for cadres of bureau-chief rank and above were kept by higher authorities, all others were kept within the ministry. Those for Party members and those for non-Party cadres were separated, however. The former were maintained in the Party Committee's office and the latter in the Personnel Bureau. These two organizations, which were in adjacent locations and were closely linked organizationally, simply exchanged dossiers as needed.

The dossiers were an important element in the general system of personnel management. A dossier was set up for each state cadre as soon as he first went to work for any Party or government organization; the dossier then followed the individual from job to job throughout his career. One of the first and most important documents in each dossier was a lengthy summary (*tsung chieh*) written by the individual, of his personal history (*tzu chuan*) since childhood, his professional experience, family class background (*chia t'ing ch'u shen*) and individual class status (*ko jen ch'eng fen*), friends and relations (*she hui kuan hsi*, literally, "social relations"), and ideological development. To this were attached one's references. For Party members, the initial document was one's application for Party membership (*ju tang shen ch'ing shu*), a similar document, but even more elaborate and complete.

At the end of each year, and after every special campaign, detailed annual "assessments" (*chien ting*) were added to the dossiers. In addition, of course, the dossiers contained all important papers relating to transfers, promotions, and so on, plus the results of any special investigations concerning the individual involved. Over the the years, the dossiers for most individuals became very large indeed. Because they were classified and could be seen and handled by only a limited number of people, when a cadre was transferred his dossier was usually forwarded to his new place of assignment by "military post" (*chün yu*), the special service for classified matter run by the Postal and Telecommunications Ministry.

Annual and Special "Assessments"

The written "assessments" of each cadre, prepared annually and during almost every major political campaign, formed a particularly important part of every cadre's dossier, and the process of preparing them played a very significant role in the general system of personnel control and management. At the end of every year, each cadre in Ministry M, as in all state and Party organizations throughout the country, wrote a personal summary of his work, activities, and thought. Then, in small group meetings in every section of the ministry, several half days, or full days, were devoted to thorough discussion of these statements. In such meetings, each cadre orally presented his own summary (or, alternatively, all group members read it), and then the entire group commented on and criticized the individual's self-evaluation. The group leader noted the main points in the discussion and recorded them, together with his own comments, on each individual's statement, which was then passed up the hierarchy (with unit heads at each level adding comments if they wished) to be placed in the individual's dossier.

One reason that these Party-directed evaluation sessions were so important to the personnel management system was the fact that every cadre was fully conscious, throughout the year, that at year-end his performance and, perhaps even more important, his general attitudes and behavior would be subjected to rigorous examination and group discussion; that the collective judgments made about him would be based on Party-defined standards and values; and that the ratings given him by his working colleagues, above all by the Party and YCL members in his own unit, would become a part of his permanent record. Conflicts or frictions in relationship with the key Party members in a cadre's unit were almost certain to be reflected in his year-end ratings. Consciousness of this fact bolstered the authority of these Party men throughout the year.

The ratings received by a cadre in these assessments influenced his entire future career. Poor ratings immediately increased the likelihood of a shift to a relatively undesirable post or of "transfer downward" (*hsia fang*) to the countryside. They also increased the possibility of future criticism or attacks during political campaigns. During major campaigns, in fact, each cadre's dossier was generally subjected to a thorough review. This was the starting point for systematic investigations of all those whose records made them vulnerable to criticism. Such investigations were first conducted by Party organs and the Personnel Bureau in the ministry, but in certain cases the preliminary checks were followed up by field investigations which might involve the public security agencies. During most major campaigns, moreover, lengthy special assessments, in which political thought and behavior rather than work performance were emphasized, were prepared by each cadre. In these special assessments, cadres had to resummarize much material already contained in previous statements, and if a person was under special investigation his latest summary could be carefully cross-checked with earlier ones.

Sources of Personnel

In Ministry M, the Personnel Bureau was responsible for roughly one thousand cadres. They had been drawn from a number of sources. At the time of the Communist takeover, most ministries had relied heavily on "retained cadres" (*liu yung kan pu*) inherited from the Nationalist regime. Right from the start reliable Party cadres had been placed in key positions, but many non-Communist bureaucrats who had worked for the Kuomintang government were kept on, and some ranking pro-Communist fellow-travelers, the "democratic personages" (*min chu jen shih*), were also absorbed into the bureaucracy. Gradually, however, the number of such persons working in the ministries declined. By the mid-1950s in Ministry M there were no well-known high-ranking "democratic personages" and a declining number of "retained cadres." Of the latter, most were older men with indispensable or irreplaceable skills and experience. Some of these had been—or would have been by that time, if the Nationalist regime had survived—fairly high-ranking bureaucrats. Now, however, they were all in subordinate positions, under the direction of Party men. While their technical expertise was utilized, they lacked political power and did not play a major role in important decision-making. Gradually they were being superannuated, and replaced by newly trained, younger men.

All the strategic posts and commanding heights in the upper levels of the ministry were occupied by Party members, the majority of whom were "old cadres." While some of these old cadres were men who had, or who quickly acquired, technical skills relevant to the work of the ministry, others lacked technical qualifications. They were all, however, politically dependable and experienced organization men; and the top ones demonstrated real skill in running the organization and ensuring the implementation of the Party's general policies.

Middle-level posts in the ministry were also dominated by Party cadres, both old and new. There were many sources for such cadres. Some were drawn from Party organizations, others from former army men, and still others from different government agencies. Most of those from other government organizations came from agencies within the same general functional system as Ministry M. Some were cadres who by demonstrating special competence in provincial departments had to come to the attention of the ministry and had been transferred upward at its request; these were among the ablest younger Party cadres in the ministry. Vertical mobility was fairly limited, however, while lateral transfers were more frequent, and apparently a larger number of cadres had been shifted from other central agencies than from the provincial departments.

One of the most important sources of new younger cadres, both Party and non-Party, consisted of recent graduates from institutions of higher learning. Every year the regime assigned a sizable number of new graduates to the ministries, and many of these had at least some specialized training relevant to their assignments. This steady flow of young people was a major channel for the infusion of new talent into the central bureaucracy. Assignments to work in the central ministries not only were rated as important by the regime but also were viewed as desirable by most graduates, and some of the ablest young people in the country were drawn into the ministries —although ability was judged on the basis of one's political activism as well as intellectual accomplishments. Frequently, these young people were sent for a preliminary period of training in the ministry's cadre school before being assigned to regular posts in the ministry itself. The percentage of educated young cadres, roughly from twenty-five to thirty-five years in age, steadily rose over the years, therefore, and they filled a sizable proportion of rank-and-file ministry jobs. A great many of them belonged to the YCL, and a few were Party members, when first recruited into the bureaucracy.

Another source of personnel was the army. Although most of the servicemen released each year were either sent to collective farm organizations in their home villages in rural areas or assigned to low-level (e.g. county) organizations, a few every year, especially ex-officers and Party men, were absorbed into the ministries. In Ministry M some of these ex-servicemen presented definite problems. Because of their status and rank, they often had to be assigned to fairly good jobs, but only a few had experience or technical skills immediately relevant to the work of the ministry. Often they were given supervisory posts requiring administrative and organizational rather than technical competence, and there was some resentment in the ministry among those whom they supervised.[23]

Advancement Opportunities

The competition for advancement in the bureaucracy was very intense, but the opportunities for promotion were much fewer than in the period immediately after 1949. In the early years, the effort to create an essentially new elite to displace the bureaucrats left over from the old regime, plus the rapid expansion of government functions and organizations, meant that there were a great many opportunities for advancement, and many fairly young "old cadres" were catapulted into jobs with impressive ranks and responsibilities. Before long, however, the new group filled the leading posts in the ministries, and the tendency was for them to become well entrenched and to hang on to their jobs, with the result that it became increasingly difficult for able new cadres to mount the ladder of success to the top levels.

In theory the regime's ideal was to create a new elite that was both "red and expert"—that is, both politically reliable and technically competent. The emphasis placed on these criteria for success and advancement shifted from time to time, but at no time was the basic importance of political criteria overlooked. In "liberal periods," technical specialists were allowed to operate with reduced political control and interference, but the Party's organization men, and especially "old cadres," continued to dominate a high percentage of the key positions of power and authority. In recent years, however, technicians who are also Party members appear to have increased steadily in both numbers and influence.

---

[23] Another group in the ministry that prompted some resentment consisted of wives of high-ranking Party members. Although quantitatively insignificant in terms of the ministry's entire staff, there were enough of them to attract attention and, rightfully or wrongfully, ordinary cadres often felt that they received special treatment.

The political criteria for advancement were partly related to thought and behavior which the individual cadre could control or influence. For example, whether a cadre was successful in becoming a "new socialist man" in the eyes of the Party depended greatly on whether he had the will and determination to do so. But certain criteria which the individual could not control, such as family class background (*chia t'ing ch'u shen*), also had a significant influence on advancement opportunities. Cadres (especially non-Communist cadres) who had a "bourgeois" class background, as many pre-1949 and not a few post-1949 intellectuals did, were automatically the target of some suspicion on the part of those who did not. Many were unable to overcome this handicap. Even those who did overcome it realized that because of their background they might always be vulnerable if they made serious mistakes.

In practice, therefore, because political factors were fundamental in determining advancement, promotions to leading posts were largely monopolized by Party and YCL members. Many of the most ambitious Party cadres, furthermore, tended to move into "Party work" and other organizational activity. These fields often seemed to offer the greatest opportunities for enhancing one's power and authority, even though they might be less rewarding financially than technically specialized fields. Many non-Party cadres in Ministry M, including numerous higher intellectuals, apparently had relatively little expectation or hope of promotion to leadership positions. For at least some of these cadres, the main aim was simply to "hold their own" in the bureaucratic structure and to avoid getting into trouble.

Cadres with scarce technical skills, including non-Party cadres as well as Party men, were obviously considered to be very important by the regime, however, and even though the non-Communists among them were the objects of suspicion by the Party's "old cadres," who dominated the system, and were discriminated against in assignments to politically important leadership positions, they were relatively well treated financially. The salaries of all technical specialists tended, in fact, to be higher than those of administrative cadres, and in many of the basic units of Ministry M there were specialists whose salaries were actually higher than those of their section or division chiefs. This anomaly created some tensions in the system. Not surprisingly, the political generalists tended to resent the financial discrimination in favor of the technical specialists, who in turn tended to resent the monopoly of leadership posts and authority by the "old cadres."

Impersonal and Personal Factors

Relatively speaking, over time, performance—judged by the Communists' own standards stressing political reliability as well as technical competence—had become more important, and personal factors (including family connections) less important, in determining advancement. In fact, if a person attempted in the traditional Chinese way to capitalize on personal relationships, the attempt could boomerang, since it was likely to be interpreted as evidence of "bourgeois" or even "feudal" attitudes. But this did not mean that personal factors were totally ignored.

In actual decisions on promotions, both the Personnel Bureau and the heads of basic units in the ministry played an important role. The former, in cooperation with Party leaders in the ministry, made the decisions, but the recommendations of unit chiefs were important. To get ahead, therefore, it was important for a cadre to have good relations with his immediate boss, and many ambitious cadres consciously cultivated special relationships with their chiefs. In contrast with the situation in China before 1949, however, when such cultivation might have involved entertaining the boss, presenting him with gifts, or even bribing him, now it consisted mainly of giving strong support to his views and being especially responsive to his leadership.

In other subtle ways, too, personal factors reportedly had an influence on the opportunities for advancement of some cadres. For example, ex-cadres assert that young men or women who were related to high Party members, as well as the wives of such officials, generally were given special consideration by both their unit chiefs and the Personnel Bureau—a fact which often, although not invariably, gave them an advantage in the competition for advancement. This was generally a result not of direct intervention by their influential relatives, but rather of independent action by lower-ranking persons in their own organizations. These persons might rationalize the preferential treatment of the individuals involved by arguing that their class and family background obviously made them politically advanced and reliable, but they were probably motivated at least in part by a desire to avoid offending the high Party officials involved.

Raises, Promotions, and Transfers

Without access to detailed personnel records or statistics, even cadres who worked in the ministries could not have accurate knowledge of the rates or patterns of salary raises, job promotions, and transfers in their organization, but the impressionistic judgments of ex-cadres are significant nevertheless.

Cadres in the ministries apparently felt that the rate of salary increases was very slow. Periodically, there was a general readjustment of salaries, involving raises for large numbers of persons, but then there were long periods in which the salaries of many cadres were virtually frozen. For reasons of economy, the regime tried to hold the line as long as possible, and only when the pressure for change became irresistible would a major adjustment be carried out. In short, a rational system of slow but steady salary raises based on performance seemed to be lacking, and for long periods between adjustments many cadres felt that they had almost no chance for a raise. This meant that financial incentives were not a particularly important or effective device to encourage good performance. The situation tended to have an adverse effect on cadre morale. This was probably more than counterbalanced, however, by the fact that most cadres —including non-Party cadres, who had many fundamental complaints about the system as a whole—recognized that they really belonged to a privileged group. As indicated earlier, most cadre salaries were not especially high, but then practically no one in the country received very high incomes, and cadres realized not only that their incomes were relatively good compared to those of ordinary peasants and workers but also that they enjoyed a greater degree of financial security than the majority of the population. Moreover, cadre status qualified them for free medical care, low-rent housing, cheap food, better than ordinary accommodations while traveling, and access to comparatively good schools for their children.

The rate of job promotion was also felt to be low by cadres in Ministry M. This feeling was probably strongest among non-Party cadres, but it was shared by many Party members as well. There was a feeling that because "old cadres" with seniority tended to monopolize most top leadership positions, it was difficult for even an extremely able young Party cadre to move up to the top levels.

Mobility of Personnel

While vertical mobility in the bureaucracy was felt to be restricted, the rate of lateral, and downward, mobility was apparently high. Cadres were frequently transferred (*tiao tung*) from one job to another within the same ministry, or to a related ministry-level agency, or to lower-level bodies. No statistical information is available to provide a clear quantitative picture of the frequency, but an ex-cadre who worked in Ministry M believes that it was very high.[24] Some ex-cadres assert that it was quite common for many cadres working in the government to shift jobs every two to four years.

A possible explanation for frequent transfers of cadres, in the view of some ex-cadres, was the regime's desire to combat "bureaucratism" (*kuan liao chu yi*), "localism" (*ti fang chu yi*), and "departmentalism" or "vested-interestism" (*pen wei chu yi*, or "excessive loyalty to one's organizational unit"). Whatever the exact rate of transfers, it was probably high enough so that it did tend to inhibit personal attachments to specific organizational units on the part of most rank-and-file cadres. Many cadres, in fact, tended to feel that they were simply small cogs in a huge bureaucratic machine, subject to moves at any time, at the whims of the Party leaders who controlled the personnel management system.

This presented some real problems to ordinary cadres and helped to create a prevalent sense of organizational instability or insecurity. Many cadres never even attempted to create permanent homes or to

[24] He estimates that in one year there was a turnover of perhaps two hundred cadres, or about one fifth of the total staff of the ministry, and that this was not abnormal. Ex-cadres who have worked in other ministries, however, believe that this estimate is probably too high.

sink strong, lasting roots in one place. They tended to avoid accumulating bulky personal possessions, such as furniture, since it was difficult or impossible to move such things from place to place. Instead they lived, by preference as well as necessity, in furnished government housing. Cadres who were not performing well often had a nagging anxiety that they might be transferred to remote and undesirable posts. Most northerners hoped to avoid assignments in the south, and most cadres in central agencies disliked the idea of transfer to border regions and rural areas in general.

Transfers also created numerous family problems. A fairly high proportion of cadres in central government agencies consisted of married men and women, and in a great many cases both man and wife were state cadres, often in different organizations. Among families connected in any way with the bureaucracy, in fact, "housewives" were apparently a disappearing breed. Reportedly, most educated wives married to cadres in the ministries positively wished to work themselves, and it was generally expected that they would. Even if they did not wish to do so, it was quite often necessary. Though a couple might in some circumstances be supported on a single cadre's salary, it was essential for the wife to become the second breadwinner if a family had several children. It was not uncommon for transfers to split families in which both husband and wife were working cadres. As a result of persistent efforts on the part of both, assignments might eventually be arranged to reunite the family, but often this took a prolonged period, sometimes years.

Frequent transfers also created some problems for the bureaucracy itself, since they inevitably resulted in interruptions and discontinuities in the work of basic organizational units. Apparently, however, the disruption of work was not as serious as one might assume, for several reasons. For one thing, higher-ranking cadres, such as unit chiefs, reportedly were not transferred as frequently as rank-and-file staff members. Moreover, most basic units appeared to maintain intact a fairly stable core of dependable "backbone cadres" (*ku kan kan pu*), who could keep things running reasonably well even if there was a relatively high turnover of others. These "backbone cadres" usually were reliable Party people whose main skills were organizational or administrative. They were not always able to maintain high levels of technical performance when there was a high turnover of specialists in their units, but they were able to keep their units operating.

Periodic drives for economy and personnel retrenchment in the central ministries were another cause of substantial transfers. The fact that many basic units in the ministries kept on performing reasonably well even after large-scale reductions of staff suggests that between retrenchment drives "Parkinson's Law" operated in China as elsewhere and that many central agencies tended to be overstaffed. When there was a cutback in personnel, cadres in basic units in the ministry simply doubled up on jobs, and apparently this was done in at least some instances without too serious a reduction of organizational efficiency.

"Transfer Downward"

From 1957 onward, the geographical, and downward, mobility of cadres in the central ministries was greatly increased. At that time the regime began systematically to carry out the policy of "transferring cadres downward" (hsia fang kan pu). This policy had roots that could be traced to the early history of the Chinese Communist Party, but as developed from 1957 onward it was something new. Over time millions of cadres, including many thousands from the central ministries, were sent from urban centers to lower levels of the bureaucracy and to the countryside. Some were sent on permanent or semipermanent transfers, but many went on temporary assignments. The motives behind this policy were too complex to be summarized briefly; they varied, moreover, at different periods. Retrenchment of personnel in high-level organizations in the bureaucracy, the education and indoctrination of cadres through physical labor in rural areas, the strengthening of leadership at local levels, reduction of the population in major cities, and punishment of errant cadres, all have been elements in the policy at one time or another.

In the "transfer downward" of personnel from many of the central ministries, the goals of combating bureaucratism and educating cadres through labor were particularly important. A great many cadres were sent on temporary assignments, often for a year, to engage in physical labor in rural communes. Frequently, their work had nothing whatever to do with the specialized skills they possessed, and their assignments did not always contribute to strengthening central leadership over work at the local level. In a fundamental sense, therefore, such assignments were often both wasteful of the talents of the cadres involved and disruptive of the normal work in the ministries from which they were drawn. Apparently, however, the regime felt that these costs were justified by the educational and political effects of the experience, and the psychological impact it had, or was expected to have, on the cadres.

Exactly what these psychological effects were is difficult to assess. Some ex-cadres who participated in this type of "transfer downward" suggest that the results were definitely less than the regime hoped for. They say that it probably is true that many cadres, after being exposed to firsthand experience of rural conditions, became more understanding of the conditions and problems of work at the local level. However, many cadres also clearly resented being forced to undergo the hardships of life in the countryside. Often, moreover, there was little reason to believe that the great and real gap between high-level, urban-based bureaucrats and the cadres and masses in rural areas was significantly closed by the transfers. According to some ex-cadres, though, there may have been one unanticipated side effect on at least some cadres. Reportedly, not a few cadres returning to ministry jobs after a year of hard labor in rural areas tended to be less critical of things they had previously complained about in Peking. Problems that had seemed important before now seemed relatively minor after exposure to the difficulties of village life.

Bureau of Supervision

Although, as indicated earlier, the Personnel Bureau served in some respects as a watchdog agency and was responsible for certain types of investigations of cadres, there was also another watchdog unit in Ministry M—the Bureau of Supervision (*chien ch'a chü*)—the responsibility of which was to check continuously on the ministry's entire staff, in order to ensure that all cadres observed existing rules and regulations and effectively carried out current policies.

This bureau was an integral part of the ministry's organization, but it was also linked to a government-wide system headed by the Ministry of Supervision. (This system was separate and distinct from the Party's own Control Committee, or Commission, system.) There is a long tradition in China of establishing special inspectorate agencies of this sort in the government, and the Chinese Communists continued the tradition from the time of their takeover until the late 1950s through their organs of supervision within important government units.

In Ministry M, the Bureau of Supervision was a small one and was not divided into subordinate divisions or sections. Because of its watchdog functions, and because its staff dealt with many classified matters and frequently in the course of its investigations found it necessary to participate in meetings of various Party units, the bureau's cadres were almost all Party members. Many, also, were persons who had had some sort of special training or experience in investigation work.

Most of the work of the bureau consisted of special investigations of individuals or problems—cases of corruption, violations of discipline, and the like—which were brought to its attention in a variety of ways. At times, top ministry officials or bureau chiefs suggested investigations. Sometimes the bureau itself initiated them. Occasionally, information or complaints in "people's letters" (*jen min lai hsin*) to the ministry led to investigations. And from time to time top provincial officials, especially those in departments under the ministry's supervision, requested them. Not all of the bureau's investigations focused on specific, pressing problems, however; sometimes members of the bureau were sent simply to check up in a general way on the work of particular bureaus or provincial departments. Regardless of how a probe was initiated, the bureau's staff could require any organization or person within the ministry, or in subordinate provincial units, to provide them with needed information.

When conducting investigations at the provincial level the bureau invariably sent persons to work on the spot. These investigations were sometimes requested by provincial officials, even though the province itself had supervision personnel, because they felt that cadres armed with the authority of a central ministry might be able to handle particularly difficult cases more effectively than local people.

(Similarly, provincial supervision personnel sometimes conducted investigations at lower levels.) When it had completed investigations at the provincial level, the bureau sent copies of its reports to both the ministry and the provincial government, and the latter had to report later on what action it had taken.

The power of the bureau was limited, however, by the fact that it was purely an investigatory body. On the basis of its investigations, it could and did recommend certain actions; but the power to mete out administrative punishments rested with personnel organs or Party authorities, and the most serious violations of law were turned over to public security organs, the Procuracy, and the courts for police and judicial action.[25]

[25] In 1959 the Ministry of Supervision was abolished, perhaps because it was felt to be unnecessary in view of the existence of a variety of other special investigation agencies, which included both special Party organs such as the Control Committees, and other government agencies such as the public security organs, the Procuracy, and so on.

Patterns of Work

Meetings

THE NORMAL PATTERN of day-to-day work in Ministry M involved a variety of different types of meetings within the organization. The small, regular staff meetings of the top leadership, including the all-important sessions of the Party Fraction, have already been mentioned. Another important category of meetings consisted of those labeled, at least in Ministry M, "report meetings" (*ch'uan ta pao kao hui yi*),[26] in which the minister or other top ministry officials passed on important directives and information received from higher levels. These frequently took place immediately after the minister had attended regular sessions of the State Council or conferences with Central Committee personnel. Their purpose was to brief key people within the ministry on major policy matters or other important developments already defined or discussed at higher levels. Frequently the minister himself delivered the main report at these meetings. Although the reports sometimes dealt with matters directly relevant to the ministries' work, at other times they concerned broad national policies or programs which the regime's top leaders felt all key cadres in the central agencies should know about. Occasionally, cadres were briefed in such meetings on major events or problems that had not yet been mentioned in the official press.[27] Attendance at such "report meetings" was sometimes restricted to chiefs of units within

[26] Another term used for these meetings was *t'ing ta pao kao hui yi*.

[27] Cadres were informed in a variety of ways on the decision to move from lower to higher agricultural cooperatives, the planned retirement of Mao from the chairmanship of the government, and the rising tension between China and the Soviet Union, before these were widely publicized in the press.

the ministry. At other times the meetings were "enlarged" (*k'uo ta*), and on occasion all working cadres attended.

Another type of large staff meeting consisted of those convened on the initiative of the minister himself, working through the Ministry Staff Office, to deal primarily with problems and policies relating to the ministry's own work, rather than, as in the case of the "report meetings," information or directives from higher levels. Labeled "ministry affairs meetings" (*pu wu hui yi*), these were generally held about once a month in Ministry M, and usually were attended by bureau chiefs and others of equivalent rank. The minister himself often made the major report of these sessions, too.

Bureau chiefs in Ministry M generally convened their own staff meetings, labeled "bureau affairs meetings" (*chü wu hui yi*), about once a month. In some divisions, staff meetings were more frequent, often weekly. The sections rarely held formal staff meetings, however.

At all levels, including the sections, there were frequent *ad hoc* meetings, convened as needed, to discuss program matters. They were referred to as "face-to-face meetings" (*p'eng t'ou hui li*). These meetings could be quite frequent; in one division in the ministry, for example, the chief generally held at least two or three, and sometimes more, such meetings a week, in addition to the regular staff meetings.

Secrecy and Security-Consciousness

One striking characteristic of the atmosphere in which all the work in Ministry M was conducted was the high degree of secrecy and security-consciousness that prevailed. The work of Ministry M did not belong to a field considered particularly sensitive by the regime for either political or defense reasons. Yet the system of security that operated even in this ministry, and the atmosphere of secrecy affecting all its cadres, were comparable in many respects to those characteristic of highly sensitive national security agencies in a country such as the United States.

The stringency of security measures in all central ministries in China has changed from time to time, but even in relaxed periods it has been notably great. The regime's leaders appear to feel a continuing need for total control of information, partly to prevent "class enemies" at home as well as abroad from obtaining information that might be used against the regime. The leaders' long history of conspiracy as well as open struggle prior to their achieving power may well have been a major factor conditioning their attitudes on security after 1949.

There was a well-defined security system (*pao mi chih tu*) in Ministry M, with comprehensive rules on how written materials and other information should be handled; and every new employee joining the ministry's staff had to study and learn it. A high proportion of all written material handled in the ministry was restricted or classified. There were three main classifications stamped on documents, which might be translated roughly as "top secret" (*chüeh mi*), "very secret" (*chi mi*), and "secret" (*mi chien*). In addition to having security classifications on them, many documents were also marked with stamps restricting access to personnel of a certain job rank (such as bureau chiefs). The material that was classified included many types of statistics and other information that in most Western countries would be considered relatively unimportant or routine— or even desirable to publish. Classified material could not normally be taken out of the ministry, nor, in fact, be shown to a person outside of one's basic unit, except when permission was granted to do so. (As indicated earlier, certain units and lines of work—e.g. personnel—were surrounded by extra security precautions.) Within the ministry, classified material had to be locked up when office personnel were not present, and loss of such material was a serious offense. Access to the ministry building was regulated by an efficient system of building security involving passes for ministry personnel and "letters of introduction" for others; this system will be described later (see p. 98).

Since there was a large flow of classified material in and out of the ministries, special classified channels of communication throughout the country were required. Within the postal and telecommunications system, special units existed at all levels to handle classified documents; this channel was referred to as the "military post" (*chün yu*). There were also designated personnel and special procedures at all levels to handle classified telegrams.

In addition to official government documents, other sorts of materials circulated to ministry personnel were also classified. For example, in Ministry M a confidential news service, called "Reference News" (*ts'an k'ao hsiao hsi*), was distributed to cadres of section-chief rank and above.[28] This mimeographed service contained news items, especially on world affairs, that were not printed in the official press; much of its news was simply drawn from Western news sources. The purpose of the service was to ensure that higher cadres were somewhat better informed than the mass of the population, who had to depend on the public press; but what cadres could read was still carefully selected. (Similar services existed at lower levels of the bureaucracy too.) Cadres who had access to this service were expected to treat the material in it as classified, and were not allowed to show it to, or discuss it with, either lower-ranking cadres or persons outside of the bureaucracy.

Party members in Ministry M lived and worked under a security system and in an atmosphere of secrecy that was even more rigid and restrictive than those affecting non-Party cadres. They could not discuss their Party meetings with non-Party people. A variety of classified Party documents (*tang ti wen chien*), some of them regular journals, were circulated to Party members—often distribution was restricted to Party members of a specified rank or job. Since none of these materials could be shown to non-Party people, and since at times Party members felt it necessary to take some of these materials home, most Party members had to work out special facilities at home, such as a locked desk or room, where classified materials could be kept in a secure place.

According to ex-cadres this restrictive security system clearly achieved effective informational control. Cadres were generally wary about even discussing their work with anyone outside the bureaucracy. The restrictions apparently did more than this, however. Reportedly, the general atmosphere of security-consciousness also im-

[28] According to other reports, there are at least three publications of this general sort, varying in completeness and objectivity, that circulate in some institutions in Communist China. One, which is the most exhaustive and complete, is said to go only to the offices of deputy ministers and above, while another called "Reference Material" (*ts'an k'ao tzu liao*) goes to slightly lower-ranking cadres, and "Reference News" goes to the lowest cadre ranks provided with such materials. In some places "Reference News" is said to be available to some cadres below section-chief rank.

posed constraints on cadres which made them careful even in exchanging information with other members of the bureaucracy, such as persons in other ministries, or in some cases, persons in other units within their own ministry. It was, therefore, undoubtedly a factor which in some respects limited the flow of information throughout the bureaucracy.

Rhythm of Work: Daily and Weekly Patterns

In Ministry M, as in most large bureaucratic organizations, there was a regular daily and weekly schedule of normal work. In addition there tended to be a distinctive rhythm of activity over longer periods. The ministry operated on an eight-hour day and a six-day week, of which five and one-half days were devoted to ministry work and one half-day (Saturday afternoon) to political study. Some holidays were interspersed throughout the year, the most important of which included New Year's Day (January 1), the Chinese New Year (called the Spring Festival and based on the lunar calendar), May Day (May 1), National Day (October 1), and a few others.

The average winter workday in Ministry M began at 8:00 A.M. and continued until 5:30 P.M. Each new period of the day was announced by bells which rang throughout the ministry, in a fashion most familiar in the West, perhaps, in schools or military establishments. After the 8 o'clock bell, work went on for over two hours, and then the next bell, at 10:15, announced a fifteen-minute period of physical exercise, consisting of organized calisthenics, led by a physical instructor. Work was resumed from 10:30 to 12:00 noon. There was then a one-and-a-half hour break for lunch and rest. Although a few cadres either went home to eat or brought box lunches, the majority had a quick lunch in the ministry's mess hall and then relaxed in their offices; many napped on their desks. A bell at 1:30 P.M. announced the resumption of work. From 3:30 to 3:45 there was another fifteen-minute exercise period, after which work resumed until 5:30. (In summer the hours were different and the workday did not end until 6:30.)

Evenings were the time for political meetings, which were a very important part of the cadres' way of life. Many cadres spent the majority of their evenings in meetings. These included not only the regular Friday-night Party and YCL meetings and the meetings of the Labor Union on Wednesday nights but a wide variety of other special meetings and rallies. During campaigns, particularly, meetings could occur almost every night. Evening commitments even for average cadres tended to be so numerous that they had relatively little "free time." In fact, it seemed to be the conscious policy of the regime to see that free time was severely limited. Married couples with children had to organize their lives so as to ensure that their children would be cared for during their frequent evenings out. If they could, they were generally inclined to put their children into boarding schools.

Plan Periods and Political Campaigns: Tension and Relaxation

Over the course of the years, the rhythm of life and work in Ministry M was predetermined to a large extent by the system of planning which regulated all work in the ministry, as throughout the bureaucracy. All work was supposed to be geared to long-term policies (*fang chen*), long-term plans or programs (*kuei hua*), short-term policies (*cheng ts'e*), and short-term plans (*chi hua*). Operationally the most important of these were the annual, or short-term, plans, which were broken down into semiannual and quarterly periods. For each of these periods, in economic agencies at least, a variety of control figures or targets (*k'ung chih shu tzu*) for achievement were set, and the success of a unit was measured largely on the basis of whether the targets were fulfilled or, hopefully, "overfulfilled." Consequently, at predictable periods during the year, as the end of plan periods approached, the pace and tension of work increased. Especially toward the end of the year, the entire bureaucracy tended to go into high gear, and each cadre was expected to exert his maximum effort to ensure fulfillment of his unit's target.

Less predictable, but in some respects even more important in their effects on the general rhythm of life and work, were the major campaigns periodically promoted by the regime. As indicated earlier, these occurred at fairly frequent intervals, and the most important of them involved periods of almost frenetic activity and extreme tension. These campaigns played an extraordinary role in the operational dynamics of the bureaucracy in China. At the height of a campaign, cadres devoted virtually full time to meetings and other activities related to it and had virtually no time for "private" individual affairs. Every campaign was exhausting—and unnerving, too, for many cadres—and a significant amount of time and energy went into getting over the last campaign or preparing for the next one. In a sense, therefore, life and work went through alternating periods of tension and relaxation that were determined by the schedule of major campaigns.

Campaigns are still important today, but over time, especially since the late 1950s, in a slow and subtle way the regime has found it increasingly difficult to mobilize the cadres and inject a high level of tension into the system. Repeated campaigns have tended to inure many cadres to them, and some cadres appear to have gradually built up certain defense mechanisms, with the result that while they may go through the same motions as in the past they are sometimes able to avoid the same degree of psychological involvement.

Channels of Authority
and Patterns of
Communication

IN THE highly centralized structure of power in China, all ministries, as indicated earlier, are directed by higher Party and government authorities, through the Party departments and State Council staff offices which are responsible for the broad functional "systems" into which the ministries are grouped. At the same time, however, each one forms the apex of, and directs, a specialized functional hierarchy of its own that reaches from the ministry level down to the local level through provincial departments (*t'ing*) and county bureaus (*chü*). Involved also are comparable units at some intermediate levels—for example, at the special district level, between province and county—and possibly (although it is not wholly clear at present) at the level of the Party's large new regional bureaus.

There was a constant flow of written directives and instructions to Ministry M from the related Central Committee department and State Council staff office, and a steady return flow of reports upward. There were also frequent direct contacts with personnel at higher levels. The minister regularly attended both State Council sessions (about once a month) and conferences convened by either the Central Committee department or the State Council staff office. Personnel from these latter two organizations also sat in at ministry affairs meetings from time to time, and even, on occasion, at meetings convened by particular bureaus within a ministry.

Since the work of many ministries, especially those within one general functional "system," tended to be fairly closely interrelated, and sometimes overlapped to a degree, there was considerable need for contact, consultation, and exchange of information among ministries. In the case of ministries concerned with economic matters, liaison was particularly close with organizations such as the State Planning Commission, State Economic Commission, and Ministry of Finance, which, because of their special roles in the planning process, exercised certain coordinating and watchdog functions throughout most of the bureaucracy. Contacts took place not only between ministers but also between lower-level ministry personnel; generally communications were between persons of equal status—for example, bureau chiefs dealt with bureau chiefs. Apart from written communications, some interagency business was done by phone, but this was inhibited by fears of compromising security. Consequently, there was a good deal of visiting between ministry-level agencies. Most of this was fairly formal, in the sense that a cadre generally had to have an official "letter of introduction," chopped by his own ministry or bureau, in order to visit another ministry to discuss substantive matters. These letters often specified the subjects authorized for discussion, and because of the prevalent security-consciousness, cadres (at least those of lower ranks) usually restricted their discussions to the prescribed topics and avoided anything that could be interpreted as unwarranted probing into the affairs of another organization.

Downward Flow of Authority

A great deal of the ministry's work throughout the country was actually conducted through regional organs, at the provincial level and below, which operated under the ministry's direction; thus, effective communication downward was crucial in the operation of the system. In many respects, the provincial departments belonging to the functional system headed by Ministry M (and bearing the same title as it did) could be regarded as branches of the ministry. It is true that the degree of autonomy and initiative granted to provincial departments varied in different fields and from one period to another, and at times it was substantial in some fields. But fundamentally, provincial and other local organs had no inviolable autonomy. The powers they exercised were only those delegated from the center, and the center could centralize or decentralize authority as it saw fit. Consequently, the vertical chain of command was all-important in the system, and orders from above were always binding on lower levels, even though the spheres of responsibility which a ministry kept in its own hands or delegated to provincial departments were variable.

From the point of view of a provincial department, however, the lines of responsibility were complex. All government bodies in China, including the provincial departments, operated under both "vertical leadership" (*t'iao t'iao ling tao*), exercised by equivalent government bodies at higher levels within their own functional system, and horizontal or regional leadership (*k'uai k'uai ling tao*), exercised by the top over-all government body at their own administrative level (e.g. the Provincial People's Council). Moreover, as in the case of the ministries themselves, they were responsible to and controlled by not only higher government bodies but also by Party organizations at their own level (e.g. the Provincial Party Committee and one of its departments). In short, they operated under what was often called "dual leadership" (*shuang ch'ung ling tao*) but in reality was usually multiple leadership (*to ch'ung ling tao*, or *chiao ch'a ling tao*), and was sometimes labeled as such. Typically, therefore, a provincial government department was answerable to a central ministry, the local Provincial People's Council, and the local Provincial Party Committee (plus one of the Party Committee's departments). All of these were important. Evidence from ex-cadres suggests that in the system to which Ministry M belonged, the leadership of the local Party Committee was most important politically, and the local People's Council played an important coordinating role, but a great deal of the supervision and control over the substantive work—the "business" (*yeh wu*)—of the provincial departments was exercised directly by the central ministry.

For the most part the central ministries dealt with provincial departments and let the latter deal with lower administrative levels. At times, however, Ministry M could and did issue instructions and orders directly to lower units. This practice, called "skipping levels" (*yüeh chi*), was said to be frowned upon, but it nevertheless did occur.

The flow of written communications to and from Ministry M was

large. Apart from official letters (*kung han*), the downward flow
from the ministry to lower-level organizations included many types
of informational documents as well as regulations (*kuei ting*), rules
(*t'iao li*, also translated as "regulations"), orders (*ming ling*), instructions or directives (*chih shih*), circular notices (*t'ung chih* or *t'ung
pao*), and a variety of other authoritative documents, while the flow
upward to the ministry included a large number of regular reports
(*pao kao*), as well as requests (*ch'ing shih*).

Central Authority and Local Flexibility

Actually, in the "legislative process" in Communist China—if this
term is interpreted broadly to mean all authoritative rule-making—
legislatures and formal laws (*fa ling*) play a relatively minor role.
The greatest flow of "legislation" comes, on the one hand from the
Party (e.g. its "resolutions," *chüeh yi*) and, on the other, from
executive and administrative bodies in the government, including,
at the top level, the ministries as well as the State Council.

To a large extent, according to ex-cadres, the instructions sent to
lower levels by Ministry M, as by most other central bodies, tended
to be fairly generalized. Rather than specifying in great detail exactly how a general policy or program was to be implemented, they
frequently allowed considerable leeway for, and in fact called for,
local adaptation and interpretation. When concrete regulations were
issued, these sometimes were in draft (*ts'ao an*) form. Some important Party directives were actually transmitted not in the form of
specific directives at all but as regulations or outlines of "model"
(*mo fan*) institutions or programs.

Therefore, even though the chain of command was, in a basic
sense, unchallengeable at lower levels, central bodies made a conscious effort to build into the system a significant element of local
flexibility—primarily in policy implementation rather than in policy
formation—to counterbalance the high degree of centralization of
ultimate authority. This undoubtedly was an important factor in
making the system work as well as it did. The central authorities
issued an unending flow of directives down the chain of command,
and these were actually implemented at the local level to an extent

perhaps unprecedented in China, but in implementing them local authorities were both able and expected to take account of local conditions. If, instead, the central authorities had attempted to specify rigidly and in detail how all directives were to be uniformly implemented throughout the country, they probably would have encountered insuperable obstacles, in a country as enormous and varied as China.

Another distinctive characteristic of the process of disseminating directives and information from the ministries downward was the frequent use of what might be called a "filtering process." This involved dissemination stage by stage, from one level to the next, down the administrative hierarchy. In this process, instead of announcing policies and plans simultaneously at all levels throughout the country, the top authorities held meetings first to brief cadres in the central organs; then similar meetings were held in succession at the provincial level, the county level, and finally at the commune level. Generally, at each level steps were taken to inform the "leading cadres" first, then the rank-and-file cadres. Frequently also, at each level, Party cadres were informed before non-Party cadres.

One interesting innovation in the system of communications linking the ministry with the provincial departments was the institution of "urgent telephone conferences" (*chin chi tien hua hui yi*). When matters of great importance and urgency required quick consultation between the minister and the chiefs of provincial departments, a national hookup linking all the provincial organs was arranged. These conferences were irregular, but reportedly Ministry M held them several times a year.

Official Business Visits to and from the Ministry

Frequent visits of personnel both from the ministry to the local levels and vice versa played a very important role in the system of communication within the bureaucracy. A large number of cadres from the ministry made periodic inspection visits or other types of business trips, which took them not only to the provincial-level offices but also on occasion to the counties, communes, and villages. Generally, a cadre going to the lowest levels would "touch base" with each intervening level in the hierarchy. Such trips were made by ministry personnel of every rank, from the minister himself to low-level ordinary cadres. Sometimes they lasted for weeks, or even months. They served a variety of general purposes, apart from enabling the cadres involved to perform specific, immediate, assigned tasks. When visiting lower levels, cadres from the ministry briefed local cadres on current policies and programs, inspected the work of local agencies, and familiarized themselves with local conditions and problems.

These trips certainly helped the ministry to keep in touch with developments at a grass-roots level throughout the country, and to an extent contributed to combating bureaucratism and preventing central cadres from becoming desk-bound. However, they did not automatically ensure that the ministry was well informed about local conditions or eliminate the great gap existing between cadres at the center and those in local areas. Ex-cadres who made many trips of this sort, and who also, while themselves on extended "transfer downward" assignments in rural areas, observed other cadres from the ministries making them, state that it was extremely difficult for ministry-level cadres to establish close rapport with rural cadres or to probe beneath the surface appearance of things. Status-consciousness in the bureaucracy was such that at the village level all cadres from the ministries, even low-ranking non-Party cadres, were treated with great deference and were regarded with something close to awe. Local cadres often referred to them simply as "central cadres" (*chung yang kan pu*) or "Peking cadres" (*pei ching kan pu*) and assumed that since they came directly from the center of national power they must all have enormous authority. Wishing to make a good impression, local cadres also generally tried to provide the best possible accommodations and meals for such visitors and often attempted to paint as favorable a picture as possible of local conditions rather than stress difficulties and problems which they faced. In short, despite the regime's emphasis on the "mass line," antibureaucratism, and the need for direct knowledge by bureaucrats of local conditions, the psychological as well as geographical gap between the central authorities and the local areas was not an easy one to bridge. Nevertheless, frequent trips by ministry personnel to the local level were certainly an important element in the operation of the system.

The flow of personnel from lower levels, and especially from the provinces, to the ministry was even greater and more important in the operation of the system than the flow downward. A large number of people from the provincial departments went every year to attend meetings or training courses arranged by the ministry. Roughly once a year, Ministry M convened a national conference of the heads of all subordinate provincial departments, to discuss current programs and future plans. Bureaus within the ministry also held periodic meetings of provincial-level personnel working in their specialized fields. Sometimes conferences of provincial personnel in particular regions were held in major cities other than Peking. From time to time both the ministry and its bureaus organized conferences of particular categories of specialists from provincial departments. The ministry also ran a variety of cadre courses and training classes to which personnel from the provinces came. All of these were important, not only in channeling information and directives down the hierarchy but also in keeping the ministry informed about the operation of subordinate bodies under its direction.

One further channel by which information about the operation of the system reached the ministry deserves mention, even though it was of relatively minor importance. At all levels of the bureaucracy in China, there was a certain flow of "people's letters" (*jen min lai hsin*), from the "masses" to the bureaucratic organizations. Some of these contained requests, while others registered complaints or criticism of policies or personnel. It was standard practice to answer, or at least acknowledge, all such letters, and on occasion the letters led to investigations or other action. In Ministry M the staff office first received most of these letters. Occasionally it answered some of the letters itself, but generally it forwarded them to one of the bureaus for reply and, if necessary, action. A number of letters went to the Bureau of Supervision, for possible investigation. In a bureau, the reply frequently would be drafted by division-level personnel and then sent to the bureau chief for approval. If the matter was fairly routine it then went out in the bureau's name and with its chop, but if it was important it might be forwarded to the staff office to be sent with the ministry's chop.

A large proportion of the letters were handled in a routine way, and the answers were rather *pro forma*, but from time to time major complaints or charges of cadre misconduct received serious attention. To a degree, therefore, these letters provided a channel through which the ministry received some information and opinions from outside its own organization concerning the personnel and work of its subordinate bodies. Apparently, however, in practice such letters were not of very great importance in influencing the operation of the ministry.

In sum, the over-all picture provided by ex-cadres of the internal communications system in the bureaucracy indicates that Ministry M had excellent means of communications with lower levels (far better than those existing between the central and provincial governments before 1949), but that for a variety of reasons dissemination of directives down the hierarchy was more effective than the flow of information upward. The most important reason for this was not any lack of adequate channels for communication upward; rather it was because the system was so highly centralized, because authority was concentrated to such an extent at the top, and because existing patterns of authority created a great gap between higher and lower levels. Despite a conscious effort by the ministry to encourage flexibility and initiative at lower levels, the concentration of ultimate decision-making power at the top was unquestioned, and in practice all personnel at the lowest levels felt under great pressure to carry out policies and achieve targets defined at the top. Operationally, therefore, the most important element in the system was the downward flow of directives through the chain of command.

The Planning Bureau

Planning, statistical work, financial work, and accounting are obviously required in all large modern bureaucracies, but they are clearly of special importance in government organs in a Communist-ruled society, particularly in economic agencies whose operations are dominated by the necessity of achieving annual targets.

The Planning Bureau (*chi hua chü*) in Ministry M was a large one, under which there were three divisions: the Long-Range Plans Division (*kuei hua ch'u*), the [Short-Range] Planning Division (*chi hua ch'u*), and the Investigation and Research Division (*tiao ch'a yen chiu ch'u*).

The Long-Range Plans Division, a relatively small body, was concerned, as its name implies, with the problem of formulating plans covering several years, especially five-year plans, and it maintained close liaison with the State Planning Commission. Because realistic long-term plans for any one sector of the economy required considerable knowledge of other, related economic sectors, the State Planning Commission made available to the division a fairly broad range of classified statistical publications. These included comprehensive volumes of "statistical materials on the national economy" (*kuo min ching chi t'ung chi tzu liao*) that were not only unpublished but were not available to most other employees of Ministry M, who by and large could see only statistics with low classification which were directly relevant to their own work. Moreover, with letters of introduction from their minister, the staff of this division could visit the State Planning Commission and see additional material. The most highly classified materials in the commission, however, were made available only if they directly concerned the work of the ministry.[29]

The Investigation and Research Division of the Planning Bureau conducted a variety of studies. Some involved problems in the collection of statistics, but others were concerned with basic, underlying factors affecting the statistical system and trends in ministry work, as revealed by available statistics. Its investigations usually centered on fairly broad problems, however, and although they might require surveys, these were apparently not as important to the process of formulating short-term plans as other field investigations, conducted at the provincial level, which will be described below.

The most important division of this bureau was the one concerned with drawing up annual and other short-term plans.

The Planning Process

Even though Ministry M helped to determine the plans of all subordinate regional and local bodies under its supervision, it actually played only an intermediate role in the over-all planning process.

[29] Published statistics were not different from secret ones—i.e. there was not a double set of statistical books—but a great many, in fact most, statistics were classified and therefore unpublished.

The most important general policy decisions were made at an even higher level, at the top of the Party and government hierarchies. In theory, only tentative, preliminary, general "control figures" or "targets" (*k'ung chih shu tzu*) were supposed to be set at the top, to define the range within which lower units should set their own specific targets. The subsequent planning process was described as "from top to bottom and from bottom to top" (*yu shang erh hsia yu hsia ehr shang*), meaning that preliminary targets went down from the top, and then revised draft targets went up from the bottom. In reality, however, the preliminary targets set by the highest authorities tended to crystallize and set at least the minimum over-all targets permissible for lower units; generally the targets established by top authorities were divided into targets for lower administrative levels, and often lower levels could not do much more than "adjust" the targets suggested to them. Sometimes they felt under pressure, in fact, to try to set their final targets higher than the preliminary figures suggested to them.

At the highest level, the over-all framework for planning was established by the basic policies and goals defined by such top Party and government authorities as the Party Central Committee, the Politburo, and the Politburo Standing Committee, plus the State Council. (The People's Congress each year formally adopted an over-all annual plan, but its role was entirely *pro forma*.) On the basis of the plans and policies defined by these bodies the State Planning Commission was responsible for working out long-term plans, and the State Economic Commission, which was split off as an independent body in 1956, was responsible for short-term ones; operationally the latter were the most important. As indicated earlier, though, both the Central Committee departments and the State Council staff offices apparently also played an important behind-the-scenes role in the planning process. Also, the Ministry of Finance was significantly involved in across-the-board planning since it was responsible for coordinating the financial aspects of the plans.

Ex-cadres report that the initial steps to formulate annual plans generally started in the summer before the year of the plan, with the State Economic Commission taking the main initiative. Reportedly, the personnel of this commission first independently studied the general economic situation, and subsequently consulted with all the ministries. Then they attempted to make preliminary estimates of probable output or performance during the current year—which provided the most essential starting point for setting future plans— and to analyze the factors likely to affect future production. On this basis they cautiously sketched out possible future targets and discussed these with personnel in the State Council, the Central Committee, the State Planning Commission, and the Ministry of Finance, to make sure that their thinking fitted into the regime's broad policies and to check feasibility in a preliminary way. After further discussions with the ministries, resulting in inevitable adjustments in the initial figures, the State Economic Commission proceeded to prepare preliminary targets for all the ministries (these were national targets for each of the fields directed by the ministries), as well as over-all provincial targets. The ministries were then responsible for adjusting and subdividing their national targets for the provinces, which in turn subdivided them among the counties. The specific types of targets set for each ministry varied, depending on the type of work in which the ministry was engaged.

The planning process involved bargaining at every level. In general, units at higher levels, when setting targets for lower units, tried to set them as high as possible within the limits of estimated feasibility. Personnel in lower units were under conflicting pressures. On one hand, they were anxious to be certain of fulfilling or "over-fulfilling their targets" (ch'ao o wan ch'eng chi hua) without undue strain, but at the same time, they were under pressure to demonstrate their competence and enthusiasm by setting targets as high as possible. As a result, although there were sometimes "adjustments" downward in the bargaining process between higher and lower levels, in other cases lower units might actually set figures higher than the preliminary targets passed down to them. Generally, however, the preliminary targets initially set by the higher authorities were not radically altered at lower levels.

Roles of the Ministry and the
Provincial Departments in Planning

From the viewpoint of Ministry M, its major job in the annual planning process generally started in the fall,[30] when it received the preliminary target figures proposed by the State Economic Commission and Ministry of Finance (sometimes these were issued, however, in the State Council's name). The Short-Range Plans Division then set to work and, on the basis of the over-all figures given to it, established preliminary targets to send to the statistics divisions (*chi t'ung ch'u*) in all the provincial departments under the ministry's supervision. In theory, the provinces were then supposed to set preliminary targets for each county, which in turn defined proposed targets for all rural collective units. Then, starting from the bottom, definite draft targets were supposed to move up the hierarchy.

In practice, however, because of the limited time allowed for completing the planning process, and perhaps also because at the county level and below in many places there were few persons qualified to formulate plans intelligently, the provincial governments often were not able to send preliminary targets to the counties and obtain their comments and proposed adjustments prior to the time when the province itself had to send draft targets to the ministry. Consequently, the provinces frequently simply set general targets for their counties with minimal consultation with them.

At the provincial level, however, once preliminary figures had been received from the ministry, there was generally a serious attempt within the time available, to study the figures, investigate the actual current situation in the province, study the factors likely to affect future performance, determine what might be feasible in the coming year, and then decide whether they should try to adjust the preliminary targets either downward or upward. This involved much work and numerous meetings at the provincial level; generally, also, the provincial department's Statistics Division sent out investigators to the county level to make up-to-date spot surveys of the work of

[30] Prior to this, of course, the ministry started to evaluate its own performance for the year, which was a necessary first step before starting planning for the next year.

subordinate bodies and of conditions throughout the province that might affect their work. However, because time was limited (provincial departments sometimes had to send back draft targets to the ministry within one to two months after receiving the preliminary targets[31]) these surveys had to be made quickly. Nevertheless, they were extremely important, since they were the main basis for attempting to make realistic local estimates of what might be feasible.

Only rarely was there time for a provincial department to make general surveys (*p'u pien tiao ch'a*) covering all or most counties. Generally, all that could be attempted was a rapid survey, based on simple sampling techniques, and "keypoint investigations" (*tien hsin tiao ch'a*), focusing on selected areas or keypoints (*chung tien*). There were various ways in which this was done. One was a method labeled the "top-middle-bottom" (*shang chung hsia*) system. Simply stated, this was a system under which the provincial department sent investigators to three counties in the province—one where performance was believed to be outstanding, one where it was average, and one where it was notably poor—for intensive investigations. Then, in each of these counties three districts (later, communes) were selected, and in each of them three specific local areas. These too were supposed to represent examples of outstanding, average, and poor performance. The provincial investigators, working with local Party and government leaders, mobilized local cadres to help them investigate each of these selected localities. At the lowest level there were numerous meetings to discuss problems and prospects, as well as direct observation by the investigators of the current situation. The results of these investigations were then used at the provincial level as a basis for making crude estimates of the current situation and the next year's prospects for the province as a whole.

Draft and Final Plans

By a defined date, the provinces had to send back their adjusted figures to the ministry. These were still called "draft-plan" (*chi hua*

[31] Another ex-cadre asserts, however, that generally the provincial departments had two to three months after receiving targets from the ministry before they had to send in their draft plans.

ts'ao an) figures. Not long after all of these had been received, Ministry M convened a large national conference in Peking. This conference was attended by all provincial department chiefs (*ch'üan kuo t'ing chang hui yi*) and also by three to five other cadres from each department, including the chief of the Planning and Statistics Division, perhaps two other statistical experts, and the chiefs of one or two other important divisions under the department. During such a meeting, which normally lasted about a week, the ministry's draft-plan figures were hammered out, on the basis of the provinces' figures, in a series of intensive meetings and consultations, and the necessary adjustments were made in the figures sent in earlier by the provinces. Finally the ministry sent its draft plan to be approved by the highest authorities, including the State Economic Commission and the Finance Ministry. At this stage the plan, for all practical purposes, became operational, even though it did not formally become a "final plan" (*ting an*) until the State Council presented its over-all national plans to the National People's Congress and received the latter's approval. The ministry then divided its over-all national targets into definite targets for each province, which in turn divided theirs into targets for units at lower levels. On the basis of further consultation with the provinces, also, the ministry divided the annual targets into seasonal or quarterly ones.

Although in theory this entire process was supposed to be completed by the start of the plan year, in fact it was generally not brought to a close until some months later; however, most units had a reasonably good idea of what their targets were likely to be by the start of the year.

The annual planning cycle involved a great investment of time and effort by ministry personnel throughout almost the entire year (even more than does the annual budget cycle in U. S. government agencies, which is time-consuming enough). The process was fairly simple in many respects, however, and in a fundamental sense it was the policy decisions made by personnel at the top of the system rather than the data or ideas from lower levels which determined the general shape of the plans ultimately adopted.

Bureau of Statistics

A considerable amount of time and effort was also devoted by ministry personnel to the collection of statistics on all phases of work done by agencies operating at all levels under the ministry's direction. The Bureau of Statistics (*t'ung chi chü*) in Ministry M was another large unit, therefore. It had under it two divisions: the Statistics Division (*t'ung chi ch'u*), which collected nationwide statistics on both a functional and a regional basis, and the Comprehensive [Statistics] Division (*tsung ho ch'u*), which analyzed and processed the statistics in a variety of ways.

Statistical reports were transmitted up the governmental hierarchy through more than one channel. At each level of regional administration there was a specialized statistical unit for the government as a whole (for example, a county committee or bureau, a provincial department, etc.) which collected over-all statistics for the region; the apex of this specialized hierarchy was the State Statistical Bureau. In addition, however, within each nationwide functional "system" headed by a ministry, including the one headed by Ministry M, there were also statistical personnel and units at each level (for example, sections or divisions for statistics, or planning and statistics, within the county bureaus and provincial departments); these reported to equivalent units at the next higher level, and culminated in the ministry's Bureau of Statistics.

Two types of statistical reporting to the ministry took place from the provincial departments under Ministry M. First of all there were numerous, detailed written statistical reports (*shu mien t'ung chi pao kao*). In addition, there were telephone reports (*tien hua hui pao*). Because statistics were particularly important to the type of work done by Ministry M and its subordinate bodies, the reporting schedule called for more frequent and detailed reports than in some other ministries. Actually, each provincial department was required to send by mail a fairly detailed daily statistical report, which was based on similar reports from lower levels. In addition, every five days they provided selected statistics in telephone reports to the ministry; within the ministry's Bureau of Statistics, personnel designated to specialize on particular provinces received these reports on a regular schedule.

The statistics gathered and processed by the bureau were mainly for the ministry's own operational use and were distributed throughout the ministry on a regular basis as needed. One of the assistants to the minister was specially responsible for keeping an eye on the statistical system; the bureau sent him a special monthly consolidated report. The bureau also sent reports to the State Statistical Bureau and, as requested, to the State Council staff office and the Central Committee department supervising the ministry. If any of these organizations wished to have interim reports, they simply telephoned their request to the minister, and the minister instructed the Bureau of Statistics to prepare whatever was required. All statistics prepared within the ministry, being intended for operational use, were considered to be provisional; only those issued by the State Statistical Bureau were regarded as "final."

The quality of statistics flowing to the ministry in this system improved gradually,[32] but there were some real problems in obtaining accurate and reliable information from lower levels. The greatest problems, actually, were at the lowest levels, where cadres with very little statistical training were responsible for gathering and reporting a wide variety of statistical material. Not only were these cadres relatively unskilled, but their reporting was sometimes influenced by the fact that local units felt under continuous pressure to prove good performance. Obviously, the final statistics emerging at the ministry level could be no better than the primary information fed into the system at the bottom. At higher levels there were also some problems in working out effective reporting forms and schedules and in processing data so that they would be really useful operationally to ministry personnel. But clearly the weakest link in the system was at the local level.

[32] During the "Great Leap Forward," from 1958 on, however, all statistical services in Communist China deteriorated, mainly as a result of political pressures.

Bureau of Finance and Accounting

The Bureau of Finance and Accounting (*ts'ai k'uai chü*) in Ministry M was responsible, as were comparable units in most ministries, for general management and control of finances for the ministry. It reported and was responsible to the Ministry of Finance as well as to the top cadres within its own ministry. It too served, therefore, as an important watchdog and control agency, not over political matters, as in the case of the Bureaus of Personnel and Supervision, but rather over the substantive aspects of the ministry's work. Financial data provided one basic measure for checking on general performance and fulfillment of plans, and financial controls were among the most important means of regulating the operations of all units under the ministry's direction, including those at lower administrative levels. The Bureau of Finance and Accounting itself, therefore, checked on and helped to regulate all units under Ministry M. In addition, the bureau's most important monthly, quarterly, and annual reports, which went to the Ministry of Finance, provided the latter with a basis on which it could evaluate and help to regulate the work of Ministry M.

The Bureau of Finance and Accounting was a large one, with three divisions: the Finance Division (*ts'ai wu ch'u*) responsible for over-all financial planning including preparation of the annual financial plan or budget; the Accounting Division (*k'uai chi ch'u*), which, as its name implied, kept the records; and the Systems Division (*chih tu ch'u*), a small unit that studied and recommended systems and procedures, on the basis of general principles defined by the Ministry of Finance.

Operating funds provided by the Ministry of Finance to Ministry M were channeled through this bureau and were then allotted to operating units under the ministry on the basis of budgetary plans. Disbursements for the ministry's administrative expenses were made through the General Affairs Division.

Expenditures for "capital construction" (*chi pen chien she*) were handled separately, through the independent Division of Capital Construction (*chi chien ch'u*), roughly equivalent to a bureau in status. This division supervised a special ministry enterprise, the Building

Construction Company (*chien chu kung ch'eng kung szu*), which was "economically independent" (*ching chi tu li*)—that is, it was operated as an independent accounting unit, as such enterprises generally were—but was controlled and directed by the division. The construction division and the Company together were responsible for all construction and repair of the ministry's physical facilities. It is not entirely clear whether this division was in the catagory of the "administrative" or the "business" units in the ministry, but it probably belonged to the former.

In-Service Training and Education

Most ministries in Peking are engaged in training and education in a variety of ways. Virtually all of them run in-service training courses or classes for cadres. At times, some ministries have administered large special cadre schools providing specialized training relevant to their work. In cases where there are other independent institutes providing such training, the ministries maintain close liaison with them. In addition to their involvement in cadre training, the ministries also generally operate nurseries, and sometimes other schools as well, for cadres' children.

In Ministry M, there was an Education Bureau (*chiao yü chü*), which was responsible for cadre training and also ran nursery schools for the children of ministry employees.[33] This was a medium-size bureau and had two divisions: the Educational Materials Division (*chiao ts'ai pien yi ch'u*), responsible for over-all planning of cadre training and preparation of instructional materials; and the Education Division (*chiao yü ch'u*), which actually administered all ministry-run training classes and schools.

Ministry M at one time operated two levels of cadre training institutions: a Higher Cadre School (*kao teng kan pu hsüeh hsiao*) and a lower-level Cadre School (simply called *kan pu hsüeh hsiao*). The former was particularly important while it existed, but it was eventually converted into a separate, independent institute, or college. While in existence under Ministry M, it accepted students with

---

[33] In some other ministries the Personnel Bureau had an education division or other subunit responsible for this work.

the equivalent of either higher or lower middle school educations. These students belonged mainly to two categories. Some were assigned by provincial departments to receive specialized training in the school; these were generally cadres with a good deal of experience. While receiving in-service training at the school, the cadres continued to be paid their regular salaries, and generally they later returned to their own provincial departments. The second major group of students consisted of young, recent graduates of middle schools assigned by the Party and government to work in the ministry or in subordinate organs supervised by it. For them, attendance at the school provided a general introduction to the work of the ministry, and preliminary professional training. All students attending the school took courses that exposed them to many of the different sorts of work done by the ministry, but there was also concentration on particular specialties. The courses often lasted a year or more. The low-level Cadre School, on the other hand, was considered to be an institution of roughly middle-school level, and ran shorter in-service training courses. When both these schools were in existence several hundred students could be accommodated in them at one time.

As already mentioned, the Education Bureau of Ministry M managed nursery schools for cadres' children. The person in charge of these was the minister's wife, herself a Party member and "old cadre." These nursery schools were important to the cadres, since many cadre families in which both husband and wife worked had small children, and very few families included another relative, such as a mother-in-law, who was capable of caring for small children. Moreover, as stated earlier, the frequency of evening meetings created real problems of child care even after working hours. Therefore, cadres generally desired, if possible, to send their children to the ministry's boarding nursery school, where they spent six out of seven days, returning home for one day every weekend. This was the largest school in the ministry, with about 150 children. There was also, however, a day nursery school, with roughly sixty children. These two schools could not accommodate all the small children of cadres in the ministry; thus there was strong competition for admission. The schools were considered well-run, and fees were fairly reasonable. The day nursery cost Y12 a month per child, which included three meals a day. The boarding school cost Y18 a month per child.

Research

In the years since Communist takeover, "research" of many kinds has been significantly expanded by government organizations in China, and many ministries now operate research institutes of varying sorts.

Ministry M's Research Institute had a staff of about forty. It was roughly equivalent in status to the bureaus, but unlike the bureaus it was an "economically independent" institution and, as such, formulated its own annual plans, kept independent accounts, and received funds directly from the Ministry of Finance. It was located in Ministry M's main building, and reimbursed the ministry for use of this space. It also reported directly to the head of Ministry M, who was the institute's formal director. The person actually responsible for running the institute, however, was its deputy director, who was one of the assistants to the minister. Since the deputy director had many other responsibilities as well, the head of the Research Institute Staff Office (*pan kung shih chu jen*) carried much of the day-to-day administrative load. This person, a woman, was a Party member and an "old cadre"; she had no special technical qualifications for the job but was an able administrator. Three other cadres worked for her in the institute's staff office: a personnel staff member (*jen shih kan shih*), an accountant (*k'uai chi yüan*, or *k'uai chi* for short), and a cashier (*ch'u na*).

The institute was divided into several units: a Library and Materials Office (*t'u shu tzu liao shih*), a laboratory (*shih yen shih*), and four research groups (*yen chiu tsu*). The research groups, numbered one to four, were the main working bodies. They varied in size from four to seven persons. Each group was headed by a chief (*tsu chang*), and concentrated on a particular area of research.

The personnel of the institute had been drawn from several sources. As in virtually all central government organizations, there were a few "old cadres"—Party members—who occupied the key leadership and administrative positions; here they tended to be persons with relatively good education, however. There were also a few transferred army men; since they did not have research skills, they were assigned to jobs considered to be relatively unskilled, such as those in the library. The research personnel, including both Party and non-Party cadres, were almost all university graduates. Some, including the most highly qualified ones, had been drawn directly from universities and other government organizations in various parts of the country. A few were non-Party intellectuals who had taken the initiative themselves in applying for such research work. There were also a few recent graduates of institutions of higher learning.

The research workers, although generally considered in Ministry M to be state cadres, were rated and paid according to a special twelve-grade scale that differed from the system applied to administrative cadres. They also were divided into four main professional categories: researchers (*yen chiu yüan*), the top category; associate researchers (*fu yen chiu yüan*); assistant researchers (*chu li yen chiu yüan*); and research trainees (*shih hsi yen chiu yüan*). Their pay was somewhat higher than that of administrative cadres of roughly equivalent status.

However, in the Research Institute, as in other ministry subunits, power and authority were concentrated in the hands of Party cadres. There were ten Party members, one fourth of the total staff, who were organized into a Party Branch. These included not only the top leaders and administrators, but also four of the younger researchers, three of whom headed research groups. The Party Branch, headed by a secretary (*shu chi*), had committeemen (*wei yüan*) for organization (*tsu chih*), propaganda (*hsüan ch'uan*), and youth (*ch'ing nien*).[34] The propaganda committeeman was responsible for the weekly study meeting for both Party and non-Party cadres in the Research Institute; the youth committeeman was in charge of YCL work. The ten YCL members in the institute did not have their own branch, and therefore participated in a branch in one of the ministry's bureaus.

The actual research work in the institute was based on both long-term plans or programs (*kuei hua*) and short-term plans (*chi hua*). The research staff took the initiative in defining some of the research

[34] This branch had no united front committeeman, although branches of this sort often do.

topics, but many were based on proposals that came both from bureaus in the ministry and from provincial departments. All proposals for specific research projects were thoroughly discussed in general "institute affairs meetings" (*so wu hui yi*). Once the annual work plan was defined, specific topics were assigned to each researcher. It was assumed that there should be about a three-to-one ratio between the time spent on research and the time required to write up results. It was also assumed that normally a researcher should be able to turn out about 100,000 words of finished research reports a year. Thus, a researcher generally would spend more than eight months each year on research and more than three on writing.

Most research consisted of individual rather than group work, and the research groups operated rather informally. There were no formal staff meetings in the groups, although there were frequent *ad hoc* "face-to-face" discussion sessions. On an average of about once a month, the institute's deputy director convened institute affairs meetings at which all personnel reported on work in progress, and both problems and plans were discussed. Except for these meetings, the average researcher did not have very much direct contact with the deputy director, since the latter generally dealt with the staff through the group heads.

Once a year, toward year-end, the institute convened an important meeting to discuss research papers (*k'o hsüeh lun wen t'ao lun hui*). At these meetings, which might take three days, members of the staff presented summary reports of their work to meetings attended by persons from the bureaus and some from provincial departments as well as the institute's staff. They prepared papers, about forty in one year, that were reproduced and distributed beforehand, and these were thoroughly discussed at the meetings. These sessions helped both to disseminate the results of research and to determine future research priorities.

There is little doubt that the research done by the institute was of assistance to both the ministry and its subordinate units. The problems and questions dealt with by the institute's researchers were generally ones of fairly practical importance to the work of the ministry itself. They were therefore not the kind likely to receive equal attention in other types of research programs, such as those conducted in universities or by the institutes under the Academy of Science.

They were, moreover, questions which personnel working in the ministry were not likely to find the time or opportunity to study in detail themselves.

However, the usefulness of its research was limited by a number of factors. The top ministry leaders did not always turn to the institute for advice on major problems. Sometimes, in fact, even the applied research done by the institute was regarded by others in the ministry as being too theoretical to provide practical solutions to current problems; this was probably true in some instances. Perhaps even more important, the constant intrusion of politics, here as everywhere in the bureaucracy, affected the institute's work adversely in a number of ways. Normally, relations between Party and non-Party cadres in the organization were reasonably good; but the concentration of leadership in the hands of "old cadres" without technical training meant that on occasion their uninformed views prevailed over the views of more highly qualified researchers, even including the younger Party members. As everywhere, political study competed to a degree with normal work, even in politically relaxed periods; and during major campaigns, work was severely disrupted for long periods. Also, as a result of the many political pressures operating on the cadres, and particularly as a result of the major campaigns, there was a tendency to "play safe," and many cadres were normally chary of writing analyses that were too critical of existing practices.

Publishing

Many ministries in China run their own publishing houses, which put out various publications including national journals or "organizational papers" (chi kuan pao) relating to their work. Such publications are of considerable importance in the functioning of the bureaucracy, because they provide an important link in the internal communications system between the top leaders of a particular functional system and all the cadres working within the system throughout the country. Most material in such publications is viewed by the cadres as providing guidelines and directives for work at all levels.

Ministry M did not, during the period of its existence, get into the publishing business. However, through certain official publications put out by other organizations that concentrated on work related to its own field, it was able to disseminate information and instructions to cadres working under its direction throughout the country.

"Administrative Support"

THE MINISTRY units whose structure and functions have already been discussed include only those which carried general responsibility for running the organization and managing its staff; similar units exist in most top-level bodies in the central government bureaucracy in China. In addition, there were in Ministry M eight medium-size and large bureaus which were responsible for conducting the bulk of the ministry's substantive work. These eight bureaus will not be described here, for two reasons: First, they cannot be discussed in terms which would preserve the anonymity of the ministry; and second, the work of each was in a sense *sui generis*, rather than typical of organizations found throughout the bureaucracy. If one were attempting to understand the substantive work of Ministry M, one would have to analyze these eight bureaus above all. However, in this analysis of the organization and functioning of Ministry M as an example of how bureaucracy is structured and works at the highest levels of the Chinese government, the various administrative "affairs" units that have been described thus far are the ones which are most pertinent, because they are most typical of the bureaucracy as a whole.

In these terms, there remains one large unit in Ministry M which must be described: the General Affairs Division. Of all the major units in the ministry, it was the one most concerned simply with the routine bureaucratic functioning of the organization, and with the day-to-day needs of the bureaucrats which it employed, rather than with the substantive work of the ministry.

General Affairs Division

Any large, modern, bureaucratic organization requires a fairly elaborate administrative support structure to run the "housekeeping" functions which keep the organization going and to service the staff members doing the organization's substantive work. In Communist China, this is particularly true because the life of cadres in the bureaucracy, especially those working in national-level organizations such as the ministries, has been "collectivized" to a very large degree. A ministry must concern itself with housing its cadres, feeding them, educating at least some of their children, and performing many other functions that in a different sort of society would be individual responsibilities. "Collectivization" of the way of life of cadres in central government organizations goes well beyond what might be described simply as paternalistic treatment, however. It reflects the regime's positive goal of creating disciplined, regimented, semimilitarized patterns of work and behavior.

The primary administrative support unit in Ministry M was the General Affairs Division (*tsung wu ch'u*). This division worked in close contact with, and under the direct supervision of, the Ministry Staff Office. When the chief of the division encountered particularly difficult problems arising from competing demands for space, supplies, or services, for example, he could, and did, refer them to the staff office director, whose decisions carried more weight than his own.

With a personnel roster of between one and two hundred employees, it was an extremely large unit. (Not all of its employees were state cadres; also included were drivers, cleaning staff, and various other types of general service personnel.) However, it was classified as an independent division rather than as a bureau, probably because of the relatively low prestige associated with much of its work.

The division had seven section-level units: the Supplies Section (*wen chü k'o*), Printing Section (*chien yin k'o*), Library (*t'u shu kuan*), Security Section (*pao wei k'o*), "driver's group" or "car pool" (*szu chi pan*), Mess Hall and Guest House Section (*shih t'ang chao tai k'o*), and Housing Management Section (*fang wu kuan li k'o*).

Routine Administrative Services

The Supplies Section's responsibilities were not exceptional; it simply provided the necessary materials for the day-to-day operations of all units in the ministry.

The Printing Section, which provided typing, mimeographing, and printing services for the entire ministry, was more important, however, than comparable units in Western bureaucracies would be. Because the written Chinese language is complex, most typewriters are relatively complicated and expensive machines which require skilled operators. It is therefore not practical for all low-level bureaucratic units to have them. In Ministry M, as in many if not most large Chinese organizations, reproduction of written materials, including everything from correspondence to official reports, was centralized. Virtually all documents were first prepared in handwritten form and were then taken to the central reproduction center run by the Printing Section. Ordinary documents which required multiple copies and originated in lower-level ministry units (divisions and below) were normally written on sheets that could be immediately reproduced on mimeograph or other duplicating machines. Documents originating at the bureau level or above generally were first written by hand, then taken to be typed by the Printing Section's typing pool, and finally mimeographed or otherwise duplicated. Many of the most important documents, especially those originating from high-level ministry officials, were taken in handwritten draft form to the Printing Section, which set them in type and printed them. To service the ministry as a whole, then, the Printing Section had a typing pool and duplication unit, an editing and correcting staff, and a full-scale printing shop, which altogether had over twenty employees.

The General Affairs Division's Library maintained a fairly sizable general library. All ministry cadres had free access and borrowing privileges. This library was separate from the specialized research library maintained by the ministry's Research Institute and open only to authorized personnel.

Building Security and Ministry Transport

The physical security of ministry buildings was the responsibility of the Security Section. The section supervised a small Guard Unit (*wei ping pan*)[35] consisting of more than twenty public security men assigned to protect the buildings. Together, the Security Section and Guard Unit ran the Communications Reception Center (*shou fa shih*, literally "receiving and sending office") at the front entrance of the main ministry building.

While the stringency of physical security measures varied from time to time, a fairly tight system was normal. During one period of relatively low general political tension, for example, the system operated thus: Twenty-four–hour guard posts were maintained on a three-shift basis at both the front and the rear entrance to the main ministry building (usually four guards at front and one in the rear). The guards checked the credentials of all persons entering or leaving the premises. Ministry personnel carried identification cards (*kung tso cheng*, literally "work cards"), which were issued twice a year, and which gave the bearer's name, age, and unit, as well as a photograph of him. All nonministry personnel had to check in with the guards and register at the reception center. If a visitor was from another government organization and came on official business he brought not only his own identification card but also a "letter of introduction" (*chieh shao hsin*), chopped by his ministry or bureau, stating whom he had come to see and what his official business was. After signing a registry book (*teng chi shu* or *teng chi pu*) at the reception center, he received a pass which permitted him to go to a guest room (*hui k'o shih*) on the floor where the cadre he had come to see worked. Each floor of the ministry building had one of these guest rooms, and all official visitors were met there. If the ministry cadre being visited was a unit chief, he usually then took the visitor to his own office, but if he were a low-ranking ordinary cadre he generally talked with the visitor in the guest room, if necessary bringing

[35] In some ministries, this unit was called the *ching wei pan*.

pertinent reports or materials there with him. On leaving, the visitor signed his pass, returned it to the guards at the front entrance and was checked out of the registry book. Visitors making personal, non-official calls on cadres in the ministry went through comparable procedures, but instead of going to a guest room on an upper floor they were met and talked with in the main guest room on the ground floor near the ministry entrance. These procedures were not particularly onerous but were restrictive enough to reinforce the general atmosphere of security-consciousness prevailing in the ministry.

Ministry transportation was managed by the car pool, which maintained a fleet of over twenty automobiles, about five large buses, several trucks, and numerous bicycles. The right to use various types of ministry transportation was based primarily on rank. Each of the three top ministry officials—that is, the minister and his two deputies—was assigned a car and driver for his personal use. The assistants to the minister and the leading unit chiefs could request the use of a car with full assurance that they would obtain it. Lower-ranking cadres, however, could not normally use automobiles; when on official business, they either obtained a bicycle from the ministry's pool or used public transportation, in which case they could later obtain reimbursement for expenses. The ministry buses were used for many purposes, such as transporting large groups of cadres to meetings, or taking cadres' children to the ministry-run schools.

Collective Living: Mess Halls and Guest Houses

The large majority of ministry employees ate at the ministry's own mess hall (*shih t'ang* or *ch'ih t'ang*). The hall, which was run by the Mess Hall and Guest House Section, was located in a special building adjacent to the main ministry building and the ministry's large meeting hall (*li t'ang*). It provided very low-cost food, and for most cadres, the convenience and economy of using this public facility outweighed the possible objections to eating mass-produced meals. In this, as in most matters affecting the life and work of the cadres, however, privileges were based at least to some degree on rank. A small executive dining room was maintained for those of bureau-chief rank and above, while all other cadres ate in one large dining hall.

The Mess Hall and Guest House Section was also responsible for managing three ministry-run guest houses (*chao tai so*). Such guest houses, each of which is in effect a special, low-priced hotel for visiting cadres, play an important role in the life of the bureaucratic elite in China. Almost every important organization in Peking maintains at least one guest house, and often several, for use by personnel within its functional system, from the provinces or lower government levels, who come to visit the capital on business. Guest houses exist also at all lower levels in the administrative hierarchy, down to the counties. At lower levels, however, they are usually maintained by the major Party and government bodies, such as the county Party committees and people's councils, rather than by specialized agencies. As noted already, there is a great deal of business travel by cadres in China; and traveling cadres almost always stay together with other cadres in these official guest houses.

Altogether Ministry M's three guest houses, one adjacent to the ministry and two not far away, could when necessary accommodate a maximum of several hundred visiting cadres, although normally they did not have that many, of course. Cadres from the provinces constituted the majority of the users. These included persons attending a wide variety of meetings, conferences, and training classes at the ministry. Accommodations varied by rank, but for all cadres the guest houses provided convenient and cheap housing while in Peking. From the organization's point of view, it was not only convenient to keep all visiting cadres together, it also facilitated maintenance of security; the guest houses kept the cadres relatively isolated from persons outside the bureaucracy, and even, in fact, from persons outside their own line of work.

Collective Living:
Apartment Buildings, or Dormitories

The development of state-run apartment buildings or dormitories (*su she*) for cadres and their families has also been an extremely important "collectivizing" influence shaping the lives of the bureaucratic elite in China, especially those cadres working in national-level organizations. Ministry M had five large residential buildings run by the Housing Management Section of the General Affairs Division. These buildings accommodated about 60 percent of the cadres in the ministry (in many ministries the proportion now is considerably higher).

In line with the stratification of privilege, based on rank, that characterized the ministry as a whole, the minister and his two deputies lived in individual ministry-owned houses; assistants to the minister, as well as bureau chiefs and persons of equivalent rank, lived in one of the apartment buildings; and lower-ranking cadres lived in the other four buildings. Party and non-Party cadres were mixed in the residence buildings, but Party members generally received preference—or, at least so non-Party cadres claimed—in the allocation of the best space. Since accommodations varied considerably, there was strong competition for desirable space. The newer buildings, which accommodated only about one third of the total personnel, had the best family apartments. Although small, most of the new apartments had individual kitchens and bathrooms; sometimes, however, two families had to share these facilities. Two thirds of the cadres living in ministry-run apartments occupied older buildings that had been converted to residential use, and they usually had to be satisfied with communal kitchens and bathrooms that served from two to ten families. All the apartments were provided with government-owned furniture, which varied only slightly from one apartment to another.[36]

The 40 percent or so of ministry employees who were not provided with apartment space—mostly low-ranking non-Party cadres —lived in rented "private" housing elsewhere; the Housing Management Section was responsible, however, for helping to find such housing, as well as for making assignments to ministry-owned space.

In each of Ministry M's apartment buildings there was an elected "family dependents' committee" (*chia shu wei yüan hui*), which maintained close links with the nearest residents' committee (*chü*

---

[36] Office furniture in Ministry M was differentiated considerably on the basis of rank, however; for example, only high-ranking cadres, generally bureau chiefs and above, were allotted overstuffed furniture for their offices.

min wei yüan hui). Apparently, however, these were not especially active and did not impinge excessively on people's lives.

Nevertheless, the lives of the cadres and families who lived in these buildings were basically "collectivized." Privacy was very limited, and for some almost nonexistent, not simply because of the elements of communal living involved but also because of the sense of close mutual surveillance that characterized the general atmosphere in which they lived. No one seriously attempted to maintain secrecy about what he ate and wore, whom he saw, or what he did with his spare time. Not only would it have been impossible to maintain secrecy, but the attempt to do so would have created suspicion. Everyone, in short, lived in a fishbowl.

Decline of Personal Life

According to ex-cadres who lived in such apartment buildings, most people in them had very little "personal life." Entertaining among friends was rare, and even casual visiting was fairly limited. There were several reasons for this. Most cadres could not afford frequent entertaining, and almost all were so busy that they had little time for social life. In addition, the development of personal friendships was inhibited by the fear of drawing criticism from Party members, who were suspicious of almost all close relationships that developed outside organizational channels. Even in normal day-to-day contacts with neighbors, most cadres reportedly showed considerable restraint and caution. In the prevailing atmosphere of mutual surveillance everyone was presumed to be observing and judging everyone else's attitudes as well as behavior, and it was assumed that from time to time, especially during political campaigns, these judgments would have to be passed along to the Party. Caution extended further and often tended to create inhibitions even in relations within the family. Parents were frequently wary of speaking frankly in front of their children, because the children might unwittingly repeat to others casual remarks which might be open to censure. And to a degree at least, some husbands and wives refrained from telling each other things which they felt might compromise the other if and when (the question in most cadres' minds was really when, rather than if) he, or she, were later under pressure, such as in small group self-criticism sessions, to dissect all aspects of his personal life. Ironically, all these inhibitions appeared to be most restrictive on the lives of Party members. In fact, many former non-Party cadres agree in asserting that Party cadres in China operate in the most restrictive environment of political control, while non-Party cadres are somewhat better off in this respect, and the persons who are most free in many ways are the *lao pai hsing* ("common people"), since they are least subject to direct bureaucratic controls.

Obviously, a great many factors have contributed to the decline of personal life among the cadres, but collective living, while perhaps not the most basic factor, certainly has been one of them. However, there was little evidence that cadres in Ministry M strongly objected to, or tried to avoid, being housed in the ministry's apartment houses. On the contrary, because state housing was generally the best and cheapest obtainable, most cadres in Ministry M, including non-Party cadres, did their best to live in the ministry's residential units. In fact, whatever resentment existed regarding the housing situation seemed to be caused by the belief that Party cadres received preference in obtaining living space, not the fact that it was necessary to live under such collectivized conditions. Perhaps this could be explained in part by the fact that traditionally the Chinese have not considered privacy to be a necessity, at least not to the same degree as people in some other societies; in such an overpopulated country, privacy has always been a luxury. Clearly, however, it was also due to a widespread feeling that the actual material advantages of living in state-owned housing outweighed any theoretical personal advantages that might result from having individual accommodations, since in the controlled political atmosphere created by the Communist regime, genuine privacy could not really be achieved no matter where one lived.

As was stated at the start, Ministry M no longer exists. But the bureaucratic practices and forms of organization which characterized it do. While they can be expected to change and evolve over time, they are likely to continue bearing the stamp of both the Chinese Communists' revolutionary experience and deep-rooted Chinese traditions of bureaucratic behavior.

Part II
A COUNTY

Position of the County in the Administrative System

IT IS not surprising that in a nation as large as China the pattern of administrative division of the country is complex. Although a centralized system of authority and a fairly uniform pattern of organization are prescribed, there are inevitably numerous regional variations. Over time, also, there have been many administrative changes, as Chinese leaders, including the present ones, have continued the difficult search for a workable political system. Despite the regional variations and the changes over time, however, the administrative continuities are in many respects as striking as the changes, and in some instances the uniformities are as important as the variations—except, perhaps, at the lowest subcounty levels, where both the changes and the local variations have been greatest.

Administrative Divisions from the Central Government to the Counties

Traditionally in China, the provinces and the counties have been the most important levels of regional administration between the central government and the village level.[1] They remain so today. But today as in the past there are also a number of other layers of

[1] Village-level organization will be discussed in Part III rather than here.

administration which play significant, though secondary, roles in the system.

In late imperial times, at the end of the nineteenth century,[2] China had twenty-two provinces, each headed by a governor or *hsün fu*,[3] and over fifteen hundred county-level units, which included 1,303 regular counties (*hsien*),[4] 145 departments (*chou*), and seventy-five subprefectures (*t'ing*). The provinces were grouped into larger units under viceroys, or governors general (*tsung tu*). Generally two or three provinces made up each large unit, although some governors general administered only a single province. Altogether there were eight governors general. Between the provinces and the county-level units there were two other administrative levels: circuits (*tao*); and prefecture-level units, which included 185 regular prefectures (*fu*), forty-five independent subprefectures (*chih li t'ing*) and seventy-two independent departments (*chih li chou*).

During the Nationalist period—after the 1911 collapse of the empire and the interregnum of warlordism—when the Kuomintang attempted to construct a modernized political system, provinces and counties continued to be the key units, but their number increased substantially from 1928 on. This was in large part a result of the regime's integration of outlying borderland areas into the regular Chinese administrative system and the elevation of a number of major cities to a status equivalent to the provinces. By mid-1947,[5] there were forty-eight provincial-level units in China, including thirty-five provinces (*sheng*); one large territory, Tibet;[6] and twelve centrally administered municipalities (*chih hsia shih*). At the county level, there were now 2,244 units, including 2,023 regular counties, thirty-

[2] See Ch'ü T'ung-tsu, *Local Government in China Under the Ch'ing* (Cambridge, Mass., Harvard University Press, 1962), p. 2. The data used here is for 1899.

[3] Tibet and Mongolia are not included in this total, since they were under special administrations of a colonial type.

[4] *Hsien* is sometimes translated as "district"; but "county" seems more appropriate and also avoids confusion with *ch'ü*, which is usually translated as "district."

[5] See *China Handbook, 1950* (New York, Rockport Press Inc., 1950), p. 3.

[6] Tibet was still claimed by China even though it was not then under effective control.

four "preparatory counties" (*she chih chü*), one "administrative bureau" or "management bureau" (*kuan li chü*), 132 banners (*ch'i*),[7] and fifty-five municipalities (*shih*) subordinate to the provinces.

The Nationalists did not establish any formal administrative organs at the regional level, above the provinces. However, the need for regional coordination continued, and to meet it the "office of the president" (*tsung t'ung fu*) stationed "personal representatives" (*hsing ying chu jen*) in all the major regions of China. The supervisory role of these representatives was analogous in some respects to the more formally constituted administrative organs which existed at this level both previously and subsequently.

In the mid-1930s the Nationalists did formally establish a new administrative level between the provinces and the counties. It was called the "special commissioner's district" (*chuan ch'ü*). In 1947 there were 208 such districts, each under a special commissioner (*chuan yüan*) responsible for helping the provincial government supervise its counties.

Since their takeover of power in 1949, the Communists, despite their drastic reorganization of the body politic in China and their introduction of revolutionary and totalitarian methods of rule, have not radically altered this pattern of over-all administrative division. They have introduced some innovations and have made numerous changes over the past seventeen years in specific administrative boundaries; but the general pattern has not been fundamentally altered. Provinces and counties have remained the two most important administrative units above the local level; and the Communist regime, like its predecessors, has developed—or experimented with—regional groupings of provinces, as well as intermediate administrative organs between the provinces and the counties.

Constitutionally, the "basic" levels of regional and local government in Communist China today are the following: (1) at the provincial level, the provinces (*sheng*), autonomous regions (*tzu chih ch'ü*), and municipalities that are directly administered by the central government (*chih hsia shih*); (2) at the county level, regular counties (*hsien*), autonomous counties (*tzu chih hsien*), and ordinary municipalities (*shih*); plus (3) at the local level, prior to 1958 ad-

---

[7] Banners were units equivalent to counties in Mongol areas.

ministrative villages (*hsiang*),[8] market towns (*chen*), and autonomous administrative villages (*tzu chih hsiang*), and then after 1958, the communes (*kung she*), which replaced the administrative villages as the lowest "basic" units of local rural administration.[9] At each of these "basic" administrative levels there is an elected People's Congress, which chooses a People's Council as the principal organ of local state power.

Between the provinces and the counties, in the administrative system as it now exists in China, the Communists have retained special districts (*chuan ch'ü*) very similar to those that existed in the Nationalist period. In theory these are regarded as "dispatched organs" (*p'ai ch'u chi kou*) with delegated powers, established simply to help the provinces supervise the counties, rather than as regular organs of state power.

At the regional level the Chinese Communists first established "great administrative regions" (*ta hsing cheng ch'ü*), each encompassing several provinces. From 1949 to 1954, when these existed, they were much more than simple coordinating bodies and at first acted as full-scale regional governments. The great administrative regions were abolished in 1954, but, as will be noted below, regional organs were reestablished at this level in 1961. Ostensibly these new bodies are simply regional bureaus of the Party Central Committee and are not government organs. Actually, however, they appear, in some respects, to have become hybrid, Party-government organizations which possess at least some of the institutions and exercise some of the functions normally associated with the government rather than the Party.

---

[8] *Hsiang* is sometimes translated as "township." The term "administrative village" seems most descriptive, however, since *hsiang* are rural administrative units composed of one or several natural villages. The character for *hsiang* literally means "countryside" or "village." One difficulty is that in Chinese Communist writings there are also occasional references to *hsing cheng ts'un*, which literally also means "administrative village." However, *hsing cheng ts'un* have only recently been referred to, they are not part of the regular administrative system, and they are not discussed in this study.

[9] In some provinces and autonomous regions where large minority populations exist, there is another "basic" level, the autonomous department (*tzu chih chou*), between the province and county.

Great Administrative Regions

When the Chinese Communists, during their initial years in power, divided the country into great administrative regions they established six units, covering (1) north China, (2) northeast China, (3) northwest China, (4) east China, (5) central south China and (6) southwest China. Except for the northeast, where a "people's government" was organized, a "military and administrative committee" was established in each of these areas as the highest local organ of state power, responsible for managing all the provinces within their jurisdiction, on behalf of the central government. At first these committees had substantial power and exercised a significant degree of autonomy. Before long, however, the regime, fearing the growth of regional autonomy, took steps to centralize power, and in 1952 it substantially reduced the functions of these regional bodies and changed their name to "administrative committees." Two years later, in 1954, it tightened central controls still further and totally abolished the administrative committees as well as the six regional bureaus of the Party Central Committee, which had existed in the same areas. Both political and administrative considerations dictated this move. Politically, Peking was obviously alarmed by what it considered to be dangerous trends toward autonomy, especially after the challenge to central authority made by two Central Committee members, Kao Kang and Jao Shu-shih, who had been top regional leaders in northeast and east China, respectively, and who were purged in 1954–1955 in conjunction with the abolishment of the great regions. Administratively, the regime wished to centralize control in order to facilitate economic planning during China's first Five Year Plan, which was initiated in 1953.

For over six years after 1954 there were no Party or government agencies between the central government and the provinces. But the lack of any administrative agencies at the regional level created many problems, as well as solving others. Consequently, in early 1961, the Party publicly revealed its intention to reestablish Party bureaus in the six large regions. Actually, steps pointing in this direction had been taken even earlier. As early as 1958, for example, the regime had apparently divided the country into seven large economic cooperation regions, and considerable discussion of the need to handle economic problems on a regional basis had taken place—although what the role of large economic areas might be was unclear and almost nothing was said at first about any institutional innovations that might be involved. Preliminary steps to reestablish Party organizations at the level of the six large regions may have started not very long thereafter, and concrete action to set them up probably took place during 1960 before the Party's formal announcement of their establishment in 1961.

Even after formal reestablishment of the Party bureaus, very little general information was released concerning them. In time, however, the fragmentary data which became available suggested that in addition to having the standard Party departments, at least some of the new regional Party bureaus possessed staff offices comparable to bodies existing under the State Council, as well as certain commissions and bureaus, dealing particularly with economic matters such as finance and planning, comparable to ministry-level bodies in the central government.[10] The seemingly hybrid, Party-government nature of the regional Party bureaus appeared to reflect a trend toward direct Party rule, and toward Party encroachment in fields theoretically assigned to government administration, which characterized the regime as a whole in the period of the Great Leap Forward and immediately afterward. It also seemed to indicate that Peking's leaders once again felt the need for governmental functions as well as Party tasks to be performed at the level of the great administrative regions.

In all probability, however, the Chinese Communists have always been, and will continue to be, ambivalent about the desirability of establishing regional bodies between the central government and the provinces. Conflicting pressures operate on them. On the one hand, China is so large that it is extremely difficult for the central authorities to administer the entire country directly; there are strong arguments, therefore, in favor of establishing regional organs, at least to help supervise the provinces. On the other hand, the basic predisposi-

[10] For example, as of 1965, various articles in the Chinese Communist press had mentioned the following organs under the East China Bureau: departments for propaganda, and finance and trade; offices for agriculture and forestry, water conservancy, finance and policy research; and committees for planning, economic affairs, and science and technology.

tion of China's leaders toward effective centralization of policy-making, and their fear of excessive regionalism, militate against the delegation of unrestricted authority to regional bodies—even though the existing ones appear to have been delegated considerable power. In all likelihood, therefore, the regime can be expected, in the future as in the past, to vacillate in its attitude toward the idea that significant regional administrative organizations should be interposed between the central government and the provinces.

Provinces and Equivalent Bodies

The Communists have not tinkered very much with the traditional Chinese provinces. It is true that the number of provincial-level administrative units has been gradually reduced in the period since 1949. Whereas immediately before Communist takeover there were forty-eight such units, by the 1960s there were only twenty-nine, including twenty-two provinces (*sheng*),[11] five large autonomous regions (*tzu chih ch'ü*), and two centrally administered municipalities (*chih hsia shih*).[12] However, very little change has taken place since 1949 in the provinces in the central portions of China proper. One new province, Pingyuan, was established in this area in 1949, but it existed only briefly and was abolished by 1952.

The principal changes at the provincial level since 1949 have been in outlying, borderland regions. Step by step, in 1952, 1954, 1955, and 1958, the regime abolished the majority of old provinces in these areas and in their place set up three new and larger provincial-level autonomous regions—Inner Mongolia, Sinkiang, and Tibet—plus two other large autonomous regions in the areas that formerly made up the provinces of Kwangsi and Ninghsia. These autonomous regions are the highest level of administration established by the Communists in areas with large minority populations; similar units have been set up at lower levels, including autonomous departments (*tzu chih chou*), autonomous counties (*tzu chih hsien*), and even autonomous administrative villages (*tzu chih hsiang*). The fact that the adminis-

[11] This figure includes Taiwan, which the Communists claim but the Nationalists rule; if Taiwan is excluded the total is twenty-one.

[12] For the source of these figures see p. 115, n. 13.

trations in these areas are labeled "autonomous" does not mean, however, that they have important powers which other administrative units lack. All "autonomous" areas in Communist China are totally integrated into the regular centralized administrative hierarchy. They are different from other units mainly because within them concessions are made to local minority customs and languages and special efforts are made to absorb minority cadres into the local administrations.

The reduction from thirty-five provinces and one territory to twenty-two (or twenty-one, excluding Taiwan) provinces and five autonomous regions has really not, therefore, involved very significant changes in the administrative system as a whole except in minority and borderland areas. The provinces in most of China have proven, so far, to be comparatively stable units of administration. There are good reasons for this. As the provinces have evolved, over time, the configuration of many of them has come to reflect basic topographical, economic, social, and even linguistic factors; they are not arbitrarily defined administrative units. Consequently their boundaries are not easily altered.

Inherent in this situation, where provincial boundaries continue to reflect social factors that periodically in the past have nourished localism, there is, of course, the continuing potential danger of trends toward undesirable forms of provincialism. In the past, the development of provincialism in extreme forms often led, during periods of weakened central power, such as the one immediately preceding Communist takeover, to political fragmentation of the country. Since 1949, however, while preserving the province as a key unit of administration, the Communists have effectively and thoroughly destroyed the old bases of provincial warlordism that existed just prior to their takeover, and to date they have successfully maintained strong central control. Whenever disturbing signs of incipient provincialism have appeared, they have taken drastic measures to suppress it.

The reduction in the number of centrally administered municipalities, from thirteen in 1949, to twelve, then to three, and finally to two (Peking and Shanghai) has not radically altered the general administrative system. The result has been simply to shift responsibility for direct control over these cities from the central government to provincial-level units.

Intermediate Units
Between Provinces and Counties

Between the provinces and the counties, the Communists, as already noted, have retained intermediary units similar to those that existed under the Nationalist regime. Throughout most of the country, these are still called special districts (*chuan ch'ü*), as they were before 1949.

As stated earlier, in theory these special districts are considered to be not regular organs of state power but simply "dispatched organs," with delegated powers, established to help the provinces supervise the counties. In practice, however, the real role of the special districts is not wholly clear, and it seems to have varied from area to area and at different times. In some areas, the special districts at times since 1949 appear to have developed what in effect are full-scale governments which, though they do not have elected representative bodies —that is, people's congresses—have possessed virtually all the important administrative agencies found in governments at both the provincial and county levels. When this has been the case, special districts, rather than functioning simply as coordinating and supervising bodies assisting the provinces, seem in practice to have functioned as an additional layer of regular government, interposed between the provinces and counties. Moreover, in many areas the Party Committees at the special district level appear to constitute a well-defined, regular level of authority in the Party hierarchy, exercising powers similar to those wielded by other levels in the regular Party chain of command rather than acting as mere supervisory bodies.

There are now 151 special districts in China.[18] Usually their head-

[18] This figure and the following figures on all administrative units at special district and county levels are for the year 1963; they are official figures published in the 1963 *People's Handbook* (*Jen Min Shou Ts'e*). Changes since that time, at least until mid-1966, appear to have been minor.

quarters are located in either a municipality (*shih*) or a county seat (*hsien ch'eng*), and more often than not the special district is named after the place where its headquarters is situated. Generally, this municipality or county seat is one of the units supervised by the special district, but in some cases it is an "independent" municipality or one directly administered by the province, in which case it is not included in the special district's jurisdiction.

Special districts supervise both counties and municipalities. While the number of such units under each special district varies, the average for the country as a whole is about a dozen. For the nation as a whole, the average number of special districts per province is roughly eight.

In some minority areas, as mentioned earlier, there are, in addition to special districts, autonomous departments (*tzu chih chou*), between the provinces and counties. A total of twenty-nine such units exist in nine provinces. While these departments are roughly equivalent to the special districts, they have been described in some official Chinese Communist publications as being a regular level of government rather than simply "dispatched organs." [14]

In the Inner Mongolia autonomous region, instead of special districts there are seven leagues (*meng*), based on traditional Mongol units which existed under the old Chinese Empire. They are equivalent to the special districts, and in all essentials appear to be similar to them. The only other special units which should probably be classified as belonging to this same general level of government in China now are the so-called administrative districts (*hsing cheng ch'ü*). There are three administrative districts located in three different provinces; it is not clear what special characteristics, if any, they may possess.

There is only one province in China, Liaoning, which does not now have any sort of intermediary level of administration between the province and the counties. Liaoning has abolished all such units, and has placed its counties directly under the supervision of the major municipalities in the province.

[14] See article by "Shie I-yuein" on China's administrative divisions, *People's China*, May 16, 1955.

Counties and Equivalent Bodies

The most important administrative unit in rural China now, as in the past, is the regular county. This has been true for two millennia, and it remains so today. Most counties have tended to be relatively stable administrative units, because more often than not they have constituted natural centers of transportation, communications, industry, and commerce. Traditionally, the county seat has served not only as an administrative headquarters but also as the economic and social center of a fairly well-defined region.

At roughly the county level in Communist China, there are now[15] 2,291 units: 1,978 regular counties (*hsien*), fifty-eight autonomous counties (*tzu chih hsien*), forty-nine banners (*ch'i*), three autonomous banners (*tzu chih ch'i*), two management bureaus (*kuan li chü*), three work committees (*kung tso wei yüan hui*), one "town" (*chen*), and 177 municipalities (*shih*), plus twenty districts (*chü*) in China's two centrally administered municipalities.[16]

The Communists have merged some counties and split others. They have redrawn many boundaries. And, during one period in the latter half of the 1950s, they apparently tried to increase the size and reduce the number of counties in a fairly radical way. The details of exactly what happened to the counties in the period of communization and immediately thereafter remains to be reconstructed in detail. However, it is clear that during a short period a great many changes were introduced at the county level. In the country as a whole, the number of counties dropped by close to one quarter. In some provinces, the number was cut in half. In many areas, though, the changes may have been more apparent than real, since some counties were simply attached, without very significant changes in

---

[15] As stated earlier, these are official figures for 1963.

[16] The autonomous counties are in minority-inhabited areas. All the banners, regular and "autonomous," are in Inner Mongolia. The management bureaus are in Kiangsi, the work committees in Tsinghai, and the "town" in Yunnan; little is known about most of these special units, and they are not important in the over-all administrative system. (Curiously, the term for the "town" is the same as that normally used for units at the subcounty, administrative village level.)

their character, to large municipalities. In other areas, however, more basic changes were introduced, as many counties were merged or otherwise enlarged and given new boundaries.

This period of drastic experimentation proved to be short-lived, however, and soon—by exactly what process is still not wholly clear —the number of counties rose to roughly what it had been before communization. The striking fact is that the total number of rural county-level units now in China is remarkably close to what it was before Communist takeover. Excluding urban county-level areas (that is, municipal units), there were by 1963 2,093 units at this level, compared with 2,190 in 1947.

The position of the county in the over-all administrative system in China has been changed somewhat, however, by the fact that formal government and effective political control have been pushed down to the village level as never before. Under the old Chinese Empire, the county formed the bottom level of the centralized bureaucracy. Now, under the Communists, the centralized bureaucracy reaches, in both formal and real terms, to a much lower level. First, from 1949 to 1958, the administrative villages, and then from 1958 onward, the communes—rather than the counties—have been the lowest "basic" level of state power in rural China.

This does not mean, however, that the importance of the counties has been substantially reduced. County governments in Communist China today are far more complex institutionally and have much broader responsibilities functionally than subordinate units such as the communes. It is eminently clear, in fact, that in the performance of many government functions the counties are still by far the most important governmental units directly affecting the lives of people in the vast rural areas, where the overwhelming majority of all Chinese live.[17]

[17] There remain, however, great gaps in status both between provincial and county officials and between the county apparatus and the commune apparatus. The rank of a county magistrate or Party first secretary, for example, is only equivalent to that of some of the higher-level office workers in the provincial apparatus; and the level of literacy of the county officials is far below that of provincial personnel. However, officials at the county level in turn see an enormous gap between themselves and "the countryside" down below. All functionaries in county govern-

The counties in China today vary greatly in population, from a few thousand to over a million. However, for the country as a whole, the average is probably now close to 300,000. The number of counties per provincial-level unit also varies tremendously, from sixteen in the Ninghsia Hui Autonomous Region to 186 in Szechwan; but in the majority of provinces there are currently between sixty and one hundred county-level units. A few counties are directly administered by provincial governments without any intervening level of supervision or control. The overwhelming majority, however, are supervised or controlled by special districts or autonomous departments.

"County-level" administrative units also include, in addition to rural units, 177 municipalities, and twenty urban districts located in the two centrally administered municipalities.[18] The municipalities are cities of various sizes and sorts, roughly two thirds of which come under the jurisdiction of special districts or equivalent units, and about one third of which are directly administered by provincial governments. The steady increase in the number of county-level municipalities—there are now roughly three times as many as there were shortly before Communist takeover—has been due in part simply to the redefinition of the status of urban areas and in part to real urban growth.

All of these administrative units between the central government and the village level play significant roles in the political system in China today. Today as in the past, however, the rural county governments unquestionably have far more direct contact with the mass of the population in the vast Chinese countryside than any higher

---

ment and Party organizations are official state cadres, entitled to a stable fixed salary, with welfare benefits, and are considered to be a responsibility of the Party and the state, which control their assignments. At the commune level, by contrast, some functionaries are not state cadres but are paid by the commune; if they encounter difficulties as cadres they are likely to have no option other than to return to farm work for a living.

[18] The twenty urban districts classified as equivalent to counties are located in Peking and Shanghai. They include only the urban areas of these two municipalities. The suburbs consist of counties under the municipalities' jurisdiction. There are also districts in other large cities, but they are not normally included in official listings of county-level units.

levels of administration. Consequently, knowledge of how rural counties are organized and function is of particular importance to an understanding of the political system in China. What follows is a detailed examination of one such county—which will be called County X—as it operated in the early 1960s.

Characteristics of County X

County X was a fairly large unit, with a population of close to half a million, located in a coastal area of south China. Formed in the late 1950s by a merger of two small counties (which will be called Y and Z), it was, like almost all counties in China, primarily an agricultural area.

The one sizable town in the area, which served as the county seat (*hsien ch'eng*), had a population of roughly sixty thousand, about half of whom lived in the urbanized sectors of the town, and the other half, in its agricultural suburbs. This town had previously been the county seat of one of the two small counties that merged to form County X. The county seat of the other had been detached at the time of the merger and converted into a municipality under direct provincial control, which was the seat of the special district to which County X belonged.

The county seat, in addition to being the headquarters for the government and Party organization of the area, was also organized as a city commune (*ch'eng kuan kung she*), under which there were eight residents' committees (*chü min wei yüan hui*) composed of persons living in the urbanized areas.

Since it was located in a primarily agricultural area, County X had, apart from its county seat, only three other significantly urbanized areas. These were all small market towns (*chen*), each with a population of roughly one thousand households (*hu*), or somewhat over five thousand people. Being a coastal county, it had a sizable fishing population. Like many if not most other Chinese counties, at least in south China, it was characterized topographically by low hills and small, agricultural valleys. As in much of southeastern China, the population was generally clustered into small village settlements containing an average of one to two hundred households, although there were some larger villages containing several hundred households.[19]

Administrative Divisions of County X (1962)

In the mid-1950s the two counties that were later merged to form County X had been divided into thirteen districts (*ch'ü*) and eighty-three administrative villages (*hsiang*). When communization occurred, in 1958, the districts were converted into communes (*kung she*), and each of the administrative villages became a "production brigade" (*sheng ch'an ta tui*). In addition, two new production brigades were created for the fishing population in coastal areas. After the merger to form County X had taken place, one district was separated from the county and attached to the former county seat which was converted at that time into a municipality (*shih*). Subsequently, still further adjustments were made, and the county was divided into eleven communes (one of which was located in the county seat) and eighty-five production brigades.[20]

In many areas of China, communes were formed in 1958 out of one or several administrative villages—that is, units smaller than districts. In much of coastal south China, however, the most common pattern was the one followed in the area of County X. Generally, the districts were converted into communes, and the administrative villages were transformed into production brigades.

Representativeness of County X

It would be difficult to maintain that County X is a "typical" Chinese county. The south China coastal area is unique in some respects.

[19] Before communization, each *hsiang* normally consisted of a number of average-size villages, although a very large village could constitute a single *hsiang* by itself.

[20] Beginning in 1961, communes in most parts of the country were decentralized, and many were reduced in size. The average size of communes, on a nationwide basis, was cut to one third the former size, although developments varied a great deal from one locality to another. It is possible that this process affected County X after the major informant for this study had left the county.

Distinctive local dialects, strong links with overseas Chinese (a great many of whom originate from this region), and continuing conflict between Communist China and the Chinese Nationalist regime on Taiwan, which makes security and defense a special preoccupation, are factors which distinguish the area from others in China. However, this does not mean that the region or County X should be regarded as essentially "atypical." It would be difficult, in fact, to label any single area of China as perfectly typical. In a country so large, there is tremendous regional variation, and many areas are unique in some respects. However, despite the wide variations in dialects and customs, and the existence in local areas of many special economic and political problems, the Communists have imposed a remarkably uniform pattern of government administration throughout the country. From the evidence available, the basic organizational features of County X are similar to those of other county-level organizations throughout mainland China.[21]

[21] This statement seems justified despite the special characteristics of the region mentioned above and despite the fact which will be noted later, that County X contains some organizations, such as the Party's Seacoast Department and the government's Overseas Chinese Affairs Section, that are not found in many parts of the country.

The Party in County X: Organization and Operation

Party Primacy

TWO PARALLEL, interlocking hierarchies governed County X. One was the county government, whose top authority was the County People's Council (*hsien jen min wei yüan hui*, or *jen wei*, for short) headed by the magistrate (*hsien chang*). The other was the county Party organization, headed by the County Party Committee (*hsien tang wei yüan hui*, or *hsien wei*, for short), whose chief was the county's Party first secretary (*ti yi shu chi*). Of the two, the Party Committee had unchallenged primacy. As will be seen below, the Party was not only acknowledged to be the highest policy-making authority within the county; it was also directly involved in the governing process in many ways. Especially during the Great Leap Forward, starting in 1958, it encroached on government administration so extensively that there was no very clear line of demarcation between the respective spheres of Party and government responsibility. After 1961, an effort was made to sharpen the distinctions between Party and government responsibilities, so that the government would take responsibility for routine administrative work and much of the technical work. But this effort was not wholly successful and in any case the government administrative agencies remained definitely subordinate to the Party, with their primary task being to implement—or to help implement—Party-defined policies.

Over-All Growth of the Party

At the time of Communist takeover in 1949, the Party membership in the area later to become County X was very small. It consisted mainly of those who had belonged to small guerrilla units in nearby mountain areas plus a few soldiers from the north, who came with the victorious army. Immediately after takeover, the Party was cautious about too-rapid expansion. Peasant organizations were established in the villages, and while local leaders were chosen for their sympathy to the Communist cause, as well as for their ability, they were by no means necessarily Communist Party members.

With the advent of land reform, special land reform work teams were sent from higher levels into the villages. The county served as the principal headquarters for organizing these work teams, each consisting of about seven members who went to live for two to three months in an administrative village to carry on the work of land reform. In this period there was ample opportunity for county-level cadres to observe potential Party members in action, and subsequently many promising young local men were selected to begin training for possible Party membership. After a period of study and work alongside cadres at higher levels, those who "proved themselves" were admitted to the Party. As of 1953, however, even after land reform had been completed, there was still only one or two Party branches per district.

Party membership increased only slowly following land reform, and for a fairly long period of time few Party units existed below the district level. But when, soon after land reform, the program for "unified buying and selling" and cooperativization developed and penetrated into rural areas during 1953–1955, there was a much greater need for reliable cadres at the local level. Although the central government could not hope to include all new cadres on the state payroll, it could at least offer them Party membership, which would increase their incentives to carry out orders from above.

A large Party recruiting campaign was launched during the 1955–1956 period, in which an attempt was made to establish a Party unit in each administrative village, to serve as the key unit for organizing basic-level cooperatives. During the big collectivization campaigns, demobilized servicemen and cadres from higher government and Party offices were sent down to the administrative villages to assist both in early organizational work and in the selection and training of new Party and Young Communist League members.

The typical pattern was to have a Party branch in each administrative village, although two small administrative villages might combine to form one branch. Ordinarily, at least one leader from each cooperative became a Party member, although this too varied somewhat, depending on the size of the cooperative. Whatever their size, the Party branches at the administrative village level linked the cooperatives into coordinated units, and they became the basic local channels through which county leaders worked in implementing their policies.

Despite the many vicissitudes and subsequent changes involved in higher-stage cooperativization, communization, decentralization, and the various rectification campaigns conducted by the Party, the Party branches at the level of the administrative villages (and their equivalents since communization) have remained the key local Party units. Membership in the branches has occasionally been reduced slightly, as a result of the expulsion of some Party members during Party rectification campaigns, but as of 1962 there were some six thousand or more Party members in County X as a whole, constituting between 1 and 2 percent of the population of the county.

Party Organization: The Party Congress

In theory, the top local authority in the Party organization in County X was the Party Congress (*tang tai piao ta hui*), composed of representatives elected by all subordinate Party committees and branches in the county. Each of the eleven commune Party committees (*she tang wei yüan hui*, or *she tang wei*, for short), each of the ninety-three Party branches (*chih pu*) in rural production brigades and urban residents' committees, and each of the twenty-one "organization branches" (*chi kuan chih pu*) in county-level Party and government units, elected at least one, and in a few cases more than one, delegate to the congress. Altogether there were between 130 and 140 representatives—roughly 2 percent of the total Party membership in the county.

In practice, however, the importance of the Party Congress was limited at this level, as at higher levels in the Party organization in China. Its primary function was to meet at fairly infrequent intervals —theoretically once a year, but in practice less frequently—to review the work of the Party and to elect the Party Committee, which was the top governing Party body between congress sessions. Even in the performance of these responsibilities, the role of the congress was often simply to endorse decisions made at higher levels in the Party rather than to exercise local initiative. Whenever the Party Congress met in County X, the Special District Party Committee (*tang ti fang wei yüan hui*, or *ti wei hui* or *ti wei*, for short) sent a representative, who was always a high-ranking cadre and sometimes the secretary of the committee; and all choices of County Party Committee members were subject to approval, or veto, by the special district committee. Ordinarily, unless changes were to be made in the officials, the congress simply endorsed the existing officeholders. When changes were to be made in officeholders, the names would be selected by the county committee leaders and approved by the special district committee; in the selection of the highest county officials, approval by the Provincial Party Committee (*sheng tang wei yüan hui*, or *sheng wei*, for short) was required. Although some members of the congress could express their opinions informally before the meetings, a slate of selected candidates was presented to the congress, and the "election" of Party officials at the congress was merely a *pro forma* endorsement of this slate.

The congress, moreover, simply "elected" the twenty-seven regular Party Committee members (*cheng shih wei yüan*) and two alternates (*hou pu wei yüan*) without designating their functional posts in the local Party hierarchy. The first secretary then allocated job assignments among the committee members, after having obtained special district committee approval. Once the key job assignments had been made, the County Party Committee elected a Standing Committee (*ch'ang wu wei yüan hui* or *ch'ang wei*, for short). Nominees for this committee also required the approval of the Special District Party Committee. In 1962 the Party Standing Commit-

tee consisted of fourteen men and included all those assigned to key
Party posts (with two exceptions) plus a few holding important government jobs.

In County X the key Party posts designated by the first secretary
from among those elected to the Party Committee included the following: the secretary (*shu chi*), the five deputy secretaries (*fu shu
chi*), the secretary of the Control Committee (*chien ch'a wei yüan
hui shu chi;* this committee was called *chien wei hui*, for short),
and the heads (*pu chang*) of all the departments (*pu*) under the
Party Committee.

In County X the Party had nine departments: the Organization
Department (*tsu chih pu*), Political and Legal Department (*cheng fa
pu*), Armed Forces Department (*wu chuang pu*), Seacoast Depart-
ment (*yen hai pu*), United Front Department (*t'ung chan pu*),
Propaganda and Education Department (*hsüan chiao pu*), Rural
Work Department (*nung ts'un kung tso pu*), Finance and Trade
Department (*ts'ai mao pu*), and Industry and Communications De-
partment (*kung chiao pu*). No personnel were assigned to the Armed
Forces Department; Party members in the government's Military
Service Bureau (*ping yi chü*) handled the functions of the depart-
ment, which existed on paper only.

Top Party Leaders: Party Committee
and Standing Committee

Unlike the Party Congress, the Party Committee was an extremely
important decision-making body. Its twenty-nine regular and alternate members met for regular sessions about four times a year and
whenever there were important political movements or campaigns
(*yün tung*). It was supposed to meet even more frequently—bi-
monthly—but in practice this was not feasible. However, all its meetings were occasions for major work reports and discussion of major
policies.

Between the meetings of the full Party Committee, its fourteen-
member Standing Committee met on an average of once a month.
Since the Standing Committee could exercise all the powers of the

full committee, for most of the year it was the body that actually ran day-to-day Party affairs—and county affairs as a whole.[22]

The members of the Party Committee and its Standing Committee occupied not only all the key operational posts in the Party hierarchy but some major government positions as well. Only the first secretary held no other concurrent post in either Party or government; his general Party tasks, and over-all responsibility for county affairs, fully occupied his time. The other thirteen Standing Committee members (*ch'ang wu wei yüan*) held additional jobs concurrently. The Party secretary, number-two man in the Party hierarchy, was chairman (*chu hsi*) of the People's Political Consultative Conference (*jen min cheng chih hsieh shang hui yi*, or *cheng hsieh*, for short), the principal united front body in the government. Of the five deputy Party secretaries, one was county magistrate, three headed important Party departments (the Organization, Political and Legal, and Rural Work Departments), and one was head of the government Military Service Bureau. Another member of the Standing Committee was a deputy magistrate in the government. One member was the secretary of the Party Control Committee; one was chief of the Public Security Bureau (*kung an chü*) in the government and a deputy head of the Party Political and Legal Department; and one was chief of the People's Court (*jen min fa yüan*) as well as a deputy head of the Political and Legal Department. The remaining three members headed the Party's United Front, Finance and Trade, and Industry and Communications Departments.

The only heads of Party departments who did not belong to the Standing Committee were those in charge of the Seacoast Department and the Propaganda and Education Department. Normally, the chiefs of these departments would have been members of the Standing Committee; but the men holding these posts in 1962 were fairly

[22] In addition to holding regular Party Committee and Standing Committee meetings, the Party Committee called large numbers of special meetings to deal with specific problems. To discuss important issues they might call an "enlarged cadre conference" (*kan pu k'uo ta hui yi*) and to consider more technical questions they might call a "work conference" (*kung tso hui yi*) or a special "forum" (*tso t'an hui*). Most Party Committee members attended such meetings, but participants also included others directly concerned with the topics to be discussed.

new appointees. Both men were, however, members of the larger Party Committee and in time could expect promotions to the Standing Committee. The government bureaus most notably represented on the Standing Committee were, as indicated, those responsible for key security and control functions.

The other thirteen regular County Party Committee members (*tang wei wei yüan*) also held important Party or government posts. One was the head of the Procuracy (*chien ch'a yüan*) and a deputy head of the Party's Political and Legal Department. Another was chief of the government Grain Bureau (*liang shih chü*). The other eleven were secretaries of commune Party committees.

These top Party bodies had primary authority to define major policies for the county as a whole and were, in practice, much more important than any equivalent county government bodies. They exercised tight control over all government agencies, which they simply used, in effect, to help implement Party-defined policies. Although only a few bureaus or other top government bodies were headed by Party Committee members, virtually all county government agencies—with minor exceptions that will be noted later—were headed by Party members subject to close Party direction and discipline, exercised by the Party Committee, its staff office (*hsien wei pan kung shih*), and the various Party departments, as well as by the Party's "organization branches," to which they all belonged.

Social Characteristics of Party Leadership

The social characteristics of the top ruling elite that emerged in this particular area of rural China after Communist takeover is revealed by an analysis of the highest Party leaders in County X as of 1962. The majority of these leaders consisted of "old cadres" (*lao kan pu*) who had come from outside the area. The very top leaders, in fact, were northerners who did not even know the principal local dialects. With few exceptions they had had military experience of some sort. Most had had only limited formal education—less, in fact, than many persons working under them in both the Party and government hierarchies. Despite having had ten to twenty years of experience working for the Party, most were still in their forties, although there were a few in their late thirties or early fifties. The absence of women in the top stratum of county Party leaders was striking.

Most leaders had worked their way up gradually within the power structure of the Party; but in the early years when manpower was limited and the Party organization was expanding rapidly, some had been promoted very quickly. Although these men had risen through a number of different career lines, Party organizational activity and work in the political and legal field had been particularly important. All of them were essentially "organization men" of proven ability and reliability; few had any notable technical experience or qualifications. To a large extent, a small group of these men had dominated the power apparatus in this area ever since Communist takeover.

The first secretary of the Party Committee in County X was a "northerner" from Anhwei Province ("northerner" was used locally to describe persons from central as well as north China). He was also a "Yenan cadre." [23] A graduate of primary school, he was about forty-five years old. Just before "liberation" he had been working in a political work team (*cheng kung tui*) in the People's Liberation Army (*chieh fang chün*), or PLA for short, and was sent as a "southbound cadre" (*nan hsia kan pu*) to join the guerrillas in Fukien Province. At the time of Communist takeover, he was first appointed magistrate of County Y. Later he became secretary of the Party Committee there, before finally being designated first secretary of the Party Committee in County X in 1959. A roughhewn, simple man, he was an excellent public speaker.

The Party secretary, a northerner from Shantung Province, was about forty years old and had graduated from lower middle school.[24] He had served as a political commissar (*cheng chih wei yüan*) in the army, participating in the Korean War, and was transferred to work in this area only after the war had ended in 1953, later than most of the other top county leaders. When first assigned to this area, he became head of the Party Organization Department in County Y, then deputy secretary of the Party Committee there, and finally Party secretary in County Z, prior to appointment to his current post.

[23] See p. 188 for an explanation of this term.
[24] Lower middle school in China is equivalent to junior high school in the United States.

The first deputy secretary, concurrently county magistrate, was a man about forty years old and was a graduate of lower middle school. A northerner from Tientsin, Hopei, he was also a former political commissar in the army. He had been sent to Fukien before "liberation" as a "southbound cadre," had taken part in the land reform campaign, and then had become Party secretary of a district in County Z. Subsequently, he became chief of County Z's Public Security Bureau, then the county's magistrate, and finally its deputy Party secretary, prior to appointment as deputy Party secretary and magistrate of County X.

The second deputy secretary, concurrently head of the Party's Organization Department, was a northerner from Shantung Province and was still in his late thirties. Better educated than most of the other top leaders, he had graduated from higher middle school, and then had been sent to Fukien as a "southbound cadre" by the army. At the time of "liberation" he was assigned to head a district in County Z. Then he became, in succession, chief of the Grain Bureau in County Z, chief of its Personnel Section (*jen shih k'o*), deputy magistrate, and finally staff secretary (*mi shu*) of the County Party Committee's Staff Office (*hsien wei pan kung shih*), before assuming his current posts in County X.

The third deputy secretary, concurrently head of the Party's Political and Legal Department, was a northerner from Honan Province. About forty years old, he had attended but had not graduated from higher middle school. Also sent as a "southbound cadre" to join the Fukien guerrillas, before "liberation," his first assignment after 1949 was as a section chief (*k'o chang*) in the Public Security Bureau of County Z. All his subsequent posts were in the political and legal field. After working up to be deputy chief of the Public Security Bureau in County Z, he became head of that county's Procuracy, then head of its Public Security Bureau. After training at a public security college (*kung an hsüeh yüan*) in Shanghai, he was transferred to be chief of the Public Security Bureau in County Y, before assuming his current posts in County X in 1959.

The fourth deputy secretary, concurrently head of the Party's Rural Work Department, was about fifty years old—the oldest of the top group. A northerner from Honan Province, and a "Yenan cadre," he had had a primary school education. His first major post in this area was that of deputy Party secretary in a district in County Z, and soon thereafter he became its secretary. Subsequently, he was promoted to be head of the County Party Committee's Rural Work Department (then called *nung yeh sheng ch'an ho tso pu*, or "Department of Agricultural Production Cooperation") in County Z. In 1959 he was elected to the Party standing committee of County X, and not long after that he assumed his current posts.

The fifth deputy secretary, who was concurrently chief of the county government's Military Service Bureau and was, therefore, considered to be the head of the Armed Forces Department in the Party, was in his late forties—this was considered fairly old—and had completed lower primary school. A northerner (province unknown), and an "anti-Japanese war cadre" (*k'ang jih chan cheng kan pu*) who had joined the Party during the Sino-Japanese War, this man was, and remained, primarily a military cadre. He came to County Y in 1956 to head its Military Service Bureau. Formerly a regimental commander (*t'uan chang*) in the PLA, he continued to wear a military uniform and maintained close liaison with the army even after his assignment to county posts.

All of these top seven men, in sum, were not only "outsiders" but also northerners. All had had military experience, either as commanders or political commissars, and most had come directly on assignment from the army. Two of the men, the "Yenan cadres," one of whom was the first secretary, had had only primary school education. Four had attended middle school but had not completed it. Only one man had finished higher middle school; and none of them had had any university-level education. Their careers had been almost entirely in military, Party, and government "organization" work, or in political and legal work (chiefly public security); except for one man, who had headed a Grain Bureau, none of them had ever held any important job in other lines of activity.

The other twenty-two men belonging to the Party Committee in County X had characteristics fairly similar to those of the top seven. Among them, however, there was a slightly higher percentage of persons with some middle school education, there were a few younger men (the youngest was twenty-seven), the career lines of advancement of the men were somewhat more varied, and there were several local men.

Outsiders Versus Local Leaders

The relationship between local men and outsiders among the County Party leaders deserves special note. Of the total of twenty-nine regular and alternate members of the county Party Committee, fifteen were northerners (eleven of whom were on the Party Standing Committee), seven were "outsiders" from other counties in Fukien (two of these men were on the Standing Committee), and seven were local men from the area of County X (only one of whom was on the Standing Committee).

The predominance of outsiders in key posts at the county level has probably been more extreme in the coastal regions of south China than in some other areas of the country, partly because this area, which traditionally has had strong tendencies toward localism, and is more exposed to external contacts, seems to have been viewed with a considerable degree of suspicion and uneasiness by leaders from other parts of the country. However, the use of outside cadres has been an important device used to ensure central Party control in many other parts of the country as well.

In County X, as in many areas of south China, the presence of the northerners, especially in top positions, has been a source of considerable strain, and there have been significant tensions in their relations with local cadres. Most of the northern cadres have been able and hard-working, and the majority of them have won the respect of the local cadres. However, when not on duty, most local cadres still speak their local dialect, which most northern cadres still have not learned. The language used in offices is Mandarin, and local cadres who have not spoken Mandarin in the course of conducting official business have been accused of "regionalism." Some local cadres learned Mandarin while in the army, but until 1956 interpreters were still needed at all large Party meetings. At such meetings, a side room was often reserved for those who did not know Mandarin, and the interpreter would stand at the head of the room to translate the proceedings. In 1956, a big campaign was launched for the study of Mandarin, and the interpreters were abolished. The use of Mandarin now poses no problem at the county level; but at the commune level, even in 1962, only state cadres were required to speak Mandarin, and at the brigade level virtually no one was able to speak it.

One source of tension between local cadres and outsiders has arisen from the fact that working in the villages has been considered very undesirable and almost invariably it has been the local cadres who have been sent to the villages, since the northerners have not been able to converse in the local dialect. This problem was greatly exacerbated during the "transfer-downward" (*hsia fang*) campaign,[25] since it was generally the local cadres who were selected to go to the countryside. In 1959, when this campaign was already in full-swing, "localism" became an increasingly serious issue; and as one might expect, the higher officials came down very strongly against those who were guilty of "regionalism."

Another source of tension has arisen from the fact that northerners have generally held higher positions than local cadres of equal competence and have had better opportunities for promotion. In 1959, for example, after the "anti-rightist tendency" campaign, when a number of local Party and government positions became vacant, not only were more local cadres criticized and demoted but more northerners were promoted. Although local cadres could agree to the promotion of northerners who were obviously competent, there was considerable discontent about the promotion of those who were considered less able.

Party Secretaries

The committee system which runs the Party machinery in Communist China places strong emphasis, in some respects, on collective leadership.[26] At the same time, the top man in any Party committee carries enormous responsibility and generally wields the power to go with it. In County X, the county first secretary, who was approved and sometimes designated by higher authorities, was clearly recognized as the most powerful man in the county. His opinions carried

---

[25] See pp. 60–61 for a discussion of this campaign.

[26] This was especially true immediately after 1956, in the aftermath of de-Stalinization in the Soviet Union, when there was particular sensitivity about arbitrary one-man rule.

more weight than those of any other individual, and he was responsible for directing the entire range of work carried out by both Party and government organs. He was assisted by the secretary and five deputy secretaries, and also by an important Party Committee staff office (*hsien wei pan kung shih*) headed by a staff secretary-general (*mi shu chang*).

In many, if not most, major political institutions in Communist China—both Party and government—there are several deputy chiefs, who divide their work along functional lines, each supervising and coordinating one or more broad areas of the institution's activities. In County X, the Party secretary, as second-ranking man, acted as general assistant to the first secretary; but each of the five deputy secretaries supervised one or more general fields of work. One was in charge of political and legal work and united front activities. Another directed armed forces work and military affairs. The other three supervised broad economic fields: rural work, including all activities related to agriculture; finance and trade; and industry and communications. Areas of Party responsibility that did not fall into these categories—for example, Party organization work and propaganda and education—were directly supervised by the first secretary and the secretary.

Party Committee Staff Office

The Party Committee Staff Office was responsible not only for assisting both the first secretary and the secretary in all their activities but also for helping the deputy secretaries in supervising, coordinating, and servicing the Party Committee's departments. The head (*chu jen*) of the staff office—the staff secretary-general—was an able, young, local man in his late twenties, who had joined the Party while still in his teens in school. Relatively well educated (a graduate of middle school), he was an alternate member of the Party Standing Committee and was one of the most influential local men in the Party, despite his youth. His close relationship with the first secretary made him a rising figure in the local Party hierarchy. His salary grade was seventeen.[27]

[27] For an explanation of the ranking system, see pp. 190–92.

Not only the secretary-general but most of his staff were very young. The nature of their work—reading and writing documents—required that they be well educated and literate. A large number of top Party officials, coming from poor and middle peasant backgrounds, had had little formal education. Though many of them could read fairly simple documents, they had to rely heavily on younger men who were also from the "proper" class backgrounds and yet had nevertheless had a chance to become literate.

The staff secretary-general was expected to keep well informed on all documents coming down from higher levels of authority and to brief the Party first secretary and other Party leaders about them. In addition, he was responsible for overseeing the preparation of periodic summary reports and for drafting most of the first secretary's major reports and speeches. As editor-in-chief (*tsung pien chi*), he exercised general supervision over the county newspaper published by the Party Committee.

The staff office also served as a clearinghouse for most documents going to higher levels. Specialized reports were written by personnel in the Party's departments, but they were often edited in the staff office before being sent to higher levels. Since some reports were written by cadres of marginal literacy, the problem in editing the reports often involved stylistic rather than substantive problems.

Under the staff secretary-general, eleven cadres, all Party members, worked as permanent employees of the staff office. One was deputy head (*fu chu jen*). Two made up the permanent staff of a small, special Work Group (*kung tso tsu*). Most of the others were engaged in clerical or secretarial work: Two kept the archives and files (*tang an kuan*); one was a general affairs cadre (*shih wu kan pu,* or *shih wu*, for short); two were secretarial clerks (*wen yin*); and two were receiving and sending clerks (*shou fa*).

The permanent personnel were supplemented by cadres who served temporarily in the staff office. These were normally assigned by the Party's Organization Department, on the request of the first secretary, to work either in the special Work Group or in the "*ad hoc* campaign staff offices" (*lin shih yün tung pan kung shih*), which were established as needed to promote current political or other campaigns. On occasion, YCL members, or even non-Party cadres, instead of Party members, received such assignments.

The two cadres (grades twenty-three and twenty-five)[28] who ran the files and archives of the staff office kept copies of all important reports and correspondence channeled through the Party Committee, although subordinate Party departments also kept their own files. The two secretarial clerks acted as a typing and mimeographing pool to service the Party departments as well as the staff office itself. The two receiving and sending clerks registered and distributed all documents going through the staff office.

The staff office also had four "messengers" (*t'ung hsün yüan*), who were general service personnel (grades twenty-seven to twenty-eight) rather than state cadres. One of them regularly delivered communications to all Party and government organizations in the county seat. Another dealt primarily with the post office, through which most communications upward or downward were sent. Many secret or special communications were sent via the post office's classified postal system (*chün yu*, literally "military post"), which made deliveries to the special district every morning and brought mail from the special district each afternoon. This mail was generally delivered by cadres from the staff office, who traveled by bus or car. Mail service to and from the communes was less regular. Service from county headquarters to Peking ordinarily took four or five days. The other two "messengers" working for the staff office only occasionally dealt with communications. Most of the time they served as clerical assistants and cleaning men.

The staff office's two general affairs cadres (grades twenty-three to twenty-five) were responsible for performing a variety of "housekeeping" tasks and providing a number of services to the personnel of all units under the Party Committee. They ran a mess hall (*fan t'ing* or *shih t'ang*), which served three meals a day, prepared by two cooks (*ch'ui shih yüan*, or *ch'ui shih*, for short), who were general service personnel rather than cadres. All cadres in the Party departments could eat there, and the majority did so, although married cadres usually ate at least some meals at home. The cost of food was

[28] The grade levels given here and subsequently, in discussion of County X, are based on data provided by the primary informant for this section. Although possibly subject to minor errors, they indicate the general range of grade levels. When grade levels are not indicated, no information has been obtainable.

low; three meals a day for a month cost Y10.05 in 1962. Messes of this sort were available to all Party and non-Party state cadres at the county level.

The general affairs cadres also managed a dormitory (*su she*) for single cadres and helped to arrange housing for others. The dormitory was located on the floors above the offices and was available not only to all unmarried cadres but also to married cadres living apart from their wives. Except for higher-ranking cadres, the cadres in the dormitories generally lived two to a room. In recent years a slight majority of the cadres have been married, but because of the policy of limiting migration from rural areas to the towns and cities, cadres' wives have generally been discouraged from coming to the county seat. Hence many local cadres have left their wives with their families in rural areas, seeing them only on weekends. A cadre might either return home for the weekend or arrange for his wife to stay in the official guesthouse at the county seat. In some cases, the wives of cadres lived in factory dormitories at the county seat and saw their husbands on weekends.

The top-ranking married cadres in County X, all "outsiders," were provided with state-owned housing at extremely low rents, often as little as Y1.10 a month. Although some of these cadres dispensed with household servants in 1958, when pressure was exerted on domestic workers to get regular jobs, a number still had servants in their homes in 1962.

The general affairs cadres tried to help some married cadres find small apartments in town where they could live with their families, but this was often difficult; it was especially so in the early part of the Great Leap Forward when housing was extremely tight because of the migration of people from rural to urban areas.

The staff office's general affairs cadres also handled the payment of salaries (*kung tzu*), with funds that came from the county government, to all Party Committee cadres; distributed allowances for office supplies (*pan kung fei*) to all organs under the committee; and handled the procurement of office equipment. A small working library (*t'u shu shih*), containing periodicals and study materials, was also under their supervision and was located in the staff office.

The staff office handled visits and letters to the Party Committee from people of all sorts. One room in the office was called the "reception office for people's visits" (*jen min lai fang chieh tai shih*); and the staff secretary-general or other staff office personnel met and talked with visitors there. "People's letters" (*jen min lai hsin*) received by the Party Committee were generally forwarded by the staff office to the appropriate Party departments, or sometimes to government agencies, for replies. All letters were answered, and the staff office was responsible for checking on this, seeing that subordinate units sent out replies, or in some cases, answering the letters itself. On occasion some such letters—for example, complaints about the misconduct of specific cadres—led the staff office to request investigations and remedial action by Party or government investigatory and control units. And some letters were published in the county paper, which maintained a special section for "people's letters."

Special Work Group

The staff office's small, permanent, special Work Group was, in a sense, a task force to deal with special problems which arose; but it had particular responsibility for rural programs. Unlike the Party's Rural Work Department, or the regular county government agencies concerned with activities in rural areas, it did not concern itself with day-to-day programs. Instead it concentrated on carrying out investigatory work (*chien ch'a kung tso*) on special problems and organizing "keypoint experiments" (*shih yen tien hsing*) to test alternative ways of implementing the Party's current "central work" or responsibilities (*chung hsin kung tso*) or major programs in rural areas. In addition to its two permanent cadres, this work group usually had at least two or three other cadres temporarily assigned to it, and sometimes more.

The role of the group in testing new programs and policies was an important one. The pattern of policy implementation, and adaptation, at the county level, at least in this area, usually called for local experimentation before new policies outlined by higher authorities were generally applied. With very few exceptions, important new policies did originate at higher levels, often in Peking, but it was expected that in implementing them the county authorities, in consultation with higher authorities, should adapt them to local conditions.

The most common pattern of policy transmission and implementation was one in which higher authorities would send fairly general directives or instructions (*chih shih*), outlining new policies or programs, down the hierarchy of regional administrations, each of which would interpret and adapt them to some degree. At the county level, when such instructions were received from the provincial or special-district authorities, the Party Committee—in practice often the Party Standing Committee or first secretary—would instruct the staff office's Work Group to test them out. Generally, the Work Group would then conduct an experiment in one brigade for a period of a month or two. On the basis of this experiment, it would write a summary report (*kung tso tsung chieh*) for the Party Committee, recommending how best to adapt and implement the policy locally. The Party Committee would then issue its own instructions to the communes. Sometimes, it would also convene a large conference (*hui yi*) in the brigade where the experiment had been conducted, to which all communes and brigades in the county were asked to send representatives to be briefed on the results of the experiment and on the Party Committee's conclusions regarding how best to implement the policy throughout the county. Officials at various levels kept in close touch with each other through telephone calls and visits, and ordinarily there was a great deal of consultation before final decisions were made on how specific policies or programs should be implemented.

Temporary Campaign Staff Offices

The *ad hoc* campaign staff offices, established as needed under the Party Committee Staff Office, also played an extremely important operational role in the system. For almost all major (*chung hsin*) movements, whether political or nonpolitical, the County Party Committee first received instructions from the Provincial Party Committee. These might come as written instructions (*wen chien chih shih*), or the provincial committee might call a large meeting (*ta hui*, literally, congress) of representatives of all county committees to discuss methods of carrying out the campaign. After receiving provincial instructions, whether written or oral, the county first secretary would usually convene a meeting of the County Party Committee, or Standing Committee, which would discuss methods of implementing the campaign and would decide whether or not it was necessary to establish a temporary campaign staff office, and if so how large it should be. The size of campaign staff offices varied from a few to over twenty staff members; often there were nine, eleven, or thirteen members. To establish such an office the first secretary would instruct the Party Organization Department to select and temporarily assign (ch'ou tiao) a certain number of cadres for this specific purpose to the Party Committee Staff Office. One of these would be designated head (chu jen), and the others might be divided into small groups (hsiao tsu), as needed, for different types of work. The first secretary then usually convened a large meeting, lasting several days, to brief representatives from all communes and brigades about the campaign. Sometimes, following such a meeting, the communes would themselves establish ad hoc campaign small groups (lin shih yün tung hsiao tsu) to manage the campaign.

Campaign Approach to Policy Implementation

In most major campaigns some effort was made to adapt methods of implementation to the local situation (yin ti chih yi ling huo yün yung); frequently, therefore, experiments were conducted before new policies were generally applied. Then the responsibility of the Campaign Staff Office was to organize and supervise, under the Party Committee's over-all direction, the implementation of the campaign throughout the county. Often this involved coopting very large numbers of Party and non-Party cadres from both government and Party agencies for temporary duty. The Organization Department handled such assignments, training the cadres selected, organizing them into small groups, and sending them on temporary duty to lower levels.

This approach to policy implementation applied not only to special major campaigns but also to the annual local campaigns initiated

by the County Party Committee itself.[29] As a result, there were usually one or more campaign staff offices in existence at any time, and
sometimes as many as half a dozen or more operated simultaneously.[30]

Several aspects of this mode of operation deserve special note. It
meant, first of all, that the County Party Committee tended to rely
on the special mobilizational techniques of mass campaigns, rather
than on routine government administration, to implement many, if
not most, important major policies. Clearly, these techniques enabled
the Party authorities to implement priority programs in a way that
was remarkably effective in some respects. Measures such as the concentration and training of large numbers of cadres to be sent to
the local level, and the systematic briefing at the county level
of cadres from all communes and brigades, helped to guarantee that
priority programs were actually implemented at the grassroots level.
At the same time, however, it is clear that reliance on the campaign
approach also involved significant costs and liabilities. It tended to
disrupt the more normal tasks of government and Party administration. It resulted in neglect of problems that were not the focus of
current campaigns. It involved considerable waste of time and effort
on the part of cadres diverted from their regular work. And, in general, it probably inhibited the development of an effective government administration of a more routinized sort.

It is noteworthy that it was the County Party Committee, rather
than the County People's Council, which organized all these campaigns. This meant, in effect, that many if not most priority programs
were implemented directly by the Party rather than by the government, and direct Party rule was substituted for more regularized government administration. While this ensured Party control, it did not
contribute to the effectiveness of the government agencies responsible for the bulk of day-to-day administration.

[29] These included campaigns for spring planting, summer harvesting
and fall planting, fall harvesting, the division of crops after harvesting,
fertilizer gathering, postharvest rectification, and others.

[30] In some counties there was excessive proliferation of such *ad hoc*
campaign staff offices, and strenuous attempts were made periodically to
reduce their number. See, for example, an article in the Peking *People's
Daily*, October 22, 1956, on Taiku Hsien, Shansi, which lists sixteen
campaign staff offices.

Total Staff of County Party Apparatus

Under the top Party leadership, and serviced by the Party Committee staff office, the main operating organs of the Party Committee included not only the nine Party departments (eight with personnel, one a paper organization only) but also the Party Control Committee (*chien ch'a wei yüan hui*) and Party School (*tang hsiao*). In addition, three Party-directed mass organizations—the Young Communist League (*ch'ing nien t'uan*), the Women's Federation or Women's Association (*fu nu lien ho hui*, or *fu lien hui* or *fu lien*, for short), and the General Labor Union (*tsung kung hui*)—functioned as Party subsidiaries and looked to the staff office for assistance of various sorts.

There was a total of 137 posts in the County Party Committee's entire apparatus, if one includes the mass organizations and disregards overlapping positions. In addition to the twenty-nine members of the Party Committee and the twelve cadres in the staff office, sixty-five state cadres worked for the Party departments, the Party Control Committee, and the Party School, and thirty-one state cadres for the three mass organizations. If one excludes the cadres working for subsidiary mass organizations and takes into account overlapping positions, there were 106 Party posts, filled by slightly under one hundred cadres. All of these, with the exception of two YCL cadres working for the Propaganda and Education Department, were Party members.

In addition to these cadres, there was a sizable number of general service personnel, who served as office boys, messengers, cleaners, cooks, and the like. Security-sensitive positions—messengers, for example—were generally filled by Young Communist League members. Since many of these general service personnel were young, the able ones who proved themselves through their work might later become cadres; some were either officially or unofficially considered to be "cadres in training."

Party Control Committee

The Party Control Committee consisted of four men, a secretary (*shu chi*), who held grade seventeen, and three staff members (*kan shih*), who held grades nineteen to twenty-two. In practice, these men were appointed by the first secretary rather than elected by the Party Congress. They worked under the supervision of the Party Committee, and were serviced by its staff office. Its primary task was to ensure that effective discipline (*chi lü*) was maintained among all Party members in the county. It was expected, on its own initiative, to check continuously on the performance of Party members to ensure that they implemented Party policies, followed Party regulations, and fulfilled the eight great standards (*pa ta piao chun*) of conduct expected of them. In practice, however, partly because its staff was small, the Control Committee was generally restricted to investigations of major violations of Party discipline, usually ones that had been brought to its attention either by the Party's Organization Department or by lower Party committees and branches.

The Control Committee did not itself mete out punishments. Instead, after making its investigations, it simply made recommendations on appropriate action. The final decisions on administrative punishments were then formally made by the Party branches to which the errant members belonged, or, when branch leaders were involved, by the next higher units. However, except for the lightest punishments —for example, education through criticism—Party branches did not mete out punishments unless and until concurrence had been obtained from the Control Committee. Furthermore, before a final decision was reached, the Party member subject to punishment was allowed to defend himself at a meeting of his Party branch.

Very close liaison was maintained by the Control Committee with both the Party Organization Department and the county government's Public Security Bureau. This was partly because the latter units were able to conduct more thorough investigations than the Control Committee itself could, and partly because questions might arise as to whether serious cases should be handled administratively within the Party or be transferred to the government's law-enforce-ment agencies to be treated as criminal cases. When possible, the Party preferred to handle the disciplining of its members through its own Party machinery and to use administrative measures rather than criminal procedures. Even when it was felt that formal judicial action had to be taken against Party members, the Party preferred to make its own decisions before action was taken by the Public Security Bureau or the Court (except, of course, when Party members were apprehended in *flagrante delicto*).

When necessary, informal *ad hoc* committees representing the Control Committee, the Organization Department, and the Public Security Bureau met and reached joint decisions on borderline cases. To cite a specific example: When the chief of the county government's Finance and Tax Bureau discovered that a Party cadre in his bureau was guilty of corruption, he reported this fact to the Party's Organization Department, the Control Committee, and the county government's Personnel Section. If the guilty person had been a non-Party cadre, his case probably would have been turned over immediately to the Public Security Bureau and the Procuracy for action. Since he was a Party member, however, representatives of the Organization Department, Control Committee, and Public Security Bureau first met and discussed the case. They decided to recommend criminal proceedings carried out by the Public Security Bureau, rather than Party disciplinary measures, because the offense was a clear-cut case of criminal action. Nevertheless, their recommendation was first sent to the man's Party branch; only after the branch had formally made a similar decision, endorsed by the Control Committee, did the Public Security Bureau and Procuracy act to arrest and indict the man.

Administrative Punishments

Five different kinds of administrative punishment (*ch'u li*, or *ch'u fen*) were used within the Party: (1) education through criticism (*p'i p'ing chiao yü*), which was very light; (2) warnings (*kao*), which might be either "light" or "serious," both of which, however, were considered to be fairly light punishments; (3) the recording of errors or transgressions on one's Party record (*tang nei chi kuo*), which was more serious;[31] (4) probation (*liu tang ch'a k'an*), which was even more serious;[32] and (5) expulsion from the Party (*k'ai ch'u tang chi*), which was the most serious punishment of all.[33] In County X perhaps 1 percent of all Party members were expelled, and another 5 percent punished in other ways, in a year when there were no major political campaigns. These figures rose to as high as 3 percent and 7 percent in some campaign years.

Non-Party state cadres in the government were also subject to five different kinds of administrative punishment. In their case, however, the Party Control Committee was not involved, nor, obviously, were the Party branches. These punishments were decided upon jointly by the government's Personnel Section and the Party's Organization Department; this, in practice, meant final decision by the latter. The five types of punishment in County X were: (1) warnings (*kao*); (2) registration of errors (*chi kuo*) in one's record; (3) job and/or salary demotion (*chien chih chien chi*); (4) dismissal from one's job (*ts'e chih*); and (5) dismissal from service as a state cadre (*ch'ing hsi k'ai ch'u*).

Party cadres were subject to both types of punishment, that is, those relating strictly to their Party membership and those relating to governmental units in which they might be employed. The Party Organization Department, by virtue of its control over the Personnel Section in the government, could coordinate both kinds of punishment, which could be meted out either simultaneously or at different times. For example, a cadre who committed a serious crime might be both expelled from the Party and removed from his job in the government.

All disciplinary actions were entered in a cadre's personnel dossier (*tang an*) and became a part of his permanent record. Even the lightest punishments were taken very seriously. A cadre's dossier followed

[31] In some places differentiation was made between "serious errors" (*ta kuo*) and "minor errors" (*hsiao kuo*).

[32] Probation was usually for a definite period—several months, or even years, during which time a person had to participate in "Party life" but could not vote or hold responsible posts. If his behavior was good, he was taken off probation at the end of the period.

[33] Generally expulsion was permanent, since it was extremely difficult, once expelled, ever to reenter the Party.

him everywhere, and blemishes of any sort on his record clearly affected his future opportunities for advancement. In a relatively monolithic society, where alternative career lines were limited—in fact almost nonexistent for most people—criticisms in one's dossier were much more damaging to the individual than they would be in a more pluralistic social setting.

The punishments listed above were not the only ones that could be meted out administratively, rather than through judicial procedures, to state cadres. As will be noted later,[34] much harsher punishments could be administered by the Public Security Bureau without going through the courts.

Party Departments

The bulk of the day-to-day work of the Party in County X was carried out by its various departments. (As already stated, there were nine such departments, of which eight were important operationally, while one existed only on paper.) Although the number of persons working in each of these departments was not large—the smallest had four cadres and the largest ten—the departments were extremely important in the political system. Under the over-all direction of the Party Committee, each department in effect acted as the primary directing body for its general functional "system," or field of work, throughout the entire county. Each not only supervised the activities of Party personnel engaged in work related to its "system," but even more important, exercised primary control and direction over all county government agencies and mass organizations involved in it.

To a large extent, the staff members of the departments were generalists rather than technical specialists. They were reliable Party organization men who could be depended upon to ensure that Party policies, whatever they might be, were implemented, and that the technical specialists in government agencies and other organizations functioned under efficient Party direction. Nevertheless, in another sense, they were specialists, within the context of the Party's own organization, who were responsible for effective Party and government operations within a defined area of concern and therefore de-

[34] See section on public security on pp. 219ff.

voted their major attention and effort to activities in one functional "system" of Party and government work.

Each department had responsibility, although not exclusive responsibility, for providing administrative management (*hsing cheng kuan li*), leading substantive work (*yeh wu chih tao*), and determining personnel assignments (*jen yüan tiao p'ei*), for all government as well as Party organs and personnel in their functional "system." They engaged in planning, conducted investigations, and checked on work performance. They regularly issued instructions to, and received reports from, both the county-level government agencies under their direction and lower-level Party personnel responsible for work in their field. They also convened periodic work conferences (*kung tso hui yi*) or enlarged cadre meetings (*kan pu k'uo ta hui yi*) of key Party and government cadres working within a system.

Even though they were subject to the over-all direction of the County Party Committee, operationally they maintained direct lines of communication with equivalent Party departments at higher levels, with all the government agencies under their direction at the county level, and with lower-level Party committees and branches as well as the communes and brigades. Only the most important of their reports, instructions, or other communications, whether directed to higher or lower levels, had to be cleared through the County Party Committee before being dispatched; the majority of routine communications were sent directly (*chu sung*) to the addressee, with only an information or file copy (*pei an*) sent (*ch'ao sung*) via the staff secretary-general to the top Party Committee leaders. All important general instructions sent to lower-level organs throughout the county (*ch'uan hsien chih shih*), however, were first cleared through the Party Committee; in practice this sometimes meant simply obtaining an endorsement from the staff secretary-general, although on the most important matters, approval by a deputy secretary or the first secretary was required. Informal discussions were also held with higher authorities before most important decisions were made, to ensure that the local unit would not be solely responsible for errors.

In written communications with either higher- or lower-level organs, the principal action copies of documents were generally sent by the departments only to the next level in the hierarchy. When levels were skipped, however, as they occasionally were, information copies were supposed to be sent to every intervening level. For example, a majority of reports upward were sent to or through a department in the Special District Party Committee, with an information copy going to the Provincial Party Committee's department; but if the principal copy was sent directly to the province, an information copy was sent to the special district. In either case, an information copy was always sent to the County Party Committee. Similarly the principal copies of most communications sent downward went to commune Party committees or management committees, but on occasion they went directly to branches or brigades, with information copies to commune-level organs.[35]

Ordinarily, messengers traveled daily between brigade and commune headquarters, and between the communes and the county seat; therefore, written communications from the brigade to the county-level ordinarily required two days each way. In addition to formal written communications, there were frequent communications by telephone and many informal, direct contacts for consultation. During recent years, virtually every brigade had acquired a telephone so that daily reports could be communicated to the county Party headquarters without waiting for the mail.

The efforts of the Party committees and departments to keep well informed on the activities of lower-level units did not always work as well as intended, however. With multiple lines of leadership over specific activities, it was sometimes unclear who was responsible for

[35] To cite one example of the distribution of documents, the documents captured by Kuomintang forces in early 1963 from a county Party committee near County X reveal in detail how one important document was distributed in that county. First, 375 copies were made; three were sent to each commune Party committee, one to each brigade Party branch, one to each keypoint work team, and eleven to the Party committee of the one city in the county. Reference copies were sent to all county Party committeemen, and one each to the Party committees of the four military units in the area. One copy was sent to each department of the county Party committee and one each to the YCL, Women's Federation, Labor Union, county government, Military Affairs Bureau, and Public Security Bureau. Two copies were kept for the files. See *Fan Kung Yu Chi Tui T'u Chi Fu Chien Lien Chiang Hsien Lu Huo Fei Fang Wen Chien Hui Pien* [Documents Captured by Anti-Communist Guerrillas in Lienchiang Hsien, Fukien], Taipei, March, 1964.

certain work, and some units were not always kept fully informed of plans and policies. Because of the heavy work load at times, the periodic transfer of cadres to perform temporary duty elsewhere, the disruptive effects of campaigns, and the selectivity of reporting from lower levels, knowledge about the activities of lower units was not always complete. Nevertheless, a serious attempt was made to maintain good communications with lower levels, and the results were far more impressive than those achieved by any Chinese government before 1949. Moreover, when information on the activities of lower-level units seemed inadequate, the Party Committee could, and did, send cadres to inspect conditions on the spot.

The fact that the Party Committee departments maintained these channels of direct communication with higher and lower levels did not mean, however, that the departments were considered independent units. Theoretically, they were simply organs of the County Party Committee, working under its direction and responsible to it. They kept the committee fully informed of all their activities and obtained prior approval from it for their most important actions. Nevertheless, although they were ultimately responsible to the Party Committee, in practice the departments apparently had substantial delegated authority and were expected to carry out much of their routine work on their own.

As will be described later, within the county government there were also some mechanisms for over-all direction and coordination of agencies working within particular functional "systems." To a degree the deputy magistrates performed coordinating roles; and there were several staff offices which, though not comparable to the Party departments, were designed to aid in the task of supervising government agencies within particular "systems." (For further discussion, see p. 276.) In terms of policy direction, however, the Party departments in County X clearly played a much more important role than any equivalent bodies in the county government. Primary initiative on policy matters lay with them, rather than with comparable bodies in the government. Moreover, the meetings that they convened, which usually included key government personnel (the most important meetings were generally attended by a county deputy magistrate and the bureau chiefs) as well as Party functionaries, were said to be both more frequent and more important than equivalent meetings called by the top county government authorities.

The Party departments required frequent and regular reports from the government agencies and mass organizations under their supervision; in some cases brief written monthly reports (*yüeh pao* or *chien pao*) were specified. Periodically—at least once a year and in the case of some departments as frequently as every three months— they held enlarged cadre conferences for key cadres working in Party and government organizations involved in their "system"; these conferences always included those working in county-level agencies, and sometimes rural cadres as well. Some department heads convened monthly bureau-chief meetings (*chü chang hui yi*) that brought together the unit heads of all government agencies under their supervision; on occasion these were enlarged meetings (*chü chang k'uo ta hui yi*) which included other personnel. Some departments also held biweekly meetings which brought together selected personnel from government agencies with particular members of a department's own staff.

Party Organization Department

The most important Party department for day-to-day management of internal Party affairs in County X was the Organization Department. Its responsibilities were not restricted to internal Party matters, however, since it also exercised ultimate control over personnel actions affecting all state cadres at the county level, including non-Party as well as Party cadres and those in government jobs as well as those in Party posts.

The Organization Department had a staff of seven: a head (*pu chang*), who held grade fifteen; a deputy head (*fu pu chang*), who held grade seventeen; one special staff member (*chu pan kan shih*); one statistician (*t'ung chi yüan*); and three staff members (*kan shih*). All were highly reliable, experienced members of the Party; and because their work involved written material much of the time, their average "cultural level" tended to be higher than that of cadres in many other Party units. The majority had proven themselves in organizational or personnel work or in public security and other political and legal activities. Their control over personnel decisions gave them considerable power within the Party hierarchy, and their prospects for future advancement within the Party were excellent.

The responsibilities of this department generally fell into two broad fields. On the one hand, it was in charge of Party organization and personnel matters for the entire county. In discharging this responsibility it provided management assistance and leadership to all subordinate Party committees and branches; took the lead in developing and expanding Party membership (*chieh shou kung tso*); handled all assignments (*tiao p'ei* and *p'ei pei*), transfers (*tiao tung* and *ch'ou tiao*), and promotions (*chi sheng*) of Party members; and was involved when punishments were meted out (*ch'u li*) to Party members. It directed the study (*hsüeh hsi*) of Party members in their "Party life" (*tang ti sheng huo*) or "organizational life" (*tsu chih sheng huo*) meetings and received dues (*tang fei*) from all Party members.[36] It maintained the personnel dossiers (*tang an*) of Party members, kept systematic statistics on membership meetings and other Party activities, and sent reports on all of these matters to higher-level organization departments as well as to the County Party Committee.

In addition, the Organization Department had the power of ultimate decision concerning assignments, transfers, promotions, and punishments affecting all non-Party state cadres in the county. Generally, in dealing with non-Party cadres it worked through the county government's Personnel Section, whose staff acted, in effect, as representatives within the government of the Organization Department. Even when handling Party members who worked in government agencies, the Organization Department usually solicited the Personnel Section's views before making decisions. Nevertheless, it was the Organization Department rather than the Personnel Section which had the final responsibility for personnel management in the government as well as in the Party.

Although it was responsible to and closely supervised by the County Party Committee, the department also communicated on

[36] Dues, in theory, consisted of 1 percent of a cadre's salary, paid monthly; often the figure was rounded, however, and amounted to slightly over 1 percent.

many matters with higher organization departments, at special district and provincial levels, as well as with the organization committeemen in subordinate Party committees and branches throughout the county.

To the extent that the department's staff members specialized, or divided their tasks, the deputy head bore the major responsibility for regular transfers, promotions, and demotions; the special staff member handled most large-scale temporary assignments (*ch'ou tiao*), which took place especially in connection with mass campaigns; the statistician received all dues and maintained the personnel dossiers, as well as compiling a wide range of statistics; and the three ordinary staff members spent much of their time in investigations and field contacts with subordinate Party units, and in addition regularly assisted those in charge of the Party School.

Party Membership in the County

As stated earlier, the total number of Party members in the county, as of 1962, was somewhat over six thousand; 96 percent were regular members and 4 percent were candidate members or alternate members (*hou pu tang yüan* or *yü pei tang yüan*). These six thousand plus members in the Party in 1962 constituted only a small percentage—between 1 and 2 percent—of the total county population, and there was every indication that the Party would remain a small elite. Generally speaking, as it grew, the Party became progressively stricter and more selective in admitting new members. Most of the Party members were men and women who held leadership positions throughout the county. Relatively few members were ordinary peasants or workers.

The most important and influential Party members were those who worked as state cadres and were on the county government payroll. The majority of these lived and worked at the county level, although some were assigned to the local level. Approximately three hundred to four hundred, or roughly 5 percent, of the Party members in the county, were state cadres. They constituted about one third of all administrative cadres working for the county government and Party apparatus and about one fifth of all those who could be classified as state cadres in the county (see definition and discussion of state cadres below). These figures alone, however, do not really indicate the degree to which Party members dominated the centers of power and decision-making in the county. Apart from staffing the Party apparatus itself, they occupied a sizable majority of the posts in certain lines of government work, such as personnel and public security, which were crucial in terms of political power; and in Party, personnel, and public security work, virtually all the non-Party cadres were members of the Young Communist League. The lowest percentage of Party members was in economic agencies. In addition, Party members headed every county government bureau and major economic enterprise, and held most of the section-chief positions as well. The only county unit not headed by a Party member was the Cultural Hall (*wen hua kuan*). Even the few Party members who were simply staff members rather than unit heads in the government had a fairly high political status (*cheng chih ti wei*) despite their relatively low administrative status (*hsing cheng ti wei*). In short, Party members dominated *all* the leading posts in the county's bureaucratic structure.

The great majority of Party members lived in the countryside. While most of these were of peasant origin, and participated in farming, very few spent full time in farm work. Most of them held functionary posts either in rural Party units or in the communes, production brigades, and production teams.

The Party in County X, then, was primarily an organization of male bureaucrats and peasant functionaries. Notably underrepresented were certain population groups that one might have expected to be more important in its membership. For example, less than four hundred (only about 6 percent) of the Party members were women. At the commune and brigade levels, there were occasional women Party members with influential roles; ordinarily, in fact, one deputy chief in each commune and brigade was a woman, who had the primary responsibility for mobilizing the women in her unit. But of the 137 cadres occupying posts in the County Party Committee apparatus, only eight were women. Five of these were in the Women's Association, one in the YCL, one in the Party Committee Staff Office, and only one in a Party department—the Organization Department. Women made up a sizable proportion of the state cadres in certain lines of government work—for example, teaching, commercial work, and banking. In some organizations in these fields women constituted close to a third of the total staff, but most of these women cadres were not Party members. The traditionalism of rural women was almost certainly one factor (in addition to male resistance to the idea of women taking active parts in public life) that partially explained their underrepresentation. As traditional views were being slowly broken down among the younger women, participation in the Party's youth subsidiary, the YCL, slowly but steadily increased. As a consequence, female participation in the Party can probably be expected to increase gradually in the future.

"Industrial workers" were another group with surprisingly low representation in the Party—especially in view of the Communists' pretensions to be essentially a proletarian organization. Altogether there were five hundred or more administrators and workers in the state-owned "factories" in County X, but less than forty of these were Party members, and almost all the Party members were in managerial posts, dominating the key leadership jobs rather than working as ordinary laborers. Of course, the working force in County X's "factories," most of which were really no more than small workshops, operated in a semirural setting and hardly constituted an "urban proletariat" comparable to that existing in larger cities. Nevertheless it is noteworthy that the local Party leaders placed no special importance on recruiting the ordinary factory- or shopworkers into the Party. As in other organizations in the county, the primary concern, apparently, was simply to ensure that those occupying the positions of power—especially in administrative, as opposed to technical, work—were Party members. If an ordinary worker rose to a responsible position, he was almost automatically inducted into the Party; or conversely, if an ordinary worker was able to join the Party, he was likely soon to be promoted to at least a low-level management job.

Despite the Party's ambivalence toward intellectuals, the necessity of making good use of "intellectuals" and trying to ensure their loyalty, required the admission into the Party of a higher proportion of intellectuals—especially school administrators—than of workers or peasants. Yet many intellectuals were not admitted. In this rural setting, most of the persons labeled "intellectuals" (*chih shih fen tzu*) were teachers, but the term was also applied to all persons with specialized training or with a relatively good education. Persons with lower middle school education were almost invariably labeled as intellectuals, and sometimes the term was loosely applied to virtually everyone who was literate.

There were over six hundred school administrators and teachers on the county government payroll throughout County X. They made up roughly one third of all those who could be considered state cadres. Of these perhaps only a sixth were Party members; but the majority of the Party members were school administrators—including about a dozen on the staff of the county middle schools, plus the principals of the ninety-odd state-run primary schools throughout the country—rather than ordinary teachers. Here again the pattern tended to be one in which, if a person became a Party member, he then moved up to a relatively important administrative post, or vice versa.

The lack of Party members among ordinary teachers was somewhat counterbalanced by the YCL membership among them. A good many ordinary teachers were quite young, recent graduates, especially from middle schools. Between fifty and sixty of these, or over 10 percent of the total, were YCL members. Often there was at least one teacher, and frequently more, in each primary school, who belonged to the YCL. In time, of course, some of these can expect to be accepted into the Party.

Apart from school administrators, however, there were relatively few other intellectuals in the Party in County X. During the "hundred flowers" period, directives were sent from higher Party authorities to expand the number of "intellectuals" inducted into the Party, but they did not produce dramatic results. A limited number of new members classified as intellectuals were accepted into the Party that year, including a leading doctor, who was deputy head of the county hospital; a banking expert in the county bank; a financial specialist, who was deputy head of the Finance and Tax Bureau; a leading local "democratic personage" (*min chu jen shih*); and a few others. But the total number remained small, apparently smaller than in some other south China counties.

One explanation for the relatively low number of intellectuals—other than school administrators—in the Party in County X was the fact that some mutual suspicion existed between them and the top Party leaders. The top Party leaders, being revolutionary politicians rather than intellectuals, apparently tended to view most intellectuals, including some of the young new graduates of middle schools, as persons influenced by corrosive "bourgeois" values. The Party leaders generally expected that intellectuals would be more critical of many Party goals and policies than ordinary people—which, in fact, was likely to be the case. On their part, many intellectuals tended, in time-honored Chinese fashion, to look down upon those who, like most of the local Party leaders, had enjoyed only a limited education.

Party Committees and Branches

All the six thousand or more Party members in the county participated in regular organizational "Party life." The Party Organization Department was responsible for supervising the various committees and branches to which they belonged. These included (1) eleven Party committees (*tang wei yüan hui*), one in each commune; (2) six general branches (*tsung chih pu*)—one supervising the twenty-one "organization branches," to which county government and Party cadres belonged, one supervising the four political and legal organization branches, one supervising the four residents' committee (*chü min wei yüan hui*) branches in the county seat, and one in each of the three major market towns (*chen*);[37] and (3) 110 branches (*chih pu*), including the twenty-one "organization branches" (*chi kuan chih pu*) in county Party and government organs, one each in the county's eighty-five brigades, and four in the eight residents' committees. Although the theoretical "average" membership for all Party branches in the county was about sixty each, most county-level "organization branches" were smaller than that, and some other branches were substantially larger.

[37] At an earlier date, when higher cooperatives grew beyond the boundaries of the administrative villages, there were for a while general branches in rural areas, in the larger cooperatives.

"Organization Branches"

The "organization branches" were particularly important in the total structure of the Party, since they included all Party members working as state cadres in county Party and government organs. Altogether there were twenty-one of these branches, with well over three hundred members. Supervising them all was one "organization general branch" (*chi kuan tsung chih pu*), whose secretary was the staff secretary-general of the County Party Committee.

The assignment of members to these "organization branches" was only partly on a functional basis; that is, some but not all Party members who worked in organs within a particular functional "system" were put together in one "organization branch." Sometimes other factors, such as the physical location of the offices where cadres worked, determined who would be assigned to what branch.

Two County Party Committee branches[38] (*hsien wei chih pu*), numbered one and two, included most Party members who worked in Party organs located in the Party Committee's compound. One, with close to forty members, included those in the Party Committee Staff Office, Control Committee, Organization Department, Party School, United Front Department, and Seacoast Department, plus the Party members working in the government Labor Bureau and Overseas Chinese Section. Its secretary was head of the Party School. The other, with roughly thirty members, included those in the Party's Propaganda and Education Department, Rural Work Department, Finance and Trade Department, Industry and Communications Department, and in the government Radio Station and Finance and Trade Staff Office. The head of the Party Propaganda and Education Department was its secretary.

In the political and legal field, there were four political and legal branches (*cheng fa chih pu*), numbered one, two, three and four, supervised by the Political and Legal General Branch. Two of them —one with slightly under forty members and the other with just

---

[38] At times the primary informant for this section reported that there were two such branches, and at other times, three. Unfortunately, there is no way to resolve the inconsistency, although conceivably the number varied at different periods.

over twenty—included members of the public security apparatus. They were headed, respectively, by a deputy chief of the Public Security Bureau and the chief of that bureau's People's Police Unit (*min ching tui chang*). Two, each with less than ten members, were headed by a deputy head of the People's Court and a deputy head of the People's Procuracy, and included all Party members from those two organs.

The head and deputy heads of the Party Political and Legal Department, including the chiefs of the Public Security Bureau, the Court, and the Procuracy, also formed an important Party Fraction (*tang tsu*), which, as will be noted below, was in effect also the Party Political and Legal Department.

Another "organization branch," called the Military Service Bureau Branch (*ping yi chü chih pu*), contained over ten members. It had as its secretary the deputy political commissar (*fu cheng wei*) of the Military Service Bureau, and it included all Party members in that bureau. Still another, the Party Mass Organization Branch (*tang ch'ün chi kuan chih pu*), included all Party members in the YCL, the Women's Association, and the General Labor Union. It also had less than ten members, and its secretary was the chairman of the Union.

Two People's Council branches (numbered one and two, *jen wei chih pu*) were headed respectively by the chief of the government personnel section and the chief of the Forestry Bureau; they included Party cadres from a variety of government organs. One, with over twenty members, included those from the People's Council Staff Office, the Personnel Section, the Civil Affairs Section, the Education Bureau and its subsidiary bodies, the Office for Elimination of Illiteracy, the Bureau of Culture and its subsidiary bodies, the Bureau of Health (but not the county hospital), and Committee on Physical Education and Sports. The other, also with more than twenty members, included Party cadres from the Agriculture, Forestry, and Water Conservancy Staff Office, the Agriculture Bureau (including its fertilizer factory and other subsidiary organs), the Bureau of Agriculture and Land Reclamation, the Forestry Bureau, Bureau of Water Conservancy, Bureau of Industry, Construction Bureau, electric plant, printing factory, and the Planning and Statistics Committee.

One small "organization branch," the Medicine Branch (*yi yao chih pu*), consisted of only a half-dozen members. It included Party cadres from the County Health Center or Hospital (*wei sheng yüan*) and "joint clinic" (*lien ho chen so*), the Medicine Company (*yi yao kung szu*), and the New China Bookstore (*hsin hua shu tien*). Its secretary was the hospital director. Another, the School Branch (*hsüeh hsiao chih pu*), had the principal of middle school No. 1 as its secretary; its dozen or more members were administrators and teachers in the county's middle schools.

The other nine "organization branches" were all composed of Party cadres working in various economic fields. One, the Finance and Tax Branch (*ts'ai shui chih pu*), had just over a half-dozen members; with a former head of the Tax Bureau as its secretary, it included all Party cadres working in the Finance and Tax Bureau. A much larger one, the Grain Branch (*liang shih chih pu*), had more than thirty members from the Grain Bureau and the rice mill; its secretary was chief of the Personnel Section (*jen shih ku*) of that bureau. There were two commerce branches (*shang yeh chih pu*), numbered one and two, made up of Party members in the Commerce Bureau. Each had over ten members; one was headed by the bureau chief and the other by the chief of the bureau's Personnel Section. A small Aquatic Products Branch (*shui ch'an chih pu*), with under ten members, consisted of Party members who worked in the Aquatic Products Company and the Navigation Management Station; its secretary was manager (*ching li*) of the former. Party cadres in the County People's Bank belonged to the Bank Branch (*yin hang chih pu*), which had more than ten members, with the bank manager as secretary. The Communications Management Branch (*chiao kuan chih pu*), with about ten members, included Party members from the Communications Bureau and its subsidiary organs, the Transportation Control Station, and some of the Party members working in the Postal and Telecommunications Bureau (the others belonged to one of the political and legal branches); its secretary was chief of the Transportation Bureau. And finally there were two factory branches (*kung ch'ang chih pu*), with Party members from all factories other than those already mentioned above. Each of these branches had about twenty members, and the two secretaries were the manager of the wine factory and the manager of the machine repair and building factory.

Personnel Management and Control

One of the prime requisites for effective operation of the political system in Communist China is the maintenance of a high degree of discipline and commitment among basic-level cadres, most particularly among the Party cadres who dominate the system. The regime has evolved many techniques of ideological indoctrination and political control designed to achieve this end.

The Chinese Communists' methods of personnel management, if one may call them that, have a variety of objectives: to promote revolutionary values and goals, to combat bureaucratism, to suppress corruption, to maintain a strict, almost military sort of discipline, to train cadres in the skills necessary for the tasks they perform, and to develop certain operational work techniques (the "mass-line style of work") designed to ensure that local cadres are both responsive to instructions from above and effective in dealing with the general population.

There is no doubt that the methods which the regime has evolved to work toward these ends have been effective in many respects. But there is also no doubt that persistent and growing tendencies toward bureaucratization have posed a continuing threat to the leaders' efforts to maintain an elite characterized by revolutionary *élan*. In Communist China today the cadres at the local level, in areas such as County X, are both bureaucrats and revolutionaries. Moreover, the trend over time has inevitably been increasingly toward bureaucratization. Consequently the battle against bureaucratism has had to be a constant, unending one.

"Party Life"

One of the most important means by which the Party attempts to maintain a high degree of discipline and commitment among its members is the requirement that all members must belong to basic Party branches and must regularly participate in what is called either "Party life" (*tang ti sheng huo*) or "organizational life" (*tsu chih sheng huo*). The latter is a broader term and includes YCL as well as Party activities.

"Party life" must include attendance at regular, frequent branch meetings as well as active participation in all Party-sponsored programs. In County X, every Party member was expected to attend a Party meeting once a week, normally on Saturday afternoons for about two hours—or in the evening, if "Party classes" were held that day (see below). Ordinarily each branch met once a week, but if a branch was divided into small groups (cells), the small groups might meet on two or three Saturdays a month, and the branch on the other Saturdays. Certain special branches, such as the one composed of rural educators, might meet only once or twice a month; on the other Saturdays, these Party members would attend the branch meeting at their local commune. Certain higher officials might sometimes attend one branch meeting, sometimes another. Regardless of whether the meeting was of a branch or a small group, the weekly meeting constituted the basic "organizational life" of the Party.

At these meetings, not only was there thorough discussion of any instructions or study materials which had been sent from higher Party authorities (via the Organization Department which was in over-all charge of these meetings) but each member was expected to summarize and discuss his activities during the week. Every meeting was an occasion for self-criticism (*tzu wo chien t'ao*, or *chien t'ao*, for short) and criticism (*p'i p'ing*)—that is, for systematic group evaluation of the performance of each member of the branch and, when necessary, organized group pressure to bring laggards or deviants into line in order to maintain high performance standards. "Party life" meetings were also an essential channel for keeping all Party cadres fully informed on current policies; frequently, important new policies were revealed to Party members in their meetings before they were disclosed to non-Party cadres. In addition, since each branch ordinarily had responsibility for some administrative unit or units, the branch members evaluated the work of that unit, and determined what was to be done in the unit during the week ahead.

The top Party leaders, the members of the County Party Committee, did not always attend branch meetings if they had other pressing duties (it was estimated that they generally attended about half the time). Other Party members, however, were normally expected to be present at all the meetings of their own branch, unless they were on detached duty elsewhere; and they were subjected to strong criticism if they were absent. Absence for six months resulted in expulsion from the Party.

When Party cadres working in county-level organizations were sent on temporary assignments to the countryside for periods of more than several days, as they frequently were, the Organization Department normally gave them a temporary letter of introduction (*lin shih chieh shao hsin*) to the leaders of some Party branch in the rural area where they were to be based, and they were expected to participate in "Party life" meetings there. When permanently transferred, Party cadres were given an administrative letter of introduction (*hsing cheng chieh shao hsin*) addressed to the Organization Department in the area to which they were going, and they were expected to report immediately on arrival and to be assigned as soon as possible to a branch so that they could start participating in its meetings with a minimum of delay.[39]

In addition to keeping watch over the branch meetings, the Organization Department about once a month convened large meetings called "Party classes" (*tang k'o*), which all Party members in county Party and government organs were expected to attend. Held generally on Saturday afternoons, these meetings were occasions for fairly important work reports, as well as speeches on a variety of subjects including Party history, organizational or ideological problems, and current policies, delivered usually by the Party first secretary or one of his deputies, the head of the Organization Department, the head of the Party School, or the staff secretary-general.[40]

[39] In the countryside, "Party life" meetings were, of necessity, less regular or frequent, however. Generally, branches attempted to meet about every two weeks, except in the busiest farming seasons.

[40] Some forms for reporting monthly activities of Party branches were captured by Kuomintang forces in 1963 from a county near County X. These forms require monthly information on (1) total membership; (2) Party study—number of participants, names and positions of speakers, topics covered; (3) "Party life"—number of participants, time spent, chairman; (4) branch committee meetings—participants, time spent, chairman, contents of meetings; (5) number of applicants; (6) names of those who for six months failed to pay dues, attend study meetings, at-

Political Study

In addition to attending their branch meetings, Party members also had to participate in the regular political study (*cheng chih hsüeh hsi*) sessions that were organized for all state cadres, Party and non-Party, in county-level organs. In County X these study meetings were held every morning, from 7:00 to 8:00 A.M., six days a week, all year round. Party and non-Party cadres met together in small study groups (*hsüeh hsi hsiao tsu*) consisting normally of ten to twelve members. These groups were set up by the Personnel Section, if in government agencies, or the Organization Department, if in Party organs. Generally they were organized on the same unit basis as the Party branches but included all non-Party as well as Party cadres in these units. Each group had a designated head; usually, although not always, he was a Party member, sometimes the branch propaganda committeeman.

Study sessions almost always involved prolonged discussion and, periodically, criticism and self-criticism as well. Instructions and study materials were sent to the groups by the Party Propaganda Department, which collaborated with the Personnel Section in dealing with groups in government organs. Sometimes specially prepared documents provided the basis for discussion; at other times the Propaganda Department simply designated certain editorials or articles in major newspapers and journals as the focus of study. Frequently, study concentrated on the county's current central tasks as defined by the local Party Committee. During major political campaigns or movements, the amount of time spent in political study meetings was increased greatly. Depending on the intensity of the campaign, extra meetings might be held nightly, or every afternoon, or even all day, for periods lasting from several weeks to several months.

In addition to organized political study, there were two other types of study group meetings conducted for county cadres. The General Labor Union set up cultural study groups (*wen hua hsüeh hsi hsiao*

tend "Party life" meetings, or attend branch meetings. See *Fan Kung Yu Chi Tui T'u Chi Fu Chien Lien Chiang Hsien Lu Huo Fei Fang Wen Chien Hui Pien* [Documents Captured by Anti-Communist Guerrillas in Lienchiang Hsien, Fukien], Taipei, March, 1964.

tsu) or staff and workers study groups (*chih kung hsüeh hsi hsiao tsu*), which emphasized literacy training and basic general education. Some low-ranking cadres with limited education were permitted to attend these meetings instead of those of the political study groups. And quite a few government organs established so-called "business" or substantive work study groups (*yeh wu hsüeh hsi hsiao tsu*), which in effect were night schools that provided training and instruction directly related to the substantive work of the unit.

Altogether, cadres spent an enormous amount of time, both "working time" and "spare time," in these various group meetings, even in normal periods; and during major campaigns such meetings became almost the dominating activity of the cadres' lives. Organized study provided a very important mechanism, therefore, through which Party leaders transmitted instructions and policies to all cadres, obtained reports on cadres' attitudes and opinions (all study groups reported regularly to their supervising bodies), carried out continuous and systematic indoctrination, checked on cadres' work performance, ensured constant surveillance of all cadres' thought and behavior, promoted collectivist rather than individualist patterns of activity, and mobilized effective social pressure to maintain discipline among the cadres.

There was some tendency, almost inevitably, for these group meetings to slip into patterns of relatively routine study during periods of comparative relaxation between political campaigns. Whenever major campaigns took place, however, study group meetings became extremely important in the lives of all the cadres, and no cadre could afford to regard them as routine even if he wished to do so.

Personnel Dossiers

Another extremely important mechanism for controlling and checking on the performance of all cadres, Party and non-Party, were the personnel dossiers (*tang an*) maintained for all of them, and the annual and special "assessments" which were prepared regularly and filed in them. Such a dossier was established for each Party member and state cadre when he first entered the Party or became a state cadre, and it followed him wherever he went in his subsequent career, providing the basis for decisions regarding his assignments, promotions, and so on.

In County X, the Organization Department kept these dossiers for the three to four hundred Party members in the county who were state cadres, including those working at the commune level. The Personnel Section kept the dossiers for the more than twelve hundred non-Party state cadres working in the government. Both of these units had ready access to the dossiers kept by the other (the Personnel Section's staff was composed entirely of Party members). Rural Party members in the county who were not state cadres did not have individual dossiers, but every local Party branch maintained an annual personnel record book (*chi lu*) with a page for each member. These books, maintained by the local Party secretary, provided simple personnel records on all members and were available for examination by visiting Party cadres from the county level.

The first basic document in the dossier of every Party member was his application for Party membership (*shen ch'ing ju tang chih yüan shu*), which included among other things a detailed statement on his personal history (*ko jen li shih*), relatives and friends (*she hui kuan hsi*, literally, social relations), thought (*szu hsiang*) and standpoint (*li ch'ang*), and family class background (*chia t'ing ch'u shen*) and individual class status (*ko jen ch'eng fen*), plus the recommendations from his sponsors. Similar information about personal background was prepared by all non-Party cadres and went into their dossiers.

Personnel Assessments

Perhaps the most important materials added regularly to the dossiers were the "assessments" (*chien ting*) of every state cadre, which were prepared at the end of each year and at the close of every major political campaign. In some respects these assessments were comparable to the general fitness reports on one's performance which are common in bureaucratic institutions everywhere, but they were also more than that. For one thing, they put great stress on evaluations not only of work performance but also of general attitudes and behavior and the degree to which a person accepted the ideological premises and lived up to the moral standards set by the Party. Moreover, the collective process of preparing these reports, which involved systematic group criticism and self-criticism, was itself an important mechanism of personnel control.

At the end of each year every Party branch and government unit at the county level devoted several days of full-time meetings to the process of preparing the assessments. Each individual first prepared a written self-evaluation, on a standard year-end assessment form (*nien chung chien ting piao*), and this was circulated to all members of the unit. Then meetings were held to have group discussion of the self-evaluations. Each individual's case was discussed separately. The individual first made an oral statement, summarizing his self-evaluation and outlining his own self-criticism; then he and his statement were subjected to comment and criticism by all the other members of the unit. The head of the branch or the chief of the government unit in which the assessment was made recorded this discussion, and entered the main points, along with his own comments, on the back of the individual's statement. Then it was sent to either the Party Organization Department or the government Personnel Section to be filed in the individual's dossier.

For a non-Party cadre, this process took place entirely within his government work unit. A Party member's assessment, however, could be discussed in either or both his government unit and his Party branch, the latter generally being more important. A county-level cadre on assignment in the countryside sometimes returned to the county seat at year-end to have his assessment prepared, but if this was not practical the assessment was prepared in meetings of either the branch or commune unit where he was currently working.

In addition to these regular year-end assessments, individual assessments of a similar sort were made at the end of almost every important "rectification" campaign. Often, these were even more thorough than the regular annual assessments, and everyone had to make a detailed statement of his personal history, social relations, thought and standpoint, and so on, recapitulating material already entered in his dossier. If a cadre were then subjected to investigations of any sort, careful checks could be made for discrepancies between his latest and earlier statements. In major "rectification" movements, in fact, detailed reexamination of cadres' dossiers was usually one of the first steps taken by those in charge of the movement.

In the countryside in County X, a small Party "rectification" campaign (*hsiao cheng tang yün tung*) was held toward the end of every year, after the fall harvest, as part of a regular commune and Party "rectification" process (*cheng she cheng tang*). In this annual checkup, every commune Party committee and brigade branch held nightly meetings during a period of ten days or more; often at least one cadre was sent by the County Party Committee to sit in on some of these meetings as an observer. While this was going on, the Commune Management Committee generally held similar meetings in the afternoons. The purpose of both the Party and commune meetings was to examine the state of the organization of every unit, to evaluate the work of every one of its members, to criticize any evidence of shortcomings, and generally to tighten up discipline.

The knowledge that every cadre's work, thought, and behavior would be scrutinized and subject to group assessment at least once a year, and that the resulting evaluations would be placed in his permanent dossier, clearly contributed in an important way toward the maintenance of strict discipline and effective Party control over the entire bureaucracy; and the collective process by which assessments were made was an important factor which helped to shape patterns of relationships within the basic Party and government groups to which all cadres belonged.

Training: Party School

Another important responsibility of the Party Organization Department was the development of various types of special training classes and programs for Party members. A large number of Party cadres received periodic training of many sorts. Some instruction was essentially in-service training for people within a particular functional "system," or line of work. Some was to instruct cadres how to implement certain specific policies or promote particular mass campaigns. And some was designed principally to raise the general level of Party performance and discipline.

Politically, the most important general training unit in County X was the Party School (*tang hsiao*). Prior to 1960 there had been only a Party training class (*tang hsün pan*), run directly by the Organization Department, but in that year a new Party School was established as an independent unit, although one still maintaining close links with, and subject to the general supervision of, the Organization Department. The Party School had a staff of only three, headed by its principal (*hsiao chang*), but it could and did call upon many other key individuals from the Party Committee to give important lectures.

Every year the school organized two or three major training programs, each attended by two to three hundred Party cadres; during an average year, therefore, perhaps five to six hundred or more cadres took part in its programs for varying periods. The large majority of these were Party cadres from the countryside. Many county-level Party cadres were sent to training classes not at the County Party School but at schools run by either the special district or the provincial Party organization. All these training programs contributed significantly to the maintenance of Party control over the cadres as well as to the development of the cadres' political and other skills.

"Rectification" Campaigns

Major political "rectification" campaigns have played a role of particular importance in Communist China in the control and management of all cadres, whether Party members or not. Almost all such campaigns have aimed at correcting specific bureaucratic weaknesses, expelling or punishing undesirable elements, generally tightening up discipline, redefining acceptable standards of performance, combating particular political "errors," and stimulating all cadres to work harder and more effectively. These movements, the most important of which have been organized on a nationwide basis, have tended to occur fairly frequently, generally every one to three years. All of them have involved periods of great tension within the bureaucracy, and most have resulted in the punishment of selected cadres, who have served as negative examples for the bureaucracy as a whole. The specific problems that have been the focus of attention have varied from one campaign to another, but almost all campaigns have been directed against the recurring basic problems of bureaucratism—corruption, arbitrary exercise of power, separation from the "masses," individualism, localism, "departmentalism" or "vested-interestism," and all other trends which appear to have weakened or undermined the selfless, disciplined collectivism desired by the Party.

One such campaign in the mid-1950s, the "campaign to clean out (purge or liquidate) counterrevolutionaries" (*su fan yün tung* or *su ch'ing fan ko ming yün tung*), was organized in County X in the following manner. When the County Party Committee first received instructions concerning the campaign from higher Party authorities, it immediately and secretly established a special Staff Office to Investigate Cadres (*shen kan pan kung shih*). Eleven people were assigned to this at the start, five from the Public Security Bureau and one each from the Organization Department, Procuracy, Court, government Personnel Section, Finance and Trade Department, and Industry and Communications Department. They started their work by studying and reviewing the personnel dossiers of all Party and non-Party state cadres, to determine which cadres "had problems" (*yu wen t'i*), in a political sense, as well as this could be determined from their dossiers. Then those who were suspected of illegal activity, compromising connections, or even undesirable attitudes, were subjected to secret investigations (*mi mi tiao ch'a*).

Two to three months later, the Party Committee enlarged this investigatory group, first to seventeen members, then to twenty-one, and converted it into an open body called the *Su Fan* Staff Office (*su fan pan kung shih*). Under this office several small groups (*tsu*) were organized, one for political work, particularly propaganda (*cheng chih kung tso tsu*), another for gathering materials on cadres (*ts'ai liao tsu*), and still another to conduct "outside" investigations (*wai tiao tsu*).

At this stage the staff office organized all state cadres working at the county level into special study groups, in which they were expected to study specially provided materials relating to the campaign, then discuss their own and others' "political problems" (*cheng chih wen t'i*), and finally engage in intense criticism and self-criticism. Each such group, composed of twelve to fifteen persons, spent eight hours a day in meetings. Every cadre had to review his personal history, explain (*chiao tai*) his political problems, and confess (*t'an pai*) both current faults and past errors. This process evolved over two months, in three stages of about twenty days each. In the first stage, all cadres participated, and regular Party and government work came almost to a halt. At the end of this stage, some cadres, in particular those who had made thorough confessions, returned to their regular work, but the others had to go through a second, similar process, and then those who were still not cleared had to go through a third. The climax, as in most such campaigns, came in a series of dramatic, mass "struggle meetings" (*tou cheng hui*), in which a few cadres selected as major targets for special criticism were subjected to organized and controlled but nevertheless extremely emotional public defamation and abuse. Prior to each such "struggle meeting," the Campaign Staff Office held small strategy conferences with selected activists, to brief them about the people to be "struggled" against; these activists then led in making accusations during the public meetings. The psychological pressures on the cadres who were the targets and victims of these "struggle meetings" were such that three committed suicide during this stage of the campaign.

In this particular campaign, over fifty cadres were formally punished, in a variety of ways. One was sentenced to reform through labor (*lao tung kai tsao,* or *lao kai,* for short). Eleven were fired from their jobs and deprived of cadre status (*k'ai ch'u kan pu*). The rest were demoted, transferred, or sent for a period of forced "study." In addition, a special assessment (*chien ting*) was prepared for the dossier of every cadre working in a county-level organ, whether or not he had been the target of any special criticism.

Actually, in all of this, not a single case of current counterrevolutionary activity was brought to light in County X. Those who were the targets of public abuse were guilty of "problems of history" (*li shih wen t'i*), that is, of committing mistakes in the past, or of covering up unsavory aspects of their past. Furthermore, the number of persons given severe punishment was rather small. Despite these facts, however, the period of the campaign, and especially the final period of "struggle meetings," was one of great apprehension and tension for all the cadres. And it resulted, as was intended, in a significant tightening up of standards and discipline within the entire bureaucracy.

The effects of these campaigns were by no means limited to the periods during which they were under way. To a degree, all members of the bureaucracy lived in anticipation of campaigns to come; and the desire to avoid becoming a target of criticism in the future provided a strong incentive to perform as the Party demanded in the present.

Bureaucratism, in its varied forms, was not the only evil which periodic "rectification campaigns" attacked. Localism was another recurring problem to the Party—particularly in many areas of coastal south China—which the Party attempted to deal with from time to time in its "rectification" campaigns. Resentment about the domination of outside cadres was one significant cause of tensions in this area; but even outside cadres working in the area were on occasion accused of "localism."

In 1959–1960, a large "antilocalism campaign" (*fan ti fang chu yi yün tung*) was conducted in County X, simultaneously with a "campaign against rightist tendencies" (*fan yu ch'ing yün tung*). It resulted in the purge of several high-ranking leaders, including a county deputy Party secretary, a deputy chief of the Public Security Bureau, two Party secretaries at the commune level, and a deputy chief of the Agriculture Bureau. A purge of some high-ranking cadres accused of localism took place at the same time in this area at the special district level. Most of those punished were simply "transferred downward for labor" (*hsia fàng lao tung*) in the countryside.

Manual Labor by Cadres

The policy of fostering manual labor by cadres is another important, and in many respects unique, mechanism for personnel control and management in the bureaucracy in Communist China. The Chinese Communists act as if they have a genuine faith that regular cadre participation in manual labor can effectively combat tendencies toward bureaucratization and prevent backsliding toward "bourgeois" attitudes among the cadres. Their attitude in this respect may date back to the period immediately before the founding of the Party, when a number of Chinese students, including some who were later to become Communist leaders, went to France to participate in a work-and-study program. The policy certainly developed further during the Communists' long struggle for power, and particularly during the Yenan period of the Sino-Japanese War, when cadre participation in labor was a necessity as well as a virtue. It continued even after the achievement of power, however, and received renewed emphasis following the "hundred flowers campaign" in the spring of 1957, when intellectuals gave evidence—as the Communist Party saw it—that they lacked discipline and had become "separated from the masses."

In County X, the majority of cadres in county-level organs regularly contributed some spare time, especially in the evenings, to the care of small agricultural plots, mainly for the cultivation of vegetables. Such plots were maintained by almost all Party and government units. They were located either in hilly areas surrounding the county seat or on empty lots within the city.

In addition, most cadres also spent some time during the year performing "labor service" (*yi wu lao tung*) on public work projects in the countryside, or participating in various annual campaigns for developing water conservancy projects, gathering fertilizer, planting trees, planting and harvesting grain, and so on. Although such labor was considered voluntary—in a formal sense it was; volunteers were "requested," but virtually all cadres "volunteered"—the mobilization, organization, and assignment of cadres participating in such labor was directed by the County Party Committee and the Organization Department. Moreover, the Organization Department set quotas of man-days of labor which various county-level units had to fill. On some projects, county-level cadres were sent to the countryside to work for fairly extended periods, and during many campaigns every Party and government unit sent the majority of its cadres, in rotation, with each individual involved going out to work for perhaps one or two days a week. In County X the peak for this type of cadre participation in manual labor was in 1958–1959, when each county cadre was given a work book (*lao tung shou ts'e*), in which the number of days he participated in manual labor was formally entered.

In the countryside, many Party branches and other rural organizations in County X which had state cadres working for them maintained small experimental plots (*shih yen t'ien*) on land assigned to them by the communes, and the cadres cultivated these plots in their spare time. Grain crops, as well as vegetables, were grown on some of these. The cadres were expected to use advanced methods, achieve high yields, and set a good example for the ordinary peasants.

In 1959 the Party Committee and Organization Department in County X took steps to place manual labor by cadres on an even more systematic and regularized basis.[41] They held a large conference of county-level cadres to discuss making "productive labor the first front" (*lao tung sheng ch'an ti yi hsien*)—i.e. the priority task— and it was decided to introduce a system under which all cadres would spend thirty days a year in productive labor, to be scheduled by the basic Party and government units to which they belonged. By 1962, however, although some units and cadres were already following this system, it had not yet been put completely into operation in County X.

"Transfer Downward" of Cadres

Another extraordinary personnel management policy energetically promoted by the Chinese Communists from the latter 1950s onward was the "transfer of cadres downward" (*hsia fang kan pu*). While related to the aim of having all cadres participate in labor, the "transfer downward" policy had much more complicated motivations. Started in a systematic fashion in 1957, over the ensuing years the policy stressed a variety of aims at different periods: retrenchment of personnel in higher levels of the bureaucracy, reform and indoctrination of cadres through participation in labor at "basic levels," punishment of errant cadres, and strengthening of leadership at lower levels by sending down higher-level cadres.

In time the "transfer downward" policy came to be linked to other aims, such as combining labor and study in education, and reducing the urban population. Consequently, it involved increasing numbers of ordinary urban youth and workers. Some persons were transferred downward for relatively brief periods, a few months to a year; some for more extended periods; and some semipermanently or permanently. In the country as a whole the total number of persons

---

[41] In some counties this move took place earlier.

transferred downward in the seven or eight years after 1957 was certainly in the millions.[42]

The number of cadres transferred downward from higher levels to County X was apparently smaller than the number of similar transfers in many other areas in China, at least according to ex-cadres' estimates. In 1959, for example, the number of cadres transferred from the special district and provincial levels to County X was said to be only twenty to thirty. Of these, only a few were sent to strengthen county-level leadership, although one became a Party deputy secretary and another a department head. The majority were assigned to labor in the brigades.

Over the years, however, a substantial number of county-level cadres were transferred to commune and brigade levels. A distinction was made locally between: (1) transfers to lower-level administrative posts (*hsia fang kan pu*), mainly to strengthen basic-level leadership (*chia ch'iang chi ts'eng ling tao*); and (2) transfers downward to do ordinary labor (*hsia fang lao tung*), mainly to indoctrinate cadres or, in some cases, to punish them. The former usually involved able, reliable cadres, and although sometimes their assignments were short, they often went for extended or semipermanent stays. The latter generally involved less able cadres, including ones with serious "political problems"; the assignments could be either short-term or for extended periods—that is, one or two years. In either case the cadre transferred downward remained a state cadre, on the county payroll, and he continued to receive his regular salary from his original county-level unit. After a period of time, however, a cadre who remained at the local level was sometimes taken off the state payroll, and his local unit (commune, brigade, or team) was then responsible for his support.

In County X, the more sizable numbers of both long-term and short-term transfers downward to lower administrative posts took place during communization in 1958 (earlier, during cooperativization, there had been similar transfers but not with this label) and during the 1961 period of major adjustment of the communes (this was during the "movement to rectify and build communes" [*cheng she*

[42] One official statement claimed that forty million youths had been sent to the countryside since 1949 (see *Current Background*, No. 735). However, this may well have been an exaggeration.

chien she yün tung] following the Party's issuance of the so-called "sixty articles" [*liu shih tiao*] [43] calling for changes in the communes). Some transfers, of both general types, occurred almost every year, however. In one year, in County X, more than fifty county-level cadres were transferred downward to lower-level administrative posts, and more than one hundred cadres were transferred to participate in ordinary labor, according to the estimates of ex-cadres.

Geographical Mobility of Cadres

The transfer-downward policy contributed substantially to a long-standing characteristic of the bureaucracy in Communist China, namely its high degree of geographical mobility, especially lateral and downward mobility. Both Party and non-Party cadres did a very great deal of traveling in connection with their work (*ch'u ch'ai*), to inspect and participate in work at lower levels. They were also sent very frequently on temporary assignments to lower, including "basic" (i.e. bottom), levels in connection with periodic campaigns and to participate in manual labor.

In County X, for example, reportedly every state cadre spent some time each year working in rural areas, on temporary assignment. Some county-level cadres were estimated to spend as much as half or more of their time in work away from the county seat, and it was estimated that during some of the most important campaigns, between a quarter and a half of all cadres in county-level organizations left the county seat for at least brief periods to undertake temporary assignments in the countryside. Certain cadres were on the move, on detached duty, so often that although they maintained a home base in one of the county-level organizations, in reality they felt almost like itinerant cadres; such persons were humorously referred to as "tiger balm cadres" (*wan chin yu kan pu*). *Wan chin yu* is the brand name of a popular Chinese medicine, generally called "tiger balm"

[43] The formal title of the "sixty articles," issued secretly in March, 1961, by the Central Committee, was "Draft Regulations for the [Operation of] Rural People's Communes" (*nung ts'un jen min kung she t'iao li ts'ao an*). They were never published on mainland China, but a copy was obtained by the Chinese Nationalist Government.

in English. The Chinese name literally means "ten thousand gold balm"; thus *wan chin yu kan pu* means "cadres who were used in ten thousand ways"—i.e. who were constantly moved.

Frequent movement of cadres seemed to be consciously designed to combat certain aspects of bureaucratization and routinization of Party and government work; and to a degree it was effective in preventing cadres from becoming deskbound and in ensuring that bureaucrats would have periodic contact with the problems of implementing policies at the lowest levels, where it was necessary to have direct relations with the "masses" rather than simply with lower-level bureaucrats. Whether by conscious design or not, the practice probably also reinforced a sense of dependency on Party and government organizations, and a feeling of personal instability, that seemed to be shared by most cadres, since it impressed upon the cadres the fact that Party and government leaders had virtually unlimited authority to send them almost anywhere at any time, regardless of their individual wishes. The policy involved definite costs, however; the day-to-day operation of Party and government agencies at the county level was disrupted when personnel were sent elsewhere for detached duty that might, in many cases, have no direct relation to their regular work.

Mobility in the Bureaucracy

Regular administrative transfers, and promotions and demotions— as contrasted with the temporary transfers and detached-duty assignments discussed above—were less frequent; but by the late 1950s and early 1960s the pattern of movement of cadres shifting jobs was one in which downward or lateral transfers seemed to be as common or even more common than moves up the hierarchy. In any case, many cadres felt that promotion upward—either in job level within the county or from the county to higher levels—was extremely slow, and in practice it doubtless was for most of them.

On the basis of the limited available data, the following generalizations appear to be true about cadre mobility and the recruitment of new talent into leadership positions in County X. (Admittedly these generalizations are based primarily on the impressionistic judgments of ex-cadres, rather than on adequate statistical data.) At first, in the years immediately after Communist takeover, there was striking upward mobility in the leadership in County X. But before many years had passed, most key posts of power and influence were filled, the chances for advancement to top jobs at the county level declined sharply, and the situation was stabilized—one might say it was almost frozen.

The takeover period was one of virtually complete change in leadership, economic and social as well as political, within the county; and advancement opportunities were created for a very large number of people. Not only did new people take over old government functions, but many new posts were created as the regime rapidly expanded the government's functions. At the very top levels of Party and government, however, "old cadres"—mainly outsiders sent south just before 1949, plus former local guerrillas—moved into the key posts. Thereafter a small group of "old cadres" tended to monopolize virtually all the leading positions, and still do today, to such an extent that after the initial period, opportunities for others to advance to top-level positions were very limited. This situation still exists today, and it appears likely to continue without fundamental change until the takeover generation passes out of the picture. Thus, at the county level, as at the national level, continuity and stability of the top leadership, which for a period of time was clearly a source of great strength to the regime, now appears to have become a real problem, and a potential source of weakness. The persistence of the first generation of revolutionary leaders in maintaining their power and authority as long as possible, and the failure of the regime to work out effective policies of superannuating them and replacing them with able, younger leaders, are both to blame.

Although a relatively few "old cadres" have dominated the top posts in County X ever since the takeover period, opportunities for advancement have been somewhat better at lower levels in the county hierarchy. Not only was there a rapid turnover of leadership at the start, but throughout much of the 1950s there was a continuous, if slower, recruitment (with periodic spurts) of new people into the bureaucracy and power structure. Opportunities for advancement were mainly due, however, to the rapid expansion of the Party and the bureaucracy. The number of administrative state cadres (not counting teachers) increased, for example, from about two hundred in the early years to over one thousand by 1962, and the number of Party members from a few hundred to over six thousand by 1960. (A great many of these were not state cadres but were commune, brigade or team cadres.) As Party and government expanded, and society became increasingly organized, a large number of new posts opened up, not only in the Party and government bureaucracies but also in peasant associations (in the early days) and other mass organizations, cooperatives, communes, military and police units, and so on. Since the overwhelming majority of persons who moved into such posts had never held leadership positions of any sort previously, it is clear there was substantial and continuing upward mobility at the lower levels, and the regime was able to absorb a great deal of new talent.

By the late 1950s and early 1960s, after communization, however, advancement opportunities declined even at the lower levels. Fewer new positions of power or authority were created. Moreover, those who had already achieved such positions in the early years continued to cling to them; and cadres "transferred downward" took over some posts that had previously been open to local people.

Recruitment of New Party Members

For most people in County X who had ambitions to mount the ladder of success, membership in the Party was a major prerequisite. Over-all responsibility for development of the Party organization, including the recruitment of new members, lay with the Organization Department. However, general recruitment policies were defined by the Party center, and actual responsibility for accepting new members rested with the local Party branches.

The largest single source of new members recruited over the years into the Party in County X were the activists (*chi chi fen tzu*),[44] who generally emerged, particularly in rural areas, during the course of mass campaigns. By the late 1950s, however, most new Party recruits were drawn from the membership of the YCL, which

[44] "Activist" was a definite classification of status, determined by local Party branches.

served as a testing ground for potential Party members. Not all YCL members could expect to obtain Party membership, however.

Even though the Party attempted to expand its membership rapidly at times, joining the Party was never easy. An ambitious activist or YCL member who wished to become a member, or whom a Party branch felt should be encouraged to join, first had to obtain the backing of two Party members who were willing to introduce and endorse him for membership in a particular branch. The applicant then filled out a detailed application form (*shen ch'ing ju tang chih yüan shu*) which, as already mentioned, contained an account of his personal history, social relations, class status, individual status, and so on, plus a statement on why he wished to join the Party. If a potential recruit were being actively cultivated by a branch, the branch leaders usually assigned a reliable Party member to get to know him as well as possible and, in some cases, to take him to Party classes (*tang k'o*). Once a person had submitted a formal application, the Party branch carefully investigated and discussed his qualifications during a regular branch meeting. If the branch members approved him as a candidate, this was reported to the county Organization Department. If the Department then gave its endorsement, the applicant was made a candidate, or alternate, member (*hou pu tang yüan* or *yü pei tang yüan*) for a specified period of time, during which he participated in all Party meetings and activities, but without voting privileges or the right to be elected to any post.

In County X, the Organization Department asked all branches to submit recommendations for new members twice a year. By the early 1960s, however, Party expansion had slowed down, and the branches tended to be highly selective and careful in choosing new members. Consequently, the number of new members proposed in each period was not very large; and sometimes a branch might not recommend any new members for a year or two.

After a candidate had been thoroughly tested during his probation period, the branch again discussed whether to admit him to regular membership. If the branch again recommended admission, and the Organization Department again gave its endorsement, the recruit became a regular member. If branch members were seriously divided in their views at this stage, they could decide on an extended probation period, or could reject the applicant.

Persons recruited to be new, low-level state cadres to serve in either the Party or the government bureaucracy were drawn from several sources. The largest number were selected from organizations in rural areas—Party and YCL branches, cooperative and commune organs, militia units, and so on. While these persons did not have to be Party members to serve in the government bureaucracy, the majority of new state cadres were able young Party men. A very sizable number came from schools and training classes, located not only within the county but also at the special district level. These young new graduates constituted not only the majority of the county's teachers but a large number of the other new state cadres as well. And in addition a steady flow of new cadres came from among transferred army men (*chuan yeh chün jen*) who returned to the county after completing their military service.

Prospects for Advancement

Even after becoming a Party member and a state cadre, most young men found that progress up the ladder of success was fairly slow. The jump from jobs at the commune or brigade level, where the majority of rural cadres started their careers, to positions at the county level, was not easy. Promotion from county to higher (that is, special district or provincial) levels was even more difficult, and most county cadres felt that unless they were unusually fortunate they were not likely to be promoted to work at higher levels, outside their own county.

The ultimate power of decision regarding transfers, promotions, and demotions of all state cadres, whether Party or non-Party, theoretically lay, as stated earlier, in the hands of the Party Organization Department; but in practice the department spent most of its time dealing with Party members, and the government Personnel Section handled many of the routine personnel actions for non-Party state cadres. However, in virtually all cases involving transfers of cadres out of the county, and in particular promotions to levels above the county, the initiative was taken by authorities at either the special district or provincial levels, not at the county level.

Within County X, it was estimated that perhaps 5 to 10 percent of all county cadres changed jobs on regular transfers (usually within the county) in an average year, although of course the figure varied from year to year. Since many of these were essentially lateral transfers, and some were downward (at least geographically), the number of real job rank promotions (*sheng chih*) was usually smaller. Salary-grade promotions (*sheng chi*) within a particular job were more common than job promotions. A great many transfers—probably the majority—were within one functional "system"—that is, from one job to another, or one area to another, but in the same general line of work—and within the boundaries of the county.

Although there were some differences of opinion on what career lines offered the most attractive opportunities, the majority of ambitious young Party cadres tended to feel that the best prospects lay in Party organization work, including jobs in the Party committees and branches, the Organization Department and, to a lesser degree, other Party departments, the Party Control Committee, and personnel units in the government, or in political and legal work, especially in public security organizations. These institutions were regarded as crucial centers of power and influence, and as the best stepping-stones, therefore, to posts at higher levels. Furthermore, because of the importance of these organs, their cadres usually had better working conditions and were less likely to be called upon to take part in labor projects. However, the advantages of work in these institutions were somewhat counterbalanced by several factors that made cautious cadres have mixed feelings about them. Because they were staffed almost entirely by Party members, the competition for advancement was greater in these fields than in others, and because they involved important and politically sensitive work, there tended to be a greater risk that a cadre could make a costly mistake which would seriously damage his career. By contrast, various types of economic work, as in commercial agencies of the government, were not generally regarded as giving cadres unusual access to power and influence. But in some respects job promotion possibilities in this field were relatively good for Party cadres because there were fewer other Party cadres to compete with, and because the agencies involved were often large and there were generally more leadership posts.

Non-Party cadres had few opportunities for promotion to the top posts in any line of work in County X, unless they could at some point join the Party. Apparently many of them simply accepted this as a basic fact of life and adjusted their ambitions to fit the realities of the power structure of the system.

Young Communist League

The Young Communist League in County X, as throughout the country, acted as the Party's subsidiary for youth. It was guided by the County Party Committee, one of whose members, designated youth committeeman (*ch'ing nien wei yüan*), was directly responsible for this work. The secretary of the YCL (*t'uan wei shu chi*) was a Party member, but in County X he was not, as in many other places, a member of the Party Committee.

The organization of the YCL paralleled that of the Party itself. With a secretary and a committee at the top, it was divided into branches on the same basis as the Party. Each production brigade, for example, had a League branch (*t'uan chih pu*).[45] Procedures for admission to the YCL were similar to, although not as complicated as, those followed by the Party; and YCL members, like Party members, were obligated to participate in regular "organizational life" meetings in their branches. Members also paid regular dues; for those who were state cadres, dues amounted to 1 percent of salary.

Established as an organization of youth between the ages of fourteen and twenty-five, the YCL actually had a good many members who were overage (*ch'ao ling t'uan yüan*). Such members fully participated in the work of the organization, and held top leadership posts, even though theoretically they were not supposed to have voting rights. In 1962, an estimated 16 percent of the members in County X were overage.

A total of fourteen YCL state cadres, three of them Party members, worked for the YCL Committee in County X. The Party members included the secretary (*shu chi*), the staff secretary (*mi shu*), who concurrently was deputy secretary (*fu shu chi*) and also

---

[45] Many brigades also had a special youth shock production unit, called the *ch'ing nien t'u chi tui*, which was composed largely, although not exclusively, of YCL members.

headed the YCL's Organization Department; and the head of the
School Work Department (*hsüeh hsiao kung tso pu*). These had
been assigned by the Party Organization Department, which had
ultimate control over assignments of all YCL cadres. There was one
other YCL department, the Rural Work Department (*nung ts'un
kung tso pu*); but it was not headed by a Party man.

Apart from providing a reservoir from which many new Party
members were recruited, the YCL was extremely active in assisting
the Party in all its work. YCL members took part in virtually all
Party-directed activities and programs. They played particularly
important roles in propaganda work, and also in the annual conscription and production drives.

As of 1962, there were over eight thousand YCL members in
County X. Roughly twenty-four hundred of these, or 30 percent
of the total, were young women and girls, a higher proportion of
female membership than in the Party itself. Since YCL members
functioned under direct Party leadership and were subject, in effect,
to Party discipline, one might say that the top elite in County X,
including both Party and YCL members, consisted of more than
fourteen thousand persons, or over 3 percent of the population—
rather than 1 to 2 percent, the figure if only Party members were
counted.

Young Pioneers

Itself responsible to the Party, the YCL in turn was in charge of
organizing and running a subsidiary organization for children, called
the Young Pioneers (*shao nien hsien feng tui*, or *shao hsien tui*, for
short), made up of youngsters aged nine to fifteen. The YCL's
School Work Department directed the Pioneers' activities, which
consisted for the most part of recreation and indoctrination designed
to inculcate basic Party-approved values and attitudes into children.
The Pioneers were organized mainly in the schools. Perhaps 35 to
40 percent of primary school children—including many, if not most,
of the brightest and most energetic ones—took part in its programs.[46]

[46] Some ex-cadres assert that in many places 50 to 70 percent of all
primary school children belong to the Young Pioneers.

Understandably, the YCL drew a significant number of its members from those who had come to its attention because of their activities in the Pioneers. The YCL and the Pioneers constituted, therefore, a pipeline for recruitment to the Party elite that enabled the leaders to select, train, and test potential Party members from a very young age.

Mass Organizations: General Labor Union and Women's Association

There were two mass organizations established by the Party in County X, which were direct subsidiaries of the Party: the General Labor Union (*tsung kung hui*) and the Women's Federation (*fu nü lien ho hui*, or *fu lien hui*, for short). In theory, these organizations—unlike the mass organizations composed of nonproletarians, which were the objects of united front work—were "on the side of the people" and therefore represented the working classes. Theoretically, the General Labor Union was an organization established for "workers" throughout the county, including state cadres as well as industrial and commercial workers. In practice, however, not many Party members participated actively in its programs, and its activities were designed for non-Party state cadres even more than for ordinary workers.

The county headquarters of the union had a staff of eight state cadres. Only one, the chairman (*chu hsi*), was a Party member, although some of the others belonged to the YCL. Under the chairman, there were a clerical secretary (*wen shu*); four welfare cadres (*fu li kan pu*), who also acted as cultural workers (*wen hua yüan*); one statistician (*t'ung chi yüan*), who collected the monthly dues; and a management cadre (*kuan li yüan*).

Each large government organization and economic enterprise in the county had a branch of the union, but the organization of the branches was minimal, generally with just a single cadre designated as head (*fu tze jen*). In government organs, the personnel cadre or cadres were normally responsible for union work.

Altogether, there were perhaps four to five hundred members in the union in County X. They paid 1 percent of their salary monthly as dues, but collection of these dues was much more lax than in Party organizations. Every Saturday, during the period when the Party branches met, the union convened meetings of its own, attended by non-Party cadres.

The union maintained one sizable headquarters building and also had space in several other locations for "cultural palaces" (*wen hua kung*) and recreation clubs (*chü lo pu*). Its main activities were in the fields of welfare, recreation, and propaganda. In addition to operating the cultural and recreational centers, it maintained a library and ran a night school which provided literacy training.

In political terms the union was not a very important organization in County X, partly because the number of workers in "factories" and other economic enterprises was relatively small. It did, however, provide some useful services to the non-Party working force, especially those persons employed in the county seat.

The Women's Association, as would be expected, concerned itself primarily with activities of special interest to women throughout the county. The headquarters of the association was staffed by nine cadres, seven Party members and two non-Party cadres. Headed by a chairman (*chu hsi*), the staff included a secretary (*mi shu*) and seven other women's work cadres (*fu nü kan pu*). It had its own building, a fairly large one, located in the Party Committee's compound. At the local level, there was both a women's work cadre and a branch of the association in most communes and brigades.

Concerned with political as well as welfare work, the association had a variety of responsibilities. During every major campaign, its specific task was to organize special propaganda directed at women, and to mobilize them to support the campaign. It also had primary responsibility for organizing, or at least helping to organize, women to participate in all programs that were aimed specifically at them, such as implementation of the marriage law or the fostering of family planning. The association provided an important outlet for the energies of many activist women, both Party and non-Party members, and it assisted the Party considerably in many different ways. However, its organization was fairly loose, and could not really be compared, in terms of usefulness to the Party, with a more disciplined organization such as the YCL.

State Cadres on Party and Government
Tables of Organization

As already stated, by the early 1960s the total number of state cadres in County X who were on the state payroll, and on the tables of organization of either the county Party organization or the county government and its numerous agencies, was between fifteen and sixteen hundred (see p. 39 for definition of state cadres). Of these, between one thousand and eleven hundred were administrative cadres, and over five hundred were state-paid teachers who worked for the most part in rural primary schools. Of the administrative cadres, who filled roughly 140 positions in the county Party apparatus and over one thousand positions in county government agencies (these figures include overlapping), perhaps seven hundred or more worked mainly in the county seat and over three hundred were assigned to work at the commune level or in rural offices of county government agencies.

Despite the domination of top posts by "old cadres," the average age level of state cadres in the county as a whole was quite low, since many of the new cadres who had been recruited into the bureaucracy from schools, the army, and so on, were very young. The age level varied in different lines of work, however. The lowest, apparently, was in public security work, where the average age was reported to be in the mid-twenties; in commercial and some other types of economic work, the average age was considerably higher, in the mid- or late thirties.

All state cadres in the county clearly belonged to the bureaucratic elite, and were so regarded by noncadres. But here, as at higher levels in the Chinese bureaucracy, the state cadres could be divided into many different groups, with varying power, prestige, and influence. The most important differentiation, as everywhere in China, was between Party members (*tang yüan*) and non-Party cadres (*fei tang kan pu*). The three to four hundred Party members who were state cadres constituted an elite within the elite, and dominated the key posts throughout the government as well as the Party bureaucracy. If a Party member were transferred from work in a Party department to a government bureau, he generally became a bureau chief, or at least a section chief; relatively few Party members working in the government were ordinary cadres (*p'u t'ung kan pu* or *yi pan kan pu*). All Party members working in the government had a special political status (*cheng chih ti wei*) deriving from their Party membership, their participation in closed Party meetings, and their access to restricted Party documents.

Social Stratification of the Elite

As is the case throughout China, seniority in the Party was one of the most important criteria on the basis of which the Party cadres in County X were divided into numerous categories. Labels were attached to virtually all Party cadres which denoted when they had joined the Party (*ts'an chia tang*) or, in a few instances, when they had "joined the revolution" (*ts'an chia ko ming*). All old cadres (*lao kan pu*) were differentiated from new cadres (*hsin kan pu*); these were variable terms, to a degree, but in County X all persons who had joined the Party before 1949 were definitely considered to be old cadres, while only a few who joined after 1949 were.

This was only the beginning, however, of the complex stratification based on seniority. Many other distinctions were made among the leaders on the basis of when they began their service. In County X there were no "land revolution cadres" (*t'u ti ko ming kan pu*), a title given those who had served in the Kiangsi Soviet in the early 1930s; but there was one "long march cadre" (*ch'ang cheng kan pu*), who had participated in the Communists' move westward in the mid-1930's. There were several "Yenan cadres" (*yen an kan pu*), who had worked at the Communists' wartime revolutionary headquarters in the late 1930s and the 1940s; "anti-Japanese war cadres" (*k'ang jih chan cheng kan pu*), who had joined the Party at any time during the Sino-Japanese War; "liberation war cadres" (*chieh fang chan cheng kan pu*), who had joined during 1947–1949; "uprising cadres" (*ch'i yi kan pu*), who had come over to the Communists' side at the time of Communist victory (most of these were non-Party men, but a few were Party cadres); "southbound cadres" (*nan hsia kan pu*), who were sent south by the Party just before or at the time of "liberation" (these cadres were further subdivided into *huai hai chan yi kan pu*, or "Huai Lake Battle cadres," and *tu chiang* [*nan hsia*] *kan pu*, or "Yangtze crossing [southbound] cadres"); and "land reform cadres" (*t'u ti kai ko kan pu*), who had joined the Party during the post-1949 land reform. (In the early 1960s a majority of the "land reform cadres" in County X were still local cadres, rather than state cadres.) [47]

Apparently, virtually all cadres in County X could, and frequently did, categorize other cadres—at least the leading ones—according to these divisions based on seniority. Although such titles were informal labels, they were not simply polite honorifics. Not only were persons with seniority generally treated with deference and consideration, but to a remarkable degree, job status and rank, and therefore power and authority, in the local hierarchy tended to follow the lines of seniority in the Party.

Other Cadre Ranking Systems

In County X as elsewhere, another ranking system divided cadres according to their job status. There was a broad distinction between all leadership cadres (*ling tao kan pu*), who held high-ranking posts in Party and government organs, and ordinary cadres, who were simply staff members. Leadership cadres were further divided in County X into the following groupings: (1) county-level cadres (*hsien chi kan pu*), or higher-ranking leadership cadres (*kao chi ling tao kan pu*); these included all County Party Committee members, the staff secretary-general, the Party department heads, the secretary of the Control Committee, the magistrate and his deputies, the chiefs of the Court and the Procuracy, and the chiefs of the Bureaus of Public Security, Military Service, and Grain; (2) district-level cadres (*ch'ü chi kan pu*), or middle-rank leadership cadres (*chung chi ling tao kan pu*), a category which included all other chiefs of bureaus, independent sections, and equivalent organs, the section chiefs in the three bureaus mentioned under (1) above, the heads of public

[47] In County X, people were aware of the term "1938 cadres" (*san pa kan pu*) but did not use it locally.

security substations, the top staff members (*kan shih*) in Party departments, and a few others; and (3) lower or "small" leadership cadres (*hsiao ling tao kan pu*), a category which included all other section chiefs, and some higher staff members in government agencies.[48]

In addition to these informal job-level rankings, all administrative state cadres in County X, Party and non-Party, were, of course, formally ranked, as everywhere in China, in the nationwide salary system. There could be minor discrepancies between job ranks and salary grades, but, as would be expected, the two tended to be equated over time; that is, generally, job promotions were eventually followed by salary-grade promotions, and vice versa.

Official Ranking System: Salaries and Benefits

The official ranking system for state cadres was gradually introduced in the early 1950s. It was officially revised in July of 1956, and it has remained virtually unchanged since then. According to this system, counties across the country were grouped into eleven categories depending on the cost of living. Since the cost of living in County X was somewhat higher than the national average, the county was assigned to Category 7, along with many other counties on the southeast China coast. According to the official documents published in 1956, the grades and salaries of county-level officials in County X fell within the ranges shown in the table opposite.

The same ranking system applied to all state cadres, whether employed in the Party apparatus or in the government. The highest-ranking cadre in County X was the Party first secretary who held grade fourteen. The clerical staff members, through grade twenty-six, were considered cadres; but the general service personnel, below grade twenty-six, were considered noncadres even though they were on state payroll. Some persons who were being considered for cadre status were assigned grade twenty-seven and were called temporary or provisional cadres (*lin shih kan pu*), to set them apart from other general service personnel.

[48] Among staff members in the bureaucracy, a *chu pan kan shih* generally ranked just below a deputy bureau or section chief or equivalent, a *kan shih* was slightly lower, and a *k'o yüan* was just an ordinary cadre.

GRADES AND SALARIES OF CADRES IN COUNTY X
(and other counties of Category 7)[a]

Grade	Salary (in Yüan)	Position
13	159.5	
14	141.5	
15	127.5	Magistrate and deputy magistrate
16	113.5	(hsien chang and fu hsien chang)
17	101.5	
18	89.5	
19	80.0	Section and bureau chiefs (chü k'o
20	72.0	chang) and their deputies
21	63.5	
22	57.0	Section member
23	50.5	(k'o yüan)
24	44.5	
25	38.5	Clerical staff
26	33.5	(pan shih yüan)
27	30.5	
28	28.5	General service personnel
29	26.0	(ch'in tsa jen yüan)
30	23.5	

[a] This data is taken from *Chung Yang T's'ai Cheng Fa Kuei Hui Pien* [Central Government Financial Regulations], 1956, pp. 224ff.

The official ranking system, along with "Party age," official position in the bureaucratic hierarchy, and official position within the Party, was one of the very important ways of ranking cadres. This grade, in fact, tended to sum up the total of a cadre's status, and changes in grade were considered very important as key indicators of how well a cadre was doing in his career. Inasmuch as most changes in rank were usually made only after much discussion among peers and superiors, rank also represented a kind of collective judgment concerning a cadre's status.

Invidious comparisons based on rank were actually more important than the salary differentials, for salaries were not high in any case. Much of a cadre's material rewards came not from his salary but from the various other benefits which accrued to all state cadres. They received free medical care (although if the costs went above a certain amount they had to request, and usually received, special financial help from their organizations); they could also request and usually obtain subsidies to cover one half of their family's total medical expenses. Housing was provided to them at very low rents—in 1962, about Y0.50 a month for bachelors and Y1.00 for married couples. Home furnishings were provided on loan, and utilities rates were nominal. Food was also subsidized, and cadres who wished to eat at Party or government messes could do so very economically; in 1962 the cost for three meals a day for a month in these messes was Y10.05.

Despite the low salary levels, therefore, because of the many subsidized services and benefits available to them, cadres without large families in County X were generally able to live on their salaries without great difficulty. A married cadre with several children could not support his family easily on his own salary, but he could easily manage if another member of the family was also a breadwinner; consequently a substantial proportion of such cadres' wives worked and obtained a second income. All cadres were considered to be privileged to a degree, because of their relative financial security; but in County X they did not enjoy living standards that were very much higher than those of ordinary people and they were thus not generally regarded as a highly privileged economic group.

The highest-ranking state cadre in County X, as indicated above, might receive roughly four times the monthly salary of the lowest-ranking one, but despite this fact there was apparently less sense of differentiation based purely on income and other perquisites and privileges than at higher levels in the bureaucracy in China. Even though top-level county cadres were allotted relatively spacious housing, their home furnishings and office equipment were not notably different from those of ordinary cadres. When traveling outside the county, county-level cadres received a slightly higher per diem allowance (Y1.00 instead of Y0.50) than those of lower rank; they were also permitted to travel "soft class" (*juan chi*) on the trains, but reportedly most of them did not take advantage of this privilege because they felt that this might indicate a lack of genuinely "revolutionary" attitudes. (Cadres working at the national and provincial levels were not notably affected by this inhibition.)

The stratification among state cadres was not, in short, reflected in material ways to the same extent in County X as at higher levels in the bureaucracy. But rank-consciousness and rank-differentiation were extremely important, nevertheless, in terms of power, influence, and job responsibilities. Quite clearly, by the early 1960s, there had already been, in these terms, a steady trend toward bureaucratization even at the county level, as cadres increasingly thought in terms of status in the system, and as the rankings became much more crystallized and important than they had been in the pre-1949 revolutionary movement.

Work Schedules

Many ex-cadres who worked at different levels in the bureaucracy in Communist China appear to feel that in general the work load on individual cadres tends to increase as one goes down the hierarchy. At the top levels of the bureaucracy, although some leading administrative cadres may have a wide variety of responsibilities and work in many different positions, in general there is a greater degree of specialization and division of labor. At lower levels there is a tendency to pile a multitude of tasks on fewer and fewer people. Many cadres at lower levels constantly feel under very great pressure from higher authorities. It is at the lower levels that plans, policies, and programs originated by numerous different agencies up the line must be translated into concrete action affecting the mass of the population; and higher authorities are constantly exhorting "basic-level" cadres to complete the myriad tasks assigned to them.

In County X, the normal summer work day of county-level cadres started at 5:45 A.M. and continued—counting evening meetings—until 9:30 P.M. In the winter it lasted from 6:30 A.M. to 9:00 P.M. The summer schedule for an ordinary day was roughly the following: 5:45–6:00 A.M., reveille and preparation for the day; 6:00–7:00, military-training physical exercises (*chün hsün t'i yü*); 7:00–8:00, political study; 8:00–8:30, breakfast; 8:30–11:30, work; 11:30–12:00

noon, lunch; 12:00–12:40 P.M., rest; 12:40–2:00, rest and preparation for work; 2:00–3:30, work; 3:30–5:30, either work or periodically, individual activity; 5:30–6:00, supper; 6:00–7:30, individual study or recreation; 7:30–9:30, generally (a majority of evenings) meetings or political study; 9:30, retirement to bed. In winter,
the schedule varied slightly: 6:30–7:00 A.M., reveille and preparation
for work; 7:00–8:00, political study; 8:00–8:30, breakfast; 8:30–
11:30, work; 11:30–12:00, lunch; 12:00–1:40 P.M., rest; 1:40–2:00,
preparation for work; 2:00–5:00, work; 5:00–5:30, supper; 5:30–
7:30, individual study or recreation; 7:30–9:00, generally (a majority
of evenings) meetings or political study; 9:00, retirement to bed.

While on paper these schedules included reasonable time for rest,
in practice there was little leisure or opportunity for recreation. The
regular work load kept people extremely busy, and if cadres found
that they did have any spare time, they usually devoted it to additional work or study. During campaigns, moreover, the work hours
for everyone were greatly extended. During the Great Leap Forward, which was admittedly the most frenetic period of activity for
almost everyone in China, it was not uncommon for cadres to work
until 1:00 A.M. In theory, county organizations were supposed to operate on a six-day week, with the seventh day off. In practice, however, county cadres frequently felt it necessary to continue various
types of work on the seventh day; consequently, they had fewer
weekends or other periods of real rest or recreation than ordinary
cadres at higher levels in the bureaucracy.

Party Political and Legal Department

While the Organization Department of the County Party Committee was principally concerned with the organizational and personnel
matters that have been described so far, the responsibilities of almost
all the other departments were concerned mainly with the direction
of various substantive aspects of the work of the government. It is
true that some of them, including the Seacoast Department, United
Front Department, Propaganda and Education Department, and Rural Work Department, carried out certain programs that could be
considered essentially "Party work," in addition to supervising the

work of government agencies. But the heaviest work load of most departments consisted of supervision of activities that for the most part were actually carried out by government rather than Party agencies.

The most powerful department of the County Party Committee, in terms of its impact on the population as a whole, was the Political and Legal Department (*cheng fa pu*). The newest of the Party's organs in County X, it was established in 1959 to unify leadership and control over the entire political and legal field, that is, over the work of three government agencies: the Public Security Bureau (*kung an chü*), the People's Procuracy (*jen min chien ch'a yüan*), and the People's Court (*jen min fa yüan*). For some time prior to 1959 there had been serious problems in coordinating the work of these three agencies, whose activities were closely interrelated. All three agencies were involved, for example, in cases involving arrest and formal court proceedings, and disagreements among them could and did involve embarrassing complications.

As early as 1955, soon after promulgation of the 1954 national constitution and at the time when the local Procuracy was first established in County X, a Joint Political and Legal Office (*cheng fa lien ho pan kung shih*) had been set up in the county government, to provide some mechanism for coordination. The organization of the Party Committee's Political and Legal Department in 1959 went further, however, and established genuinely unified control over these three fields. The result was much more than simply an improvement of administrative coordination of the agencies involved. The new department established direct Party control over these fields. In a sense, the Party was welded to these administrative organs to form a single unified administration under Party direction. The reorganization also reflected the rise in importance of the Public Security Bureau and its increasing dominance over the Procuracy and the courts. Cadres in County X tended to link these trends in their area —the increasing direct Party intervention in and public security's domination of the entire political and legal field—with what they felt to be similar trends on the national level following the 1957–1958 and 1959 campaigns against rightists and rightest tendencies. (In 1959, the national Ministries of Supervision and Justice were abolished, the functions of the latter being absorbed by the Supreme

People's Court. In the same year there was evidence of the growing influence of Lo Jui-ch'ing, the Minister of Public Security, when he was appointed a deputy premier. In the period immediately following these developments, the increasing importance of political and legal personnel, most particularly public security men, was indicated by the fact that a large number of them moved into more influential Party and government posts at both the central and the provincial levels.)

Among the Party departments in County X, the Political and Legal Department was unique in that it was simply a leadership group or collegium of the chiefs of three government agencies, all of whom were high Party members, led by an even higher-ranking Party leader, and did not have a separate staff of its own other than the organs it administered. The head of the department was one of the deputy secretaries of the Party Committee. The deputy heads included the chiefs of the Public Security Bureau, the Procuracy, and the Court and a deputy chief of the Public Security Bureau. As stated earlier, these five men also formed a special Party Fraction, and together they made up the entire membership of the county government's Political and Legal Staff Office (*cheng fa pan kung shih*) as well. They maintained two offices: one, which was labeled the department's office, was located in the Party Committee headquarters; the other, labeled the Staff Office, was in the Public Security Bureau building. They had no special employees, and the office personnel of the Public Security Bureau performed the necessary staff and secretarial work for the Political and Legal Department.

Even though the 1959 reorganization resulted, *de facto*, in effective operational unification of the three government agencies involved, and established clear Party and public security control over the entire political and legal field, the organizational merger was concealed from the public. All three agencies continued to maintain their own buildings and staffs, but the principal office of the Political and Legal Department was located in the Public Security Bureau's building. One reason for this was the fact that because the 1954 constitution had established the Court and the Procuracy as independent agencies (they were supposed, in fact, to be equivalent in status to the County People's Council rather than to bureau-level subunits such as the Public Security Bureau), it was felt desirable not to subordinate them in any formal or open sense, which would have been a violation of the constitution, but rather to establish Party and public security dominance by more indirect means.

The five members of the Political and Legal Department met whenever major cases arose or important policy questions required decision, and they jointly determined the best course of action. Generally, they decided not only what the charges should be in a particular case, and how the case should be handled, but also, in major cases, what punishments should be meted out by the Court. If they wished, they could and sometimes did hold enlarged meetings, bringing in other personnel from the Party or from their own government agencies. In these meetings, differences of opinion did, on occasion, arise among the three agencies; for example, they did not always agree even on whether a particular case should be brought to the Court or not. On most such occasions, the public security man's viewpoint prevailed.

Party Seacoast Department

The Party Committee's Seacoast Department was responsible for special security work among boatmen, fishermen, and others in coastal areas throughout the county. This department existed only in a few[49] coastal Chinese provinces, areas where there were special tensions and problems resulting from the continuing conflict with the Chinese Nationalist regime on Taiwan.

The work of the department supplemented that of other agencies, which also had special responsibilities in the area. The Public Security Bureau and special militia units handled regular police security measures in this area, as throughout the county. The Aquatic Products Bureau organized fishermen for production, but did not specialize in security work. Regular army units, not under county supervision, were responsible for military defense. The Seacoast Department's responsibility, as a Party organization, was to mobilize Party personnel in special ways to strengthen security in the area. Specifically, it was expected to promote programs to increase the

[49] Probably four; Kwangtung, Fukien, Chekiang, and Shantung.

level of general vigilance against enemy (i.e. Chinese Nationalist) infiltration, and to prevent defections.

Perhaps the most important counterdefection measure instituted by the department was the organization of Party and YCL members to act as special security personnel on the fishing junks and other boats along the coast. It tried to ensure that there would be at least one reliable Party member on every sizable boat in the region and at least one YCL member on all smaller ones. And every time a boat went in or out of port, it was checked by a public security unit that worked closely with the Seacoast Department.

Defections were apparently not, however, an enormous problem in this area. In 1958 there had been a number of defections to the Nationalists, but in most periods they were reportedly quite rare, partly, of course, because of the effectiveness of the control system.

The staff of the Seacoast Department consisted of eight men. Under a department head and deputy, there was one "custodian" (*pao kuan yüan*), who also acted as a statistician, and five staff members (*kan shih*). Beyond this, the department had no other staff or forces of its own located in coastal areas but rather worked through regular Party channels and the Public Security Bureau.

Party United Front Department

The Party's United Front Department had special responsibility for assisting, mobilizing, indoctrinating, and controlling a number of special population groups in the county, including overseas Chinese and their relatives, former businessmen, and to a lesser extent, local intellectuals. It worked mainly through several non-Party but Party-controlled government agencies and mass organizations. One of these was the People's Political Consultative Conference (*jen min cheng chih hsieh shang hui yi*, or *cheng hsieh*, for short), the PPCC, which, as the major united front representative organ in the government, contained "representatives" of all the non-Communist elements which the Party at any particular period wished to include in its united front. The others were the Overseas Chinese Affairs Section (*ch'iao wu k'o*) and the Office for the Reform of Private Entrepreneurs (*szu jen kai tsao pan kung shih*, or *szu kai pan kung shih*, for short), both of which were government agencies; and the Overseas Chinese Association (*hua ch'iao lien ho hui*, or *ch'iao lien hui*, for short) and Association of Industry and Commerce (*kung yeh shang yeh lien ho hui*, or *kung shang lien*, for short), which were Party-sponsored mass organizations.

As of 1962, apart from generally supervising the PPCC, by far the most important work of the United Front Department in County X concerned overseas Chinese affairs;[50] and actually, the Overseas Chinese Affairs Section of the government, through which much of this work was done, was more of a Party than a government organ. The section was located in the same building as the United Front Department—which had its own establishment separate from the Party Committee compound—and it was headed by a staff member of the department.

Work with businessmen and merchants had been very important in the mid-1950s, when the department played a major role in the efforts to "reform" them and convince them that they should accept socialization peacefully; but it was less demanding after the socialization drive of 1956 had virtually completed the takeover of private enterprise.

Work among ethnic or religious minorities was not important in County X because such minorities were relatively small and weak. The Organization Department and the Propaganda and Education Department shared responsibility for work among intellectuals. In urban areas intellectuals were important targets of united front work in the early years, but this was much less true in rural areas such as County X, which had so few intellectuals. Work in the countryside at that time was left largely to the Organization Department and the Rural Work Department.

As indicated earlier, supervision of the major mass organizations in the county that were directly tied to the Party and were in effect Party subsidiaries—that is, the Women's Association and the General Labor Union as well as the YCL—was exercised directly by the Party Committee and the Organization Department rather than through the United Front Department.

The United Front Department's own staff consisted of five per-

[50] This will be described later; see pp. 250ff.

sons: a head, a deputy, and three staff members (*kan shih*). Two of the staff members were concurrently members of the overseas Chinese section, and one of them headed it. The other members of the section were also, for all practical purposes, staff members of the department, even though they were not labeled as such.

Party Propaganda and Education Department

The Party's Propaganda and Education Department had broad responsibilities which involved both extensive mass propaganda and indoctrination programs conducted by Party personnel throughout the county, and the direction of all educational, cultural, health, and athletic activities conducted by government agencies and mass organizations. Its staff, totaling ten, was the largest of any department, and included, besides the head (grade fifteen), and his deputy (grade seventeen), a special staff member (*chu pan kan shih*), who held grade eighteen, a statistician (*t'ung chi yüan*, often called *t'ung chi*, for short), who held grade twenty-one, and six others (grades nineteen to twenty-four). The department head supervised the entire work of the department and also bore direct responsibility for the political education of cadres. His deputy was primarily concerned with school affairs, especially in government operated schools.

Three men in the department were primarily responsible for propaganda and indoctrination (*hsüan ch'uan chiao yü,* or *hsüan-chiao,* for short). They were in charge of all Party propaganda activities, including the organizing of newspaper reading groups (*tu pao tsu*), maintenance of blackboard newspapers (*hei pan pao*), promotion of oral face-to-face propaganda (*tui hua hsüan ch'uan*), and so on, at the local level. During campaigns their work was particularly demanding, since they were expected to give over-all direction and provide needed materials to the Party propaganda committeemen (*hsüan ch'uan wei yüan*) in all Party units throughout the county. Periodically, generally at least once or twice a year, the department called together all these committeemen for special meetings, which might last anywhere from three to five days. These three men also bore the major responsibility for getting out the county Party newspaper, under the supervision of the Party Committee's staff secretary-general, who was its editor-in-chief (*tsung pien chi*). One of them did most of the actual editing, although the secretary-general checked all material and wrote some important articles himself; both of the others did some reporting and writing.

In County X the Party newspaper, which served as the Party Committee's "organizational paper" (*chi kuan pao*), was started in 1958 as a daily but in 1959 changed to an every-other-day schedule. The paper was called the "X" (that is, the county's name) "Daily" (*jih pao*), and an average issue consisted of four pages (each page half the size of a metropolitan daily), and three to four thousand copies. It was printed by the county printing plant, located in the county government's premises, and was distributed principally by the Postal and Telecommunications Bureau.

Every commune, brigade, and team received a minimum of one copy of the paper. At the team level, there was usually at least one person, often the work-point recorder (*chi kung yüan*), who was literate enough to pass on information in the paper to illiterates, sometimes through organized reading groups; thus the paper had a very broad outreach. Some material was drawn from both the Peking *People's Daily* and provincial Party paper, but much of the paper's space was devoted to county affairs, and key articles were frequently written by important local Party and government leaders. Material was also obtained from local areas to illustrate how Party policy could and should be adapted to local conditions and be properly implemented. Local stories were sent in by designated persons acting as reporters or correspondents (*t'ung hsün yüan*) in the communes. The paper also carried a regular section for "people's letters" (*jen min t'ung hsün* or *jen min lai hsin*). In many respects the paper was the most important medium for systematic dissemination of Party propaganda throughout the county.

The three propaganda staff members of the department also directed, in collaboration with the county government's Personnel Section, the daily political study meetings, attended by all state cadres in county-level agencies. The department determined what topics were to be discussed, and either designated certain newspaper editorials, major government reports, and the like for study, or provided special materials that had been passed down from higher Party propaganda departments or were prepared by the county department itself. They also supervised the work of the County Broadcasting Station (*kuang po tien t'ai*), which will be described later.[51]

The other three staff members of the Propaganda Department concerned themselves with the work of all government activities in the educational, cultural, and health (*wen chiao wei sheng*) fields. The agencies under their supervision included the Education Bureau (*chiao yü chü*) and its schools; the Office for the Elimination of Illiteracy (*sao mang pan kung shih*); the Association for the Dissemination of Science (*k'o hsüeh p'u chi hsieh shang hui yi*, or *k'o p'u hsieh hui*, for short), a mass organization; the Bureau of Culture (*wen hua chü*) and its Cultural Hall–Library (*wen hua kuan–t'u shu kuan*), and Opera Troupe–Movie Team (*hsi t'uan–tien ying tui*); the New China Bookstore (*hsin hua shu tien*); the Bureau of Health (*wei sheng chü*) and its hospital (*wei sheng yüan*); and the Physical Education and Sports Committee (*t'i yü yün tung wei yüan hui*).[52] To give policy direction to all these organizations was a large task. In practical terms, however, work in the schools and among the several hundred teachers in the county demanded the largest share of their time and effort.

Party Rural Work Department

The Rural Work Department of the Party Committee was responsible for helping to promote all of the Party's numerous programs and campaigns in the countryside, and more concretely for directing the activities of all government agencies in the field of agriculture, forestry, and water conservancy (*nung lin shui*). Everything from helping to plan and ensure the success of agricultural production to leading the revolutionary process of political and social transformation in the countryside fell within its broad area of concern, with the result that the department's work load was extremely heavy. The government agencies that came under its supervision included the following: the Agriculture, Forestry, and Water Conservancy Staff Office (*nung lin shui pan kung shih*); the Bureau of Agriculture

[51] See p. 270.
[25] The work of these various agencies will be described later; see pp. 258ff.

(*nung yeh chü*) and its Agricultural Technology Extension Station (*nung yeh chi shu chih tao chan*), Agricultural Exhibition (*nung yeh chan lan hui*), and Veterinary Station (*shu mu shou yi chan*); the Agriculture and Land Reclamation Bureau (*nung k'en chü*), the Forestry Bureau (*lin yeh chü*), the Water Conservancy Bureau (*shui li chü*), and the Meteorological Station (*ch'i hsiang chan*).[53] The department had a staff of eight: a head, a deputy, a special staff member (*chu pan kan shih*), a statistician (*t'ung chi yüan*), and four staff members (*kan shih*).

Party Industry and Communications Department, Finance and Trade Department

The other two Party departments working in economic fields were the Finance and Trade Department (*ts'ai mao pu*) and the Industry and Communications Department (*kung chiao pu*); each had eight men on its staff. While some of the cadres working for these departments were primarily Party affairs men rather than technical specialists, they had received at least some training in specialized Party schools at the provincial level. The work of both departments consisted almost entirely of providing policy direction to the government economic agencies—and their subsidiary companies and factories—operating in their respective fields.

The Finance and Trade Department supervised the following organizations: the Finance and Trade Staff Office (*ts'ai mao pan kung shih*), the Bureau of Finance and Taxation (*ts'ai shui chü*), the Grain Bureau (*liang shih chü*), the People's Bank (*jen min yin hang*), and the Supply and Marketing Cooperative (*kung hsiao ho tso she*), together with their subsidiary companies, banking outlets, and cooperatives. The Industry and Communications Department supervised the Bureau of Industry (*kung yeh chü*), the Handicraft Cooperative (*shou kung yeh ho tso she*), the Bureau of Construction (*chien she chü*), the Bureau of Communications (*chiao t'ung chü*) and its various stations (*ch'e chan*), the Transportation Management Station (*yün shu kuan li chan*), the Postal and Telecommunications Bureau

---

[53] The organization and functions of these agencies will be described later; see pp. 276ff.

(*yu tien chü*), and the Navigation Management Station (*hang hai kuan li chan,* or *hang kuan chan,* for short), together with their subsidiary factories, cooperatives, companies, and so on.[54] As one would expect, supervision of such a large number of economic agencies involved many complex problems, and the number of government state cadres involved in their work was larger than in any other field except education.

[54] The organization and functions of these agencies will be described later; see pp. 284ff., 298ff.

The Government in County X: Organization and Operation

AS ALREADY emphasized, in County X the Party apparatus, the structure of which has been outlined above, was the highest policy-making authority in the county, but the principal administrative load was carried by the county government, which had, on its payroll, over ten times as many cadres as the Party. To oversimplify, one can say that the Party decided basic policies and the government implemented them.

County People's Congress

In the government of County X, the County People's Congress (*hsien jen min tai piao ta hui*) was, like all government congresses in Communist China, ostensibly the highest legislative body in the area. In actuality, however, it played little more than a symbolic role. "Elections," which were supposed to take place every two years, simply involved *pro forma* approval of a slate put forth by Party officials, and congress membership normally underwent little change. Its membership, totaling close to four hundred, generally met for only one relatively brief session a year. Its legislative role was clearly minimal. To the extent that policy formulation and decision-making occurred in the government in the course of the implementation of basic Party policies, it took place at the higher levels of the county government bureaucracy rather than in this diffuse representative body. However, the annual meetings of the People's Congress, like those of the Party Congress, were the occasion for some fairly important work reports on government operations during the previous year, and during each session, plans for the period ahead were outlined by the top Party leaders. Occasionally, some positive proposals were advanced from the floor during the discussions, including some by representatives from the communes and brigades.

The main function of the People's Congress was to elect the County People's Council (*hsien jen min wei yüan hui*), the magistrate, the heads of the Court and Procuracy, and the county's representatives to the Provincial People's Congress. These elections, too—like so many elections in Communist China—were in reality nothing more than a public endorsement of nominees already chosen by the County Party Committee. They were designed mainly to reinforce the legitimacy of the top local government officials.

The majority of representatives to the congress came from the communes and brigades, with population determining the number per unit; the only other regular delegates were a few elected by locally stationed units of the armed forces. In addition to these regular representatives (*cheng shih tai piao*), however, almost all Party branches and government agencies that did not have at least one of its members sitting in the congress selected one person to participate as an observer (*lieh hsi tai piao*).

The Party decisions on who was to be elected to the congress were made at the nominating stage. For example, the nominations for regular delegates from the brigades were actually made by each local Party branch. Those nominated usually included some key people in the power hierarchy, plus others who were thus rewarded for collaboration with the Party or because they provided useful symbols of the united front. Election to the congress did not in itself bring any power to the persons elected, but it was considered a desirable status symbol and carried with it a certain amount of prestige.

Each session of the congress was organized and run by an *ad hoc* presidium (*chu hsi t'uan*) elected to serve for the duration of the meeting. Far more important was the Standing Committee (*ch'ang wu wei yüan hui*, or *ch'ang wei*, for short) elected by each session of the congress. This standing committee could exercise the full powers of the congress between its annual sessions. In 1962, the Standing

Committee of the People's Congress in County X was composed of fourteen members: eight Party cadres and six non-Party members. The Party cadres included the county magistrate (*hsien chang*), three of the four deputy magistrates (*fu hsien chang*), the county staff secretary-general (*mi shu chang*), the heads of the Court and the Procuracy, and the head of the Party's United Front Department. Four of these—the magistrate, one of the deputies, the head of the Court, and the united front man—were also members of the Party Standing Committee, which provided an important overlap between these two bodies. The non-Party members included the fourth deputy magistrate, the deputy head of the PPCC, the head of the Overseas Chinese Association, and three elderly gentlemen who "represented" three major population groups: the peasants, returned overseas Chinese, and intellectuals (teachers).

County People's Council

The County People's Council (*hsien jen min wei yüan hui*, or *jen wei*, for short), elected by the County People's Congress, was the top administrative body in the county government. Prior to the 1954 constitution, the comparable body was simply called the County People's Government (*hsien jen min cheng fu*). As of 1962, the People's Council in County X had a membership of fifty-three; two thirds of these were Party members, and they included not only many of the top leaders in both Party and government but also key persons connected with the mass organizations and major social groups. Only three of the fifty-three council members were women.[55]

The People's Council in County X was theoretically supposed to meet monthly, but in practice it did not meet that often. It did, however, have sessions at least once each season (*chi tu*), or roughly quarterly; and occasionally it met more often. In these meetings it reviewed major programs and discussed basic policies, but for the

---

[55] Theoretically, according to centrally promulgated regulations, county people's councils in China are normally supposed to have no more than twenty-one members, or thirty-one in especially large counties. County X apparently exceeded these limits, and it is not wholly clear why.

most part it was not an initiator of them. A great many of its actions simply involved approval or endorsement of general plans and policies already formulated by the Party Committee.

The most important forum for discussion of the day-to-day administrative tasks and problems of government was not the People's Council, or even the Party Committee, which dealt with broad policy. Detailed consideration of these tasks and problems took place most frequently in the many "administrative meetings" (*hsing cheng hui yi*) which were convened by the magistrate. The magistrate, through his staff secretary-general, called together a variety of such meetings at frequent intervals. About once a week or so he held *ad hoc* working sessions (*p'eng t'ou hui yi*) with just his deputies and staff secretary-general. Somewhat less frequently, perhaps once a month on the average, he would convene larger meetings of all the bureau and section chiefs (*jen wei chü k'o chang hui yi*) in the county government. In addition, of course, he could and did hold other meetings, as needed, of selected people to deal with specific problems. (The deputy magistrates also convened periodic meetings of the chiefs of units within the functional "systems" which they supervised; see below.) All these meetings were important, in fact, essential, for the effective operation of the county government; they were the occasions when concrete problems were hammered out. But mostly they were concerned with routine administration, rather than with basic policy formulation, which generally took place, as stated earlier, in meetings convened by the Party Committee and its departments.

People's Political Consultative Conference

In addition to the People's Congress, there was one other "representative body" and general forum for discussion at the county level: the People's Political Consultative Conference. In theory, at the county level as at the national level, the PPCC was a body which originally was supposed to represent the will of the people in forming the government and was to exercise the powers of a people's congress until such a congress could be formally established. In the early years after "liberation" the PPCC in County X did meet fairly frequently and with considerable fanfare. After 1954, however, when people's congresses were established within the governmental organization, at the county level as in the central government, the consultative conferences gradually receded into the background. In County X it remained as a united front organ, and it occasionally held brief meetings before or after the meetings of the County People's Congress, but its role steadily decreased in importance.

In 1962 the PPCC in County X had more than sixty members, appointed from among groups and individuals considered by the regime to be acceptable and desirable for its united front, including "democratic personages" representing the "minor parties" (*min chu tang p'ai*, literally "democratic parties and groups"), overseas Chinese, and others. Their average age was higher than that of members of any other government organization in the county.

The chairman of the PPCC in County X was the county Party secretary (not the first secretary), and it had two deputy chairmen —both of whom were non-Communist "democratic personages" (*min chu jen shih*)—and a secretary-general. The Standing Committee of the PPCC consisted of its chairman, the head of the Party United Front Department, and three non-Communist members. The United Front Department played the largest role in selecting all the members of the PPCC, and it closely supervised all of its work. By the early 1960s the one annual session of the PPCC was almost always held simultaneously with the People's Congress meetings, and PPCC members generally sat in on many of the sessions of the congress. Between meetings, however, the PPCC members—to the extent that they were active—were expected to collaborate with the United Front Department in pushing all the Party's policies toward the social groups that were the main targets of united front work, and to help actively propagandize these groups. Not all these activities were confined to the local county; at times, for example, PPCC members were mobilized to write letters to relatives and friends on Taiwan and overseas.

County Magistrate and Deputies

The chief executive of the county government was the magistrate, who was elected by the People's Congress and who was the chairman of the People's Council. In County X, the man who held this position was a deputy secretary of the Party Committee and, in effect, the third-ranking Party leader in the county. Under Party Committee supervision, he was responsible for directing the work of all county government agencies.

Four deputy magistrates assisted the magistrate in his task; following a pattern already described, they divided their work along functional lines. One, a Party man who had once headed the Civil Affairs Section of the government, was responsible for all activities in the fields of planning (*chi hua*) and welfare (*fu li*). Another, a Party man who had formerly been a special staff member (*chu pan kan shih*) and the third-ranking man in the Party's Rural Work Department, supervised all agencies in the field of agriculture, forestry, and water conservancy. A third, also a Party man and previously chief of the County Finance Bureau (prior to its merger with the Tax Bureau), had over-all responsibility for finance and trade. The fourth, a non-Party man who had formerly worked in the County Education Bureau, was in charge of all activities in the field of culture, education, and health. All four of these men worked closely with, and under the supervision of, not only the magistrate but also the secretaries of the County Party Committee and the Party departments which had responsibilities roughly equivalent to theirs. The non-Party deputy magistrate was supervised especially closely by the relevant Party department; moreover, the bureau chiefs under him, in particular the chief of the Education Bureau, were Party men who in actuality had a status that was equivalent to his in many respects.

Each of these deputy magistrates was expected to keep both himself and the magistrate fully informed on current policies and actual performance in the field under his supervision. As needed they could and did call administrative work meetings (*hsing cheng kung tso hui*) of all bureau chiefs within their jurisdiction. Their offices were located in the People's Council compound, near the magistrate's office, and they were serviced by the council's staff office.

Several functional work fields did not come under the supervision of any deputy magistrates. One of these, industry and communications, was directly supervised by the magistrate. Most of the others in this category, including political and legal work, armed forces work, seacoast work, and united front work, were directed almost wholly by the Party.

People's Council Staff Office

Directly under the magistrate and the People's Council, as under the Party Committee, there was a staff office (*jen wei pan kung shih*), which performed a fairly wide range of functions. Its head (*chu jen*) was the staff secretary-general (*mi shu chang*). Like his counterpart in the Party Committee, this man was relatively young (in his late thirties), and a fairly well-educated, local Party man. He had joined the Communist guerrillas in nearby mountains just before 1949, and became first a political commissar and then instructor in a local guerrilla training school.

Responsible for helping the magistrate in all his work, the secretary-general drafted many of the magistrate's major reports and dealt with a great many different sorts of administrative problems (*hsing cheng kuan li*). He had nine cadres working under him: a deputy, two clerical secretaries (*wen yin* and *ta tzu yüan*, or *ta tzu*, for short), two receiving and sending clerks (*shou fa yüan*, or *shou fa*, for short), one accountant (*k'uai chi*), one statistician (*t'ung chi*), one management cadre (*kuan li yüan*), and one ordinary staff member (simply called *k'o yüan* even though the organization was a *shih*, not a *k'o*). Only the secretary-general and his deputy were Party cadres; of the others, four were YCL members and four were non-Party men.

The staff office's personnel performed the usual sort of service functions required for the operation of the bureaucracy in China. The clerical secretaries did typing and mimeographing for all the smaller county bureaus and sections located in the People's Council compound; only the largest bureaus in the county government had typists and machines of their own. The receiving and sending clerks registered and distributed all documents that came to the office for any of the many agencies under the county government. The statistician received copies of most important statistical reports prepared by all government agencies, including the Planning and Statistics Committee; he also prepared certain types of consolidated figures for the magistrate and provided much of the statistical material needed for the preparation of reports to higher levels.

The accountant was responsible for handling the salaries and office allowances for all units in the council's compound. Salaries were paid monthly, with funds obtained from the People's Bank; the staff office accountant obtained these funds from the bank and delivered them to all agencies in the council compound, which in turn distributed them to their individual cadres. The largest bureaus in the county government, most of which were located elsewhere, in compounds of their own, handled this themselves and obtained their funds directly from the bank. The so-called management cadre was in charge of all "livelihood" or "housekeeping" matters; he ran the council's dormitory, which had more than thirty rooms, and its mess hall (ch'ih t'ang). He also supervised the four general service employees who acted as cleaning men and messengers; one of these served as gateman and was in charge of a reception office (chieh tai shih) at the entrance to the compound. The ninth staff member was responsible for maintaining the staff office's archives and files (tang an), as well as a small reference or materials office (tzu liao shih), which contained mainly newspapers and journals.

One room in the staff office, as in many Chinese government offices, was called the "reception office for people's letters and visits" (jen min lai hsin lai fang chieh tai shih). No cadres were specially assigned to it. When people came to visit the county government, the secretary-general or his deputy generally received them. There were not a great many such visits, however. To most people in the county, the magistrate's office seemed fairly remote, and if they had complaints to make, they were more likely to go through local Party or commune channels, or to write letters, than to try to visit the magistrate's office. Some people, though, did write letters containing suggestions or complaints; all those received by the staff office were at least acknowledged. On occasion the deputy secretary-general him-self answered them, but usually they were forwarded to one of the bureaus or other county organs for reply.

Personnel Section

As has been emphasized already, throughout the government bureauc-racy in Communist China, personnel organs are viewed as being among the most important centers of bureaucratic power. Staffed al-most entirely by Party members, and in effect acting as agents, within the government, of the Party's Organization Department, they wield great influence because of their (i.e. the Party's) control over the careers of all cadres working in the bureaucracy. Generally, an aura of secrecy surrounds their work. Non-Party cadres tend to view them, in fact, as they do other key power centers in the bureaucracy, such as the public security organs, as agencies to be dealt with cau-tiously, or to be avoided when possible.

In County X, the agency in charge of personnel matters within the government was the Personnel Section (*jen shih k'o*), an inde-pendent section—that is, not under any bureau—located in an office very near the magistrate's. It was a small office consisting of only three men: the section chief (*k'o chang*) and two staff members (*kan shih*), all of whom were reliable Party cadres assigned by the Organ-ization Department.

One of the responsibilities of the Personnel Section was to main-tain the dossiers of all non-Party cadres working in the government. It worked closely with the Organization Department in making de-cisions on personnel assignments for both Party and non-Party ca-dres in government agencies. If the section had had full responsibility for this, the task would probably have been more than such a small staff could handle; but in practice, as emphasized above, the section was essentially an outpost of the Organization Department, which in consultation with the Personnel Section made the most important decisions.

Another responsibility of the section was to collaborate with the Party Propaganda Department in organizing regular political study for all cadres. Here again it was the Party Department which carried much of the actual work load, but the Personnel Section was the responsible agency within the government. It also handled certain cadre welfare problems (*fu li wen t'i*); for example, its approval was necessary on requests for subsidies to pay family medical expenses.

In addition to making frequent verbal reports (*hui pao*) to the magistrate on all personnel matters, the Personnel Section also prepared periodic written reports which were sent not only to the county magistrate and the Party Organization Department but also to the personnel organs at the special district and provincial levels. Any county government agency desiring a significant increase in personnel had to inform the Personnel Section and request a change in its table of organization (*pien chih*). If both the magistrate and the Party Organization Department, as well as the Personnel Section, endorsed such a request, the section sent it on for approval to either the special district or provincial personnel organs (major requests had to go to the latter) for approval.

In all bureaus and other units within the county government, certain people were designated as specifically responsible for personnel work, and all of them dealt with and reported to the Personnel Section. The largest bureaus had specialized personnel sections (*jen shih k'o* or *ku*), while medium-size organs had only a single personnel cadre (*jen shih kan pu*), and in the smallest agencies the unit chiefs themselves handled personnel work.

Virtually without exception, all cadres dealing with personnel matters were Party members. Because their work required constant scrutiny of all cadres' performances, they were not only essential cogs in the over-all machine for personnel management but they also served, in effect, as an important watchdog network throughout the bureaucracy.

Committee on Planning and Statistics

Most organs of the government in County X clearly belonged to one of the identifiable functional "systems" into which most Party and government agencies in China are grouped; each of these "systems" included several agencies and was supervised by a county Party department. Four small government organizations in County X, however, were apparently not operationally linked with any of the "systems," and came, therefore, directly and solely under the supervision of the magistrate and his staff office. Why this was so is not entirely clear, but one explanation given was the fact that their functions were varied and tended to cut across "system" boundaries.

The Committee on Planning and Statistics (*chi hua t'ung chi wei yüan hui*) was one of these organizations. Under a director (*chu jen*), who formerly had been deputy secretary-general of the Party Staff Office and subsequently had received training at a provincial Party school, the committee's staff consisted of a deputy chief, and four section members (*k'o yüan*). The chief, his deputy, and one staff member were Party men.

In theory, this committee was basically responsible for over-all planning and the maintenance of comprehensive statistics for the entire county government. One might have expected it, therefore, to be an extremely important unit. In some other counties in China, organs responsible for this work apparently do play a very significant role; in some counties, in fact, the Planning Committee and Statistics Committee are separate, and each may have a large staff and fairly complex organization. However, in County X, this committee's functions reportedly were limited. It did collect and process statistics from all county government organs, but it did not play a primary role in actual planning, or even in checking on plan fulfillment.

In practice, the main outlines of the major annual plans of many if not most agencies in County X were predetermined to a considerable extent by instructions and performance targets passed down from higher authorities. Within each "system" or line of work, tentative targets that had first been determined by a central ministry were sent to all subordinate provincial departments (*t'ing*), which in turn established targets for each subordinate county bureau or equivalent unit. Although, in theory, these targets were supposed to be adjusted at both the provincial and county levels, in practice many county-level organs, at least in County X, apparently had little to say about some of the targets set for them by the provincial departments, unless there were extenuating circumstances and the county organs involved could present their case quickly and persuasively. One reason for this was the fact that the time pressures were great; consequently the provincial agencies had very little opportunity to arrange thorough consultations with their county-level equivalents. In many instances, county agencies simply had to accept targets set for them by superior organs at the provincial level, and these targets generally defined at least the minimum over-all performance standards which they were expected to meet.

It is true that in this process at each level, including the county, all plans had to be adjusted and coordinated to fit into a feasible over-all plan for the area. But in County X this adjustment was said to take place late in the planning process, after targets assigned to the county by higher-level authorities had already taken fairly definite shape and had set definite limits on what the county could decide. Moreover, the Planning and Statistics Committee apparently played only a secondary role in the process. The main discussions took place, and the basic decisions on over-all plans were made, in special meetings of the Party Committee and People's Council, especially the former. Representatives from the Planning and Statistics Committee usually sat in on such meetings as resource personnel, and provided needed statistics and data, but the committee itself did not carry a great deal of weight in determining what policies would be adopted or what targets set.

Civil Affairs Section

Another of the four small agencies directly under the supervision of the People's Council was the Civil Affairs Section. In some counties this organ is a bureau; in County X, its status as an independent section was probably due to the fact that it was considered to be relatively unimportant and had a small staff, consisting of a section chief (*k'o chang*) and four section members (*k'o yuan*). Its main responsibilities were in the field of social welfare. Transferred (*chuan yeh*) and demobilized (*fu yüan*) soldiers who needed assistance, or who had family and other problems, were provided advice and aid by the section. It was also responsible for providing allowances to wounded soldiers who were unable to take productive jobs; these allowances were reasonably generous and ranged from Y28 to Y45 for different sorts of persons.

When floods and droughts (*t'ien tsai jen hai*) or other calamities occurred in the county, the Civil Affairs Section was in charge of relief activities (*chiu chi kung tso*), generally working through the communes involved. In certain cases, persons injured in accidents, for example on the roads, could, with backing from the Public Security Bureau, request assistance from the section.

The Civil Affairs Section also acted as mediator in certain types of minor civil disputes (*chiu fen*), especially property disputes. Such mediation was referred to as civil affairs mediation (*min cheng t'iao chieh*).

In some counties, civil affairs units are in charge of the mechanics of elections, and in County X the section may have had this responsibility too. Also, in some counties civil affairs units are said to be grouped with other agencies in the political and legal "system" and have additional duties, including that of handling all changes in administrative boundaries. In County X, however, this was reportedly not the case; instead the County Party Committee and People's Council directly handled these matters.

Labor Bureau

The Labor Bureau (*lao tung chü*) was another small organization which was directly supervised by the People's Council and had only limited functions. Its staff consisted of a chief (*chü chang*), and three section members (*k'o yüan*), and its principal responsibility was to help unemployed persons and unplaced school graduates find jobs. Actually, in most periods, there were not a large number of unemployed laborers in the county, so the bureau's work load was not heavy. Nor were there many unplaced school graduates. Most graduates were assigned to definite jobs by the Party and government. Both the Propaganda and Education Department and the Education Bureau participated in the determination of their assignments. However, the bureau attempted to keep itself informed about the needs for laborers or school graduates of all organizations in the county, and it assigned unemployed persons to them as feasible.

Neither labor reform nor voluntary labor came under the Labor

Bureau's jurisdiction. The former was handled by the Public Security Bureau, and the latter by Party organizations.[56]

Market Management Committee

The other county government organization that was not grouped in a formal sense with any of the major functional "systems" in County X was the Market Management Committee (*shih ch'ang kuan li wei yüan hui*, or *shih kuan hui*, for short). This committee had been established to control and supervise the few free markets that were permitted to operate in the county, especially in the county seat. (Similar committees in the communes exercised control over rural free markets.) Operationally, though, the committee coordinated its work closely with both the Bureau of Commerce and the Bureau of Public Security.

The committee's staff of four—a head (*chu jen*) and three other cadres (including a public security cadre)—spent most of their time visiting and directly checking on the operation of the free markets. In particular they were responsible for suppressing black markets and seeing that persons who offered goods for sale in the permitted markets had already fulfilled their obligations for compulsory sales to state agencies under the "planned purchase and planned supply" system. They also regulated the location of markets, the assignment of stalls, the weighing of goods, and so on. In some areas, such committees were responsible for collecting certain types of commercial taxes on transaction at the free markets, but reportedly this was not the case in County X. Local public security substations assisted the committee's personnel in performing its tasks.

[56] On a national level, the Labor Ministry has, at least in some periods, been grouped with ministries in broad fields of industry and communication, and in particular with those in the field of light industry. This may also be the case at the county level in some areas, although apparently not in County X.

Political Control:
The Political and Legal "System"

One of the most important functions of government in any totalitarian system is political control. No matter how much emphasis is placed upon persuasive instruments of rule—and in Communist China mass persuasion has been stressed perhaps more than in any other modern totalitarian society—effective coercive methods of control are necessary, in the final analysis, not only to provide the ultimate guarantee of the ruling elite's position and power against all potential threats, but also to provide essential underpinnings for even the routine operation of the system. Without an effective apparatus of political control, the Party leaders would find it difficult, if not impossible, to carry out their broad policies of social reconstruction, revolution, and forced-draft economic development, and one can argue that their intensive efforts at mass persuasion would have more limited success without the backing of effective methods of political control.

The Chinese Communists themselves frankly recognize the prime importance of what they refer to as the "instruments of state power," including not only the regular army but also the public security apparatus, the Procuracy, and the courts. Actually, in Communist China the army generally stays in the background, in reserve against any possible danger of open, violent opposition to the regime. Primary responsibility for the day-to-day maintenance of the system of political control, as it affects the mass of the population, rests principally with those civilian agencies which belong to the political and legal "system," namely, the public security organs, the Procuracy, and the courts.

As has been noted already (see above, p. 196), the entire political and legal system in County X was controlled from 1959 onward by the Party Fraction of five men—a deputy Party secretary, the chiefs of the three agencies involved, and a deputy chief of public security —who together acted concurrently as the Party's Political and Legal Department and the government's Political and Legal Staff Office. In reality public security personnel dominated the system and had a special relationship with the County Party Committee and a unique status in the county government.

In County X the chief of the Public Security Bureau was generally considered to have a status roughly equal to that of the county magistrate, and he clearly outranked all other bureau chiefs. Moreover, the bureau's most important lines of responsibility went, via the Political and Legal Department, to the Party Committee, rather than to the County People's Council. This was highlighted by the fact that although certain of its major reports were sent to both the magistrate and the Party Committee, others went only to the latter. Since most of its reports were highly classified, furthermore, some of those going to the magistrate were reserved for his eyes only and bypassed the normal reporting channel, which went through the Staff Office of the People's Council and the secretary-general.

The Public Security Bureau's special relationship with the Party was also underlined by the fact that it was the only organ in the county government other than the small Personnel Section whose entire staff of administrative cadres consisted of Party or YCL members or candidate members. As a result of these facts, the bureau was regarded by many people as an institution which was basically a Party organ operating within the government bureaucracy, similar in this respect to the Personnel Section. Or, in other words, even though it was a government bureau, it was viewed as the Party's main instrument for enforcing political control over the population as a whole. As already indicated, the importance of the public security system steadily increased in the late 1950s, especially after the 1956–1958 period of the "hundred flowers" and antirightist campaigns. By the early 1960s, with fifty-one administrative cadres in its office at the county seat, it was one of the largest bureaus in the county.

Vertical lines of responsibility appeared to be of greater importance, in some respects, for the Public Security Bureau than for other bureaus. Instructions from higher-level public security agencies were of overriding importance, and on occasion the county bureau could even bypass the County Party Committee by appealing to superior public security agencies at the special district or provincial level. To cite one example, a decision made by the County Party Committee to transfer a particular cadre out of the bureau was canceled after the bureau appealed to the Special District Public Security Office, which in turn induced the Special District Party Committee to send instructions to the County Party Committee to let the man stay in the bureau.

Public Security Bureau

In County X, there was a total of 147 state cadres on the Public Security Bureau's table of organization. Of these, fifty-one were non-uniformed administrative cadres working in the bureau; forty-nine were uniformed policemen (Census People's Police, *hu chi min ching;* and Seacoast People's Police, *yen hai min ching*) working in public security substations (*p'ai ch'u so*) or as special agents (*t'e p'ai yüan*) in the communes; and forty-seven were semimilitary armed policemen in the People's Police Forces (*wu chuang ching ch'a* or *min ching tui*). While all 147 were classified as state cadres, the first two categories, totaling one hundred, were regarded as comparable to other administrative cadres, while those in the third category were considered in some respects to have a special status, more like that of army men than administrative cadres.[57]

The Public Security Bureau was headed by a chief and two deputies. One deputy supervised political security (*cheng pao*) and organizational security (*chi pao*); the other, social order (*chih an*) work, preliminary examination of cases (*yü shen*), and the County Detention Center (*k'an shou so*).

Because of its size, the bureau had its own staff office, with seven employees: a staff secretary (*mi shu*); a deputy (*fu mi shu*); one typist (*ta tzu* or *wen yin*); a cadre who acted both as manager of archives or files and as the person responsible for sending and receiving materials (*tang an kuan li yüan*, or *tang an kuan li*, for short, and *shou fa*); two staff secretaries (*mi shu kan shih*), who did some special investigating as well as general statistical work; and one general affairs cadre (*shih wu*).

The Staff Office of the Public Security Bureau drafted most of the

[57] In addition to the above-mentioned policemen, there was a substantial number of secret agents (*t'e ch'ing yüan*) in rural local areas who were not actually on the bureau's payroll even though they reported to it.

important reports on the bureau's work. It also handled all incoming and outgoing correspondence for the bureau. Because of its size and importance, it was considered to be an independent unit authorized to issue its own announcements and reports. In addition, it provided typing and mimeographing services for all sections, kept detailed over-all statistics, and maintained archives, files, and personnel dossiers on the "five [bad] elements" (*wu lei fen tzu;* see below, p. 231, for a discussion of this term). The personnel dossiers maintained by this office on the "five [bad] elements" included only those on people who were currently undergoing labor reform or other punishment at the county level.

The staff office was also responsible for all "housekeeping" and routine administrative matters, including disbursement of salaries, maintenance of property, and management of the bureau's mess hall and dormitory space. The mess hall and dormitory space were located in the bureau's headquarters building. Sleeping quarters were upstairs in the building, and every section of the bureau had assigned space; section chiefs generally had single rooms while others slept three to a room.

Apart from the staff office, the bureau consisted of another office (*shih*), four sections (*k'o*), and the Detention Center (*k'an shou so*). The Aide's Office (*hsieh li shih*), which had a staff of only two—an aide (*hsieh li yüan*) and one other staff member (*kan shih*)—was responsible for personnel management, including maintenance of dossiers on all public security cadres, supervision of cadres' political study, control over the distribution of weapons, and cadre welfare work.

The Political Security Section (*cheng chih pao wei k'o,* or *cheng pao k'o,* for short), had a staff of ten: a chief (*k'o chang*), a deputy (*fu k'o chang*), one internal clerk (*nei ch'in*), and seven other section members (*k'o yüan*). This section supervised sensitive political security work throughout the county. One of its most important responsibilities was counterintelligence against actual or potential enemy agents; secret agents (*t'e ch'ing yüan*) scattered throughout the county reported to the section. It was also responsible for the security aspects of control over and investigation of overseas Chinese, who were the target of continuous special attention by the bureau because of their foreign travel and contacts. The bulk of the work done by the staff of this section was investigatory. Every "incident" with any conceivable sort of political implication was thoroughly investigated; sometimes investigations of particular cases took one to two years.

The Organizational Security Section (*chi kuan pao wei k'o*, or *chi pao k'o*, for short), was likewise an investigating unit, but it focused its attention on personnel in government agencies, mass organizations, factories, schools, and the like. It, too, investigated any suspicious individuals or incidents. In addition it conducted routine security checks on all army recruits, as well as on students being considered for assignment to certain educational institutions and training classes. This section had a staff of four: a chief, an internal secretary, and two section members.

The Social Order Section (*she hui chih an k'o*, or *chih an k'o*, for short) was the largest unit in the bureau and had broad and varied responsibilities. Its total staff numbered eighteen persons: a chief, three deputies, two internal secretaries, two cadres for investigating criminal cases (*hsing shih chen ch'a yüan*), one management cadre in charge of entry and exit permits for overseas Chinese (*hua ch'iao ch'u ju kuan li kan pu*), two technical specialists (*chi shu jen yüan*), and seven other section members. Of the three deputies, one was especially concerned with overseas Chinese and "internal work" (*nei ch'in*) within the section; another with criminal (*hsing shih*) cases; and the third with transportation, factory protection (*pao wei*), and "social order" in general. The two specialists were experts in detection techniques, including fingerprinting and handwriting analysis.

Among the varied responsibilities of the social order section as a whole were the maintenance of ordinary law and order, investigation of criminal cases, census registration (*hu k'ou tiao ch'a*) of the population, traffic management (*chiao t'ung kuan li*), fire extinguishing (*mien huo*), registration and control of Chinese traveling overseas, control of the "five [bad] elements," and management of labor reform (*lao tung kai tsao*) and labor reeducation (*lao tung chiao yang*).

The Section for Preliminary Examination of Cases (*yü pei shen p'an k'o* or *yü shen k'o*, for short) had a staff of four: the chief, a deputy, and two other section members. This section worked closely with the Procuracy, in the preparation of indictments, and so on, particularly after formal arrests had been made but before the cases came to court. It was also responsible for managing political education programs for persons undergoing labor reform.

The bureau's Detention Center (*k'an shou so*) was located next to the People's Court and had over twenty rooms, with separate quarters for political criminals (*cheng chih fan*), ordinary criminals (*hsing shih fan*), and persons detained—without court action—for the purposes of social order (*chih an chü liu fan*). Its permanent staff consisted of only three men: the head (*so chang*) and two "management cadres" (*kuan li kan pu*). Actual guard duty was done by units of the People's Armed Police (*min ching tui*).

The only other employees at the bureau's headquarters who were not uniformed policemen were four general service men: two messengers (*t'ung hsün yüan*) and two cooks (*ch'ui shih yüan*).

Policemen

A total of ninety-six uniformed policemen worked for the Public Security Bureau, and, as already stated, they belonged to two different categories. Forty-nine of them were classified either as Census People's Police (*hu chi min ching*) or Seacoast People's Police (*yen hai min ching*) assigned to public security substations (*p'ai ch'u so*), or as special agents (*t'e pai yüan*) assigned to the communes. There were two Census Police public security substations in the county, one at the county seat and another in a market town; each had a staff of fourteen policemen: a head (*so chang*), a deputy (*fu so chang*), one internal affairs man (*nei ch'in*), and eleven other people's policemen (*min ching*). A third substation was a special Seacoast Police Public Security Substation which had ten men: a head, a deputy, one internal affairs man, and seven other people's policemen. The eleven other people's policemen were assigned to work in the communes as special agents.

The forty-seven other armed and uniformed men working for the Public Security Bureau were called Armed Forces Police (*wu chuang ching ch'a*) and were organized into the county-wide People's Police Group (*min ching tui*).⁵⁸ This group had eight men in its headquarters: a chief (*tui chang*); a deputy (*fu tui chang*); a political instructor (*cheng chih chih tao yüan*); a clerical secretary (*wen shu*); a cultural instructor (*wen hua chiao yüan,* or *wen chiao,* for short); a health cadre (*wei sheng yüan*); a general affairs supply cadre (*kung chi yüan,* similar to a *shih wu*); and one other cadre. Under this headquarters, the thirty-nine other men were divided into three units, called people's police small groups or teams (*min ching hsiao tui*), each consisting of thirteen men headed by a group chief (*tui chang*). These three units could be used anywhere in the county, as needed—if, for example, disorders or tense situations arose—but in normal times their routine duties, which were rotated among the three groups, included (1) running the county's reform-through-labor unit or team and labor reform farms (*lao kai tui* and *lao kai ch'ang*); (2) guarding the County Detention Center; and (3) acting as a central mobile unit (*chi tung hsiao tui*), which was used to guard important cadres and visitors and was available for special use as needed.

The total number of armed, uniformed men under the Public Security Bureau—less than one hundred—was certainly not remarkably large for an area with close to half a million population. Apparently, however, it was adequate. The number of cases and incidents, whether criminal or political, which required action by armed police units was reportedly not very large. This has traditionally been the case in China, except in periods of general disorder and breakdown of authority; a relatively small number of policemen has ordinarily been sufficient for maintenance of law and order under normal conditions. The effectiveness of the public security system in County X, moreover, did not by any means rest solely on these uniformed policemen. In the background were much more powerful forces; and the entire population realized that if there were any open defiance of the regime, the regular army could easily be called in. Apparently, however, during the period of more than a decade since the Communists fully consolidated power in this area, there had never been any occasion for the local security forces to request army help to maintain local law and order.

⁵⁸ The province had a people's police general group (*tsung tui*); and the special district, a large group (*ta tui*).

In operation, the public security system was primarily preventative and was remarkably effective in deterring and suppressing potential dissidence before it reached a serious stage. Part of the explanation for this was the fact that in every organizational unit at the local level there were public security personnel or units which kept the entire population under close continuing surveillance and reported regularly to the County Public Security Bureau, enabling it to take prompt action against any potential threats to the regime's firm, effective control. In fact, the public security apparatus permeated society to such an extent that the entire population of the county lived in an atmosphere of pervasive surveillance and control.

Surveillance at the local level did not depend, of course, solely on specialized public security personnel. The Party apparatus as a whole also performed this function. But in every locality there were local cadres with specialized public security functions, all of whom reported to the County Public Security Bureau. In each commune there was a political and legal department in charge of security, and in every brigade there was either a security committee (*chih an pao wei wei yüan hui*, or *chih pao*, for short) or, at the minimum, a single security committeeman. And working under or in close collaboration with all these local cadres dealing with security problems were the local militia units.

As has been mentioned, there were also public security secret agents (*t'e ching yüan*) scattered throughout the county, perhaps two hundred to three hundred in all, who reported directly to the Public Security Bureau. These agents, who were generally not publicly labeled as such, were specially responsible for continuous surveillance of the "five [bad] elements"; and some of them operated under the guise of actually belonging to the "five [bad] elements" themselves.

The public security apparatus also included special personnel— most of whom were simply called security officers (*pao wei yüan*)— working within the county's major factories and in certain county-level government and Party organs. In County X these security men were located in thirteen government bodies, factories, and companies that were considered to be particularly important for a variety of reasons. These units were the government's Personnel Section, Education Bureau, New China Bookstore, Postal and Telecommunications Bureau, Commerce Bureau, Finance and Tax Bureau, People's Bank, Water Conservancy Bureau, Navigation Management Station, electric plant, machinery repair and assembly factory, Construction Company, and Lumber Company. Interestingly, there was also a special security man in the Party's Organization Department. All these men reported regularly to the Public Security Bureau; and on occasion they were brought in to participate in some of the bureau's meetings.

Characteristics of Public Security Personnel

Of the 147 state cadres on the Public Security Bureau's own payroll, more than sixty were Party members; these included all the administrative cadres, the key unit chiefs of the uniformed police groups, and a few others. Most of the remainder were YCL members. The bureau's employees were predominantly young; the average age of the entire group was estimated to be in the mid-twenties. The majority of the cadres were unmarried and lived in the bureau's dormitory accommodations.[59] These cadres had been drawn from several sources. A large percentage of the administrative cadres had previously been officials of Party or YCL branches. Some, however, were transferred army men. A few had worked their way up from the ordinary People's Police. Some, also, had had special training in higher public security schools. A large percentage of the People's Police either were demobilized servicemen (these included all unit chiefs) or had been active in local militia units.

The chances for promotion to desirable posts were relatively good for most public security personnel. Some even moved on to jobs in county Party departments; and a few were promoted to jobs at the special district level and above.

[59] To marry, a public security cadre had to be investigated and have his proposed marriage approved by the bureau, as well as by his Party branch.

Weapons Control

The Public Security Bureau had over-all responsibility for weapons control throughout the county. Soon after Communist takeover in 1949, the regime registered and collected all firearms that had been in private hands. Thereafter, strict control was maintained over the distribution and use of all weapons; unauthorized possession of any firearms was an extremely serious offense. Apart from weapons allocated to militia units, however, possession of firearms was authorized for quite a few cadres in County X. All county public security personnel, including the administrative cadres, were authorized to carry firearms, normally pistols. Almost all "bureau-level" cadres in the county apparatus—except for certain ones in commercial work —and all cadres in the Procuracy and the Military Service Bureau, were also authorized to carry pistols when necessary, although they generally did not do so except on special occasions, or when they traveled in the countryside at night. In the communes, Party secretaries, commune chiefs, and the chiefs of political and legal departments and armed forces departments (*wu chuang pu*) were permitted to carry weapons when necessary, as were the secretaries of all Party branches in seacoast areas.

Use of Violence

The actual use of physical violence by public security personnel in dealing with the population had declined since the days just after Communist takeover. During the early land-reform period, public executions by public security personnel were numerous, generally following kangaroo trials conducted by *ad hoc* people's tribunals, which were closely directed by security personnel. The regime at that time insisted on violent class warfare in every village to destroy the prestige and power of the old leaders of state and society. In this area, it was said to have been a matter of policy to choose at least one landlord, and usually several, in virtually every village, for public execution. In one of the two counties that were ultimately merged to form County X, over four hundred persons were reportedly killed at that time. In the entire area comprising County X, an estimated 80 percent of the old chiefs of administrative villages (*hsiang chang*), 10 to 20 percent of the *Pao* chiefs, and over 20 percent of all landlords, were said to have been killed, mostly in the period of land reform. There was apparently some, and perhaps considerable, popular peasant support at the time for a violent policy, in many although not all villages, as passions were aroused and the masses were encouraged to vent their feelings against the old elite for both real and imagined grievances. Whatever the popular reactions to the violence may have been, there is no doubt, in any case, that the killings had a lasting imprint on the attitudes of everyone, including the ordinary peasants; it impressed upon them the power of the new regime and its capacity to use arbitrary and extreme violence, if and when it wished, against all persons classified as enemies of the state.

Methods of Political Control

From about 1956 onward, despite the increasing influence and expanded activities of public security agencies, the use of violence reportedly was consciously minimized, and other methods of political control were increasingly emphasized. This was done after 1958 under the slogan "reduce arrests and killings and increase [political] control" (*shao pu shao sha to kuan*).

By this time, the Party and public security agencies had developed a wide range of nonviolent methods of political control over dissident elements. One of the most severe of these was "reform through labor" (*lao tung kai tsao*, or *lao kai*, for short). In County X, as throughout China, this was a penal sentence,[60] and therefore had to be meted out by the County People's Court. It involved unpaid, forced labor which could last anywhere from a few months to several years, or, in actual practice, for an indefinite period. Generally, most of those sentenced to relatively long periods of labor reform were sent to labor reform institutions outside the county, run by organiza-

---

[60] Officially, all penal sentences in Communist China are, in one sense, considered to be "reform through labor," but in rural areas this generally involves assignment to a penal "farm," which may or may not be the case for people in urban areas.

tions at higher levels, while those sentenced to serve a year or less were kept within the county.

The County Bureau of Public Security organized all those serving labor reform sentences within the county into labor reform teams or groups (*lao kai tui*) and assigned them to work on two labor reform farms (*lao kai ch'ang*), which the bureau itself ran; one was near the county seat and one in the mountains not far away. Generally, there were at least thirty to forty, or more, persons working on these two farms—at certain periods there had been many more—under the eye of one of the three units of the bureau's People's Armed Police.

Labor reeducation (*lao tung chiao yang*) was another form of punitive political control, but it was considered to be less serious and could be meted out administratively, without formal court action. Party and government organs themselves decided which errant cadres and others would be sent for labor reeducation, but public security organs supervised those so punished. Although those sent for labor reeducation were supposed to be sent for definite periods (which could be adjusted for good behavior), in practice those undergoing labor reeducation in 1962 were assigned for indefinite periods.[61] (Quite a few cadres were sent to provincial-level "farms.") Release was dependent upon evidence of ideological reform, which ostensibly was the main objective of labor reeducation. In practice it generally involved shorter periods than labor reform; cadres punished in this fashion remained on the tables of organization of their basic units and continued to receive their regular salaries—a fact which was very important to those involved.[62]

There were several other forms of detention or special political control which were also handled administratively rather than juridically. Detention for social order (*chih an chü liu*) was a form of punishment under which, in County X, a person could be placed under security detention for up to fifteen days, or thirty days if pun-

[61] Later, because of objections about the length of labor reeducation, definite terms were instituted in practice.

[62] Some ex-cadres say that at least some cadres sent to take part in labor reeducation are actually fired from their jobs and do not receive salaries, while those sentenced to supervised labor (*chien tu lao tung*) do remain on their tables of organization and receive reduced salaries. The conflicting reports suggest that practices may vary.

ished simultaneously for two offenses. Commune authorities could recommend this form of punishment, but the County Public Security Bureau's Social Order Section had to approve. Under "administrative detention" (*hsing cheng chü liu*), any person could be arrested on suspicion for up to twenty-four hours. The twenty-four–hour limit actually had little meaning in practice, however, because if the Public Security Bureau wished to hold a person for a longer period of time, it simply converted the person's arrest status to that of detention for social order.

Two other types of punishment involved forms of "control" which were lighter but involved longer periods. For example, a great many unreformed "five [bad] elements," including the most "serious" cases, involving persons who had not made any progress toward "changing class status," were placed under so-called political control (*cheng chih kuan chih*). A person so classified had to report regularly to his local public security unit (at one time he had to report weekly in County X, but this was later changed to fortnightly), and he could not leave his area of residence without special permission. Some people remained under political control for long periods, in fact indefinitely. However, others, on the recommendation of their commune leaders or other local authorities, were released from this status, or placed under so-called production control (*sheng ch'an kuan chih*), which was less severe. (Political control and production control were, in practice, very similar, but the former was more punitive because of its greater stigma and the more formal legal procedures involved.)

Control over the "Five [Bad] Elements"

Production control was a somewhat less severe form of supervision than political control and was imposed particularly on the "five [bad] elements," but also on some others, by public security agencies on the recommendation of either communes or brigades. Frequently, such control was imposed for a period of a year or so.

Continuing surveillance and control of all persons labeled as "five [bad] elements" (*wu lei fen tzu*) was one of the major responsibilities of public security personnel. The continued maintenance, seventeen years after Communist takeover, of a special status for these politically ostracized persons, labeled enemies of the regime, is perhaps one of the most remarkable features of the Chinese Communists' social and political control at the village level. As used by the Chinese Communists, the term "five [bad] elements" includes landlords, rich peasants, counterrevolutionaries, rightists, and other less well-defined "bad elements" (mainly habitual petty criminals)—or rather all those whose background puts them in any one of these categories (obviously there have not been any actual landlords since collectivization) and who have not been able, as a few have, to "change their class status." Being classified as a member of any of these groups has very serious implications and consequences. All persons labeled as "five [bad] elements," for example, are denied the political rights of citizens, including the right to vote or hold public office. They must, if they live in rural areas, participate in agricultural work as ordinary members of production teams, but they cannot vote or hold office in them or in other commune units.

In County X the names of all persons who were labeled as members of the "five [bad] elements" were posted in the brigades' offices, and a special dossier on each was kept by public security personnel at the commune level (this practice was said to have been started in 1958 in this area). The dossiers were sent to the county public security bureaus if the persons involved were sentenced to labor reform or other stricter forms of control. All members of the "five [bad] elements" were kept under either political control or production control and had to report (*hui pao*) regularly to local public security personnel. In addition, three or more local people were often designated to keep a check on each member of the "five [bad] elements." These measures not only isolated and made possible close continuing surveillance of all members of the "five [bad] elements"; they also pin-pointed these persons as actual or potential subversives, and in addition made them symbols of the disastrous consequences of being classed as enemies of the regime. As political pariahs, these unfortunates also provided a ready target for abuse whenever the regime wished to intensify the atmosphere of class warfare, as it has at frequent intervals over the years.

As of 1962, in County X, more than two thousand persons were included in the "five [bad] elements." Of these, over seven hundred were ex-landlords, over six hundred were former rich peasants, three to four hundred were ex-counterrevolutionaries, and two to three hundred were miscellaneous "bad elements." Only a negligible number of persons were labeled as rightists in County X, as in most rural areas. The total number of "bad elements" in County X was under 1 percent of the total population. This was less than in some other nearby areas, where as many as 3 percent or more of the population were reportedly placed in this general category.

In theory, any members of the "five [bad] elements," after a fairly long period of good behavior, during which they had convincingly demonstrated a change of class outlook, could request the Party and public security authorities formally to redefine their class status (*kai pien chieh chi ch'eng fen*). In actuality, however, the total number of persons bearing this label had not dramatically declined over the years in County X. Although periodically a few had been "uncapped" (*chai tiao mao tzu*), to use the accepted term for a formal change of status, there were others who were periodically "capped" (*tai mao tzu*). Nevertheless, a few had been able to change their status; twice every year, in fact, the County Public Security Bureau's Social Order Section carried out a county-wide movement (*p'ing hsing yün tung*) during which at least a few people were able to change their class status.

Control over Population Movement

Control over all population movement in the county was another routine function of the Public Security Bureau. While in County X there was no requirement that all ordinary people carry regular identity cards (*shen fen cheng*), as has sometimes been the case in China, and while most people—except for those who were labeled as "five [bad] elements" or were condemned to some sort of political control—could travel within the county without special public security permission, public security personnel nevertheless kept a close watch on all travel. Moreover, all travel outside the county did require special permission from them. Every person permanently moving his residence to some other place had to obtain a special moving certificate (*ch'ien yi cheng*), and anyone going on a visit out of the county had to obtain a travel certificate (*cheng ming*) from public security personnel—from commune-level personnel if the individual were merely going to a nearby county, but from the County Public Security Bureau if he were going out of the province. Furthermore, all outsiders visiting the county had to report to, or be reported to, the bureau or a substation or local public security personnel; this procedure also applied, of course, to persons from County X when they were making visits elsewhere. Possession of a radio also required a special certificate.

"Social Surveys"

The Public Security Bureau was also responsible for conducting periodic social surveys (*she hui tiao ch'a*)—especially during important campaigns—which were designed to determine public attitudes on the regime's current policies. Sometimes in carrying out these surveys the bureau itself sent personnel to conduct special investigations, but to a large extent it relied on reports sent in by local public security personnel, including security committees or committeemen, and by its secret agents in the countryside. In making their reports, local security people usually relied heavily on trusted activists in their area to help assess prevalent attitudes. Invariably they paid special attention to the "five [bad] elements," to try to determine whether there were any ominous signs that they were actively opposing current policies or attempting to stir up trouble. Whenever the bureau conducted a special survey of this sort, it submitted a detailed report to both the County Party Committee and the Provincial Public Security Department.

These public security social surveys were, of course, supplementary to the continuous regular reporting on local attitudes that went on through the Party's own channels. Even though it seems likely that the bureau's surveys could hardly avoid reflecting the bias of the policemen's outlook, at least to some extent, bureau personnel were urged to report the actual situation as they saw it, and apparently the bureau's leaders believed that they were able to obtain fairly accurate assessments of public attitudes. Their surveys did not always paint a uniformly favorable picture of public reactions to current Party policies. For example, when voluntary cooperatives were first promoted in County X, a social survey of this sort apparently indicated that while about 70 percent of the peasants in the county, including most poor and lower middle peasants, favored the formation of cooperatives, roughly 30 percent including most families with good land as well as those with relatively few members and therefore little labor power, tended to oppose them. A similar survey conducted when lower cooperatives were introduced on a wide scale indicated that 50 percent favored the cooperatives, 30 percent appeared to be neither strongly for nor strongly against them, 10 to 12 percent verbally approved but were judged to be really opposed, 8 percent were openly opposed, and 0.5 percent were suspected of planning sabotage. Still another survey conducted during the early phase of the movement to establish higher cooperatives reportedly indicated that, in very rough terms, only 30 percent or so of the peasants (in particular the poorest peasants) were really enthusiastic supporters of the movement at that time, while 20 percent were clearly opposed to it, and roughly 50 percent were reluctant to express their views.

The Public Security Bureau was also responsible for making regular semiannual reports on the population of the county (*jen k'ou t'ung chi*). These were rather simple census reports giving over-all population figures, plus a breakdown by age and sex. They were compiled on the basis of forms, sent in by the brigades in the countryside and the residents' committees in the county seat, which listed the name, age, and sex of every resident.

Public Security Reports

The social surveys and census reports were only a minor part of the regular reporting for which the Public Security Bureau was responsible. It had, in fact, one of the heaviest reporting schedules of any county-level organization. Among the regular reports which it had to submit to county Party authorities and other higher public security organs, for example, were sixteen different reports covering all aspects of the security situation in the county; most of these were sent monthly.

The staff office of the bureau made out a number of regular reports, among them the following: reports on any changes in class status of the "five [bad] elements" (*wu lei fen tzu pien hua pao kao*), reports on all arrests made in the county (*pu jen pao kao*), reports on all court sentences (*p'an hsing pao kao*), and reports on the activities of enemy agents (*t'e ch'ing pao kao*). The Political Security Section compiled the following: reports from public security secret agents (*t'e ch'ing an chüan pao kao*); monthly reports on enemy secret agents (*t'e yüeh pao kao*); reports on investigations of cadres (*kan pu shen ch'a pao kao*); and six different types of reports on "political cases" (*liu lei cheng chih an chien pao kao*), including reports of any evidence of reactionary propaganda activities (*fan tung piao yü pao kao*), organized riots (*tsu chih pao tung pao kao*), defectors (*hsia hai t'ou ti pao kao*), or sabotage of important military installations (*p'o huai chün kung yao ti ho chiao lien pao kao*), as well as reports on counterrevolutionary groups and organizations (*fan ko ming chi t'uan tsu chih pao kao*), and all political murders (*cheng chih mou sha an chien pao kao*). The Organization Security Section made out regular reports on incidents occurring in factories or bureaucratic organizations (*kung ch'ang ho chi kuan shih ku an chien pao kao*). The Social Order Section made out the following: reports on criminal cases (*hsing shih an chien pao kao*), reports on unnatural deaths (*fei cheng ch'ang szu wang pao kao*), reports on social conditions (*she ch'ing pao kao*), reports on arrivals and departures from the county of overseas Chinese (*hua ch'iao ch'u ju kuo pao kao*), and reports on "social order detentions" (*chih an chü liu pao kao*).

The fact that the bureau regularly prepared reports such as these did not mean that there were large numbers of cases in each category, however. In fact, during long periods there were no cases at all in certain of these categories. For example, there were almost no political murders (*cheng chih mou sha*); and reportedly only one or two nonpolitical killings took place in an average year (these were either *ch'iu sha*, planned killings or deliberate murder; or *hsiung sha*, accidental killings or manslaughter). According to ex-cadres from the region, up to 1962 there had been no cases of major organized riots in the county. There were generally said to be two or three cases involving enemy agents from abroad each year, and perhaps a similar number of special political investigations of cadres. From time to time there were a few defectors, but not many. All in all, apparently there were relatively few political cases in most of these categories, which was testimony to the effectiveness of the over-all system of political control, as well as to the lack of organized overt opposition to the regime.

The Public Security Bureau not only sent a large volume of reports to higher authorities but also received a large flow of instructions from above. Several classified journals played a supplementary role in briefing cadres throughout the public security system. Public security personnel in County X, for example, received regularly at least nine classified newspapers and journals issued by higher authorities, some by the central public security agencies and some by the provincial authorities. One of the journals issued by national authorities, classified as top secret (*chüeh mi*), was made available only to cadres of section-chief rank and above in the bureau; the others were reportedly classified as very secret (*chi mi*). One of the provincial publications, a newspaper, was said to have the widest circulation; the bureau carried sufficient subscriptions to supply one copy to every one or two cadres on its payroll. These publications provided an important continuous link with public security work elsewhere.

People's Procuracy

The political and legal "system" in County X included two other organizations subordinate to the Public Security Bureau. The People's Procuracy and People's Court in China were constitutionally independent government agencies with considerable power;[63] but in County X they were, in practice, clearly subordinate elements in the political and legal system and worked under the direct and close supervision of the Party and public security personnel, especially from the late 1950s onward. As stated earlier, the emergence of public security personnel into roles of increased influence at that time

[63] Whereas the People's Court had been established in 1949, the law establishing the Procuracy had not been promulgated until 1954 and in most places it went into operation in 1955.

was accompanied by many nationwide trends that could be described as antilegalistic. The ideas of codification and stabilization of law, for example, were indefinitely postponed, and the primacy of Party policy over law was reasserted and reemphasized in numerous ways.

The function of the Procuracy in County X, as elsewhere, was to investigate violations of law, to issue warrants for arrest, to prepare indictments, and to act as prosecutor for the state. In County X, it had a staff of eight cadres: a chief procurator (*chien ch'a yüan chang*); a deputy; a staff secretary (*mi shu*); an accountant (*k'uai chi*), who was also in charge of general affairs (*shih wu*) and acted as typist (*ta tzu*); and four ordinary staff members (*chien ch'a yüan*). It also had one messenger, in the general service personnel category. Most of the regular staff of eight were Party members. The top four, in fact, were all bureau-level cadres and therefore persons of some status. The routes which they had traveled prior to obtaining jobs in the Procuracy included service as section chiefs in other political and legal agencies, such as the Public Security Bureau, and training in the Provincial Political and Legal Cadres' School.

The Procuracy had been established in County X during 1954–1955, after promulgation of the 1954 constitution. Following the 1959 reorganization, which linked the Procuracy with the Court and Public Security Bureau under unified direction, the Procuracy was considered to be the Procuracy Section of the Political and Legal Department. The former head of the Procuracy became deputy chief of the Political and Legal Department; and the former deputy head became head of the new Procuracy Section. Otherwise, however, the organization remained essentially the same.

One of the major reasons for linking the Procuracy closely with public security was the difficulty previously encountered in coordinating the work of the two. Procedures had been cumbersome because it had been necessary for the Procuracy to give permission to the Section for the Preliminary Examination of Cases (*yü shen ko*) of the Public Security Bureau, which then issued the order to make an arrest; sometimes the Procuracy could not issue the warrant as fast as the Public Security Bureau desired. After reorganization, the procedures were better coordinated; the Procuracy Section was more responsive to public security demands and could issue warrants for arrests directly to the Social Order Section of the Public-Security Bureau, which then made the arrest.

After a person was arrested, the Procuracy Section investigated the suspect, who was held at the County Detention Center, in preparation for presenting formal charges to the Court. According to regulations, it had to make a decision within seventy-two hours after arrest, or the person had to be released. The Court ordinarily made no change in the charges brought by the Procuracy Section but did make a judgment on the severity of the punishment. Rejecting the accusations of the Procuracy might make court officials—though they would be technically within their rights—vulnerable to charges of being too soft on the accused, of being "rightists." Rarely did they acquit the accused.

Many of the cases handled by the Public Security Bureau were not channeled through the Procuracy, however. In handling misdemeanors or routine cases involving the "five [bad] elements," public security officials did not have to clear through the Procuracy and Court. Even political cases could be handled by the Political Security Section without clearing through the Procuracy. The Procuracy dealt only with cases where a person had committed or was suspected of having committed a specific crime, was officially arrested, and had his case formally presented to the Court for judgment. All cases of labor reeducation could be handled administratively by public security officials, but cases involving reform through labor had to be cleared through the Procuracy and the Court.

People's Court

The County People's Court, which had been established when the government was first organized after Communist takeover in 1949, had a staff larger than that of the Procuracy. Its employees totaled thirteen, of whom nine were Party members, three were YCL members, and one was a non-Party man. Included were the chief judge, or president, of the Court (*yüan chang*); a deputy; a staff secretary (*mi shu*); three cadres who acted as judges (*shen p'an yüan*); two court clerks (*shu chi yüan*);[64] four men who handled the organization and operation of people's tribunals (*fa t'ing yüan*); and one court policeman (*fa ching*), who also acted as court messenger.

The People's Court in the county seat met as needed, which was infrequently, to hear formal cases. For several reasons its case load was not excessively heavy. For one thing, a great many cases were handled, and many types of punishments were meted out, administratively rather than juridically, that is, by the Party and the Public Security Bureau, rather than by the Court. Secondly, probably an even greater number of disputes, especially civil disputes, were settled by mediation. Some mediation was done at the county level; the Civil Affairs Section's role in this has been mentioned already. But most of it was carried out at commune and brigade levels.

Traditionally, the Chinese have much preferred mediation to formal litigation, and the Communists have been influenced by this fact in developing their legal system. In many communes and brigades in County X there were well-organized mediation committees (*t'iao chieh wei yüan hui*). In some places, these had been combined with local security committees into groups called security and mediation committees (*chih an t'iao chieh wei yüan hui*). Even where no formal mediation committee existed, usually one or several persons at the commune and brigade levels—sometimes a public security man— was specifically designated to be responsible for mediation. The great majority of disputes at the local level, including family disputes (*chia t'ing chiu fen*), divorce disputes (*hun yin chiu fen*), property disputes (*ts'ai ch'an chiu fen*), and other conflicts or quarrels (*ta chia*), were settled by these mediators. Only the most serious cases, particularly criminal cases, were sent to the county Court.

In addition to holding sessions at the county seat, when necessary the Court also organized itinerant tribunals (*fa t'ing*), which held sessions at the commune level and handled both criminal (*hsing shih*) and civil (*min shih*) cases. Some cases brought before these tribunals were deliberately selected because it was felt that they would be good demonstrations to "educate" the masses.

While both secret arrests (*mi pu*) and secret trials (*mi mi hs'üan p'an*) took place in County X, all court decisions (*p'an chüeh*) and

[64] These court clerks sometimes participated in investigations, and in some minor cases might take part in disposition of the cases.

punishments in the county reportedly had to be publicly announced. Generally, people's assessors or jurors (*jen min p'ei shen yüan*) sat in and offered their opinions during the hearings; usually three or so were selected for each case by either the residents' committees in the county seat or by the Party branches in the brigades. They rarely played more than a figurehead role in criminal cases, however.

In a basic sense, though, the most important court hearings and decisions were ritual performances. Ordinarily, prior to the hearings, the five-man Political and Legal Department of the Party had already thoroughly discussed the cases involved and had reached a consensus on how they were to be handled.

Military Service Bureau

Together with the maintenance of political control and basic law and order, military conscription and the organization of local defense forces have long been among the basic responsibilities of government in China. Under the Communists these activities have been systematized and developed more than ever in the past.

The government agency in County X responsible for these func tions was the Military Service Bureau (*ping yi chü*), established in 1955. After military affairs and government administration in China were organizationally separated, a civilian organ within the government was necessary to handle the coordination of civilian and military affairs. One of the first tasks was the implementation of the Military Service Law, which introduced a nationwide system of conscription. Prior to 1955, recruits for the regular People's Liberation Army (PLA) had been, in theory at least, volunteers (*chih yüan ping*); but thereafter they were selected under the regularized, nationwide military service system; they were referred to, at least in County X, as compulsory service soldiers (*yi wu ping*). The distinction between these was not as clear-cut as it might seem. In practice, prior to 1955 "volunteers" were often first selected by Party cadres and then pressured to join the army, and even after 1955 volunteering played a role in the recruitment process. One of the most significant changes in 1955, however, was the fact that the obligation of military service was made universal—even though the actual choice of recruits continued to be highly selective—and the selection process was systematized.

In addition to handling conscription and supervising militia organization and training (see below), the Military Service Bureau had a skeletal organization prepared to give logistical support to the PLA in case of emergency. The bureau in County X had a staff of sixteen cadres. All were military officers who continued to wear uniforms even though they had been transferred to civilian posts and were now directly responsible to the county Party and government rather than to the PLA. They also continued to maintain close liaison with the PLA. Most had been assigned to the bureau by the Special District Military Subdistrict (*fen ch'u*). Many had originally served in guerrilla units. Thirteen of the sixteen were Party members, two were members of the YCL, and only one, an older man, belonged to neither the Party nor the YCL. As mentioned earlier, the thirteen Party members had their own Party branch.

The top men in the bureau were its chief (*chü chang*) and political commissar (*cheng chih wei yüan*, or *cheng wei*, for short). The rest of the staff was divided into four sections: the Staff Secretariat Section (*mi shu k'o*) responsible for logistical support, the Military Service Section (*ping yi k'o*), the Militia Section (*min ping k'o*), and the Military Training Section (*chün hsün k'o*). (The bureau also had one messenger, who was a former army man.)

Conscription

One of the Military Service Bureau's principal responsibilities was conscription, which was managed by the Military Service Section. Almost every year the Party and the bureau organized a "movement to join the army" (*ts'an chün yün tung*), when and as directed by higher authority. In preparation for this annual movement, the Provincial Party Committee and the military district authorities would first convene a meeting of military-service-bureau chiefs and political commissars from all counties, at which time quotas for conscriptees, based mainly on population, were assigned to each county. Then, on a schedule subsequently outlined by the Military Subdistrict, each county proceeded to organize the movement in its area.

In County X, this usually began with a meeting of cadres from the Military Service Bureau, the Party Organization Department, the Public Security Bureau, and other agencies to discuss how to organize the campaign. Then, the County Party Committee normally established an *ad hoc* military service work group (*ping yi kung tso tsu*) to manage it. Quotas of conscriptees were set by this work group for each commune, which in turn set quotas for every brigade. Although the major purpose of the campaign was to recruit soldiers, it was also a device to propagandize the good works of the PLA and to promote good relations between the army and the people.

All young men, upon becoming eligible for military service, were registered; but the number to be selected was always a very small percentage of those eligible, so the selection process involved careful screening of persons who "volunteered." The volunteering took place at the brigade level. Always the number who wished to enter the services far exceeded the quotas that had been set. In fact, according to ex-cadres, a very high percentage of young men between the ages of eighteen and twenty-one, who were most eligible, genuinely hoped to be selected, for several reasons. One reason was that living conditions in the army were relatively good. Another was that service in the army was regarded as an excellent means to obtain further education and training. And, perhaps most important, service in the military forces was felt to be a good way to get ahead, to advance one's status in society. At the end of their period of service (in the early 1960s it was still three, four, or five years, depending on the service, although subsequently it was raised to four, five, and six), those who had not become at least platoon leaders (*p'ai chang*) were discharged either as transferred army men (*chuan yeh chün jen*) or as demobilized army men (*fu yüan chün jen*). The former generally were assigned to posts as state cadres; and even the latter, when returned to their villages, usually became activists or local cadres and enjoyed more prestige and status than they could have expected without having undergone military service. A high proportion of soldiers were admitted to either the Party or the Young Communist League, and they kept their membership when they returned to civilian life as veterans.

Because of all these factors, the county authorities were able to be highly selective in choosing conscriptees from among the lists of potential recruits sent in by the communes.[65] Those chosen, in fact, were said to be among the brightest, most energetic youth in the county. Virtually all were literate. Students currently in school were not selected to be infantrymen; but they were eligible, and were sometimes selected, for service in the specialized branches such as the artillery, air force, and navy. A fairly high percentage of all those selected had already had experience in the YCL, or the militia, or both. If a young man was an only child, he was usually not accepted for any of the services, unless his parents approved. Married men could be accepted, but only if they had no children.

All potential recruits were given preliminary screening by the communes and were thoroughly investigated by public security personnel. Generally these investigations were carried out by personnel at the commune level, but the county bureau participated in the investigation of some persons being considered for the specialized services. Particular attention in these investigations was given to the class background (*chia t'ing ch'u shen*), political history (*cheng chih li shih*), and social relations (*she hui kuan hsi*) of potential recruits, and only those who had desirable backgrounds and were considered to be thoroughly reliable in a political sense were seriously considered. The final choice of those to be conscripted was made by Party officials within the Military Service Bureau. Those selected were then given thorough physical examinations by military personnel sent by the PLA authorities.

The number of recruits conscripted annually was fairly small. In former years it had been larger, but by the early 1960s, reportedly only about two hundred men were selected each year in County X. There is little doubt that, because of the high degree of selectivity involved, the general quality of recruits for the military services was much higher than in the past in China.

Militia Forces

The development and organization of militia forces throughout County X was also the responsibility of the Military Service Bureau,

[65] There is some basis for estimating that perhaps only 8 to 10 percent of those who volunteer are finally accepted.

and specifically of the bureau's Militia Section. Three of the bureau's cadres spent most of their time working to develop the militia, visiting rural areas and supervising militia activities in the communes and brigades.

Militia units were first organized in this area in the period immediately after Communist takeover, and they had existed continuously thereafter. But the stress placed upon the importance of the militia varied over the years. After a period of relative neglect in the mid-1950s, Peking greatly stepped up its efforts to expand and strengthen local militia forces in 1958, during the period of the Great Leap Forward. Proclaiming the slogan of "everyone a soldier" (*ch'uan min chieh ping*), it frankly promoted a policy of militarizing (*chün shih hua*) society, in conjunction with the communization drive then under way. The motives behind this policy were obviously complex and varied. Perhaps most important, the militia forces were regarded as an important mechanism for improving the organization and discipline of the work force and strengthening political control at the local level. However, the regime also believed the militia would improve local defense capabilities against possible external threats, at least in some areas, including this coastal region.

In County X, at the time of the 1958 militia drive, the over-all militia headquarters unit for the county was the Militia Regiment (*min ping t'uan*), whose commander (*t'uan chang*) was the magistrate, and whose political commissar (*cheng wei*) was one of the Party deputy secretaries. Under the leadership of this headquarters group, expansion of units in the communes and brigades was vigorously pushed. In the county seat, all state cadres were organized into either militia battalions (*ying*) or companies (*lien*), generally on the basis of units which belonged to one or more of the Party's "organization branches"; these were called "Organization Militia" (*chi kuan min ping*). More systematic training was introduced, and competitions to select the best militiamen and units were held to spur improved performance. At the height of this campaign, virtually all able-bodied men and women in County X who belonged to certain age groups (eighteen to forty-five for men, eighteen to forty for women) were enrolled in militia units.

However, by 1962 the campaign's momentum had greatly declined in this area, and the numbers of persons actually participating in militia activities had dropped significantly. The distinction between "Basic Militia" (*chi kan min ping*) and "Ordinary Militia" (*p'u t'ung min ping*) now became much more important. In reality only the Basic Militia units were effectively organized or active; the Ordinary Militia became little more than a roster of eligible persons (which, incidentally, excluded all members of the "five [bad] elements") in the proper age groups.[66] The Basic Militia was composed of able-bodied people, mostly men, aged eighteen to twenty-eight, who maintained at least minimal readiness for active duty, by annual rifle practice. At each level the Basic Militia served as an active nucleus around which the Ordinary Militia could be mobilized and trained if necessary.

The "Organization Militia" became essentially a latent structure, a kind of civil defense corps which could serve as a headquarters regiment for organizing the entire county in time of emergency. Except for the very small number of full-time staff members within the Military Service Bureau, virtually all posts in this headquarters regiment were filled by officials whose main work was in other Party and government posts. Their assignments in the militia, however, were generally at least related to the work they regularly performed in the government or Party, and they were expected to be ready to mobilize their units of the Headquarters Regiment in time of emergency. They were assigned to the following units:

1. The Staff Division (*ts'an mou ch'u*), also known as the War Bureau (*tso chan chü*), which was located in the Military Service Bureau and had general responsibility for planning militia activities, calling meetings, and organizing military training.

2. The Political Division (*cheng chih ch'u*), which was under the direction of the Organization Department of the County Party Committee. It concerned itself with militia organizational problems and assigned men to different units. In time of emergency, it would have responsibility for militia mobilization.

3. The Security Division (*pao wei ch'u*) was responsible for investigating personnel security problems and assigning weapons.

4. The Rear Services Division (*hou pu ch'u*), supervised by the

[66] During 1964–1965, as stated elsewhere, the aim of drawing the bulk of the population into active militia work was revived once again.

Finance and Trade Work Department of the County Party Committee, was the unit which would have responsibility for the issuing of food, clothing, medicine, and other supplies in time of emergency.

5. The Communications and Transport Division (*chiao t'ung ch'u*), supervised by the Industry and Communications Department of the County Party Committee, had responsibility for both land and sea transport.

As of 1962, it was estimated that there were somewhat over eight thousand members of Basic Militia units throughout County X. Each rural commune had an armed forces department (*wu chuang pu*), usually with two or three cadres, which was responsible for militia work. Only a command structure existed at the commune level, however; the actual operating units of the Basic Militia were in the brigades, each of which had one militia group (*min ping tui*). Frequently, the militia group chief (*min ping tui chang*) was also the head or deputy head of the brigade's Security Committee, while the Party branch secretary was political instructor or director (*cheng chih chih tao yüan*) of the militia group. The size of these brigade groups varied, but many had sixty to eighty active militiamen; generally four fifths or more of them were men. While men in the Basic Militia continued to take part in agricultural labor, they also received at least some simple military training. They were not assigned arms permanently, but were issued them when the authorities felt it necessary and desirable. In the county seat, state cadres continued to participate in "Organization Militia" units and, during part of the year, they had regular early-morning training.

In addition to the Basic and Ordinary Militia organization, the areas along the seacoast had a militia specialists' group (*min ping chuan yeh tui*). This group was assigned a special plot of land adjacent to the seacoast communes, in which it grew crops to support its members; these members also received a small stipend from the County Military Service Bureau but were nevertheless classified as ordinary citizens and did not wear military uniforms. If they were married, they left their wives in other parts of the county. They engaged in regular military training and maintained readiness to cope with either raids from Taiwan or local disturbances.

The Military Service Bureau had over-all responsibility for developing and assisting all these various militia units. Periodically, it convened special meetings to instruct or brief all militia cadres (*min ping kan pu*) from the communes and brigades. In addition, it assigned quite a few demobilized or transferred soldiers to act as part-time militia cadres to help in organizing and training the units. These cadres were often called military instructors (*chün shih chiao yüan*), particularly when they worked in the "Organization Militia" units in the county seat.

Despite the slackening of militia activities in the early 1960s, at least by comparison with the Great Leap period, the militia forces continued to play a significant role in County X. They were prepared to enforce political control when necessary and at all times helped to mobilize and discipline the work force. They also provided a useful reservoir of potential army recruits, as well as an important outlet for soldiers returning from military service. In a sense, furthermore, they contributed to some extent to the "militarization" of the population as a whole, by familiarizing an important section of the village-level population with military organization and techniques and subjecting almost the entire population to ideas of military discipline and control. In the early 1960s, however, the idea of drawing the bulk of the population into active militia work slipped temporarily into the background. (In 1964 it was revived when the regime again began to place increased stress on militia activities.)

The specific task of helping to train militia units throughout the county was the responsibility of the bureau's Military Training Section. For the most part it utilized demobilized soldiers for this purpose, but from time to time it also requested nearby PLA units to assign regular soldiers to serve as temporary militia instructors. At least once a year it held a three- to five-day meeting of all militia cadres from the communes and brigades to discuss training programs.

Understandably, demobilized soldiers played an important role in all militia activities throughout the county. As of 1959 roughly three thousand of them had returned to County X over the years. In some respects they were treated as a special group, and a definite effort was made to keep up their morale and stimulate them to be activists. At brigade and commune levels, meetings of demobilized soldiers were held annually, and at least once a year the Military Service Bureau, cooperating with the Party Organization Department, convened a county-wide discussion meeting or forum (*tso t'an hui*) of representatives of demobilized soldiers. At these meetings outstanding ex-soldiers were singled out for special praise.

Relations with the Regular Army

Although the County Military Service Bureau, as well as other key county organs, maintained liaison with the commanders of regular PLA troops stationed within County X, it had no control over them. The number of such troops varied considerably over time. Because this was a coastal defense area, the number was increased significantly in periods of international military tension. But normally, according to ex-cadres, only about one regiment (*t'uan*), with perhaps somewhat over one thousand men, was permanently stationed there.

The regular army troops in County X were isolated to a fairly high degree from the general population. From the mid-1950s on, they were billeted in barracks in the hills, rather than in the villages as they had previously been, and they grew most of their own vegetables, raised most of their own pigs, and avoided excessive contact with local civilians. Periodically, however, they were assigned to help in agricultural labor in nearby communes, or to take part in county-directed public works projects, partly to promote good relations with the civilian population. But apparently they did not impinge on civilian life to any great extent, as military forces often have in China in the past.

The local PLA commander and political commissar did maintain close liaison with certain key county leaders, most particularly with the secretary of the County Party Committee; and from time to time they were invited by the Party secretary to participate in important conferences called by the county committee. The Party had a separate organizational hierarchy within the military establishment, however; thus PLA personnel were not drawn into the regular "Party life" activities of county Party organizations.

Close liaison was also maintained between the PLA commanders and both the County Military Service Bureau and the Public Security Bureau. The latter, on occasion, requested the PLA to help solve certain local security problems. A rapid communications link between the military and public security authorities was provided by a special telephone line running from the county post office directly to the PLA's own military telephone system (*chün hsien*). Among county units, the Public Security Bureau was the main user of this line, although both the Party Committee and the Military Service Bureau were also authorized to use it, and sometimes did. All other county organizations were barred from using it. Adequate mechanisms existed, therefore, for liaison between the Party and government authorities in the county and the regular army units stationed there; but by and large they operated separately and independently, and military personnel stayed for the most part in the background.

United Front Work

United front work has always played an important role in the Chinese Communists' strategy of political action. While insisting that the Party's disciplined elite must provide leadership, they have relied heavily on united front tactics to mobilize and manipulate non-Party allies and to neutralize all other "middle forces" belonging to groups not classified as outright political enemies.

During their struggle for power, the Chinese Communists adopted as one of their most basic operational principles the proposition that political success required the building of a broad united front of non-Communists who were subject to Communist Party leadership and direction. The usefulness of united front policies did not end, as they saw it, with the achievement of political victory and the establishment of a Communist-controlled government, even though the importance of united front work did decline once power had been effectively consolidated. To pursue their revolutionary goals and implement their programs and policies, they still felt it necessary to use united front tactics to mobilize and manipulate—or, in their own phraseology, "to utilize, restrict, and reform"—a wide variety of non-Communist groups. For this purpose, they developed a number of special institutions, including government agencies and mass organizations as well as Party organs, to conduct united front work on a continuing basis.

As stated earlier, direction of united front activities in County X was in the hands of the County Party Committee's United Front Department. This department carried out much of its work, however, through a number of other organizations. Most of these were institutions which worked with one definable group in the population, and each was expected to develop programs aimed at mobilizing the talents and obtaining the cooperation of the people involved, or, to the extent that this was not possible, at controlling and manipulating them.

The People's Political Consultative Conference (PPCC) was one important arena for united front activity. As elsewhere in China, the PPCC in County X was composed of persons selected and appointed by the Communist Party. But, in contrast to similar bodies at higher levels, the PPCC in County X consisted largely of individuals without definite political affiliations. At higher levels of the government, the minor "democratic parties" (*min chu tang p'ai*) were permitted to maintain their own organizations under strict Party control; but in County X the Communist Party did not tolerate the existence of any other political parties.

Altogether there were between ten and twenty individuals in the county who did have, or had had, affiliations with one or another of the minor parties. Among them were persons connected with the Kuomintang Revolutionary Committee, the Democratic League, the September Third (*chiu san*) Society, and the Peasants' and Workers' Democratic Party. Most of these individuals were appointed as delegates to the PPCC, but as individuals rather than as representatives of any parties. No branches of the minor "democratic parties" were permitted in the county, nor were any organized party activities allowed. In short, there was no pretense at the county level of maintaining a multiparty united front base for a "coalition government," as was the case at the national level. The principal united front organizations in the county were Communist-directed mass organizations rather than minor parties.

Overseas Chinese Section and Association

Perhaps the most important united front activities in County X were those which focused on the overseas Chinese community (*hua ch'iao*). Although activities in this field were partly aimed at persons who actually lived abroad, mainly in southeast Asia, major attention was given to returned overseas Chinese (*kuei ch'iao*) and to the families and relatives of overseas Chinese (*ch'iao chüan* or *ch'iao shu*), residing in the county.

The Communists' special interest in the overseas Chinese and their relatives was traceable to a variety of factors. To begin with, they regarded all overseas Chinese as citizens of China, whom the regime should support and attract. They also regarded them as important in numerous ways in relation to China's foreign policy toward the areas where they lived. Moreover, all those with overseas connections were exposed to greater external influences than the mass of ordinary Chinese. As a result, many of them possessed special knowledge and skills considered to be useful by the regime. At the same time, many were viewed as carriers of potentially subversive "bourgeois" influences. Not least important, remittances sent by overseas Chinese to relatives in China were of great economic importance, not only to the coastal areas where most of their relatives lived, but also to the country as a whole because they provided essential foreign exchange.

In County X, over forty thousand persons, belonging to an estimated eight thousand households, were either returned overseas Chinese or relatives of Chinese still overseas; these groups made up close to 10 percent of the population. Many of these people were scattered in villages throughout the county, but some were concentrated in special areas. Over five hundred persons lived in an "overseas Chinese new village" (*hua ch'iao hsin ts'un*), which had been built in the late 1950s to accommodate Chinese returning at that time from southeast Asia, mainly from Indonesia. (Another overseas Chinese village was run by the special district; it was located on the boundary between County X and a neighboring county.)

Construction of this new village was only one of a number of special measures taken by the county authorities to provide assistance to families of overseas Chinese. Such families enjoyed a variety of special privileges and received preferential treatment in many ways. For example, special schools were established for their children (see p. 260); and some of the Party's programs were modified when applied to overseas Chinese. Since most of them also received remittances from abroad, their general standard of living was noticeably higher than that of most people in the county. At the same time, however, they were also subjected to closer surveillance by the Public Security Bureau as well as by united front organs, because of the regime's ambivalence and suspicion concerning them.

The county government agency primarily responsible for work among this group was the Overseas Chinese Affairs Section (*hua ch'iao shih wu k'o*, or *ch'iao wu k'o*, for short). Located in the same building as the Party's United Front Department, this independent section operated virtually as an arm of the Party apparatus. It had a staff of four: the section chief (*k'o chang*), who was a Party member; two non-Party section members (*k'o yüan*); and the chairman of the Overseas Chinese Association, who was a state cadre but was not a Party member. The section carried out various sorts of activities on a continuing basis. It helped returning overseas Chinese to find employment. It pressured the families of overseas Chinese to urge their relatives abroad to keep up, or increase, their remittances. And it regularly propagandized the members of the overseas Chinese community in an effort to obtain their general support for the regime and cooperation in implementing current policies.

As already stated, the county authorities were particularly concerned about keeping up the flow of remittances from overseas Chinese. When these dropped, the task of trying to stimulate a renewed flow generally became the top priority function of the Overseas Chinese Section. This was the case, for example, during 1958–1959, when, as a result of communization in China, the overseas Chinese greatly reduced their remittances to relatives at home, partly because they were uncertain as to whether their relatives could keep and use such funds and partly because, as the agricultural crisis developed in China after the Great Leap, they started sending food packages instead of money. Remittances to people in County X, which reportedly had totaled HK $700,000 in 1957 (remittances were calculated in Hong Kong dollars because they were channeled through banks in Hong Kong), dropped to an estimated HK $370,000 in 1958, and then to HK $280,000 in 1959. Alarmed by this trend, the Overseas Chinese Section, working with and through the local Overseas Chinese Association, and with the participation of public security personnel, convened a series of meetings of overseas Chinese families throughout the county to urge them to write to their relatives assuring them that remitted funds could be kept and used by those to whom they were sent. These meetings culminated in a large congress of overseas Chinese (*hua ch'iao tai piao ta hui*), attended by representatives from all brigades which contained relatives of overseas Chinese. Partly as a result of these measures, remittances to the county started to climb upward again in 1960, when they reportedly totaled HK $500,000 to HK $600,000.

Meetings such as those mentioned above, and many other activities of the Overseas Chinese Section, were, as already indicated, carried out in large part through the Overseas Chinese Association (*hua ch'iao lien ho hui*, or *ch'iao lien hui*, or *ch'iao lien*, for short), the mass organization established by the Communists to deal with this group. Headed by a chairman who, as stated earlier, was a state cadre and a staff member of the Overseas Chinese Section even though he was not a Party member, this association was loosely organized but nevertheless provided a very important link between Party and government organs and the entire overseas Chinese community in the county.

Association of Industry and Commerce, and Office for the Reform of Private Entrepreneurs

Another group that was a major target of united front work in County X was the business and merchant class; and in a pattern similar to that used for dealing with the overseas Chinese, the Party's United Front Department implemented the programs it directed at this group largely through one government agency and one mass organization.

The government organ dealing with businessmen in County X was the so-called Office for the Reform of Private Entrepreneurs (*szu jen kai tsao pan kung shih*, or *szu kai pan kung shih*, for short). Its main responsibility in the mid-1950s was to propagandize, indoctrinate, and organize private businessmen to prepare them for ultimate socialization. Testimony to the success of its efforts was provided in 1955–1956, when virtually all shops and other remaining private enterprises in County X, as elsewhere throughout most of China, were rapidly converted into either "joint state-private enterprises" (*kung szu ho ying ch'i yeh*) or "state enterprises" (*kuo ying ch'i yeh*), with no significant open opposition.

The Chinese Communists' policy of "utilizing, restricting, and reforming" businessmen—that is, gradually absorbing them into the socialized sector of the economy—has been a unique feature of the socialist revolution in China, as Chinese Communist leaders themselves have rightly pointed out. By moving gradually and taking over private enterprises step by step rather than suddenly, the regime was able to socialize industry with a minimum of violence or disruption. In County X, as in most of China, most shopkeepers, merchants, and other businessmen continued to work in their enterprises after socialization, but as state employees led by Party members who took over the key decision-making posts. Although a few of these former businessmen in County X ultimately became administrative state cadres, the number was not large; the majority of them were simply transformed into commercial cadres or salesmen (*ying yeh yüan*) working in subordinate positions. In the villages, most small shops became sales outlets (*men shih pu*) or agents (*tai hsiao tien*) for the government and were supervised by the state-controlled supply and marketing cooperatives. Although, over time, some former private entrepreneurs were gradually transferred to other employment, the great majority continued to work where they had worked before socialization.

The relative smoothness of this transformation, and the notable lack of significant open resistance, was due, in a basic sense, to the fact that by this time the business class had been so effectively impressed or intimidated by the regime's over-all policies and political controls, including its police controls, that they felt powerless even to try to resist implementation of the decision to liquidate private enterprise. The ease of the transformation was also due, however, to the groundwork that had been laid by the United Front Department working through the Office for the Reform of Private Entrepreneurs and the Association of Industry and Commerce.

With the virtual completion of socialization in 1955–1956, the main task of the Office for the Reform of Private Entrepreneurs was really ended. In time, similar offices were abolished in some other counties. In County X, however, it continued in existence at least until 1962, with a reduced staff of two cadres. After 1956 its main tasks were to help ex-businessmen adjust to and accept their new situation, and to continue programs of propaganda and indoctrination directed at them.

The Association of Industry and Commerce (*kung yeh shang yeh lien ho hui,* or *kung shang lien,* for short), the mass organization set up by the regime to assist in dealing with the business class, consisted, in County X, of over one hundred businessmen chosen by the United Front Department. Many of these men were considered to be progressives (*chin pu jen yüan*), or even activists (*chi chi fen tzu*), because of their willingness actively to support the Communists' policies and to play major roles in propagandizing and indoctrinating their fellow businessmen. Headed by a businessman, the association contained virtually no Party members or state cadres; but it was nevertheless closely and effectively controlled and directed by the Party's United Front Department and the Office for the Reform of Private Entrepreneurs. Following socialization, it, too, rapidly declined in importance, since its main task had been completed; but it was kept in existence because it still served as a useful mechanism to deal with problems relating to former businessmen.

Minorities, Religious Groups, Societies, and Clans

In many parts of China with significant ethnic minorities and special religious groups, these groups have been an important target of united front work. In County X, however, there were no significant minority or religious groups requiring special organizational or propaganda attention. The county contained a large group of Hakkas, who in some respects could certainly be regarded as an ethnic minority; but the authorities in County X did not treat them as a group to which the regime's distinctive "minorities policies" should be applied. Although there were various religious groups in the county, the Party apparently did not consider them important enough to justify establishing special mass organizations for them, such as those existing on the national level.

The most active Christian institution in the county was a Protestant church located in the county seat, near the Public Security Bureau, where it could easily be kept under close observation. The pastor, who was a member of the *PPCC*, and therefore was incorporated into the apparatus of the united front, held religious services on Sunday; but during the rest of the week he had a full-time job as a teacher in an overseas Chinese middle school. From Sunday through Saturday, the church building was used by the General Labor Union for its meetings and classes. At the Sunday morning church services average attendance was said to be slightly over fifty. Most of those attending were older people, and a majority were women. Apart from a few small children, almost no young people attended. The Party emphasized to local youth, apparently with considerable success, that active interest in religion was a dangerous sign of ideological backwardness, which obviously would harm one's prospects of getting ahead in society and could involve the risk of getting into serious trouble. Moreover, since the pastor was forbidden to proselytize, virtually no new conversions were being made.

Although Buddhism had traditionally played an important role in the folk culture of the area, it had never been tightly organized, and by the late 1950s what power it had possessed in County X had greatly declined. It still influenced people's attitudes toward life, but no active Buddhist organizations existed, or were allowed to exist, in the county. In the county seat and suburbs, it is true, a few temples were still maintained, and some older people visited them on traditional festival days, such as the fifteenth day of the eighth lunar month. Only a few temples had any resident monks, however; most were simply looked after by caretakers. A majority of temples in the county seat, and virtually all in the countryside, had been taken over by the regime and converted into granaries, warehouses, offices, or schools.

Prior to 1949, there had been a considerable number of religious "societies" (*shen kuan hui*) in County X, each with a special name and most with small temples of their own. While they had not been very active or important politically, they had played a significant role as social organizations. However, as early as the period of land reform, when much of their property was confiscated, the Communists began focusing propaganda attacks on them, labeling them "feudal organizations" (*feng chien tsu chih*) and pressuring people to dissolve them. Then and later, progressives and activists were instigated to destroy the religious symbols in the temples; and gradually the societies' membership declined. By the mid-1950s, they had all been closed down or taken over. Reportedly, most young people felt that these societies actually were not merely old-fashioned but also "feudal," and they therefore had no particular regrets about their demise. Though many older people who had belonged to the societies probably felt quite differently, it eventually became clear that it would be useless, and possibly dangerous, to try to preserve them in the face of the Party's strong opposition.

Almost all the clan temples (*szu t'ang*) in County X had also been disbanded in the early 1950s, apparently with similar feelings of regret on the part of conservative older people, and indifference on the part of youth. Most were converted into public buildings, a large number of them becoming production team granaries or warehouses. Generally, however, when the takeover occurred, people were permitted, if they wished, to remove their family plaques (*p'ai tzu*) from the clan temples and take them to their individual homes.

Mass Persuasion, Education, and a "New Culture"

One of the most striking characteristics of the Chinese Communist regime has been its great stress on the necessity of "remolding" the values, loyalties, attitudes, and patterns of behavior of the entire population—the need, in short, to carry out a fundamental ideological and cultural revolution. Perhaps more than any other modern totalitarian regime, it has given highest priority to programs of agitation, propaganda, indoctrination, education, and cultural "reform" designed to control and change the thinking not only of the leadership elite but also of the mass of the population. Mass persuasion, therefore, has been one of the principal functions of the entire Party and government apparatus of the regime.

In some respects, any attempt to draw a clear line of distinction between coercion and persuasion in the Chinese Communists' methods of rule is fruitless, because the two are inextricably intertwined.

On the one hand, the regime's methods of mass persuasion are in themselves important instruments of political control, while on the other, the effectiveness of these methods of persuasion rests to a considerable degree on the fact that they are backed by powerful and effective instruments of coercive control.

In many respects, therefore, the entire elite and Party apparatus in County X were engaged in the business of mass persuasion. However, special responsibility in this field rested with the Party's Propaganda and Education Department (*hsüan chiao pu*). As stated earlier, this department conducted a great deal of mass propaganda and agitation through the Party's own organizational channels. In addition, it led and directed all those county government agencies and mass organizations which were considered to belong to the culture and education field or "system" (*wen chiao hsi t'ung*).

The number of organizations that came under the department's supervision was very large. Included were the Education Bureau (*chiao yü chü*), the Office for the Elimination of Illiteracy (*sao mang pan kung shih*); the Association for the Dissemination of Science (*k'o hsüeh p'u chi hsieh shang hui yi*, or *k'o p'u hsieh hui*, for short), the Bureau of Culture (*wen hua chü*); the Cultural Hall and Library (*wen hua kuan* and *t'u shu kuan*); the Opera Troupe and Movie Team (*hsi t'uan* and *tien ying tui*); the Bureau of Health (*wei sheng chü*); the Physical Education and Sports Committee (*t'i yü yün tung wei yüan hui*, or *t'i wei hui*, for short); the New China Bookstore (*hsin hua shu tien*); and the County Broadcasting Station (*kuang po tien t'ai*).

Obviously, not all the activities of all these organs could accurately be labeled simply as propaganda or indoctrination in any narrow political sense. These agencies were concerned not only with propagandizing the population but also with raising its level of knowledge and skills. In a broad sense, of course, they were all involved in supporting the Party's efforts to carry out a fundamental ideological and cultural revolution.

Education Bureau and School System

The fairly rapid expansion and development of education was one of the most notable accomplishments of the Communist regime in County X. Whereas prior to 1949 there had been only one small middle school in the county, by 1962 there were twenty (eight state-run and twelve "people-operated" [*min pan ti*]); and the number of primary schools had also greatly increased.

Primary responsibility for administering and developing the educational system rested with the Education Bureau and the affiliated but independent Office for the Elimination of Illiteracy. The combined staffs of these two organizations consisted of twelve persons: the bureau chief (*chü chang*), his deputy (*fu chü chang*), a staff secretary (*mi shu*), and a special staff cadre (*chu pan kan shih*), plus eight other culture and education cadres (*wen chiao kan pu*), two of whom ran the office responsible for combating illiteracy. The bureau had over-all responsibility for supervising the largest single group of persons in the county who could be labeled state cadres, that is, well over one hundred administrators and teachers (*chiao chih yüan*) in the county's state-run middle schools and more than five hundred administrators and teachers in state-run primary schools throughout the county.

State-Operated Middle Schools

The most important educational institutions run by the bureau were the eight regular government middle schools in the county. Of these, only one was a higher middle school (*kao chi chung hsüeh*, or *kao chung*, for short), equivalent to senior high school. The other seven were lower middle schools, three of which were special schools for the children of overseas Chinese families.

The principal (*hsiao chang*) of the higher middle school, which was the top educational institution in the county and was located in the county seat, was a high-ranking Party man who had once been a deputy county magistrate. Under him were a staff of over seventy and a student body of over eight hundred. In running the school, the principal was assisted by a special Party cell (*tang hsiao tsu*), which he headed, and there was also a Party branch in this school. Although there were only about a dozen Party members altogether among the staff members of all county middle schools, several were in this higher middle school; the entire group of a dozen belonged to the Party's School Branch, mentioned earlier. A staff secretary (*mi shu*) also assisted the principal, and the school administration was divided into three main divisions: the Finance Division (*ts'ai wu ch'u*), Curriculum Division (*chiao tao ch'u*), and General Affairs Division (*tsung wu ch'u*). There was also a political instructor (*cheng chih chiao yüan*) on the staff; and several staff and faculty members formed a public security committee (*chih an pao wei wei yüan hui*), which reported to the Public Security Bureau. (The higher middle school was the only educational institution in the county which had such a committee.) The political instructor conducted special political classes (*cheng chih k'o*), usually once a week, at which he or an invited Party leader talked.

Many students in the higher middle school lived in dormitories adjacent to the school, and all the students, both residents and nonresidents, were thoroughly organized. They all belonged to the school's Student Association (*hsüeh sheng hui*), the leadership group of which was composed of YCL members. Within the school there was also a YCL branch (*t'uan chih pu*) and a student militia group (*min ping tui*).

The seven lower middle schools (equivalent to junior high school) in County X were located in several different places. One ordinary lower middle school and one overseas Chinese middle school were located in the county seat. Two, also including one ordinary middle school and one overseas Chinese school, were in a market town, while a second market town had an ordinary middle school. The other two schools were in commune areas.

Each ordinary lower middle school had, on the average, a staff of seven or eight administrators and teachers, and over two hundred students, while the overseas Chinese middle schools generally had only eighty to ninety students each. In the latter, most of the teachers were active members of the Overseas Chinese Association, and many of the students were children of persons actually living abroad. The administrative staffs of the lower middle schools generally consisted of the principal (*hsiao chang*), a director of instruction (*chiao tao chu jen*), and a political instructor (*cheng chih chiao yüan*). In each of the lower middle schools there was a student association, a YCL unit, and a militia group. Out of a total of about nineteen hundred students in all eight state-run county middle schools, more than 160, or somewhat under 10 percent, were members of the YCL.

State-Operated Primary Schools

The state-supported system of primary education, outside the county seat, was under the direction of state-operated central primary schools (*chung hsin hsüeh hsiao*). Each commune constituted a school district (*hsüeh ch'u*), and one central primary school was located in each of the districts. (There were also six state-supported primary schools in the county seat.) The principal of such a school was ordinarily a Party member. Together, the principals of all these schools constituted a Party branch which met in the county seat once a month. (During the other three weeks of the month they attended the weekly Party branch meetings in their own communes.)

The state-operated primary schools were financed by the county government. Each has about ten to twelve teachers, all state cadres, and an average of three hundred–odd students. In contrast to the "people-operated schools" (*min pan hsüeh hsiao*), which will be discussed below, these state-operated schools had a regular six-year course and maintained relatively high academic standards.

A central primary school not only served its own students but also was responsible for the entire educational effort in a commune. When the principal attended Party branch meetings in the county seat, or other meetings of principals (*hsiao chang hui yi*), he was expected to report on the activities of all the schools within his commune, including the "people-operated" schools. Although the state played only a minor role in financing the latter, the principal of the central primary school was nevertheless expected to supervise them, as well as the commune's program for eliminating illiteracy. The central primary school was also the key institution for the political training of teachers within the commune; and the principal, working closely with the commune's culture and education cadres, arranged the special meetings of teachers (*chiao yüan hui yi*) required for this purpose.

"People-Operated" Middle Schools

In addition to the state-supported schools, there were a large number of schools in the county which were called "people-operated" and were for the most part locally financed. Most of these schools were established after 1959, and they represented an attempt to expand educational programs rapidly without substantially increasing the state's budget in the educational sphere. The state might assist in the construction costs of such schools and might supply some state cadres to teach in them, but essentially the financing of the schools had to be handled locally by the communes or brigades. Many were set up as "half-work and half-study schools," and aimed to be self-supporting.

The "people-operated" schools were lower in quality than the state-operated schools, and tended to be smaller. Teachers were not required to meet the same standards as in the state-run institutions, and they were hired on a more irregular basis. Students of different grades might be grouped together, and the period of study might be shorter than in the state-operated schools.

Some communes established "people-operated" general schools at the lower middle school level, for students who failed to qualify for the state-operated lower middle schools; but more common were the agricultural middle schools (*nung yeh chung hsüeh*). There were twelve such agricultural middle schools in the county, and they were able to accommodate at least some of the students unable to enter the state-operated middle schools. They provided a shortened, two-year course.

Frequently, the communes assigned Party and YCL branch secretaries to head these schools. Their teaching staffs consisted mostly of local people who had completed at least lower, and preferably higher, middle school. Generally each school had a principal, a political instructor, a production instructor (*sheng ch'an chiao yüan*), and at least two, and sometimes three, teachers. Most had thirty to fifty students. A majority of the students, like those in the state-run middle schools, lived and boarded at school during the week, returning home on weekends.

The primary focus of the curriculum in the agricultural middle schools was on subjects and skills—such as agricultural techniques, accounting, and statistics—that would be useful to graduates when they went back to work, as it was assumed they would, in their own communes or brigades. One of the distinctive characteristics of the schools was that all their students, especially from 1961 on, combined study and labor (*lao tung yü tu shu hsiang chieh ho*). A definite portion of land was assigned to each school by its commune, and the students spent about half their time doing farm work, the produce helping to pay school expenses. There were various systems or formulas for dividing time between study and labor; in some of the schools the students studied in the morning and worked in the afternoon. The school-run plots not only helped to support the schools but also served, in effect, as experimental farms (*shih yen ch'ang*) for the communes where they were located. When good results were obtained on these plots, meetings were sometimes called to publicize them throughout the commune.

While a majority of the graduates of the agricultural middle schools subsequently were assigned to work in their own communes and brigades, many of the graduates of state-run middle schools received more varied assignments. A few were sent on for further education in schools at the special district level, usually in specialized training institutions such as normal schools (*shih fan hsüeh hsiao*), agricultural schools (*nung yeh hsüeh hsiao*), and industrial schools (*kung yeh hsüeh hsiao*). Others were given posts as administrative state cadres. Perhaps the largest number, however, were assigned to be teachers in state-run primary schools throughout the county. The Education Bureau, in collaboration with the Party Organization Department, determined these assignments.

"People-Operated" Primary Schools

Corresponding to the "people-operated" middle schools, there were roughly seventy to eighty "people-operated" primary schools spread throughout the county at the commune and brigade levels. Generally each brigade had at least one, and sometimes two, primary schools; and some communes operated other primary schools in the market towns, mainly for students who had failed to qualify for the state-operated central primary schools.

Because children could engage in little productive labor, these schools, unlike the "people-operated" middle schools, could not hope to be economically self-sufficient; thus the communes and brigades had to bear a heavier portion of their budgetary expenses. Students ordinarily had to pay tuition fees, which were commonly about Y4–Y5 for each of the two terms a year.

The size of the student bodies in these schools varied greatly, but frequently such a school had over one hundred students, and some had close to two hundred. Some of the schools went through to the "higher primary school" (*kao chi hsiao hsüeh*) level, grades four through six; but others were "lower primary schools," which had only the first two or three grades (*ch'u chi hsiao hsüeh*). Ordinarily the graduates of these schools did not receive an education comparable to that received by graduates of the central primary schools, and while a few went on to attend an agricultural middle school, the majority returned to work in their home production team after graduation.

Office for the Elimination of Illiteracy

The program to eliminate illiteracy operated mainly at the brigade level, although key personnel were at the commune level. Each school district, in every commune, had a cadre who operated under the direction of the County Office for the Elimination of Illiteracy. This cadre worked through the brigades, and one of his main tasks was to encourage educated people in the brigades to assist in teaching the uneducated. During major literacy campaigns, it was common for teachers to be sent down to the brigade level from higher levels (after their own regular school hours) to help organize illiterates and assist in teaching them. The attack on illiteracy in County X probably reached it peak in 1953–1955, when those adults most anxious to become literate first took advantage of the opportunities offered them. Those who remained illiterate thereafter were generally less strongly motivated or less able, and tended to be less responsive during later campaigns.

The County Office for the Elimination of Illiteracy, with two non-Party cadres as staff members, was an organization closely affiliated with the Education Bureau. It was responsible for promoting adult literacy classes throughout the county. Literacy classes were usually held at night in the rural primary schools, using local teachers or other literate local residents, especially cadres, as instructors. The county office's main function was to provide these teachers with useful ideas and materials, some passed down from higher levels, and some prepared by the county office itself.

There was no doubt, however, that by 1962 the expanded educational system as well as the literacy program in County X had already resulted in a substantial rise in both literacy and the general educational level in County X. There had been a slow but sure rise in the general level of the population's knowledge and skills since 1949.

There was also no doubt that, through the educational system, a new generation was being "socialized" to be at least aware of, and hopefully, from the Party's viewpoint, effectively indoctrinated in, the new Marxist-Leninist and Maoist ideology which the Communists were propagating. Whether or not the younger generation fully accepted the new value system, however, was hard to say.

In recent years there has been considerable evidence on the national level in China that Peking's top leaders have been genuinely worried by the persistence of old bourgeois values and the emergence of "new bourgeois influences" even among China's youth, especially educated youth, in both urban and rural areas.

In County X, there was at least some basis for such fears. Even though a high percentage of educated youth became actively involved in most of the programs sponsored by the Party, and provided a major prop to the regime, nevertheless, there was evidence that older Party leaders and public security personnel tended to regard many students, as they did all "intellectuals," with a certain amount of wariness and skepticism, fearing that they would be inclined to formulate independent views and question some of the

Party's policies rather than submit wholeheartedly and blindly to Party discipline.

Association for the Dissemination of Science

In addition to expanding and developing general education, the Chinese Communist regime has placed increasing emphasis in recent years upon the promotion of science. At the county level, however, the means to foster scientific knowledge, other than through the formal educational system, are extremely limited in most places. In County X, the organization responsible for doing what could be done to stimulate interest in science was a mass organization called the Association for the Dissemination of Science (*k'o hsüeh p'u chi hsieh shang hui*, or *k'o p'u hsieh hui*, for short). Linked to similar bodies at the national and provincial levels, the main activity of the local association was the convening of periodic meetings to study and discuss scientific topics and science policies.

One state cadre was assigned to run the association. He was a fairly well-educated man who had formerly worked in the Party's Propaganda and Education Department. His salary reportedly still came from that department, even though the association was supposed to be a non-Party organization and his office was now located in the compound of the People's Council rather than that of the Party Committee.

Loosely organized, the association's membership was open to anyone who showed a serious interest in its activities; but in practice those who joined, received membership buttons, and attended meetings regularly, were fairly few. They consisted mainly of professional and technical people, including doctors, teachers, technicians, and agricultural specialists, totaling several tens of people. Meetings were irregular and not very frequent—perhaps once every two to three months. Sometimes, but not always, materials were sent from higher levels of the association to provide a basis for discussion.

While the association doubtless provided more of a focus for promoting science than had existed previously in County X, its impact on the population as a whole was extremely limited. Almost no ordinary people attended its meetings, and it did not promote any significant mass propaganda or popular education relating to science. Nor did it engage in any systematic research.

Bureau of Culture

In their desire to revolutionize the entire "culture" of China, the Communists pay a great deal of attention not only to education and science but also to all forms of literature and art. On the national level, and in large urban centers, the regime's programs in the field of culture are very extensive, and touch virtually all of the nation's writers and artists. In rural areas, the possibilities are more limited, but "cultural" activities are still considered to be important. The Bureau of Culture (*wen hua chü*) in County X was, in effect, simply a government arm of the Party's Propaganda and Education Department, and its main activities consisted of disseminating books, showing films, promoting opera, and sponsoring recreational programs.

The bureau had eighteen cadres on its table of organization. Five of them worked in the bureau itself, while eight ran its Opera Troupe (*hsi t'uan*) and Movie Team (*tien ying tui*), and five worked at the bureau's Cultural Hall (*wen hua kuan*) and Library (*t'u shu kuan*). The chief of the bureau was a Party man who had previously been a special staff member (*chu pan kan shih*) in the Party's Propaganda and Education Department. Under him were a staff secretary (*mi shu*) and three cultural cadres (*wen hua kan pu*) who were responsible not only for supervising all the activities run by the bureau itself but also for aiding and directing cultural cadres at lower levels and promoting the organization of local recreation clubs (*chü lo pu*) in rural areas; YCL personnel played a major role in organizing and running these local clubs.

The bureau's Movie Team, with six cadres assigned to it, supervised the running of a movie house which gave daily showings, in the county seat. It also had three mobile groups (*liu tung tsu*), each consisting of two men, which exhibited motion pictures in rural areas. These groups coopted others from the bureau to help when necessary. Showings in the countryside were arranged through the brigades, and the brigades had to pay for them. The charges were surprisingly high (about Y30 per showing); but reportedly the brigades were eager, nevertheless, to arrange showings, since they provided one of the most popular forms of entertainment available in rural areas. The showings were generally given on an open sports field, if there was one, or at a local school, and were open to all members of a brigade. Some brigades had showings as often as every month or two.

The Opera Troupe ran a theater at the county seat which had frequent performances; conducted an opera school (*hsi chü hsüeh hsiao*), at the local Cultural Hall; and managed a traveling troupe, which gave occasional performances in rural areas. Only two administrative state cadres were in charge of these activities, but a fairly large number of opera performers were involved. The places where opera performances were to be given in rural areas were decided largely by Party authorities. They were generally scheduled in communes and brigades where agricultural production was outstanding; and they served, therefore, as a reward for good performance.

The Cultural Hall and Library run by the bureau were located in the county seat in a former temple, a fairly large building. Under the director (*kuan chang*), there were two library management cadres (*t'u shu kuan li yüan*), one music-group management cadre (*yüeh tui kuan li yüan*), and an accountant (*k'uai chi*). The Library was open to all and had a fairly sizable collection of books, journals, and newspapers. It obtained copies of the majority of items distributed by the New China Bookstore. Older people used it most in the daytime and younger people in the evening. One room in the building was set aside for use by singing groups organized by the staff. Another was used for instrumental music; some instruments were kept there for public use. The hall also served as headquarters for both the Opera School and Troupe and the Movie Team.

New China Bookstore and County Broadcasting Station

The local branch of the New China Bookstore (*hsin hua shu tien*) and the County Broadcasting Station (*kuang po tien t'ai*, locally also called *chan* as well as *t'ai*) were, like the Bureau of Culture and its subsidiaries, government agencies which operated under the close direction of the Party's Propaganda and Education Department. They were, in fact, among the most important instruments of mass communication in the entire Party-run propaganda system.

The bookstore had over-all responsibility for sales and distribution of all published material put out by the many state publishing companies in China, as well as for distribution of stationery. It ran one central bookstore in the county seat. In the countryside it distributed through the larger supply and marketing cooperatives. Subscriptions to magazines and journals were also handled by its staff. It had a total staff of six state cadres, including a manager (*ching li*), an accountant (*k'uai chi*), and four salesmen (*ying yeh yüan*).

The bookstore was expected to do more than simply make materials available. Following Party instructions, it was also active in promoting the sale of publications considered especially important in relation to current policies and programs. Periodically, it dispatched agricultural extension workers (*nung ts'un fu tao yüan*) to survey needs and push priority items.

The County Broadcasting Station ran a very important county-wide rediffusion system (*yu hsien tien*). Established in County X during 1956–1957, this system dramatically improved the capacity of the County Propaganda and Education Department to communicate with the mass of the rural population on a continuing daily basis. By 1962, loudspeakers (*k'uo yin chi*) wired into this system, were located in all the communes, brigades, and teams in the county. If there was only one speaker in a local area, it was usually placed in a strategic spot in front of the brigade office or team headquarters.

The usual broadcasting hours in County X were 6:30–9:30 P.M., although this could be varied. One important daily program was a half-hour of news from Peking Radio, generally at 8:30; this was picked up by radio at the County Broadcasting Station and fed into the local rediffusion system. The county station also prepared and broadcast local news and weather reports and put out various types of feature material prepared by the Party's Propaganda and Education Department as well as by its own staff. Entertainment, particularly music, was also important in the station's programming.

It was generally recognized, in fact, that programs of opera music were the most popular.

The county station was run by a staff of five state cadres. Under the director (*t'ai chang*) were a technician (*chi shu jen*), and accountant (*k'uai chi*), and two announcers (*kuang po yüan*), both of whom were young women who had been schoolteachers. The station also employed two line repairmen (*ch'a hsien yüan*, or *ch'a hsien*, for short), who were classified as technical workmen (*chi shu kung jen*).

When the Party wished to ensure that certain instructions or information would effectively reach everyone in the county, local Party propaganda personnel were directed to organize radio listening groups (*kuang po ta hui*, literally "broadcast meetings") at the brigade and team levels. Otherwise, listening was not normally compulsory. Most of the time, however, and especially in the summer, a significant number of villagers did gather to listen wherever speakers were located. It is possible that most of them were attracted primarily by the music and other entertainment provided; but whatever their reasons for listening, they were unavoidably exposed to a constant flow of propaganda and exhortation.

Bureau of Health

Public health and medicine, like education, are fields that have been energetically promoted by the Chinese Communist regime, with definite results. In County X, although facilities and personnel had not, by 1962, come close to meeting the local needs adequately, they were generally felt to be demonstrably superior to what they had been before 1949.

The County Bureau of Health (*wei sheng chü*) supervised all medical and public health personnel and institutions in the county, including the County People's Hospital (*jen min yi yüan*, or *wei sheng yüan*); the clinics or health stations (*yi liao chan* and *chen so*) run by communes and brigades; and the County Medicine Company (*yao ts'ai kung szu*). It was also in charge of annual and special health and sanitation drives or campaigns (*wei sheng yün tung*). Although the bureau, hospital, and Medicine Company were all headed by Party members, most other employees working in the health field were non-Party cadres. Because the work was essentially nonpolitical, there was relatively little Party interference or control, even by the Propaganda and Education Department which had over-all responsibility for this as well as all other fields in the culture and education "system."

The Bureau of Health had only a small staff in the county seat, consisting of a bureau chief (*chü chang*) and three other cadres (*wei sheng kan pu* or *wei sheng yüan*). The County People's Hospital had a much larger staff, totaling about thirty, which included five administrative cadres—a director (*yüan chang*), a deputy (*fu yüan chang*), a staff secretary (*mi shu*), and two accountants (*ts'ai k'uai kan pu*); three doctors (*yi sheng*); and over twenty nurses (*hu shih*).

The hospital director, a Party man, was not a doctor, but had acquired some experience in health work in the army prior to being assigned to County X, first to head the Medicine Company and then to take charge of the hospital. His deputy, a candidate member of the Party, was a Western-type doctor who had previously had a private practice. The deputy director not only helped in the administration but also served as a practicing doctor in the hospital. Of the other three doctors, two were specialists in Chinese medicine and one, a woman, was a Western-type doctor. The majority of the nurses were women. All the regular doctors and nurses were paid according to a special salary scale for medical personnel (*yi shih jen yüan*), which was different from the scale for administrative cadres; but they were regarded locally as state cadres.

County X's hospital was a fairly large one, with over one hundred beds for adults and another forty or so for children. Within the hospital, also, there was a "joint clinic" (*lien ho chen so*), which handled outpatients. This was run by former private doctors who had been "socialized" in 1955–1956, and was considered a cooperative or collective institution rather than a state organ.

Medical personnel who worked in clinics in the communes and brigades were supervised by the County Health Bureau and the county hospital, but received their pay locally rather than from the county. Commune clinics generally had one doctor, usually a practitioner of Chinese medicine, but at times one who had some minimal knowledge of Western medicine too. At the brigade level, however, there were normally only semitrained health workers (*pao chien yüan*) and midwives (*chieh sheng yüan*). While commune personnel could treat some major illnesses, the most serious cases were sent to the county hospital.

As indicated earlier, all state cadres received medical care free of charge; in County X general service personnel (*ch'in tsa jen yüan*) working for county organizations also did. The families of cadres were usually given subsidies by government or Party organizations which reduced the charges they paid by a half. Prior to visiting the county hospital or a clinic, a state cadre simply obtained from his organization a card for medical examination and treatment (*k'an ping cheng* also called *kung fei chih liao cheng*, free medical treatment card), which he then showed when he made the visit.

All persons other than cadres had to pay for medical treatment; but the fees were very low, and reportedly even peasants could afford medical care to a much greater extent than previously. In the county hospital an outpatient visit generally cost Yo.15 per visit for the registration fee (*kua hao fei*), plus the costs of medical prescriptions (*yao fei*), which were also cheap. For those hospitalized, daily charges were Yo.30 a day for most people, but only Yo.05 a day for expectant mothers. The most serious problem for many people in rural areas who were in need of treatment was not the expense, but the transportation, since there were no adequate facilities for transporting the sick from distant areas to the hospital in the county seat.

Every year health personnel throughout County X conducted at least one health campaign, directed by the county bureau. The emphasis in this campaign—which was generally held in the early spring, after the Chinese New Year and before the start of spring planting—was on improving sanitation, killing insects, and giving people certain immunization shots.

The County Medicine Company (*yao ts'ai kung szu*), which maintained close liaison with the Bureau of Health, had control over the sale of all medicines, both Western and Chinese. (Formerly there had been two companies, the *yi yao kung szu*, and the *yao ts'ai kung szu*, one selling Western and the other Chinese medicines, but they had been merged.) Headed by a manager (*ching li*), who was assisted by a personnel cadre (*jen shih kan pu*), the company had over ten salesmen (*ying yeh yüan*) who serviced several large stores or sales outlets (*men shih pu*), and a sizable number of other sales agents (*tai hsiao tien*) through whom medicine was distributed and sold throughout the county.

Committee for Physical Education and Sports

The County Committee for Physical Education and Sports (*t'i yü yün tung wei yüan hui*) also belonged to the culture and education "system" in County X and was therefore responsible to the Party's Propaganda and Education Department. It was an agency which promoted many types of athletics, arranged periodic sports meets, and directed daily calisthenic programs, particularly for cadres, students, and workers.[67] The committee in County X consisted of one head (*chu jen*) and three other cadres.

In County X, the personnel of all organizations at the county level had to participate in organized, directed, daily calisthenics sessions (*t'i ts'ao*) under the committee's over-all supervision. These were generally held early in the morning, before political study meetings, and lasted about ten to fifteen minutes. They were a regular part of the daily schedule, and were held all year round. Some rural communes organized similar calisthenics programs for their cadres, but many did not.

The committee also promoted several types of athletics and periodically held organized sports meets (*yün tung hui*). There was a military flavor to much of this activity. In fact some of it was considered part of what was called the "military-training physical-education movement" (*chün hsün t'i yü yün tung*). Many competitive programs appeared to be concerned not only with improving health standards, but also with strengthening mass discipline and "militarizing" the life of the participants. One program, labeled the "labor

[67] Three other organizations in China—the Ministry of Public Security, the PLA, and the Ministry of Railways—promoted special physical culture programs of their own, but the program of the national Committee for Physical Education and Sports, and equivalent local bodies, affected the largest number of people.

and defense system" (*lao tung pao wei* [*t'i ts'ao*] *chih tu*), pre-scribed certain standards of performance which participants were expected to achieve in a number of fields. While some were track and field events, others, such as simulated grenade throwing, were clearly military. Persons who met these standards were presented with special certificates and buttons. The two most important sports meets organized each year by the committee, with the collaboration of the General Labor Union, were held on May 1 (May Day) and October 1 (National Day). Nearby PLA units were often invited to send competitors to these. The best performers were frequently chosen to participate in subsequent meets held at the special district and provincial levels.

Expansion of Economic Functions: Three Economic "Systems"

If one compares local government in China before and after Communist takeover, one of the most significant changes has been the great enlargement of the bureaucracy's economic functions and roles. Prior to 1949, it is true, local government agencies did have some important economic responsibilities, many of them traditional ones performed over many centuries. These included tax collection, the maintenance of granaries, and the repair and development of certain major public works projects, especially in the fields of irrigation and flood control. Since Communist takeover, however, and especially since collectivization and socialization took place in the mid-1950s, the Party and government have, in effect, assumed direct responsibility for management of the entire economy, including industrial and commercial as well as agricultural activities. Moreover, they have attempted on the one hand to reorganize the entire structure of the economy, and on the other to push rapid technical innovation and economic development. Relatively few technical specialists or experts have been available at the local level to direct all these activities, although the number has slowly grown. The major economic responsibilities have fallen, however, on nonspecialized Party and government bureaucrats to a large extent. A great many of the policies that they have been charged with implementing have been formulated in general terms at higher levels of authority, but local cadres have been expected to show initiative and imagination in adapting them to local conditions.

In County X, as at higher levels in China, economic agencies and activities were grouped into three major "systems": agriculture, forestry, and water conservancy (*nung lin shui*); finance and trade (*ts'ai mao*); and industry and communications (*kung chiao*). As indicated earlier, over-all policy direction and control over these systems was exercised by three departments of the County Party Committee: the Rural Work Department (*nung ts'un kung tso pu*), the Finance and Trade Department (*ts'ai mao pu*), and the Industry and Communications Department (*kung chiao pu*).

Within the county government there were also special staff offices (*pan kung shih*) for two of these "systems": agriculture, forestry, and water conservancy; and finance and trade.[68] However, unlike the Party departments, these government staff offices, each composed of three fairly low-ranking cadres drawn from organizations within a particular "system," were not important leadership organizations in County X. Their main functions were to collect and centralize statistical data and other information from all the units in the system, to assist the deputy magistrate responsible for supervising these units (their offices were located near those of the deputy magistrates), and to help provide liaison with the responsible Party departments. The statistical and other reports which they prepared were sent to both the Party departments and deputy magistrates, and sometimes to bodies at higher levels as well.

Agriculture, Forestry, and Water Conservancy "System"

The agriculture, forestry, and water conservancy "system" in County X included four bureaus and a number of other associated institutions: the Bureau of Agriculture (*nung yeh chü*), and a fer-

---

[68] During 1958–1960 there was also a staff office for the industry and communications field, but it was abolished in 1960, apparently because it was felt to be unessential after the retreat from the Great Leap.

tilizer factory run by it; the Agricultural Technology Extension Station (*nung yeh chi shu chih tao chan*); the Agricultural Exhibition (*nung yeh chan lan hui*, or *nung chan hui*, for short) and Agricultural Exhibition Hall (*nung chan kuan*); the Veterinary Station (*shu mu shou yi chan*); the Bureau of Water Conservancy (*shui li chü*); the Bureau of Agriculture and Land Reclamation (*nung k'en chü*); the Forestry Bureau (*lin yeh chü*); and the Meteorological Station (*ch'i hsiang chan*).

Bureau of Agriculture

The Bureau of Agriculture was the principal agency in the government responsible for helping to implement all the Party's policies of collectivization and economic reorganization in the countryside; planning and promoting increased agricultural production (the main farm products in this area were rice, sugar cane, peanuts, melons, and beans); and providing technical assistance to agriculture—for example, ensuring that all commune units had adequate seed, and popularizing new farming techniques. The bureau, together with the experimental farm, extension station, and exhibition, which were closely affiliated with it, had a staff of twenty-seven. Eighteen of these were on the table of organization of the bureau itself. Under the bureau's chief (*chü chang*) were five cadres who worked within the bureau, eleven who were agricultural cadres (*nung yeh kan pu*) and spent much of their time at the commune level, and one cadre who ran the bureau's fertilizer factory (*fei liao ch'ang*). This factory was a small establishment, with six workers, which made fertilizer on an experimental basis, using local materials. Its output was small, and its main function was to develop and propagate new methods which the communes could then use to produce fertilizer themselves.

A large part of the bureau's "central work" (*chung hsin kung tso*) concerned the numerous movements or campaigns promoted by the Party in the countryside. These campaigns included not only the major socialization campaigns conducted over the years but also a variety of annual campaigns related to production. However, because such campaigns were almost invariably the current "central work" of the entire Party apparatus, because their implementation required the temporary assignment of large numbers of cadres and this had to be done by the Party's Organization Department, and because Party directives tended to carry more weight with local rural leaders than those from any government bureau, the County Party Committee itself rather than the Agriculture Bureau frequently issued the instructions for the campaigns—although the bureau was usually consulted about them.

Several important production campaigns were conducted every year in County X. One was the spring sowing and production campaign (*ch'ün keng sheng ch'an yün tung*), usually conducted not long after the Chinese New Year. Another was the summer harvest and planting campaign (*hsia shou hsia chung yün tung*), in midsummer. Still another was the fall harvest and winter planting campaign (*ch'iu shou tung chung yün tung*), organized toward the end of each year. Every fall, also, there was a campaign which mobilized "the entire Party and all the people" to collect fertilizer for agriculture (*ch'üan tang ch'üan min ta kao chi fei yün tung*).[69] On each of these occasions, large numbers of ordinary state cadres and others were mobilized by the Party and sent on temporary assignments to work in the countryside.

The county's Agricultural Technology Extension Station, which operated under the Bureau of Agriculture's leadership, ran the Agricultural Experimental Station (*nung yeh shih yen ch'ang*) to test new methods, and generally provided advice on production techniques to the communes. It had a staff of five: a station head (*chan chang*), and four extension workers called agrotechnical instructors (*nung yeh chi shu chih tao yüan*), who spent much of their time visiting rural areas. All had had at least a minimal amount of technical training, mostly in special district or provincial agricultural schools. The experimental farm consisted of about ten *mou* (roughly 1⅔ acres) of various types of land, and normally had a work force of seven, although during busy seasons the Party assigned others to help out. One of its main functions was to provide guidance and assistance to commune-run experimental farms. Twice a year the extension station convened on-the-spot meetings (*hsien ch'ang hui yi*) of person-

[69] The Agriculture Bureau also cooperated with the Bureaus of Water Conservancy and Forestry in two annual campaigns: one to repair and build conservancy works, and another to plant trees.

nel from all such farms in the county, which brought the agricultural cadres from communes and brigades to spend a period of time at the county experimental farm.

Periodically, also, the county experimental farm summarized (*tsung chieh*) the results of its experiments, and the bureau sent reports on them to both the People's Council and the Party Committee. If these reports outlined new methods which were considered both important and generally applicable, instructions were then sometimes sent to lower levels, generally by the Party Committee, directing that the methods should be widely adopted.

Not all the technical innovations in agriculture promoted in the county were sufficiently pretested by the extension station, however. Some of the most important ones were proposed in directives from higher authorities and were implemented with inadequate local testing. This was the case, for example, with the techniques of deep plowing (*shen keng*) and close planting (*mi chih*) which were promoted so energetically during the Great Leap Forward period, with fairly disastrous results. During 1958, brief local experiments with deep plowing and close planting had been carried out in County X, prior to general application of the techniques; they were successful, but the conditions under which the experiments had been performed were so special that obviously they could not be reproduced throughout the county. When use of these techniques was subsequently pushed throughout the county, the peasants were openly skeptical, but strong pressure by the cadres made them decide simply to go along with the program. The end result was a major crop failure, caused by the unsuitability of both techniques but especially of close planting.

The County Agricultural Exhibition, with a staff of three—a director (*kuan chang*) and two management workers or cadres (*kuan li yüan*)—was responsible for managing an exhibition hall in the county seat where the Agriculture Bureau gave a variety of exhibits on agricultural policies and plans, farming methods, production results, and the like, designed both to disseminate information and to illustrate progress. Communes, brigades, or experimental farms that achieved outstanding results were often publicized through such exhibits. The hall was also used for exhibits prepared by other government bureaus, including the Bureaus of Water Conservancy, Health, and Industry. Even the Public Security Bureau occasionally prepared exhibits for the hall, which usually consisted of charts with data on such matters as the current situation regarding the "five [bad] elements" throughout the county.

Over the years since 1949 there had been some gradual technical improvement of agriculture in County X, but no dramatic general increase in per-acre crop yields had taken place. While the output of some plots had risen, some of the land which formerly had been owned and run by the most successful "rich farmers" in the county reportedly was producing less under commune management than it had previously. The investment of labor on the land had increased, and expanded irrigation facilities had helped to improve output; but —at least up to 1962—there had been no great increase in such capital investments as chemical fertilizer, and the communes encountered many managerial problems. Here, as throughout much of rural China, the small private plots cultivated by individual peasants were outproducing collectivized land managed by the communes.

In addition to the experimental farm and the exhibition hall, one other agency was closely linked to the Bureau of Agriculture. This was the County Veterinary Station, headed by a station director (*chan chang*), who was the only person on the staff considered to be a state cadre. He had a staff of four practicing veterinarians, who spent much of their time traveling to rural areas to advise the communes as well as to treat sick animals. All these men were transferred army men who had received some specialized training while in the army.

Water Conservancy Bureau

Another major county government organization concerned with the agricultural sector of the economy was the Bureau of Water Conservancy. It was responsible for planning and promoting both the repair and construction of reservoirs and canals throughout the county. It carried out large construction projects itself and supervised smaller ones undertaken by communes. It also planned and managed the allocation of water resources to the communes. The bureau had a chief (*chü chang*) and a deputy (*fu chü chang*), and under them was a staff which consisted of a staff secretary (*mi shu*), a personnel cadre (*jen shih kan pu*), and more than ten conservancy cadres (*shui li kan pu*).

Technical plans for the construction of large government-run conservancy works (*cheng fu pan ti ta shui li*) were drawn up by the bureau itself and then submitted to the County Party Committee. If the Party Committee approved, the bureau and the Party Committee then organized the necessary labor force to carry out the actual construction under the technical supervision of bureau staff members. For centuries the Chinese have shown great skill in mobilizing and organizing mass labor for public works projects of this sort, but the Communists have carried out such projects on a larger scale than has any other modern Chinese government. Every level of government in China today, including the county, is involved in mass mobilization of labor for public works projects.

The organization of one large project, an irrigation canal, was carried out in County X, as follows. The areas through which the canal was to pass were divided into several work districts (*kung ch'ü*). Daily quotas of laborers were established for each district, part of the quotas to be filled by cadres and students assigned by the Party but the largest number to be mobilized and assigned to the project by communes within the districts. Commune members who were assigned to the project received wages for their work from the county government. The cadres assigned to the project were considered to be on detached duty from their own organizations or institutions and simply continued receiving their regular salaries. A total of about five thousand workers a day was required for work on the entire canal. Within each district, the workers were organized, in a semimilitary fashion, into "general groups" (*tsung tui*). Each of these groups was under a headquarters or command (*chih hui pu*) which had a chief and several staff members, including technicians provided by the bureau, and in addition had a political commissar (*cheng wei*) and a temporary Party committee (*tang wei hui*).

Smaller commune-run conservancy works (*kung she pan ti shui li*) in County X were planned by the communes themselves, but if they involved important new construction they usually required approval by the County Party Committee and technical assistance from the county bureau. (Brigades also managed some of the smallest projects.) The communes were basically responsible for routine repairs of large canals crossing their territory; when major repairs were required, the bureau could instruct the communes to undertake them as well. Every winter, also, the bureau, with the help of the Party Committee, organized an annual campaign for the repair and building of water conservancy projects (*hsiu chien hsiu li shui li yün tung*, or *hsiu chien yün tung*, for short). And once a year it held a large meeting of water conservancy cadres (*shui li kan pu hui yi*) which brought local conservancy cadres to the county seat to discuss current problems and future plans.

As already stated, the county bureau was the ultimate government authority for decisions on the use of water resources. It was responsible for allocating water from all large canals which served several communes. In performing this function it either sent its own personnel directly to the canals to open and close the canal sluice gates on a predetermined schedule, or instructed commune personnel to do this. Although water disputes were said to be less frequent than they had been prior to 1949, they still did occur between collective units, over water allocations. On occasion, also, there were even disputes between the communes and the county authorities, in which commune personnel opposed bureau instructions that they felt would be to their disadvantage. To cite one specific case, in 1958 when part of the county was threatened with flooding, the bureau worked out a plan whereby all the communes threatened would open floodgates for specified periods of time in order to equalize the water distribution and thereby distribute the probable damage to crops. The cadres in one commune refused to do this, however, asserting that it would damage their fields more than was necessary. The bureau sent representatives to ensure that the commune's cadres would comply with instructions; but they still refused. As a result, they were able to protect their own fields, and the damage to fields in neighboring communes was increased. Theirs was a Pyrrhic victory, however. Subsequently, the County Party Committee punished all those directly involved; the Party secretary plus several other key cadres in the disobedient commune were expelled from the Party and were demoted to work as ordinary peasants.

The cumulative results, over a decade and a half, of all water conservancy work in County X were reportedly fairly impressive. A number of large new canals and reservoirs had been built, and the maintenance of all existing ones had been substantially improved, by comparison with the period immediately before 1949. The percentage of irrigated land had also been increased. By the early 1960s it was roughly estimated that 50 percent of all cultivated land in the county was irrigated, and damage from floods had been significantly reduced.

Bureau of Agriculture and Land Reclamation

Another county government organ whose work was related to agriculture was the Bureau of Agriculture and Land Reclamation; its staff consisted of a chief and four cadres. Its responsibility was to plan and promote the opening up of new agricultural land. Actually, however, although there was a small amount of marginal land in County X that could be made arable, there was really not a great deal of good land that was not already being used. Consequently, the bureau was very limited in what it could accomplish. Its staff spent most of their time and effort propagandizing, encouraging, and helping the communes to develop whatever marginal land they possessed. To provide maximum incentives for them to do so, newly opened land was exempted from the land tax for three years.

Forestry Bureau and Meteorological Station

Two other small organizations completed the list of county agencies belonging to the agriculture, forestry, and water conservancy "system." These were the Bureau of Forestry and the Meteorological Station.

The Forestry Bureau was responsible both for reforestation and for protection of existing woods throughout the county. It ran an experimental tree nursery (miao p'u) and also promoted an annual tree-planting campaign (lü hua yün tung), which generally took place when the spring rains began. Like the Land Reclamation Bureau, the Forestry Bureau worked to a considerable extent through the communes, and its own staff was a small one. In addition to its chief, it had a staff of only three cadres; two of them worked in the bureau, while one was in charge of the tree nursery and the several workers employed by it.

The bureau exercised over-all control over lumbering throughout the county, and its permission had to be obtained before trees could be cut. Certain wooded areas were set aside for state use only. Timber cut in these areas, usually with labor provided by the communes, was sold by the bureau to the County Lumber Company (*mu ts'ai kung szu*), with which it maintained close liaison even though the company was directly supervised by the Bureau of Commerce. Prevention of forest fires was another concern of the bureau, and it encouraged communes to post fire-prevention watches in adjacent woods during all dry seasons.

The other agency, the Meteorological Station, was tied into a nationwide system of weather reporting, and submitted daily reports to the Provincial Meteorological Station. It also provided daily local weather reports for broadcast over the county rediffusion system. The station itself was run by a station chief and two other cadres; but some communes and brigades reportedly had local weather cadres (*ch'i hsiang yüan*)—on a part-time, extracurricular basis rather than on a regular basis—who helped disseminate weather information to the peasants.

Finance and Trade "System"

One of the general functional "systems" which had grown the most in personnel and functions in County X over the years since 1949 was the finance and trade "system." This growth was due both to the rapid expansion of traditional local government functions and to the assumption of very broad new economic responsibilities by the government. By 1962 there were five large, important government agencies in County X operating in this field.

Food Control: Grain Bureau

One of the largest and most important of these was the Grain Bureau (*liang shih chü*, also translated as Food Bureau). Even prior to Communist takeover, the collection of land taxes in kind and the maintenance of local grain reserves were among the most basic responsibilities of local government in China. After Communist takeover, and especially after a nationwide state monopoly of grain was introduced in 1953, grain management and control became even more important than before. The state now assumed responsibility for grain distribution throughout much of the economy, as well as for the control of grain everywhere, and it introduced rationing for all who were not grain producers. As a result the amount of grain handled by the state increased greatly.

By the early 1960s the Grain Bureau in County X had a payroll of more than 140 state cadres. Over seventy of these worked in the county seat, in the bureau itself and its affiliated rationing stations and grain mills, while seventy to eighty worked in grain management stations scattered throughout the county at the commune level. Of the total, about 120 were classified as administrative cadres, and the rest as salesmen.

The chief of the bureau was a ranking Party man and a member of the County Party Committee; he had been transferred from the army to County X in the early 1950s. The other key posts in the bureau, including all the section chief jobs, were also held by Party members. A majority of the cadres employed by the bureau were not Party members, however; in fact, many of those who staffed the rationing stations and purchasing stations had previously been private merchants.

The bureau possessed its own headquarters building in the county seat—a building which had formerly been one of the largest local clan temples—and it had a much more complicated organizational structure than most county bureaus. Under its chief were two deputies, one of whom had formerly been manager of the County Oils and Fats Company (*yu chih kung szu*); and it had eight sections (*ku*), each headed by a section chief (*ku chang*).

The Staff Secretariat Section (*mi shu ku*) of the bureau was responsible for general administration and personnel matters. Headed by a staff secretary (*mi shu*), its five other employees included a personnel staff member (*jen shih kan shih*), a secretarial staff member (*mi shu kan shih*), a typist (*ta tzu yüan*), a receiving and sending clerk (*shou fa yüan*), and a financial and general affairs cadre (*ts'ai wu*, or *shih wu*).

The bureau's Accounting Section (*k'uai chi ku*) maintained detailed records on all the grain transactions carried out by bureau personnel; these included figures on grain tax quotas and deliveries, state grain purchases, rationed sales, and so on. It had a staff of four section members (*ku yüan*) under a chief.

The Statistics Section (*t'ung chi ku*), with a chief and two section members, assisted in formulating the bureau's annual and other operating plans, and also kept various types of grain records for the entire county.

The Transportation Planning Section (*ch'ou yün ku*), which also had a chief and two section members, was responsible for arranging all large-scale movements of grain within the county—for example, from the rural grain management stations to the county granaries. It requisitioned the trucks for this purpose, as necessary, from the County Communications Bureau. If grain was to be transported out of the county, however, to special district or provincial agencies, the Communications Bureau itself arranged for the transport.

The Transfer Section (*tiao p'ei ku*) was responsible for decisions regarding another type of grain transfer—from one granary to another, or from one commune to another, within the county. It had a staff consisting of a chief and three section members.

The Rationing Section (*kung ying ku*), with a chief and two staff members, managed the county-wide rationing system.

The largest unit in the bureau was the Granary Section (*ts'ang kuan ku*) which was responsible for supervising and maintaining all of the county's granaries. It had a chief, a deputy chief, and over ten management cadres (*kuan li yüan*).

The Oils and Fats Section (*yu chih ku*), collaborating with the Rationing Section, was in charge of rationed sales of vegetable oil, which was distributed through the same rationing stations as the grain. It had a chief and two section members. (Previously there had been a separate vegetable oil company in County X, but this had been disbanded and its functions had been taken over by the grain Bureau.)[70]

The main task of grain collection, including the collection of land tax payments in kind and the purchase of grain sold to the state under compulsory quotas, fell to eleven grain management stations (*liang shih kuan li chan*) which were located in the communes but were really run by the bureau. Quotas for the land tax (*kung liang*, literally "public grain") were passed down from the central government to the province, then from the province to its counties. The County Grain Bureau, in deciding the size of the tax for the communes, in effect did little more than divide its quota among its communes. In the period after the Great Leap Forward, these quotas were stabilized, at least in County X, to provide increased incentives for the communes and their constituent units to exceed them; but considerable effort still had to be exerted to ensure that the quotas were met. In County X, it was estimated in the early 1960s that grain tax quotas commonly amounted to between 7 and 10 percent of the total grain output of any particular producing unit, depending on the area and the quality of land.

While the grain tax itself did not seem remarkably high, a large part of the county's grain surplus (*yü liang*), after taxes and minimum local consumption, was sold to the government under a system of compulsory sales called "unified [state] purchase and supply" (*t'ung kou t'ung hsiao*). Quotas for these compulsory sales, like the tax quotas, were set for each level by the next higher level, and these varied from year to year. In practice, the system constituted a disguised form of additional taxation, and it was not very disguised at that, since the prices at which the state purchased the grain were relatively low. In 1962 in County X, state agencies reportedly paid Y0.06 to Y0.08 to purchase a catty of unhusked grain, while their sales of similar rationed grain averaged about Y0.10 a catty, and market prices for private sales of grain ranged between Y0.30 and Y0.40 a catty. Actually, only an infinitesimal amount of grain was sold outside state-controlled channels. After the communes and their

[70] The Grain Bureau's staff also included three general service men: one messenger and two cooks. Only the largest county organizations had their own employees in these categories. Most were serviced by the People's Council Staff Office.

subunits had fulfilled their land tax and compulsory sales quotas, they were allowed to distribute the remainder of their grain to commune members, but if it was not so distributed, it generally had to be sold to state agencies. Since most individual peasants generally grew vegetables and other subsidiary crops on the limited amount of land assigned to them as private plots, almost none of them had grain to sell. Nevertheless, the price of what little grain did change hands through private sales rather than through the state agencies provided at least a suggestion of what commercial prices might have been if there had been any large free market, and the state-set prices were very low by comparison.[71]

As stated earlier, the grain management stations at the commune level bore major responsibility both for making grain tax collections and for carrying out state purchases of grain. Most of these stations had a chief (*chu jen*), a deputy (*fu chu jen*), and five to six grain cadres (*liang shih kan pu*); consequently there was a total of seventy to eighty such cadres throughout the county, all of whom were state cadres on the county bureau's payroll.

The periods of greatest activity for these stations came in mid-summer and at year-end when the main collections were made. At such times, in fact, their work load was such that it was necessary to establish numerous temporary purchasing stations (*shou kou chan*) to assist them in making collections. Sometimes as many as one hundred or more additional persons were assigned to work in these. During all major collection periods, the county bureau first drew up a detailed collection schedule, and then the communes did the same for all of their brigades, specifying how large the deliveries should be, and where and when they should be made. On the basis of these detailed plans, the collection process was generally efficient and quick. After the grain was received, most of it was then transferred to granaries managed by the bureau, although a good deal was subsequently transferred to granaries outside the county.

The number of grain storage centers managed by the bureau in the county as a whole totaled over fifty. All of these were called granaries (*ts'ang k'u*), even though some were fairly small. About thirty were located in the county seat, while the rest were in the

[71] Since 1962, however, as more food has become available, grain prices on the open market have tended to approach the price of rationed grain.

communes (these latter were in addition to the communes' and brigades' own granaries). Several of those located in the county seat were special granaries; the newest and best buildings were used for them. Two were for state reserve grain (*kuo chia ch'u pei liang*), which was controlled by higher authorities and could not be touched by the county without special permission from above— (except for periodic exchange of new grain for old). Two were for military grain (*chün yung liang*, literally, grain for military use); this was also called national defense grain (*pei chan liang*, literally, grain for preparation for war). These were supplies kept for possible use by the military in crisis situations, and were not intended for regular day-to-day army use. Two granaries were for seed grain (*chung tzu liang*); the county sold such grain to communes as needed, but provincial or other higher authorities could also requisition seed grain and transfer it to other areas which needed it. The rest of the grain storage centers were simply called ordinary granaries (*p'u t'ung ts'ang k'u*).

Most granaries in County X were kept locked and sealed except when major deliveries or withdrawals were made. Consequently, many did not need, or have, permanent guards. Bureau personnel inspected them regularly, however, and at certain times of the year, such as the Chinese New Year period, militiamen were specially assigned to guard them. Reportedly, though, few attempts were made in County X to steal from the granaries, even when food was very short and hunger prevalent; people knew that stealing from the granaries was an extremely serious offense which would likely result in rapid and harsh punishment.[72]

In County X, state sales of grain, and of edible vegetable oils, were handled by between twenty and thirty rationing stations managed by the Grain Bureau. Many of these had previously been small private shops. Over ten were located in the county seat, but each commune also had some sort of sales agent. The largest stations had seven or eight employees, and the smallest only two or three. Altogether, perhaps one hundred or more persons worked for these

---

[72] Some grain was stolen from the fields during harvesting, however. It was easier to attempt stealing in the open, and if one were caught the punishment would not be as harsh as that to be expected for attempted stealing from a granary.

stations, and perhaps twenty or more of these were state cadres, while the rest were lower-ranking salesmen.

Every nonagricultural household in the county seat was issued a grain ration card or book (*liang shih kung ying cheng* or *pu*) which permitted its members to buy a specified amount of grain and vegetable oil. All those in the countryside who were not themselves engaged in grain production were also issued ration books. The amounts of the rations varied from time to time, and were different for various categories of people. In 1962, the grain ration for ordinary state cadres in County X was thirty-two catties a month. The top ration, given to certain categories of military personnel and police, some types of workers, and a few others, was forty-five catties a month. If a person traveled on business, or moved out of the county, he had to obtain special grain ration tickets (*liang p'iao*) in order to purchase grain elsewhere.

There were three rice mills (*liang shih chia kung ch'ang*) in the county, run by the Grain Bureau. The largest was managed by four cadres and had between fifty and sixty workers on its payroll. The other two were both very small; each had a staff of two cadres and ten or more workers. These mills processed most of the grain required for rationed sales in the county. The county also had a vegetable-oil factory (*yu ch'ang*), but this came under the direction of the Bureau of Industry.

County X, like most rural areas in China, had great difficulty in meeting its obligations to the state and supplying even minimum grain supplies to the local population during the critical years 1959–1961, when agricultural output dropped. But by 1962 conditions had begun to improve, and the Grain Bureau was at least able to ensure grain rations which ended the mass hunger of the previous three years.

Finance and Tax Bureau

Despite the Communists' criticism of high taxes during the Kuomintang period, before 1949, the responsibilities of power and the great expansion of governmental and Party activities have not made it possible for them to ease the tax burden significantly since their rise to power. However, they have done a great deal to rationalize and simplify tax collection procedures, and they have distributed the tax burden very differently. The most important taxes now are the agricultural grain tax and the "turnover tax." The aim of the latter, which is modeled after a similar tax in the Soviet Union, is to tax all goods only once between the time when the raw materials are extracted until the time when they are consumed. The tax is generally handled through enterprises, and it is levied at the time when goods move from the producer either to the consumers or to commercial enterprises which sell to consumers.

Collection of taxes in County X was the responsibility of the Finance and Tax Bureau (*ts'ai shui chü*). The turnover tax was collected directly from all economic enterprises in the county. As stated earlier, grain to pay the land tax was delivered to a local grain management station, at which time certificates were issued for that portion of the grain which was to cover taxes. The certificates were then presented to one of the Finance and Tax Bureau's local tax offices as evidence of taxes paid. In addition to collecting taxes, the Finance and Tax Bureau also managed the county's general financial affairs and was in charge of preparing the county government's budget (*yü suan*) and handling financial disbursements. Earlier, there had been two separate bureaus dealing with these matters, the Finance Bureau (*ts'ai cheng chü*) and the Tax Bureau (*shui wu chü*), but these were merged in County X in the late 1950s. (Some counties in China may still have two separate bureaus.)

Somewhat larger than the average bureau in the county, the Finance and Tax Bureau in the early 1960s had a staff of twenty-seven state cadres working in the bureau itself, and perhaps more than sixty working in subordinate tax offices (*shui wu so*) throughout the county. It was headed by a fairly high-ranking Party member who previously had worked in the Public Security Bureau as a section chief. Two deputies assisted him, and the rest of the staff was divided into five sections (*ku*).

The Personnel and Secretariat Section (*jen mi ku*) handled all general administrative matters. It had a staff of five: a staff secretary (*mi shu*); a personnel cadre (*jen shih kan pu*); a secretarial staff member (*mi shu kan shih*); a typist (*ta tzu yüan*); and a general affairs man (*shih wu*), who also acted as accountant (*k'uai chi*).

The Tax Section (*shui wu ku*), with a chief and two section members, supervised the collection of the most important ordinary taxes, including the turnover tax. The special Tax Collection Section (*cheng shou ku*), with a similar staff, was responsible for handling certain other minor taxes, including, for example, import duties and an entry tax on overseas Chinese. This section was also in charge of the financial handling of confiscated opium.

Over-all tax accounts, and the control of general financial disbursements, were in the hands of the Finance and Accounting Section (*ts'ai k'uai ku*), whose staff of five included the chief, two accountants (*k'uai chi*), and two cashiers (*ch'u na*).

The largest unit in the bureau was the Finance Section (*ts'ai cheng ku*), which was in charge of over-all financial planning, and preparation of the county budget. It also supervised the finances of all the county's economic enterprises and handled profits received from them and disbursements made to them (although the mechanics of receiving and sending funds from and to these enterprises were handled by the Finance and Accounting Section, and the People's Bank).[73]

In County X, the task of actually collecting taxes, other than the land tax, fell to the sixty or more state cadres working in twelve tax offices scattered throughout the county. Each office had up to five cadres. The tax offices blanketed the county and constituted a fairly efficient apparatus for ensuring that taxes were paid.

Because it had a finger on the county's purse strings, the Finance and Tax Bureau was an influential body in the local government. However, not only did it operate under the close direction of the county's top Party and government leaders; its powers were further

[73] An ex-cadre with special knowledge of financial affairs in Communist China questions the accuracy of the above description of the internal organization of a county finance and tax bureau and asserts that normally such a bureau might have a comprehensive planning section (*tsung ho chi hua k'o*), a finance section (*tsai cheng k'o*), and a tax section (*shui wu k'o*) or revenue section (*shou ju k'o*). He also doubts whether any import duties would be handled by a county agency and asserts that he does not know of any levy on overseas Chinese or of persons assigned to the financial handling of confiscated opium. However, the information above is that provided by the ex-cadre who served as the major source regarding County X.

restricted because, in a basic sense, the county government had only limited financial autonomy. The county's budget required approval by higher authorities; its pattern of expenditures was shaped to a considerable extent by instructions from above; and fulfillment of its financial obligations to provincial and national authorities had to be given priority over local requirements.

People's Bank

Banking in County X was monopolized by the local branch (*fen hang*) of the People's Bank of China (*jen min yin hang*), the principal state bank in China. The local bank manager (*hang chang*) and his two deputies had been assigned to County X by the provincial bank, which exercised close direction over all its subsidiary branches. The manager's administrative staff, who belonged to the Personnel and Secretarial Section (*jen mi ku*), included a staff secretary (*mi shu*), two personnel cadres (*jen shih kan pu*), a typist (*ta tzu yüan*), and two bank policemen (*hang ching*)—plus a messenger.

The rest of the staff in the main county bank office belonged to three sections: the Finance and Accounting Section (*ts'ai k'uai ku*), the Deposits Section (*ch'u hsü ku*), and the Agricultural Loans Section (*nung tai ku*), each headed by a section chief.[74] In addition to its chief, the Finance and Accounting Section had four accountants and three cashiers, while the other two sections each had three banking cadres (*yin hang kan pu*).

All county government organizations maintained their accounts in the bank, which served as a watchdog, therefore, over all significant financial transactions made by them. Limits were set on the amount of cash each could keep within its own offices, and other funds had to be deposited at the bank promptly. Transfers or disbursements above minimum specified amounts had to be made by check. The bank also handled the funds required for cadres' salary payments, which were made on a definite schedule. In addition to handling the government's funds, the bank also carried private accounts, both checking and savings accounts, for either cadres or ordinary citizens.

[74] Most county banks reportedly have a section for industrial and commercial loans; this may well have been the case for County X.

Reportedly, many individuals in County X did have such accounts.

Banking services in the rural areas of the county were handled by eleven small bank offices (*ying yeh so*, literally "business departments") located in the communes. Each of these had a chief (*chu jen*) and two to three other employees, all of whom were state cadres on the payroll of the county bank. In addition, within the communes, especially at the brigade level, there were numerous credit cooperatives (*hsin yung ho tso she*), which provided some banking services. Although these were staffed by local rather than state cadres, they maintained close relations with, and were directly supervised by, the local bank offices in the communes.[75]

Management of Commerce: Bureau of Commerce

During the early 1950s the Chinese Communist regime slowly but steadily expanded its control and direct participation in domestic commerce. Then, in 1955–1956, when socialization of private enterprise was accelerated and pushed through to rapid completion, state agencies assumed responsibility for virtually all internal trade in China.

By the early 1960s, the Bureau of Commerce, responsible for domestic trade, was one of the largest organizations in the government of County X. It directed six large commercial companies, a factory, and a farm, and each of its companies ran a number of stores and sales agencies. Altogether there were between two hundred and three hundred employees on the payroll of these agencies, of whom roughly 115 were state cadres, while the rest were lower-ranking salesmen, some of whom, however, were labeled provisional cadres (*lin shih kan pu*). These state-run companies absorbed almost all of the previously existing private commercial enterprises in the county, as well as many of their employees. In fact, apart from the limited private trade conducted in the few free markets allowed to

[75] Some counties in Communist China have had a separate county-level agricultural bank. As of 1962, the functions of this institution were apparently handled in County X by the People's Bank, although this may subsequently have changed.

reopen in the period after the Great Leap Forward, these companies conducted almost all the commerce in the county by the late 1950s and early 1960s.

The Bureau of Commerce itself had a staff of thirty-six. Under the bureau chief and his two deputies, there were six sections, one labeled *ku,* and the others *k'o.* These were all headed by Party men, only a few of whom had had very much previous commercial experience. (The bureau chief, though, had previously acquired experience as head of the county's General Goods Company.) The overwhelming majority of the other cadres on the bureau's payroll were not Party members.

Like other large county bureaus, the Commerce Bureau had its own personnel unit, the Personnel Section (*jen shih ku*), which had a staff of three. It was responsible for handling personnel actions affecting all employees of all the commercial organs under the bureau, and hence it had a sizable job. The Staff Secretariat Section (*mi shu k'o*) of the bureau handled general administration. It had a staff of seven. Four staff members belonged to the Finance and Accounting Section (*ts'ai k'uai k'o*). The other sections of the bureau were the Purchasing Section (*ts'ai kou k'o*), with seven staff members; the Price Section (*wu chia k'o*), with three staff members; and the Warehouse Section (*ts'ang kuan k'o*), with nine staff members.

Commercial Companies

Under the Commerce Bureau's direction, six state-run commercial enterprises handled the bulk of commerce in County X. The General Goods Company (*pai huo kung szu*) was one of the most important of these, selling, as its name implied, a wide range of consumer dry goods and similar items. It maintained thirteen sales outlets or stores (*men shih pu*) in the county seat, three of which were large new ones. Its headquarters staff consisted of a manager (*ching li*) and a deputy, three other cadres doing administrative work—an accountant (*k'uai chi*), a statistician (*t'ung chi*), and a general affairs man (*shih wu*)—and six cadres in charge of warehouses (*ts'ang kuan yüan*). The staff of its thirteen stores, ranging from two to over ten in each store, totaled between sixty and seventy. Former merchants often staffed the smaller stores, while young salesgirls predominated in the large new ones.

The county's Textile Products Company (*fang chih p'in kung szu*), handling mainly cotton fabrics, ran about ten stores, including two big new ones, at the county seat. It had an administrative staff of seven, and thirty to forty salesmen. The Foods Products Company (*fu shih p'in kung szu*) distributed almost all types of food other than grain and vegetable oils. It ran more than twenty stores and over ten restaurants in the county seat. Thirteen persons made up its headquarters administrative staff, and it employed over eighty salesmen and other workers. Six stores in the county seat were run by the Stationery Goods Company (*wen chü kung szu*), which had a staff of four administrative cadres and twenty to thirty salesmen. The Aquatic Products Company (*shui ch'an kung szu*), which had formerly been a bureau, concentrated mainly on the procurement of fish and other products from the county's fishing population. Run by an administrative staff of twelve, this company maintained four major purchasing stations (*shou kou chan*), each of which had three to four cadres. The Lumber Company (*mu ts'ai kung szu*) manufactured and sold timber. It had a headquarters staff of four, several salesmen, and over twenty workers.

Also supervised by the Commerce Bureau were a fruit processing plant (*sheng kuo chia kung ch'ang*) and an experimental pig farm (*mao chu shih yen ch'ang*). The former canned a variety of local fruits. It had only three administrative cadres and about ten workers most of the year, but during the busy periods after harvest, when it hired many temporary seasonal laborers, its work force expanded to over eighty. The pig farm, located in a hilly area near the county seat, had five cadres and eighteen workers.

Supply and Marketing Cooperatives and Free Markets

Whereas almost all the state-run commercial enterprises in County X maintained their own stores in the county seat, in rural areas they sold largely through supply and marketing cooperatives (*kung hsiao ho tso she*). These cooperatives, ostensibly not state enterprises, were in fact directly led by the Bureau of Commerce. A sizable number of state cadres were assigned to work in them, and for all practical purposes there was little to differentiate them from state enterprises. Operationally, they extended the state trading companies' outreach effectively to all rural areas. At the county level, there was an over-all "general cooperative" (*tsung ho tso she*), and in every commune there was a local cooperative, the largest of which had several sales outlets (*men shih pu*) or sales agents (*tai hsiao tien*). These cooperatives not only served as small, rural, general stores, distributing goods sold by the state commercial companies, but also purchased on behalf of the state companies a wide variety of subsidiary agricultural products.[76]

Despite the importance of the state-operated companies and supply and marketing cooperatives, some free markets continued to exist. Nearly all sizable towns, including the county seat, had originally developed as centers of periodic markets—normally held every three to five days—where private individuals brought their wares for sale. With the growth of the state enterprises and cooperatives, the importance of these markets declined, but except for brief periods they nevertheless continued to play a significant role, as open markets, in the distribution of small-scale local handicraft products, firewood, and subsidiary foods, especially food grown by individual peasants on private plots in the communes.

The government has consistently looked with suspicion and disfavor on these private markets, and abolished them in 1955–1956 and again in 1958–1961. Even during those periods, however, and especially during 1960–1961, which was the period of greatest food shortages in China, black markets (*hei shih*) continued to do a sizable business on the side streets of the major market towns. Farmers would bring packages of food wrapped in small bundles, and sell or exchange them with eager customers. And even when open markets have been permitted, the term "free market" (*tzu yu shih ch'ang*), which is used to describe them, has had a slightly illicit connotation.

[76] In the county seat, service personnel in each occupation—for example, barbers, laundrymen, and so on—were also organized, under the residents' committees and the city commune, into special trades organizations (*ko hang ko yeh tsu chih*).

In 1961, however, following the collapse of the Great Leap Forward, the government concluded that it was essential to allow free markets to reopen—with the title of "rural trade fairs" (*chi shih*). This time, though, in order to control them and suppress black markets, the Market Management Committee was established, as indicated earlier.

During the 1958–1961 period, when private plots had been banned, the black-market trade had been primarily in food goods. These included not only some rice but also "substitute" foods—in which grain was combined with wet straw chaff and other fillers—as well as food gathered in the hills, such as wild fruit and mountain potatoes. In 1961, with the revival of the private plots, vegetable products produced on the private plots were again offered for sale in open markets, but in general manufactured goods were not, since they continued to be monopolized by the state stores and the supply and marketing cooperatives. Nevertheless, in County X's towns, shopping still tended to follow old patterns, determined by traditional marketing schedules; and even the state stores were busiest on "market days," when persons from most rural households came to town.

Industry and Communications "System"

Because the Party and government in Communist China have assumed almost total responsibility both for managing the existing economy and for promoting economic development, the industry and communications "system" has grown rapidly and has become one of the most complex functional groupings of agencies in the entire government. However, this is much more true at the national than at the local government level. In the central government, many specialized new ministries responsible for particular industries have been created over the years since 1949; and, as indicated earlier, there have been periodic mergers and splits as economic problems and opportunities have changed, and as the regime has groped for administrative rationality and efficiency. Relatively few of these changes have directly affected the over-all structure of county governments, however. Therefore, even though county governments now have much wider responsibilities and more complicated organizations in this field than did governments prior to 1949, their institutions and responsibilities are still relatively simple by comparison with those of the central government or even the provincial governments. Part of the explanation for this is the fact that, although the Peking regime has continually sought to stimulate local initiative in economic development, and has periodically attempted to decentralize development responsibilities to a degree, inevitably many of the most important tasks in the field of industry and communications, whether managerial or developmental, have required action at governmental levels higher than the county. The county governments have been expected to do what they could in this as in other fields, within the limits of their resources and competence; but few of them have been able to produce dramatic results. Nevertheless, development in the industry and communications field, even at the local level, has been greater since 1949 than it was previously.

In County X the organizations which belonged to the industry and communications "system" and were directed by the Party's Industry and Communication Department included the following: the Bureau of Industry (*kung yeh chü*), the Handicraft Cooperative (*shou kung yeh ho tso she*), the Bureau of Construction (*chien she chü*), the Communications Bureau (*chiao t'ung chü*), the Transportation Management Station (*yün shu kuan li chan*), the Navigation Management Station (*hang hai kuan li chan*, or *hang kuan chan*, for short), and the Postal and Telecommunications Bureau (*yu tien chü*).

Bureau of Industry

The Bureau of Industry was responsible for coordinating the planning and supervising the operation of all state-owned factories in the county. (Most of these were small, and elsewhere they might be labeled as workshops.) By the early 1960s every industrial enterprise that could be classified as a factory in County X, except for small commune enterprises, was state-owned; all were county-owned. In a nearby city where the special district office was located, there were a few provincial factories; and in a new industrial city roughly two hundred kilometers away there were factories owned and run by both the provincial and central governments; but all the sizable factories within County X were county-run enterprises.

The most important day-to-day tasks of administering the county's factories were handled not by the Bureau of Industry but by the factory directors (*ch'ang chang*) and administrative cadres in the enterprises themselves. Consequently, the bureau's own staff was relatively small, consisting of a chief, a deputy, and six other cadres; and unlike the larger and more complicated bureaus in the field of commerce, it was not divided into sections.

All factories supervised by the bureau did, however, submit regular and frequent production reports (*sheng ch'an pao kao*) to it. The bureau itself sent consolidated reports on output every ten days (*hsün pao kao*) and monthly (*yüeh pao kao*) to equivalent departments in the special district and provincial governments, as well as to the top Party and government units within the county. In many respects, though, the county factories operated largely on their own. For example, they made contracts (*ho t'ung*) directly with communes, rather than through the bureau, for the delivery of needed locally produced raw materials. The bureau, in short, supervised but did not directly manage them.

Industrial Factories

The enterprises supervised by the Bureau of Industry included ten factories (actually there were thirteen plants, but they were organized as ten units), run by over seventy cadres and employing well over five hundred workers. Roughly forty cadres and workers, including all managers and personnel cadres and most cadres in other leading administrative posts, were Party members and belonged to the two Party "organization branches," already mentioned, which covered industrial enterprises. The rest of the employees of the factories, including a large majority of the workers, were not Party members, although quite a number of younger workers belonged to the YCL.

The growth of industrial enterprises in County X in the period between 1949 and 1962 had been significant but not spectacular. Of the ten factories existing in 1962, four had been newly built in this period—those producing agricultural implements, cement, and sugar, and one of the two producing vegetable oil. The other six, while they had substantially expanded their facilities and output since 1949, existed before Communist takeover and had originally been private enterprises.

During the initial period of the Great Leap Forward in 1958, the Party leaders in County X, as in most local areas in China, frantically pushed the development of small iron and steel furnaces. The Party Committee established an "iron and steel headquarters" (*kang t'ieh chih hui pu*), or command, under which thousands of people were mobilized either to construct and operate the new small furnaces or to collect needed raw materials in nearby hilly areas. Not only were furnaces built throughout rural areas; every Party and government organization, and every residents' committee in the county seat, also helped to construct them. However, this major campaign proved to be abortive here, as elsewhere in China, and in 1959 all the local furnaces were abandoned. (Unlike some other rural counties, County X did not at that time develop new small-scale industries other than iron and steel.) Consequently, the Great Leap Forward failed to produce any significant net increase in county-run industries in this area.

Other industrial decentralization policies adopted by the central government in the late 1950s likewise seemed to have relatively little significant long-run impact on County X, except in an indirect fashion. They did not result in any expansion of county-run industries. However, provincial-run industries did develop during this period, and some industrial workers from the county were drawn into them; by 1962 these workers had not yet returned to the county.

Four of the factories in County X, although small, could be classified, in a broad sense, as "heavy industries." The electric plant (*tien ch'ang*), which had six administrative cadres and over thirty workers, provided electricity to the county seat and its suburban areas, supplying both industrial and home users. It had expanded output somewhat since 1949, but was not yet able to provide service to most rural areas. The machine repair and assembly factory (*chi ch'i hsiu p'ei ch'ang*) had also been built before 1949. Subsequently it had been considerably enlarged, becoming one of the most important factories in the area. This enterprise repaired all motor vehicles in the county and also assembled and repaired irrigation pumps. Apart from repair and assembly of small machines, it manufactured some spare parts. It did not attempt the complete fabrication of many items, however; most of its parts and materials were purchased elsewhere. Its eight cadres administered a working force of over sixty.

One of the most important new enterprises in the county was the agricultural implements, or machinery, factory (*nung hsieh ch'ang*). It manufactured, assembled, and repaired many small implements needed by the farming and fishing population. The tools were sold largely through rural supply and marketing cooperatives. The factory employed ten administrative cadres and over one hundred workers. The smallest of the county enterprises in the "heavy industry" category was the cement factory (*shui ni ch'ang*), which had also been newly built after 1949. With only three cadres and about ten workers, it was a very small unit. The limited quantity of cement which it produced was used mainly for road repair in the county seat; only a small amount went for building construction.

All major construction and repair of buildings in the county, other than that undertaken by the communes themselves, was handled by the County Construction Company (*chien chu kung szu*), another of the enterprises supervised by the Bureau of Industry. This company had a staff of eight cadres and over one hundred workers. Most of its work was done at the county seat.

All printing in the county, including production of the county newspaper, was done by the county printing plant (*yin shua ch'ang*), which had a staff of five cadres and over thirty workers. This enterprise, while supervised by the Bureau of Industry, maintained particularly close liaison with the Party's Propaganda Department and with the staff offices of both the Party Committee and the People's Council, since it was these organizations which provided it with most of its jobs.

The other four enterprises under the Bureau of Industry were factories which processed agricultural commodities. Two of them— one that had existed before 1949 and a new one—were edible–vegetable-oil factories (*yu ch'ang*) producing one of the most essential items for Chinese cooking. Their main product was peanut oil, most of which was sold through the Subsidiary Foods Company and the supply and marketing cooperatives, although some was exported out of the county. These two factories altogether had eighteen administrative cadres and over 110 workers. The county wine factory (*chiu ch'ang*), established before 1949, produced both rice wine and sorghum wine. It was relatively small, having only five cadres and about thirty workers. The sugar factory (*t'ang ch'ang*), new since 1949, normally had a staff of nine cadres and over fifty workers. During the periods following the sugar cane harvest, however, it operated regular night shifts, and an additional fifty or so temporary workers were employed. Some of the factory's output was exported to other areas.

Because all these factories were relatively small, the organization of their managerial staffs was generally quite simple, although it varied from factory to factory. The key person in each factory was the factory manager (*ch'ang chang*); only the largest factories had deputy managers. The largest enterprises also had personnel cadres (*jen shih kan pu*), and most had an accountant (*k'uai chi*), at least one clerk (*wen shu*), and one or more production management cadres (*sheng ch'an kuan li kan pu*). Other specialized personnel varied from factory to factory.

Workers in these enterprises were classified as either ordinary workers (*p'u t'ung kung jen*) or technical workers (*chi shu kung jen*, or *chi kung*, for short), and were paid according to graded wage scales. None of the highest grades in the national wage scales were represented among workers in county industries. Virtually all workers in the county-run factories belonged to units of the county's General Labor Union, which, as stated earlier, managed the labor insurance system and in addition ran various welfare, recreational, and educational programs and was broadly responsible for helping to maintain labor discipline.

Public-security activities in the factories were supervised by the Organization Security Section of the Public Security Bureau. In factories where there were personnel cadres, these men concurrently served as security officers (*pao wei yüan*) and reported to the bureau. Elsewhere, the factory director usually had over-all responsibility for security. All the largest factories also had "security small groups" (*pao wei hsiao tsu*), usually composed of about three workers designated by the director or personnel cadre. These groups were responsible for, among other things, helping to guarantee protection of state property and equipment.

Handicraft Cooperative

The most important handicraft enterprises in County X were managed by the County Handicraft Cooperative (*shou kung yeh ho tso she*), which was supervised in a general way by the Bureau of Industry. Although the cooperative was ostensibly neither a government organization nor a state-owned enterprise, in reality there was little to set it apart from such bodies, and it was run by a group of seven administrative state cadres. Its head (*she chang*), a woman, was the wife of the county magistrate. The largest producing unit under the cooperative was a weaving enterprise which had about fifty workers and was essentially a small factory. In addition, however, it supervised a fairly large number of very small handicraft producers, totaling altogether between two hundred and three hundred.

Outside of the County Handicraft Cooperative, there were still, in County X in 1962, some unorganized handicraft activities, mostly small family affairs, the products of which were sold on the free markets. And there were also some unorganized itinerant peddlers (*hsiao fan*) operating both in the county seat and in rural areas.

Construction Bureau

The Construction Bureau (*chien she chü*) in County X was one of the smaller organizations in the county government. With a staff consisting of only a chief and three other cadres, it was really more of a planning than an operating body. While it was responsible for all important construction in the county, actual building work was carried out by the Construction Company, which was administratively under the Bureau of Industry but operated, in practice, under the leadership of the Bureau of Construction as well.

Postal and Telecommunications Bureau

The Chinese Communists have given high priority to the development of basic communications, and as a result local rural areas are now linked much more closely to higher levels of authority than was ever the case before 1949. In County X, telephone, telegraph, and postal services were operated by the County Postal and Telecommunications Bureau. Even before 1949 postal service had been fairly well developed in this area, and regular service was provided even then to all local areas. The local telephone system, however, was an innovation after Communist takeover, and it greatly improved the links between the county and local areas. By the early 1960s, telephones had been installed not only in all important Party and government offices in the county but also in every commune and brigade headquarters.[77] The county was also linked by telephone to nearby cities and to both the special district and provincial governments. The latter periodically held telephone conferences (*tien hua hui yi*) with all the counties under their jurisdiction, as the county authorities themselves did on occasion with all the communes and/or brigades in their area.

The personnel on the Postal and Telecommunications Bureau's payroll totaled over sixty, of whom thirty to forty worked at the central office. Under the bureau chief (*chü chang*), there was a deputy (*fu chü chang*), a personnel cadre (*jen shih kan pu*), and a security cadre (*pao mi kan pu*), and three main working groups (*tsu*). The Mail Group (*t'ung hsün tsu*), which had over ten cadres, handled ordinary postal material. The Telegraph-Telephone Group (*tien hsün tsu*), which handled ordinary telecommunications traffic, consisted of five cadres. All secret (*mi mi*) or urgent (*t'e k'uai*)

[77] There were still very few telephones in private homes, however; persons who were not cadres generally had to ask permission to make private calls from a public telephone either in an office or—at the county seat—in a public security substation.

messages, however, whether telephone calls, telegrams, or mail, were the responsibility of three persons in a unit called the Secret and Important [Materials] Group (*chi yao tsu*). This unit controlled the county's telephone link with the PLA military telephone system (*chün hsien*). It handled classified mail under the system called the "military post" (*chün yu*). And it was responsible for planning and making the necessary prearrangements for all official telephone conferences. In addition to the above personnel, the bureau had two persons who handled subscriptions to all official newspapers. The rest of its staff consisted of postal delivery men.

Because of the very great importance to the regime of all communications, both ordinary and classified, there was more concern for security in this bureau than in many other government agencies. Over ten members of the bureau, including its chief, its personnel cadre, its security cadre, the cadres in the unit dealing with classified materials, those in charge of handling newspaper subscriptions, and several others, were Party members.

Communications Bureau

Over-all responsibility for operating, maintaining, and developing land transportation in County X, including the local road network, rested with the Communications Bureau (*chiao t'ung chü*, sometimes translated as Transportation and Communications Bureau). Transportation, like communications, was a field given high priority by the Communists from the start; and over the years since 1949 the road system in County X had been expanded substantially. In fact, apart from irrigation canals, roads were the principal public works that had been completed by the regime. By the early 1960s, motor highways linked the county seat with every commune in the county, and with a number of the larger villages as well, and they contributed substantially to the area's economic activities as well as to the government's ability to exercise effective political control.

The Communications Bureau had a headquarters staff of five administrative cadres, plus seven other cadres who spent much of their time in the seven work districts (*kung ch'ü*) into which the county was divided for the purposes of transportation management and development. In each of these work districts, a local "road repair group" (*p'ei yang kung lu tui*, or *yang lu tui*, for short) was organized to be responsible for continuous repair of the highways; when necessary the groups hired laborers from nearby communes to work under their direction.

Plans for all new road construction were first drawn up by the Communications Bureau. They then required approval by both the Party Committee and the People's Council, after which work assignments were allotted to the various road development groups, which organized the necessary work units, largely consisting of persons hired from the communes, to carry out the tasks assigned to them. The bureau also provided technical help, but not always financial aid, to communes undertaking to build minor local roadways.

The main public transportation in the county consisted of the county-wide bus system and the trucking network. Both were operated by the Transportation Management Station (*yün shu kuan li chan*), which, while semi-independent, was supervised by the bureau (see below). There were only three automobiles in the county, two belonging to the Party Committee and one to the People's Council; but there were more than twenty buses and over fifteen trucks, not counting a few additional trucks owned by the communes. All the buses and five of the trucks were run by the Transportation Management Station. The rest of the trucks belonged either to individual factories or to the Postal and Telecommunications Bureau. (Before 1949, by comparison, the only motor vehicles owned and based in the county were three trucks.)

Transportation and Navigation
Management Stations

The County Transportation Management Station, which had five cadres plus a number of workers and drivers, not only operated all the public buses and trucks but also had some control over the factory-owned trucks, and could requisition them when necessary. It maintained close liaison with the County Vehicle Station (*ch'e chan*), which, with a staff of almost fifteen cadres, handled the administrative side of both the bus traffic and freight trucking, including the ticketing for passengers and the documentation for freight. In addition to its main headquarters at the county seat, it maintained several substations in key spots throughout the county.

Fairly frequent bus service was provided to all communes within the county, and buses went to the special district headquarters more than once a day. The largest single group of users of this public transportation consisted of cadres traveling between the communes and the county seat. When the county Party or government convened large special meetings, a fleet of buses was sometimes organized to pick up cadres in rural areas all over the county and deliver them, free of charge, to the county seat. Ordinarily, however, a cadre paid his fare and then, if on business, obtained reimbursement from his organization. (Generally, the two front seats in a bus were reserved, until just before departure time, for postal personnel to use if they so wished.)

The Navigation Management Station (*hang hai kuan li chan*, or *hang kuan chan*, for short)—in some places this organization is a bureau—was the only other agency operating in the industry and communications field in County X. It was in charge of all maritime transport in the county. Its six cadres were in charge of over thirty wooden boats (*mu pan ch'uan*) and one motorized boat (*chi ch'uan*), and they managed a work force of over one hundred boatmen, loaders, and other laborers. The boats were used for both passenger transport and freight.

Importance of County-Level Agencies

As this inventory of agencies suggests, virtually all organized activities in County X had come under the direct supervision and management of Party and government institutions by the late 1950s and early 1960s. The regime's philosophy of "totalism" impelled it not only to expand enormously the functions of political authority, and the apparatus required to carry out new functions, but also to absorb into the sphere of Party-government responsibility many traditional activities that were formerly carried out by nongovernmental groups.

In many fields, county-level institutions are of particular importance because the county is the lowest level in the political hierarchy possessing specialized institutions to deal with these fields and it has much closer and more continuous contact with the general population than authorities at higher levels have. In this sense the county is today, as it has been traditionally in China, a crucially important level of administration. However, in contrast with the situation during China's imperial past, the county is no longer the lowest layer in the official hierarchy of administration. This hierarchy now reaches beyond the county, directly to the village level, in ways that will be described in Part III.

Part III
A COMMUNE
AND A BRIGADE

Recent Administrative
Changes Below
the County Level

IN THE seventeen years since Communist takeover, some of the greatest changes in the administrative structure of government in China have taken place at the lowest levels, below the county. Both the size and function of units at these levels have been altered many times. Most of the changes have been made on the initiative of higher-level authorities; but, not surprisingly, at the local level there has been a great deal of variation in the application of policies passed down from above. Despite the impressive centralization of power in the Chinese political system, the pattern of local administration has, almost inevitably, differed substantially in details from place to place as well as from time to time.

In some respects the many changes and variations over the past seventeen years have presented a very confusing picture of seemingly extreme fluidity and instability. However, despite the great change, much of it significant, there has also been significant continuity, more than might appear at first glance. Some of the administrative innovations at the local level have been more nominal than real. Others have been only temporary. On several occasions, when radical innovations have been introduced too rapidly, the regime has soon had to retreat, and before long has restored, partially at least, the situation that had existed previously. In analyzing the evolution of Chinese local government since 1949, therefore, one must examine both continuity and change, for both are important.

General Trends

Throughout most of the 1950s, just prior to communization, two trends were particularly important in the administrative changes taking place at local, subcounty levels. One was the development, as the result of agricultural cooperativization, of what in effect was a new structure of authority, in addition to the regular Party and government structures. Party primacy was at no time challenged, but as agricultural producers cooperatives (APC's) developed, and expanded their functions and responsibilities, many questions were posed about the relationships at the lowest levels between the cooperatives and the government. Over time, a variety of problems concerning coordination and division of functions arose in the relationships between the regular administrative bureaucracy and these new production-based organizations, and reportedly, in some places a trend toward the *de facto* merger of these two structures of organization began to take place even before any formal steps were taken in this direction, as they eventually were.

A second important trend in the 1950s was the steady enlargement, over time, of local administrative areas. There were a number of causes for this development, including the regime's strong desire to centralize and improve local political control, and its need to make the best possible use of the limited number of able, reliable cadres available to it. Clearly one of the most important reasons was the belief of key Chinese Communist leaders that, as the economic functions and responsibilities of local administrative units increased, it was essential to centralize local authority and to enlarge the basic units within which economic planning and the mobilization of resources could be carried out, in order to maximize the possibilities of economic development at the local level.

These and other trends culminated in the radical and dramatic reorganization of local government and administration that took place in 1958, when the communes were introduced. The communes represented a visionary attempt to carry out a revolutionary reorganization of both government and society at the local level. They called for the "collectivization of life" as well as the collectivization of the economy to an unprecedented degree. Initially, the regime attempted to move toward full "communism," under which peasants first were to be paid on a supply and wage system and ultimately were to be provided with all of their needs "free." Private plots and many of the vestiges of private property were actually eliminated in this period, as the regime propagated the reputed advantages of "ownership by the whole people."

Through the communes, the regime also attempted to achieve almost total mobilization of China's rural labor force, including women, in the belief that labor could be substituted for capital in many developmental tasks. To facilitate this numerous new social institutions, including nurseries, old people's homes, public mess halls, collective sewing groups, and the like, were established to care for children and the aged and to perform home duties, such as cooking, which women had traditionally performed.

Life in the villages was also "militarized" under the communes, as the regime attempted to "make everybody a soldier." Local militia forces were dramatically expanded, and the basic work groups in the countryside were regimented in a semimilitary fashion. Local political control was greatly tightened. Ideologically, primary stress was placed on noneconomic incentives; in fact, the regime attempted to substitute ideology for economic rewards. The masses were mobilized to work extremely long hours for the ultimate collective good rather than for private gain.

The communes coincided with the economic Great Leap Forward, and were in many respects an outgrowth of it. In basic economic terms, therefore, they were designed to accelerate the growth of both agriculture and local small-scale industry, primarily by unprecedented mobilization of manpower and other local resources and the stimulation of ideological fervor and hard work. They were conceived of as organizations that controlled all agricultural, industrial, and commercial, as well as political, military, and cultural affairs, within their areas of jurisdiction, and it was predicted that they would eventually become the basic social and economic as well as political units in a Communist society.

Communes: Large Units and
Merger of Government and Collectives

Administratively, the communes, as already stated, involved both a merger of the organizational structures of the local government and the collectives and a significant territorial enlargement of the basic units of local administration. In relationship to the total national scene in China, they represented a significant decentralization of power to the local level; but in local terms they resulted, temporarily, in a substantial increase in centralization of authority within the large new commune units.

It soon became clear, however, that the communes, as originally conceived, were not workable, and before long a step-by-step retreat from the original concept began. The formal merger of government administration and the agricultural collectives continued, and still exists today, and the communes together with their subordinate units have continued both to perform basic governmental functions and to manage certain large-scale economic activities. But the size, distribution of powers, and actual operation of the communes have changed greatly, though gradually.

Some economic incentives were restored. Private plots were given back to the peasants, and income was again linked directly to the output of small production groups. The most radical social innovations, such as the mess halls, were abandoned, and life was substantially "decollectivized." The militia drive and the trend toward extreme regimentation were slowed down. The efforts to develop agriculture and local industry at a forced pace slackened. In fact, when a series of natural calamities and bad harvests struck China during 1959–1961, on the heels of the disruption and confusion caused by the Great Leap Forward and communization, serious food crisis and general economic depression developed. In this crisis situation the visionary goals of the original communes slipped into the background, and local leaders in China were forced to concentrate their attention on the fundamental problem of obtaining the minimum requirements for subsistence.

Administratively, some of the most basic powers of the communes, including "ownership" of land and other means of production, planning and management of agricultural production, and distribution of output, were gradually decentralized to the communes' subunits. At first the production brigades assumed most of these powers and responsibilities, but ultimately it was the small production teams which were placed in charge of agricultural production and became the basic "accounting units," with the power to decide on the allocation and distribution of output. This decentralization of authority within the communes meant that in several important respects the regime had returned at least to the situation existing immediately before communization. Management of agricultural production and distribution of output were again put in the hands of small production units, and the need to provide some economic incentives was again acknowledged. Actually, the retreat went even further than simply a return to the situation as of early 1958, since the production teams were generally smaller units than were the higher APC's, which had been the main type of collective units just prior to communization. Moreover, many communes themselves were reduced in size, with the result that their number in the country as a whole tripled.[1]

As of 1965, therefore, the communes still existed but were very different from the image of them which the Chinese Communists had first projected. In some areas, in fact, they now appeared to be not radically different from comparable government units that had existed just prior to 1958, and their smallest subunits, the production teams, operated much as basic collective units had in the period before communization.

Nevertheless, the basic framework of the communes, including the merger of government and collective units, remained, and the regime's leaders clung to old slogans and to the hope that eventually their original concepts of what the communes should be might still be eventually achieved. If and when the leaders decided to move in this direction again, they could do so by recentralizing powers and functions within the communes, perhaps first to the brigade level and then again to the level of the communes themselves, and they

[1] Apparently, however, the degree to which communes were reduced in size varied regionally. In some places, especially in sparsely populated and mountainous areas, many were split or shrunk; in other areas relatively few of them were changed in size.

could reintroduce "collectivist" features at the expense of individual or small-group economic incentives. With the experience of the early 1960s behind them, however, it seemed unlikely as of 1965 that they would move in these directions soon or with the same impatience and lack of caution which had characterized their radical policies of 1958.

Evolution from the pre-1949 Period Onward

To understand the evolution of local administration in the years since Communist takeover, it is necessary to be at least aware of the pattern of administration which the Communists inherited.[2] In the period just before 1949, rural administration below the county in China consisted of four levels: the district (ch'ü), the administrative village (hsiang) or market town (chen), the pao, and the chia.

In most places in China the district was not a well-organized, full-scale level of government, but was simply an agency of the county government with supervisory personnel who helped the county manage a specified number of its administrative villages, in roughly the same way that special district personnel helped a province supervise certain counties.

The administrative villages, each of which usually contained several natural villages (tzu jan ts'un), constituted the most important "basic" level of government administration below the county, and each such unit had a fairly well-developed governmental structure.

[2] Statistical data on changes in districts, administrative villages, mutual aid teams, cooperatives, and communes used in the following discussion have been drawn from the following principal sources: Chao Kuo-chun, *Agrarian Policy of the Chinese Communist Party* (New Delhi, Asia Publishing House, 1960); Roy Hofheinz, "Rural Administration in Communist China," *China Quarterly*, No. 11 (July–September, 1962); Philip P. Jones and Thomas T. Poleman, "Communes and the Agricultural Crisis in Communist China," *Food Research Institute Studies*, Vol. III, No. 1 (February, 1962); *Current Background*, No. 131 (October 25, 1951), No. 157 (February 8, 1952), No. 529 (October 29, 1958), and No. 517 (September 5, 1958); *China News Analysis*, No. 30 (April 2, 1954), No. 246 (September 26, 1958), and No. 373 (May 26, 1961).

Those that had large populations and a major marketing center were classified as market towns.

Under them, the entire population was organized into units of roughly ten households, called *chia*, which were in turn grouped into larger units called *pao*, each of which had an average of about one hundred households, or ten *chia*. The so-called *pao-chia* system (*pao chia chih tu*) had a long history in China as a device not for self-government but for organizing the population for purposes of political control into groups which shared mutual responsibility for the acts of all their members. When it was revived by the Nationalists in the 1930s the prime motive was again to establish a system of effective political control at the village level; but by the late 1930s the official policy of the Nationalist regime aimed at integrating the *pao* and *chia* into the political system eventually as the lowest levels of self-government, and in some places moves were actually made in this direction.

During their struggle for power, the Chinese Communists promised a total restructuring of power relationships at the local level and proposed a few specific institutional changes, including abolition of the *pao-chia* system. When they achieved power in 1949, therefore, they immediately took over all the old agencies of rural local government and proceeded to destroy some of them, including the *pao-chia* system. Then, during the ensuing land reform period they carried out a process of violent class warfare at the village level and completely destroyed the power of the old village leadership groups, installed a new set of leaders who had been selected during this revolutionary process, and set about the task of establishing new organs of local administration. At the start, however, they retained both the districts and the administrative villages as important units of rural administration.

The districts, in fact, were not only retained but actually grew in importance in the early years. While still conceived of, as they had been previously, as "organizations with delegated powers" (*p'ai ch'u chi kou*) representing the counties, in many places they gradually became, in fact if not in theory, full-scale governments which acted as intermediate "leadership organizations" (*ling tao chi kou*) between the counties and the administrative villages. But the number and size of the districts, as of most local administrative units in China, have changed greatly over the years since 1949, as the regime has groped to solve its administrative problems. In 1955, there were roughly nineteen thousand districts throughout the country; in schematic terms, therefore, there were about nine or ten per county, and on an average each district had more than ten administrative villages under its supervision. During 1955–1956, however, in the regime's general move toward enlargement of rural units, which resulted in a halving of the total number of administrative villages, the number of districts was also reduced by over half, to nine thousand.

When the communes were finally introduced, the districts disappeared, temporarily at least, throughout China. Because the communes were themselves such large units, there was apparently no longer felt to be any need for intermediary units between them and the counties. In theory, the new communes were supposed to be based on the administrative villages, to merge with them, and to take over their governmental powers, since they had been the basic units of local self-government. However, in reality, many if not most of the new communes included more than one administrative village. When they were originally set up, roughly twenty-six thousand (then reduced to twenty-four thousand) communes absorbed the eighty thousand or so administrative villages existing at that time —and these eighty thousand already represented a great consolidation of the 280,000 administrative villages which had existed only eight years earlier. In many coastal areas of south China, in fact, communes were formed in the first instance simply by taking over the apparatus and territory of the districts; and the former administrative villages were converted into production brigades under the communes.

For several years after communization, there was almost no mention of the districts in China, but in the early 1960s, when the communes were split and reduced in size in some areas, districts again started to reemerge as intermediary units between the communes and the counties. As already stated some communes were themselves equivalent in size to the former districts. Despite all the changes it appeared that the Communist regime did not find it easy to dispense with units that were at least roughly comparable in scope, if not in function, to the old districts.

Administrative Village Level

Even greater changes have occurred over the past seventeen years in the size and structure of units at the administrative village level in China, but here too one can discern elements of continuity as well as change. Right after their takeover of power, and during the early land reform period, the Communists were more concerned with establishing control and consolidating power than with reorganization of the formal institutions of local government. One of their first moves in each administrative village was to establish a peasant association which then acted in effect as a local revolutionary junta and exercised many of the important powers of local government. For example, these peasant associations were made legally responsible, in the 1950 Land Reform Law, for carrying out land reform, which was the primary revolutionary task during this period and took place in most areas during 1950–1952. In some areas, new administrative village governments were reconstituted fairly rapidly and coexisted with the peasant associations, the two sharing governmental functions. But in other areas, no effective local governments other than the peasant associations existed at this level until new administrative village governments were organized toward the end of, or even after, land reform. However, by the period just before the adoption of a formal national constitution in 1954, effective local governments at this level had been established throughout most of the country, and these were formalized and put on a new basis when the constitution was adopted. In most places the old peasant associations went out of existence at about the time that an effective administrative village government was organized.

At this stage, in general form and function—although obviously not in personnel or policy—governments at the administrative village level in China were not too different from those which had existed before 1949, although they tended to be more complex in organization and to have somewhat increased functions. In size, however, they had already begun to change, as the regime moved gradually but steadily in the direction of larger basic units in the countryside. In the early 1950s China had had 280,000 administrative villages (encompassing perhaps one million natural villages—although there are no reliable figures on the number of villages in China, and some estimates have ranged as high as three million). By 1953 the number had dropped to 220,000. From 1954 through 1958 their size continued to increase, and their number steadily declined: from 219,000 in 1954, to somewhat over 200,000 in 1955; to 117,000 in 1956; to 102,-000 in 1957; to 96,000 in early 1958; and finally to about 80,000 in mid-1958.

Then, in 1958 came communization, and as stated already these eighty thousand administrative villages were absorbed into twenty-four thousand new communes. At the start, the average size of the communes, on a nationwide basis, was somewhat over five thousand families, or roughly twenty-five thousand people; but there were great variations in size. (In a few places, county-wide federations of communes were established for a short period.) Functionally, the communes took over the administrative village level of government, but many of them tended at first, as already indicated, to be closer in size to the old districts. They were in turn divided into roughly half a million production brigades, averaging over two hundred households each, and roughly three million production teams, averaging about forty households each. But this situation did not last for long. In the early 1960s, the number of communes rose to seventy-four thousand, a number strikingly close to the total of enlarged administrative villages which had existed just prior to communization.

Bottom Levels

At the very lowest levels of rural administration, one of the first moves of the Communists after political takeover was the abolishment of the *pao-chia* system, which had been a major target of political attacks on their part before 1949 when they had charged that it was simply a device for oppressive Nationalist control. In a few areas, they then appointed temporary village chiefs (*t'sun chang*) in every natural village, to replace *pao* and *chia* and to provide a new link between the masses of the population and higher levels of authority. But this was not done universally. In most places, in fact, it was the Party itself, plus the new mass organizations which it established, including the peasant associations, the militia units, the

Young Communist League (then called the New Democratic Youth League), and the Women's Association, which exercised effective leadership and control among the rural masses.

Even before the end of land reform, however, the Communists began taking the first steps in their three-stage program aimed at ultimate collectivization. Gradually the peasants in the villages were organized into new collective groups, which began to create the foundations for a new system of basic-level economic institutions. While not governmental organs as such, these groups played a steadily increasing role in the regime's management and control of the rural population.

The first steps in this direction were taken in some areas as early as 1950 when mutual aid teams began to be organized, initially as seasonal institutions and then as permanent ones. These were small at first. Until 1954 they averaged, in the country as a whole, four to six households, after which their average size rose to eight or nine households by 1955. They were somewhat smaller, in other words, than the *chia* had been under the Nationalist regime. The growth of these teams was rapid. Their number expanded from 2,700,000 in 1950, to 4,760,000 in 1951; to 8,030,000 in 1952; to 7,450,000 in 1953; and then to a peak of 9,930,000 in 1954, after which the number declined as more and more of them were absorbed into new cooperatives.

The first experiments in organizing agricultural producers cooperatives (APC's) also started at about this time. A definite program for developing them was drafted in 1951 and adopted in 1953. Implementation of this program accelerated from late 1953 onward, and a big national drive occurred in late 1955 and 1956, at which time virtually the entire farming population was brought first into so-called lower APC's, which absorbed the former mutual aid teams, and then into higher APC's. In the lower APC's unified management of production was introduced, but members retained at least theoretical ownership of their land and received some remuneration for land as well as labor. In the higher APC's the land was collectivized, except for small private plots, and remuneration was based wholly on labor. At first, in most places, one or two lower APC's were organized in each administrative village. Then others were gradually set up until there were generally one or two per natural village.

Finally, in 1955–1956, virtually all former poor and middle peasants were brought into them, and they were converted into the "higher" form, which was comparable to the Soviet collectives.

Lower APC's increased from under four thousand in 1952, to fifteen thousand in 1953; 114,000 in 1954; 663,000 in 1955; and almost 682,000 in 1956. At first they averaged, in the country as a whole, under twenty households; then, in 1955, twenty-six or more households, after which they dropped to under twenty again. Higher APC's increased, in rough figures, from two thousand in 1953, to twelve thousand in 1954; forty-one thousand in 1955; 312,000 in 1956; 700,000 in 1957; and finally 740,000 in 1958, on the eve of communization. Their average size also increased from sixty to eighty households during 1954–1955 to 150–170 households during 1956–1958, although some much larger ones were set up. In some areas there was a tendency, in fact, to merge all the APC's within an administrative village into one very large higher APC. In not a few places the higher APC's actually expanded beyond the boundaries of the administrative villages, which was one factor arguing for the enlargement of administrative villages in this period (i.e. to make them as large as the APC's). As they grew, in both size and importance, the higher APC's became increasingly competitive with the governments of administrative villages and, as already stated, in some places there was a tendency toward *de facto* mergers of the two structures, even before communization.

The growth of ever-larger collective units did not mean, however, that smaller groupings of peasants were abolished. Under many higher APC's there were production teams and groups comparable in size to the old lower APC's and mutual aid teams. Then, when communes were established, the tendency was for higher APC's to become new production brigades, under which were production teams roughly equivalent to the old lower APC's; and under these were small production groups not dissimilar in size (although often even smaller) to the original mutual aid teams. These were now integrated, however, into a new over-all structure which merged government and economic functions for the first time.

Changes in One County's Initial
Communist Takeover and Reorganization

The foregoing description indicates in schematic terms what some of the major administrative changes in the country as a whole have been in recent years, but local developments have varied greatly in detail from area to area. While the course of events in any single area cannot be taken to represent what happened everywhere, schematic descriptions of nationwide trends cannot have much real meaning until one knows how broad trends affected particular, specific local areas. What follows below is an account of the course of developments in one south China county, which will be called County A.

In the latter part of 1949, local Communist guerrilla units were extremely active in the coastal region of south China where County A is located. They had been reinforced since 1947 by able Party cadres sent from the north and were operating in several of the hilly areas of this region. As the regular PLA moved south, these guerrillas became increasingly aggressive, and seeing ultimate Communist victory in sight, they started to intensify underground work of all sorts preparatory to political takeover. Guerrilla sorties out of the mountains were stepped up, and local Communist forces even began arresting some leading landlords in the area, to impress their power on the peasant population and to intimidate the old power elite.

When regular PLA units finally arrived, late in the year, the guerrillas joined up with them, and they advanced together on the county seat of County A. The actual military takeover then occurred rapidly, without serious fighting, because by this time the Nationalist forces in the area were thoroughly demoralized. One day the seat of County A was in Nationalist hands; on the next, the Communists controlled it.

To establish and consolidate Communist power in County A, the new rulers concentrated at first on the county government itself, before extending their efforts to the local level. To start with, a new magistrate was immediately installed. He was a Party man from the north who had come south two years previously to work with the local guerrillas in this area, and he had been designated as magistrate well before the actual takeover of County A.

Immediately after takeover, the Communists established three military or police organizations at the level of the county government. One was a specially organized PLA unit, an independent battalion (*tu li ying*) consisting of about four hundred men, which was led by PLA officers but contained many ex-guerrillas. Besides its commander (*ying chang*), who became the top military leader in the county, the unit had a political commissar (*cheng wei*), who acted in effect as local Party leader during this initial period, before a county Party committee was organized or a Party secretary chosen. The battalion had a headquarters organization, under which were three companies (*lien*) of roughly one hundred men each; each of these was divided into three columns (*tsung tui*) of approximately thirty men each, and each of these in turn was divided into three squads (*pan*) of about ten men each. The main task of these units was to eliminate "bandits," that is, all armed resistance, and to establish over-all military control throughout the county.

A second organization established at this time was the Armed Forces Department (*wu chuang pu*), to which were assigned over forty persons. About ten of these worked at the county government level, and the rest in the districts, with three to four per district. The principal responsibility of these men—also a mixed group of PLA cadres and guerrillas—was to start organizing local militia units. The third new organization consisted of the Public Security Forces (*kung an tui*), who immediately took over the old Police Bureau (*ching ch'a chü*). At first about thirty men were assigned to this work. Most functioned at the county level, but a few were sent to work in the districts. They too consisted mainly of PLA men and ex-guerrillas, although a few former Nationalist policemen were also absorbed into their ranks.

Once these bodies were functioning, a basic apparatus for exercising control throughout the county existed, and other changes in the county government took place more gradually. At first most of the old government bureaus and personnel were retained and utilized, but over time many changes were slowly made. A Party committee was soon set up and assumed the role of primary leadership. In fact, in these early days the line between Party and government roles was very ill-defined. By 1952, however, after the nationwide "three-anti" campaign, which tightened Party discipline, a more serious attempt was made to differentiate between Party and government functions, and the county government was reorganized and enlarged. In 1954, when a national constitution was adopted, further extensive changes were made in the government structure.

In the period immediately after takeover, ultimate power in the county rested in the so-called "five big cadres" (*wu ta kan pu*). In County A these included, at that time, the magistrate (*hsien chang*); the commander of the Independent Battalion (*tu li ying chang*); the political commissar of the battalion (*cheng wei*), who was also acting Party chief; the head of the Armed Forces Department (*wu chuang pu chang*); and the chief of the Public Security Forces (*kung an tui chang*). When the local Party Committee was organized by early 1950, it became the primary center of power, but all of the "five big cadres" became members of the committee.

As soon as the basic instruments of political control had been established at the county level, which took perhaps one to two months, the new county government in early 1950 appointed and sent to each of its eight major districts a district cadre team (*ch'ü kan tui*), each consisting of six to seven men, including a designated Party secretary (*ch'ü wei shu chi*), a district chief (*ch'ü chang*), a civil affairs cadre (*min cheng kan pu*), a women's cadre (*fu nü kan pu*), and others. At about the same time, each district was assigned one column of the Independent Battalion. Soon thereafter, the county authorities organized a fairly large county land reform "regiment" (*hsien t'u kai t'uan*) and from it one land reform team (*t'u kai tui*) of twenty to thirty persons was sent to each district. The task of these units was to start preparing for land reform. Many of their members were ex-PLA men or former guerrillas, and at the end of land reform some returned to army duty.

The first changes in subcounty administrative units took place during this period. At the time of takeover, there had been six districts and fifty-six administrative villages (or equivalent market towns) in County A. In early 1950, boundaries were redrawn, and the number of Districts was increased from six to eight, while the number of administrative villages grew from fifty-six to seventy-six.

Greater emphasis than in the past was placed on the importance of the districts by County A's new Communist rulers. They felt that to carry out the revolutionary changes which they were determined to implement throughout the countryside they needed to have strong leadership organs closer to the villages than the county seat; and they still did not have enough reliable and trained cadres to establish such leadership organs in all the administrative villages. Therefore, even though the districts in County A were theoretically still only "organs with delegated powers," they soon developed, in reality, into important, decision-making leadership organizations operating at the subcounty level, although under close county direction.

The reduction in the size of administrative villages at this time had other, but related, motives. As the new county leaders prepared to carry out land reform, they felt that the establishment of smaller basic rural units would facilitate the tasks of control, organization, and indoctrination. Since land reform was to be carried out with each administrative village as a unit, they decided to cut their size by close to 50 percent.

Leadership at Lower Levels

Once the district governments had been established on a new basis, it was their responsibility to supervise the reorganization of the administrative villages, which was started in the spring of 1950. One of the first steps was abolishment of the old *pao-chia* system. Then, in most districts, one "keypoint" administrative village (*chung tien hsiang*) was chosen, and a redrawing of boundaries and reorganization of government institutions was carried out there, on a demonstration basis, with selected activists from other administrative villages observing, so that they could then go home and help carry out similar processes in their own areas.

The Communists could not yet be wholly certain about the reliability of activists selected to be collaborators, as they could be later after the land reform program had given them an opportunity to test out potential new local leaders, so they simply chose activists as best they could. Most of them were poor peasants.

It took altogether two months or so to establish the new administrative village governments. Each of these also was led by "five big cadres," who at this level consisted of the chief of the administrative village (*hsiang chang*), the public security officer (*kung an yüan*), the chief of the Militia Group (*min ping tui chang*), the chairman of the local Peasant Association (*nung hui chu hsi*), and the chairman of the Women's Association (*fu nü hui chu hsi*). The administrative village chief and other top local government leaders were formally selected in mass rallies organized by the Party leaders, but actually they were people who had already been chosen by the district-level cadres.

During this period, the district cadres in County A carried out their work to a considerable extent on the basis of so-called "joint administrative villages" (*lien hsiang*). These units, each of which included two or three administrative villages, were not formal units of administration in this area, and had no bureaucratic organizations of their own. However, the district leaders often convened meetings and took action on the basis of these joint administrative villages, which had been established and were useful because they cut across and weakened old lines of local authority. After 1951, the term "joint administrative village" was no longer used, but the district leaders continued to base certain actions on similar groupings of two to three administrative villages, which were referred to as "basic keypoint areas" (*chi pen chung tien*).[3]

In order to work effectively at the administrative village level in this period, most districts actually assigned a majority of their cadres, including those in their land reform teams, to live and work in the lower units. Only three to four cadres, usually including the district Party secretary, the district chief, and one or two others, plus the thirty-odd members of the district's military column, spent most of their time at the district headquarters. The majority of other cadres spent their time in the administrative villages. Following the reduction in the size of the administrative villages, each district could send an average of three to four cadres to each of its eight to ten administrative villages.

[3] Reportedly, there were other areas in this general region where, in this early period, local administrative organs were first established, temporarily, at the level of the joint administrative villages instead of the old administrative villages.

During this early period, a village chief (*ts'un chang*) was appointed by the Communists in every natural village in County A, to replace the old *pao-chia* leaders. In the largest villages, in fact, under the village chiefs, groupings called *chia lo*, consisting of one to two hundred households, were also set up, and each of these also had an appointed chief. These were all temporary devices, however, and they went out of existence in late 1951, after the Communist-sponsored mass organizations had been well enough organized to replace them at the village level in this area, and after initial moves had begun to set up mutual aid teams.

In 1950, virtually all the poor and middle peasants in this area were brought into the new peasant associations established by the Communists, and a great many local youth were incorporated into new militia units. Once these were set up and were operating effectively, the Peasant Association in each administrative village, under the direction of the resident land reform cadres from the district, began carrying out the long and complicated process of land reform. This process really got under way in this area in late 1950 and early 1951. After preliminary steps, including a reduction of all rents and interest rates, the first important task was to define the exact class status of every villager. After careful preliminary investigations by the Communist cadres, with the collaboration of selected local activists, class status was determined in endless mass meetings, in which the new local leaders of the mass organizations played critical parts. These meetings were followed by emotional public "struggle" meetings (*tou cheng hui*), organized by the Party cadres and directed against selected local landlords.[4] Some landlords were sentenced in public trial meetings (*kung p'an ta hui*) to labor reform; others were condemned to death in public trials before special *ad hoc* people's tribunals (*jen min fa t'ing*) and were then shot in front of mass gatherings of local villagers. In one administrative village, which was apparently in no way atypical, about half of the fifty-three local landlords were severely punished—most were sent to labor reform but eight were shot. This intense, organized, class warfare not only destroyed the old structure of authority in the

---

[4] In some places "struggle" meetings directed against landlords took place before the complicated process of class demarcation for the population as a whole.

villages; it also helped to produce a new local leadership group, since it was during this period that the Communists identified the local activists on whom they could rely, some of whom would later be recruited into the Party.

Land reform was a fairly confused process, but it was not disorderly. The outside district cadres kept it under strict control. The process went on in this area from late 1950 until 1952, by which time it was completed, and it was accompanied throughout by continuous efforts to establish and improve the organizational apparatus of the new regime. During the second half of 1952, Party committees were formally established in the districts (*ch'ü wei hui*), and during 1953 the formation of Party branches (*hsiang chih pu*) began to be widely promoted in the administrative villages. The County Independent Battalion and its district-level columns were abolished at the end of 1952, as land reform drew to a close, although the Public Security Forces not only were retained but were substantially strengthened.

Beginnings of Collectivization

The program to establish mutual aid teams (*hu chu tsu*) began soon after land reform was completed. In this region, it was started in the latter part of 1952 in areas where land reform was already completed. In any particular area, it was always initiated on instructions sent from the county authorities to the districts, which then drew up concrete plans to implement it in their own areas.

By this time the district governments in County A were fairly well organized, each with over ten permanent cadres. Again, cadres from the district were sent to propagandize and organize at the administrative village level. Apparently, however, not much pressure was required; many peasants positively favored the idea of mutual aid teams, which the regime promised would bring many benefits and in which they simply worked cooperatively while retaining full control over their own land and its output. Peasant association leaders and other activists generally took the lead in setting up the teams. Their average size in this area was about ten households, somewhat larger than the national average, and about the size of the old *chia*.

Another significant change in the size of rural administrative units took place in this area immediately after land reform. It was, in effect, an abolishment of the 1950 reorganization and a return to the status quo ante. In a reorganization campaign (*cheng tun pien chih yün tung*, or *cheng pien yün tung*) carried out in 1953, the number of districts in County A was reduced from eight to seven and the number of administrative villages from seventy-six to fifty, just below the figure for 1949. The major motive for this change was said to be the desire to centralize administration, to cut down on the number of cadres working at the village level, and to use a larger number of able, tested cadres in agencies at the district and county levels, where governmental organizations and functions had grown, rather than having them dispersed in the administrative villages.

Following the adoption of a national constitution in late 1954, both the county government and its subordinate organizations were reorganized somewhat to conform to new statutes and regulations. At this time, in County A, the peasant associations quietly went out of existence, and the governments of the administrative villages became increasingly important. Establishment of rural Party organizations was already well advanced by this time.

Major moves toward collectivization were taken in this area in the winter of 1954–1955, and the county authorities at this juncture again decided to establish special cadre units to send into the countryside. This was a little over a year after Peking had publicly announced its "general line of the state for the transition to socialism," which spelled out in detail the planned step-by-step process of collectivization. A total of fifty work teams to run cooperatives (*pan she kung tso tsu*), one for each administrative village, were organized and trained at the county level, with cadres drawn both from county-level organizations and from lower levels. Once they were ready to go to work, they were assigned to operate under the direct leadership of the districts but were expected to work down at the administrative village level.

The progress toward collectivization can best be illustrated by what took place in one administrative village, which we will call Administrative Village I. In this administrative village, roughly half of the households had been organized by early 1954—before the big push toward collectivization—into over thirty mutual aid teams, almost all of which were by this time permanent rather than seasonal teams. When the cooperativization drive began, one of the county work teams was dispatched to Administrative Village I and went right to work to organize two experimental APC's (*nung yeh sheng ch'an ho tse she*). Participation in these was quite voluntary. In each case one mutual aid team served as a center or nucleus (*chung hsin*) for the cooperative, and then other teams voluntarily joined it. If individual households in these teams did not wish to join, they could split off and join other mutual aid teams.

The original members of these two experimental APC's were all poor and lower middle peasants. However, the general attitude of most local peasants, especially the poorer ones, was reportedly quite favorable toward the lower APC's (*ch'u chi ho tso she*). The cadres intensively propagandized the idea that cooperativization would lead to dramatic increases in production, and peasants were impressed both by this propaganda and by the fact that in the lower APC's, members still retained ownership of land and received some income in return for their contributions of land to the cooperative. It was not long, therefore, before additional APC's were organized. By the end of the winter of 1954–1955, twelve lower APC's had been established in Administrative Village I, and as a result the number of mutual aid teams had declined to twelve. The majority of members of the cooperatives were still poor and lower middle peasants, but even upper middle peasants had begun to join. The size of the new cooperatives varied. A number of them had fifty to seventy households, but the largest had over one hundred.

Even though many peasants in this area had generally favorable attitudes toward the lower APC's at first, this was not the only explanation for the rapid growth of the APC's during late 1954 and early 1955. A major explanation was the fact that there was frank and open economic discrimination in favor of them and against the mutual aid teams and individual peasants. For example, during this period, although not later, the APC's in this area did not have to fulfill the quotas for compulsory sales to the state until after distributing at least minimum food grain (*k'ou liang*) to their members, whereas everyone else had to fulfill their compulsory sales quotas first.

Big Push to Collectivization

During the course of 1955, the remainder of the poor and middle peasants in Administrative Village I were rapidly organized into APC's. By the latter part of the year, as a consequence, there were sixteen APC's in the area, and they had absorbed all the old mutual aid teams. In effect, however, units comparable to the mutual aid teams continued, in the form of subunits under the APC's. Although the APC's now averaged forty to seventy households, they were divided into smaller production teams (*sheng ch'an tui*), each with approximately ten households, under which were production groups (*sheng ch'an hsiao tsu*) with six to nine persons (not households) each.

During late 1955 and early 1956, there was a nationwide push in China to establish first lower APC's and then higher APC's (*kao chi ho tso she*). In County A, and in Administrative Village I, this was the peak of the socialization movement (*she hui chu yi yün tung*), and the emphasis in this area was on the transition to higher APC's. Again County A organized special work teams to run cooperatives, and sent them to each administrative village; each had five members, this time consisting solely of cadres from the district level and above.

It was recognized by the local Party leaders that greater pressure would now be needed to get the peasants to agree "voluntarily" to join the higher APC's, which would require them to give up ownership of their land. Consequently, village-level leadership would have to be "strengthened" by the temporary assignment of county and district cadres to lower levels. The County Party Committee organized a special two-week training course for these new work teams. It also convened a very large "county-wide four-level enlarged cadre conference" (*ch'uan hsien szu chi k'uo kan hui*), a ten-day meeting which brought together cadres from the county, the districts, the administrative villages, and the APC's. At this meeting, plans and policies were outlined for establishing the APC's, especially higher APC's. (During this period, an important "forty-article charter for agricultural development" [*nung yeh kang yao szu shih t'iao*] was

sent by higher Party authorities to local levels; the charter was published in early 1956.) The county authorities described detailed plans
for the conversion of lower APC's into higher APC's throughout
the county. Then the work teams were sent to the administrative
villages to initiate the local propaganda and organization campaigns
required to prepare for this move.

Again the formalities of voluntary decision-making were observed, but reportedly the pressures exerted by the work teams were
such that local cadres could not really object to the new program
without risking the accusation of being reactionary, and the mass of
ordinary peasants was by this time fairly submissive to manipulation
by the cadres.

In Administrative Village I, the original two higher APC's continued in existence until communization. In many adjacent and
nearby areas, however, the APC's kept being expanded until most
of the higher APC's were equal in size to at least one administrative
village. Some grew until they included two to three administrative
villages and were, in effect, therefore, based on the informal "basic
keypoint areas" (*chi pen chung tien*) under the districts. In some
places, when higher APC's became coterminous with the administrative village, their administrations occupied the same building, and as
indicated earlier, a *de facto* merger of the two took place; that is, the
APC absorbed the administrative village apparatus and in reality
ran the government, even though it might still use its APC chop
rather than that of the administrative village to conduct official business.

Partly as a result of this trend, a further adjustment of local administrative units took place during a campaign in 1957 ("campaign
to incorporate cooperatives and integrate administrative villages,"
ho she p'ing hsiang yün tung). Certain administrative villages were
enlarged so as to be coterminous with the largest APC's which had
grown beyond administrative village boundaries. This adjustment
resulted in the reduction of County A's districts from seven to six
and its administrative villages from fifty to thirty-five. Under these
new enlarged units, however, special "production management districts" (*sheng ch'an kuan li ch'ü*) were established at the level of the
old administrative villages and took over the existing organizational

apparatus at this level; thus, the governments of the old smaller administrative villages really continued operating under the new title.[5]

When communes were then established in County A, in 1958, the districts formed the basis of the communes and the old administrative villages became production brigades, with the result that after communization there were initially six communes and fifty production brigades in the county.

Establishment of Communes

The move to establish communes in County A was initiated in the fall of 1958, following a meeting, convened by the Provincial Party Committee, which was attended by representatives of all county Party committees in the province. This provincial meeting was called together to transmit decisions that had already been made by the Party Central Committee, and following it the county Party leaders returned to their home areas and began systematically preparing for the establishment of communes.

In County A these preparations began when the Party Committee convened an extremely large cadre conference (*k'uo kan hui yi*) to which were invited all the key district leaders plus the top leaders from all administrative villages. Every administrative village sent its "five big cadres," who now included the Party Branch secretary, the administrative village chief, the local public security officer, the militia chief, and the Women's Association chairman. Also invited were representatives from the APC's and the YCL branches. This huge affair involved continuous lectures and small discussion group meetings over a period of two weeks, during which the communization program was outlined in detail for all these key local cadres, as well as for cadres working in county-level bodies.

The County Party Committee then set up a special campaign Staff Office for Communization, and had its Organization Department transfer over two hundred county-level cadres to serve under the

[5] In some nearby areas, "production management districts" were reportedly set up at a later period, in 1960, and existed briefly as intermediary units between the communes and brigades; normally they included two to four brigades.

office, on temporary duty. These cadres were organized into work groups (*kung tso tsu*) which were trained to operate at the local level. The size of the groups was not uniform, but many had six cadres including a chief (*tsu chang*), a deputy (*fu tsu chang*), and four others. After a ten-day period of intensive indoctrination in the county seat, the work groups were sent to the districts. In most places, it then took the groups roughly three months to convert the district governments into communes.

Collaborating with both the district Party committees and Party branch leaders in the administrative villages, the work groups held endless meetings at both the district and administrative village levels. In the administrative villages, probably the most important of these meetings initially were the so-called "congresses of cadres and activists" (*chi kan ta hui*), where the proposed communes were explained to key cadres of the Party, the local government, the YCL, the APC's, the militia, and the Women's Association.

After briefing the key local cadres, the work groups then organized intensive propaganda to reach the mass of ordinary peasants; all teachers and YCL members were mobilized to assist in this propaganda campaign. Many extreme promises of rapid economic progress were made to the peasants at this time. At most of the mass meetings ("congresses of village masses," *hsiang ch'ün chung ta hui*) convened in the administrative villages, both the chief of the county-dispatched work group and the local Party secretary gave glowing accounts of what the communes might accomplish. Finally, the masses were asked whether they wished to establish communes; they invariably decided to do so "voluntarily."

The visiting Work Group and local Party leaders then proceeded to establish commune institutions at the district level, production brigades at the administrative village level, and production teams in the villages. In the majority of areas in this general region, there was no radical turnover of local leadership; the old district cadres simply became the new commune cadres. The county did, however, "transfer downward" some cadres—including a few from the County Party Committee—to fill key posts, such as that of first secretary, in certain commune Party committees. When this was done, the old district Party secretary often took over the number two post, that of secretary of the Commune Party Committee. There were also some shifts of cadres between various district-commune areas. These personnel changes, while not numerous, did strengthen the Party's leadership in some areas where it had been relatively weak.

It is revealing of the general atmosphere of regimentation and "militarization" at the time when communization took place in this area that the various component parts of the new communes were at first referred to locally by strictly military titles. The communes (the former districts) were now called regiments (*t'uan*), the production brigades (former administrative villages) were called companies (*lien*), and the production teams were called platoons (*p'ai*). For a period of time in some communes in this area, units comparable to the early joint administrative villages were set up between the communes and the brigades and were called battalions (*ying*). The use of these military titles lasted in this area for almost two years.

Commune C

AS OF 1964 a total of seventy-four thousand communes existed in China. What follows is a detailed description of one of these, which we will call Commune C. This commune was located in the same general region of south China as the two counties, A and X, previously discussed, but it did not actually belong to either of these counties.[6]

General Characteristics and Evolution

Commune C was a very large unit, containing over eleven thousand households and more than sixty thousand people. This was considerably larger than the national average, but it was by no means unique, since there were many other communes in China which were as large. In 1958 Commune C had been formed, as was the pattern in this area, on the basis of one district; and as of 1964 it was divided into sixteen production brigades, each of which had originally been an administrative village. Typically, each brigade in Commune C contained two to four natural villages. For example, one of the brigades, which will be described in detail below (and will be called Brigade B), had three natural villages and a total population of roughly twenty-eight hundred people, or between five hundred and six hundred households. In its administrative evolution over the years prior to 1958, the area constituting Commune C had gone through a process paralleling that already described in the anal-

[6] The preceding discussion in this part of the book describes County A, rather than the county in which Commune C was located, because comparable data could not be obtained on the latter, but it is believed to have undergone a similar evolution.

ysis of County A, and even after 1958 its evolution was no less complex. As originally established, the commune lasted only a very brief period of time. As in most of China, very significant changes had been introduced by 1959, and by 1961 Commune C was a very different institution from what it had been at the start. Since the major changes in Commune C were the result of directives originating from the highest Party leaders,[7] they generally paralleled those which took place in communes elsewhere in China.

When Commune C was first organized in late 1958, it introduced many radical and revolutionary innovations which reflected the visionary goals which China's top leaders aimed for at that time. All government and collective organizations in the area were merged into a huge monolithic unit responsible for industry, agriculture,

[7] The following are among the major Communist Party directives concerning communes which were not made public by the Chinese Communists but have become available through Hong Kong and Taiwan sources: "Letter Containing the Urgent Directives from the Central Committee of the Chinese Communist Party Concerning the Problems of the Present Policy Toward the Rural People's Commune," November 2, 1960 (*Union Research Service*, Vol. XXVIII, No. 12, August 10, 1962); "Draft Regulations (Rules) on the Work of the Rural People's Communes" (*nung ts'un jen min kung she t'iao li—ts'ao an*), March, 1961 (Political Organ, Research Department, Bureau of Investigation, Ministry of National Defense, Republic of China, 1964); "Revised Draft Regulations on the Work of the Rural People's Communes" (*nung ts'un jen min kung she t'iao li—hsiu cheng ts'ao an*), September, 1962 (National Security Bureau, Ministry of National Defense, Republic of China, May, 1965); "On the Decision to Further Consolidate the Collective Economy of the People's Communes and to Develop Agricultural Production" (*kuan yü chin yi pu kung ku jen min kung she chi t'i ching chi fa chan nung yeh sheng ch'an ti chüeh ting*), September 27, 1962 (Political Organ, Research Department, Bureau of Investigation, Ministry of National Defense, Republic of China, 1964); "Central Committee Regulations on Several Specific Policies Concerning the Rural Socialist Education Campaign" (*chung yang kuan yü nung ts'un she hui chu yi chiao yü yün tung chung yi hsieh chü t'i cheng ts'e ti kuei ting*) (National Security Bureau, Ministry of National Defense, Republic of China, May, 1965); "Draft Decisions of the Central Committee Concerning Certain Problems of Current Rural Work" (*chung yang kuan yü mu ch'ien nung ts'un kung tso chung jo kan wen t'i chüeh ting*), May 20, 1963 (Intelligence Bureau, Ministry of National Defense, Republic of China, February 23, 1965).

finance, banking, retailing, education, and military affairs, as well as for all the traditional functions of local government. The commune took over ownership of all important remnants of private enterprise, except private homes; these included not only the peasants' private plots and animals but also family cooking utensils. A combination of so-called "free supply" and wages was introduced at the start in Commune C. Public mess halls were established, and everyone had to eat in them. All able-bodied women, as well as the entire male population, were organized to participate in labor; nurseries and old age homes were established to care for dependents. Work groups were organized on a highly regimented basis, and the hours of work were greatly increased. In the first months of its existence, the commune drafted very large numbers of peasants to participate in new, small-scale, commune-run enterprises, especially the "backyard steel furnaces" and activities connected with them. Labor in the fields was also greatly intensified, and several radical new agricultural techniques, including deep plowing and close planting, were energetically promoted.

Here, as elsewhere, however, the commune simply did not work as originally envisaged. Its 1958–1959 crops failed, and soon a serious food shortage developed. Its backyard steel furnaces were also a failure, and when they were abandoned in 1959 there was little to show for all the frenetic effort expended in 1958; no substantial net addition to the area's local industry remained. The diversion of substantial amounts of labor from agriculture in the early days created great confusion. In addition, the commune's administrators were simply not able to perform all the myriad functions assigned to them. Moreover, the majority of peasants, who became rapidly disillusioned, soon reacted against excessive regimentation and against the efforts of the cadres to make them work without real economic incentives, and began dragging their feet.

During 1959, following the national Party leaders' call for what was in effect a retreat, the local leaders in Commune C began to implement a process of steady decentralization within the commune. It continued through 1961 with only one brief halt in late 1959. In 1959–1960, Commune C first transferred the ownership of much land, animals, and tools to its brigades. The power of the commune to control and allocate labor and capital was restricted, the "free supply" system was limited, and payments to peasants on the basis of work points were reintroduced. The county government reasserted control over local banking institutions, the commercial cooperatives, and a number of other organizations. During this period, also, the "three-level ownership" (*san chi so yu*) system was introduced.[8] The brigades became the basic accounting units which managed production and distributed income. In 1960, all public mess halls and some other public institutions were closed down in Commune C, and the first steps were taken toward the restoration of private plots and free markets.

Then, during 1961–1962, further secret directives came from above calling for sweeping changes. The Party Central Committee issued two extremely important documents in this period, the "sixty articles" (*liu shih t'iao*) and the "twelve articles" (*shih erh t'iao*).[9] Now, in Commune C, the powers of even the brigades were restricted, and the production teams became the basic production units. Prime stress was placed on the need to increase agricultural output, and it was recognized that to this end it was necessary to restore individual incentives by allowing the development of private plots and free markets. Decentralization of powers within the commune was furthered, and both the commune and its brigades were strictly limited in the amount of labor they could employ (no more than 5 percent of the work force). Relations between the brigades and teams were now regulated by the so-called system of "three guarantees and one reward"; the teams promised to meet certain targets for output, costs, and use of labor, and they obtained bonuses if they did better than promised. Also introduced was the system of "four fixes," which assured the teams of the use of definite quantities of land, labor, tool, and animals.[10]

[8] This "three-level ownership" system was formulated by the Party resolution emerging from the Lushan meeting in August, 1959.

[9] The "sixty articles," contained in the Central Committee "Draft Regulations" of March, 1961, defined production teams as the units to manage production; but the brigades remained as the basic accounting units. The "twelve articles," contained in the Central Committee's decisions of September, 1962, made the production teams the accounting units.

[10] These measures were called for in the Central Committee's directives of November, 1962.

These various moves, emphasizing decentralization of authority within the communes and restoration of some real economic incentives, corrected many of the errors that had been made in the early period of communization, helped to restore peasant morale, and—with the help of good weather—resulted in a steady recovery of agricultural output from 1962 on. In the process, however, they changed Commune C so much that in some respects it bore little resemblance in 1964 to what it had been when first established. The description of Commune C which follows outlines its institutions and functions as of 1964, rather than as originally conceived in the first days of communization.

The Party: Roles and Organization

Political leadership was concentrated in a small group of Party elite in Commune C as throughout China. As at higher levels in the bureaucratic power structure there were also two parallel hierarchies in Commune C: that of the Party and that of the commune (*kung she*). The primacy of the Party was even clearer, however, and the interlocking of directorates even greater, than at higher levels. In fact, in Commune C, the trend toward direct Party rule was so great—in the late 1950s and early 1960s—that in many respects the Party and commune structures were merged, at least in terms of leadership, and most of the top commune officials were Party leaders wearing different hats. (This was even more true of the brigade level, as will be noted later; see p. 367.)

The Party Committee (*she tang wei yüan hui*) in Commune C, which in practice was the highest local authority in the area, was a sizable body. Included in its membership were all functionaries who held defined posts in the Party and all those who held leadership posts in the commune, as well as the secretaries (*shu chi*) of the Party branches in all sixteen of the commune's production brigades (*ta tui chih pu*). The total membership was over thirty. (Reportedly the Party committees in some other communes were smaller than this.)

Altogether there were between four and five hundred Party members in the commune, with an average of twenty to thirty in each of the sixteen production brigade Party branches. In absolute terms, this was a fairly large Party membership for a commune. But since Commune C had an unusually large population, Party membership was not surprisingly large in per capita terms; in fact it was less than 1 percent of the total population of around sixty thousand.

In theory, the members of the Party Committee in Commune C were elected by its subordinate units, the branches; but in practice the County Party Committee played a large role in choosing the members, and the commune committee invariably included all those selected for functionary posts. There were ten specific functionary posts in Commune C's Party Committee: Party secretary, first and second deputy secretaries, political committeeman, organization committeeman, propaganda committeeman, study committeeman, youth committeeman, women's committeewoman, and secretarial clerk. All persons slated for these posts had to be approved by the County Party Committee, and sometimes the county Party authorities took the initiative in designating cadres for these commune posts. In Commune C, for example, the Party secretary and political committeeman, the two most powerful persons in the commune committee, had both been directly assigned to this commune by the county committee.

The County Party Committee also had the power, in reality if not in theory, to designate persons to fill the key posts in the Commune Management Committee. Generally it let the Commune Party Committee do this, but from time to time it did intervene, either to suggest or to veto specific cadres. Since all the cadres slated to become key functionaries in either the Party or the commune hierarchy were automatically candidates for the Commune Party Committee, the "election" of the committee consisted of little more than confirmation of decisions already made by the existing leaders of both the county and commune committees.

Party dominance of Commune C's entire organizational apparatus could hardly have been greater. Altogether there were close to forty important functionary posts in the Party Committee, the Commune Management Committee, and attached organizations. Because of the significant overlapping of jobs, these posts were occupied by slightly over thirty persons. Most of these were state cadres who received regular government salaries rather than depending for their income on shares of the commune's agricultural output, distributed on the basis of work points. All were exempt from agricultural labor (*t'o ch'an*). (This contrasted with the situation at the brigade level, where most cadres were exempt from labor but were not state cadres.) Eighteen of the functionaries were members of the Party Committee, and all but two of the rest were Party members, the two exceptions being members of the YCL. In short, all the men holding important posts in this particular commune belonged to either the Party or the YCL.

At the county level, as indicated earlier, the heads of Party departments—with a few exceptions—generally were not concurrently chiefs of bureaus or other government bodies; their broad responsibilities, involving Party supervision of numerous government bodies, fully occupied their time and energy. In Commune C, however, the overlap of jobs was substantial; and at the brigade level, it became even greater. In the commune, six of the ten Party Committee functionaries held concurrent leadership posts in the Commune Management Committee. The Party's political committeeman headed the commune's Political and Legal Department, and the first deputy secretary was deputy chief of that department. The second deputy secretary was chief of the commune's Finance Department. The organization committeeman was first deputy director of the commune. The propaganda committeeman was chief of the commune's Industry and Communications Department. And the Party's secretarial clerk was also secretarial clerk of the commune. Of the remaining four Party Committee functionaries, only the secretary and the study committeeman held no other jobs. The youth committeeman and women's committeewoman headed the YCL and the Women's Association, respectively. Moreover, *all* the other leaders in the Commune Management Committee, including the director, the second deputy director, and the chiefs of the six other departments, were members of the Party Committee even though they did not hold functionary posts in the Party hierarchy.

Top Leadership

In the power structure in Commune C, five men were said to be generally recognized as the top leaders, and reportedly the ranking of these five was fairly clear, at least among the cadres. Interestingly, the commune director (*she chang*), while included in this group, was at the bottom of the list.

The undisputed top leader was the secretary (*shu chi*) of the Commune Party Committee. Since he did not hold any concurrent post in the commune itself, his authority derived solely from his Party position. The second most powerful man was the political committeeman (*cheng chih wei yüan*) in the Party Committee; as already stated, he was concurrently chief of the commune's Political and Legal Department (*cheng fa pu*). The fact that this person outranked, and clearly wielded more authority than, even the two deputy party secretaries was a very significant reflection of the special power position of those connected with the public security system, even at the commune level. The third and fourth positions in the power hierarchy were said to be occupied by the first and second deputy party secretaries (*ti yi fu shu chi* and *ti ehr fu shu chi*); as mentioned above, the former was concurrently deputy chief of the commune's Political and Legal Department while the latter was chief of the commune's Finance Department. Finally, fifth in the ranking, was the commune director, who was a member of the Party Committee but did not hold any defined functionary post in the Party structure. The fact that the commune director was considered less powerful than three men who held commune posts which were ostensibly under his direction but who outranked him in the Party apparatus, highlighted the fact that one's real standing in the power hierarchy derived fundamentally from status in the Party apparatus rather than status in the commune organization.

The social characteristics and career histories of these five men reveal the nature of the top local leadership in at least one of China's seventy-four thousand communes; and while it is not possible to assume that this one area was "typical," there is reason to believe that in many areas of south China, and perhaps elsewhere, there are numerous communes with leaders of a similar sort.

The Party secretary was an "old cadre," about fifty years of age, of poor peasant background, whose experience had been primarily in military and security work. Before 1949 he had belonged to a Communist guerrilla unit in a nearby mountain area. After "liberation" he was made chief of an armed, police-type unit (*wu chuang tui*, literally, armed forces group or team) in one of the districts (*ch'ü*) in this county. Subsequently, he was assigned for special training at a Party school at the special district level and then became chief of the district government's Political and Legal Department. From this post he was later elevated to his current position of commune Party secretary. He did not come from within the commune's own area, but he was from the same county. It was the County Party Committee which had promoted and transferred him to his current position, even though commune Party committees theoretically elected their own leaders. His formal education had been limited to primary school, but his subsequent training in the Party had raised his "cultural standard" (*wen hua ch'eng tu*) to a somewhat higher level.

The Party political committeeman, a man of about forty, was also of poor peasant origin, and had a background that was primarily military; but he was unusually well educated. In fact he had completed higher middle school before joining the Communist military forces just prior to "liberation." He stayed in the army until 1956, rising to become a first lieutenant (*chung wei*) and company commander (*lien chang*). Then he was transferred (*chuan yeh*) to be chief of the Militia Group (*min ping tui chang*) in one of the administrative villages in this general area. It was from that job that he was eventually elevated to his current posts. His home county was the one where Commune C was located but, like the Party secretary, he was not from the area of the commune itself.

The first deputy Party secretary, a local man in his early forties, also came from a poor peasant background. He had joined the Communist Party immediately after "liberation," during the land reform period. His first important post was that as head of a militia group in an administrative village. Subsequently, he became chief of the same administrative village, and then a Party committeeman in a district Party committee. This committee was ultimately converted into the Party Committee of Commune C, and it was after this change that he assumed his current posts. He was fairly well educated, having completed lower middle school.

The second deputy Party secretary was also a local man in his early forties who came from a poor peasant background and was a graduate of lower middle school. He had joined the Party soon after "liberation," and first became a secretarial clerk (*wen shu*) in an administrative village government. Subsequently, he became a district Party committeeman and then assumed his present posts when the commune was established.

The commune director was in his mid-forties. He, too, was a local man of poor peasant background and had joined the Party after "liberation." During land reform he became a secretarial clerk in his local Peasant Association (*nung min hsieh hui*, or *nung hui*, for short), then rose to be a district Party committeeman. When Commune C was first established he became head of one of its factories, and then subsequently was chosen to be commune director.

To generalize about the social characteristics of these men—and their characteristics were shared by a large percentage of the other leading cadres in Commune C—they were, first of all, local men for the most part, and even the two top leaders who did not originate from the particular area of the commune were at least from the same county. This was not true of all communes in this region; some had a larger number of leaders who were outsiders, and a few were even led by "northerners" (the county committee not infrequently sent outsiders to become Party secretaries and other key Party functionaries in communes considered to have problems). But it was true of many, and it contrasted with the situation at the county level in this region, where leadership posts were overwhelmingly dominated by northerners.

Most of the top men in Commune C were in their early forties, which meant that they had been in their late twenties at the time of Communist takeover. All had joined the Party while fairly young, either before "liberation" or soon thereafter, and therefore had had a good many years of Party experience. The very top men were "old cadres" whose Party membership predated 1949.

All the commune's leaders were classified as persons having poor peasant class origins. This reflected a conscious Party policy to select rural leaders primarily from this group.[11] Somewhat surprisingly, all had had some formal education; and some of the leaders, who had completed middle school, were comparatively well educated—better, in fact, than not a few "old cadres" who held high posts in the county-level apparatus. The very top leaders in Commune C all had had military and/or police backgrounds, with experience in guerrilla forces, the regular army, and militia, public security, or other similar groups. Some, but not all, had worked in this same area before the district government was converted into a commune.

These characteristics, needless to say, were radically different from those of the local leadership group in this area in the period prior to Communist takeover. Before 1949 comparatively affluent landlords and rich peasants had tended to dominate the local power structure here, as in most of rural China. Now, however, Commune C was led by a new breed of men, products of the Communist-engineered revolution, which had resulted in an almost total turnover of local rural leadership in the years immediately after 1949. This new breed was itself already becoming a fairly well-defined, special, vested-interest group, however, and those who had joined the Party early tended to dominate it.

Commune Organization

In Commune C the over-all organization of the commune itself included three main bodies, the Commune Congress (*she yüan tai piao ta hui*); the Commune Management Committee (*kuan li wei yüan hui*), under which were a number of subordinate departments (*pu*); and the Commune Supervision Committee (*chien ch'a wei yüan hui*) responsible for checking on the other bodies.

The congress, popularly elected by all enfranchised commune members and with representatives from each of the commune's sub-

[11] There is some evidence that during the collectivization "upsurge" of 1955–1956 the Chinese Communists reaffirmed a policy of excluding all middle peasants (except for some former poor peasants who had become lower middle peasants) from leadership posts in the cooperatives in some areas.

ordinate production units, was theoretically the top organ of authority, as elected representative bodies are purported to be at any level in China; but like all such bodies throughout the country its role in Commune C was more symbolic than real. It was supposedly elected every two years, but elections were not always held on schedule. Everyone eighteen years of age or over who was not politically disenfranchised (see p. 232) could take part in the voting, which was by show of hands rather than by secret ballot. In practice, the elections were strictly *pro forma*, since the local Party organization, in consultation with higher (county) Party authorities, drew up a single slate of nominees for each election, and those nominated were automatically elected. The great majority of those elected were cadres working either for the commune itself or for its production brigades and teams.

Theoretically, the congress had authority to decide on the commune's budget, work plans, and other major policies, and it was therefore supposed to have sessions at least twice during the year. In practice, however, the congress in Commune C met infrequently and was regarded as a body having no significant decision-making authority. Its most important function was merely to elect the commune's director, its deputy directors, and the members of the commune's Management Committee and Supervision Committee.

The Supervision Committee in Commune C was a small body, consisting of a chairman, a deputy chairman, and four other members. It was elected by the congress to supervise the over-all operation of the commune and ensure implementation of current regulations and policies.

The Management Committee, consisting of close to thirty persons, all of whom were state cadres, was the organ which actually ran the commune, although it, in turn, was closely directed by, and in fact was a creature of, the Commune Party Committee. The Management Committee met regularly—generally every week—to discuss a wide range of problems and policies. Since there was a large overlap between its membership and that of the Party Committee, and since the Party secretary usually sat in ex officio on its meetings, its operations were closely coordinated with those of the Party Committee, which itself made the most important policy decisions.

The Management Committee was headed by the commune director (*she chang*). Directly assisting him were two deputies (*fu she chang*), plus a small staff office (*pan kung shih*) consisting of a secretarial clerk (*wen shu*) and three other employees. The principal work of the committee was done by its nine departments (in Commune C these were called *pu*, although in some other communes in this same general region they were called *ku*). One of these, the Administration Department (*hsing cheng pu*), was headed by one of the commune's deputy directors and in a sense was simply an adjunct to the director's office. The other eight were: the Political and Legal Department (*cheng fa pu*); the Finance Department (*ts'ai cheng pu*); the Culture, Education, and Health Department (*wen chiao wei sheng pu*); the Industry and Communications Department (*kung chiao pu*); the Commerce Department (*shang yeh pu*); the Water Conservancy Department (*shui li pu*); the Agriculture Department (*nung yeh pu*); and the Forestry and Animal Husbandry Department (*lin mu pu*).[12]

Under the Commune Management Committee and/or its departments, there were various other organizations or institutions subject to direct commune management in this area. These included the local Market Management Committee, the Commune Credit Cooperative, a hospital, the Agricultural Experimental Station, five "factories," a pig farm, a butchery, a ferry service, a boat transportation group, several fish ponds, and *ad hoc* local labor reeducation groups.

Several important institutions located in the commune were directly managed by the county authorities. The commune exercised a degree of local supervision over such institutions, which were thus under dual leadership to a certain extent; but basic control rested with the county. These bodies included the Tax Office, the Grain Management Office and three large granaries, a branch People's

[12] The terminology used for these bodies really mixed two types of titles: those used for Party organs and those used for government organs, titles that at higher administrative levels tend to be used only for one hierarchy or the other. For example, the term *pu* is generally a Party rather than a government title at county and provincial levels. The use of such terminology in Commune C subtly reflected the fact that the line dividing Party and government organs in the commune was extremely blurred, especially in the period immediately after the Great Leap Forward. Recently, there may have been a trend toward greater differentiation between Party and non-Party organs at this level.

Bank office, a middle school, and the Supply and Marketing Cooperative.

The number of cadres working directly for the Management Committee and its departments totaled close to thirty. Apart from the director, his deputies, and the Staff Office personnel, the rest were functionaries of the departments, each of which had two to three cadres (there were two exceptions: one department had four cadres and another had only one). A chief (*pu chang*) headed each department, and if there was more than one other cadre the second-ranking man was called deputy chief (*fu pu chang*).

Functions of Various Departments

Politically, the most powerful and important department in Commune C was clearly the Political and Legal Department, whose chief and deputy chief were the second and third most influential men in the commune power structure. As the local arm of the county-directed public security apparatus, it was responsible for maintenance of law, order, and political control. Its duties included both routine work—such as the census registration of all residents, control over travel and movement, registration of marriages and divorces, and the like (the Administration Department was also involved in some of these routine activities)—and vital political work, including suppression of any political dissidence, control over the "five [bad] elements," investigation of criminal activities, and so on. There was no regular court of law in the commune, but when the county established temporary people's tribunals at the commune level, it did so in collaboration with the commune's Political and Legal Department. This department, in fact if not in theory, was also responsible for certain types of mediation in disputes between different brigades. Another of its major responsibilities was the over-all leadership and direction of militia work in the commune, which in practice meant supervision of brigade militia units, since no actual units existed at the commune level in Commune C.[13]

[13] By 1964, the bulk of the real work in Commune C, not only in militia activities but in many other fields as well, was actually performed at the brigade level, under the commune's over-all direction. Conse-

Probably the second most important department in Commune C was the Finance Department, which prepared and administered the commune's budget, controlled its funds, handled all receipts and disbursements (through the local bank; see below), and was in charge of general management of local financial affairs. Its chief was the second deputy secretary of the Commune Party Committee, and its staff of four, larger than that of any other department in the commune, included an accountant (*k'uai chi*) and a cashier (*ch'u na*) as well as the chief and his deputy. The Finance Department worked in close conjunction with five other agencies in the commune. Three of these were county-controlled institutions which, in effect, were branches of county organizations even though they were also supervised by local commune authorities: (1) the Grain Management Office (*liang shih kuan li so*, or *liang kuan so*, for short), which had primary responsibility for collecting the land—i.e. grain—tax and also maintained three large granaries (*ts'ang k'u*); (2) the Tax Office (*shui wu so*), which collected levies other than the land tax; and (3) the local commune branch (*chih hang*) of the People's Bank (*jen min yin hang*), which among other things served as custodian of the commune's funds. The other two agencies were (4) the local Commune Market Management Committee (*shih ch'ang kuan li wei yüan hui*) and (5) the commune's Credit Cooperative (*hsin yung ho tso she*, or *hsin yung she*, for short).

A third commune department, already mentioned, was the Administration Department, which had a variety of fairly routine functions. It kept records on population changes, marriages, and so on, and also helped the director in the general administration of the commune government.

The Culture, Education, and Health Department had a wider variety of responsibilities. It was responsible, for example, for all regular mass-propaganda activities in the commune (see pp. 379 ff.). All teachers were regarded as an important reserve force for propagandizing the mass of ordinary commune members, and during

---

quently, detailed discussion of many commune activities will be deferred to the section on Brigade B, which starts on p. 363. The description here of Commune C's departments will simply list their major fields of responsibility.

every major political campaign the department made special efforts to mobilize them to play active roles. The department also supervised the operation of all primary schools throughout the commune, most of which were located at the brigade level; and reportedly, it contributed financially to primary schools in the brigades. This department was also responsible for conducting regular political study (*hsüeh hsi*) for primary school teachers in the brigades, and every summer it organized special political study courses for them. The one middle school in Commune C, however, was a state-run lower middle school directly supported and managed by the County Bureau of Education rather than by the commune; thus it was not under the primary control of this commune department.

One hospital (*wei sheng yüan*, or *wei sheng so*) was operated by the Culture, Education, and Health Department, and served the entire commune. This was a small and rather poorly equipped institution, with only ten beds, and of necessity it concentrated on treatment of outpatients. Minor hospitalization cases were accepted, but major ones had to be sent on to the county hospital. The department also supervised small health stations (*wei sheng chan*) which were maintained by most, although not all, of the brigades. It also was responsible for organizing the periodic health and sanitation campaigns which were promoted and directed by the County Health Bureau.

The Industry and Communications Department was in charge of all five "factories" run by Commune C as well as for the maintenance of major local transportation facilities. The commune's factories, referred to as local state-run factories (*ti fang kuo ying kung ch'ang*), were relatively small affairs. They included a rice mill (*liang shih chia kung ch'ang*), an agricultural implements factory (*nung hsieh ch'ang*), a furniture factory (*mu ch'i ch'ang*), and a handicraft factory which manufactured bambooware (*chu ch'i shou kung ch'ang*). The most important responsibility of this department in the transportation field was maintenance and improvement of the one major road linking the commune with the county seat. In this connection the department helped to maintain a local transportation station (*yün shu chan*), which was served by county-run buses and trucks. It also controlled over thirty junks; these were organized into a boat transportation group (*mu ch'uan yün shu tui*), which operated largely within the confines of the commune. Finally, the department operated one small local ferryboat, a wooden barge which provided regular service across the largest river, or rather stream, in the commune's area.

The Water Conservancy Department was responsible for building and repairing all major irrigation works in the commune and also decided on the allocation to its various brigades of water coming into the commune from outside its boundaries. In the period during and immediately after communization, this department built, in co-operation with a neighboring commune, one large irrigation canal and two smaller ones, using labor provided by the brigades. Together with its brigades, it also organized continual repair and maintenance work on many smaller distribution canals.

The Agriculture Department of Commune C had responsibility, within the framework of general plans and instructions passed down from the County Bureau of Agriculture and other county authorities, for over-all planning of agricultural production and, perhaps most important, helping to ensure that its brigades met their regular quotas for the land tax (*kung liang*) and compulsory sales of grain to the state (locally, such grain was simply referred to as *yü liang*, meaning "extra grain"). In practice, agricultural planning at the commune level, at least in Commune C, consisted mainly of taking over-all county-defined output target figures for various types of crops, working out with the brigades a rational division of responsibilities, and then agreeing with each brigade on specific production targets for the major crops. In times of natural calamities, the Agriculture Department, with county approval, could and did make adjustments in the brigades' targets, and it also organized commune-wide antiflood, antidrought, or antipest campaigns.

This department also operated the small Agricultural Experimental Station (*nung yeh shih yen chan*), where new seeds and methods were tested. This station operated slightly over ten mou of land. It was run by three specialists who were graduates of an agricultural middle school run by the special district, and a number of agricultural workers. Commune C did not have a real agricultural research institute (*nung yeh yen chiu so*) as a few—although probably very few—communes reportedly did. In fact, it was reported that in this particular area not even the county had a fully organized research station; the nearest one was at the special district headquarters.

The Commerce Department supervised all trade in the commune and also had responsibility for ensuring that quotas for sales to the state of certain subsidiary products were met. However, the actual trade, other than that which took place in the free markets, was normally in the hands of the commune's Supply and Marketing Cooperative (*kung hsiao ho tso she*), which was closely linked to the Commerce Department but was directly supervised and controlled by the county cooperative.

In Commune C there was one over-all Supply and Marketing Cooperative serving the entire commune, which itself ran a wholesale outlet (*p'i fa pu*) and several small retail stores or sales outlets (*men shih pu*); many of these were general stores called *pai huo p'u*, located in the main market centers. The wholesale store, in turn, dealt with the small supply and marketing cooperatives, and cooperative-run stores,[14] in all the brigades. (There was one cooperative in every brigade in Commune C.) In its relationships with higher levels, the commune cooperative was not only linked to the county cooperative but also dealt with a number of specialized county-level commercial companies, each of which bought or sold certain definite commodities, and with the stations (*chan*) which these companies set up in rural areas. These stations acted as agents for the companies. The most important ones were those established for the purchase of certain agricultural commodities, especially in the areas which specialized in producing major commercial crops.

Commune C's Forestry and Animal Husbandry Department had a potpourri of tasks, some of which in other areas were divided among more than one organization. It was responsibile for afforestation programs, especially in hilly areas, and for the protection of all existing woods. It controlled the slaughtering of certain domestic animals; for example, pigs could not be killed without its permission. It set quotas specifying the number of pigs, chickens, ducks, geese, and eggs which each brigade had to sell to the state. Some of these items were important export products, and county-level purchasing

---

[14] These were sometimes referred to as branch stations (*fen chan*) and sometimes simply as stores (*p'u tzu*).

agents dealt with this department in their efforts to ensure that desired supplies would be available. The department also promoted the cultivation of fish in local fresh-water ponds. Most such ponds were managed by the brigades, but a few were directly controlled by the department.

Economic Functions of the Commune

As stated earlier, although the communes in China still combine governmental and economic functions, their role in managing local economic affairs has been greatly reduced in recent years. In Commune C, as in most places, the commune's Management Committee originally had great economic power and responsibility, and had attempted not only to manage directly all industrial, commercial, and other large-scale enterprises but also to plan, organize, and distribute the output of agriculture. At the start, it owned all land and capital goods throughout the entire commune and had virtually unlimited power to mobilize and allocate labor and other resources according to a commune-wide plan. In Commune C, as elsewhere, however, this system simply did not work as envisaged, partly because the Management Committee lacked the skill and capacity to carry out such a wide range of functions successfully, and partly because the utopian concepts on which the commune was originally based ignored fundamental peasant attitudes, and unrealistically weakened the link between labor and economic rewards.

Consequently, over time Commune C's powers and tasks were steadily reduced. Most of the basic rights and functions of the original agricultural collectives which had been absorbed into the communes—including the ownership of land and agricultural capital goods (such as tools and animals), and the management and distribution of agricultural output—were first passed down to the brigades, in 1959–1960; then, in 1961–1962 in this area, actual management of agriculture was turned over to the production teams. This decentralization was extremely important. In and of itself it restored a significant link between productive labor and economic rewards, since now the members of a team divided their own output among themselves instead of simply obtaining a share of the over-all production of the entire commune. Additional steps, including the restoration of private plots and free markets, were taken along with organizational decentralization to strengthen economic incentives for increased production.

Decentralization of important responsibilities to the team level did not mean, however, that the commune itself, or its brigades, lost all significant economic powers and functions. Both continued to be important in many fields; but by and large, their primary roles were now those previously associated with the government, such as overall planning, control of large-scale economic enterprises, grain management, tax collection, and the like, rather than those associated with the precommune collectives. Most of the collectives' functions were taken over by the teams. Information from ex-cadres clearly indicates that among the most important responsibilities which continued to be exercised by the communes even after the decentralization moves of 1959–1961 were grain management and tax collection.

Commune C, like all bodies between the top planning agencies in the central government and the basic production units, played an intermediary role in the process of formulating economic plans. It received general targets from agencies at the next higher level of authority, the county, and then, after making adjustments and consulting with its brigades, worked out targets for the brigades. (The brigades, similarly, then consulted with their teams and worked out targets for them.)

Since grain production was the most important single economic activity in Commune C, and since grain procurement was a matter of vital concern to all higher levels of government, it is not surprising that the establishment of quotas for the land tax and for compulsory sales of grain to the state were a major preoccupation of county, commune, and brigade alike. In the county to which Commune C belonged, the general land tax quotas for all communes had been stabilized in 1961, with a promise—designed to increase overall output—that no fundamental changes would be made for some years, and this promise had been observed with reasonable fidelity, at least through 1964. Consequently, in the years immediately after 1961, the commune knew fairly well what its annual land tax quotas were likely to be. Some annual adjustments were made in the quotas which it set for various brigades, after careful discussion and negotiation with them. The quotas for compulsory grain sales varied from year to year, however, so the process of establishing such quotas for each administrative level down to the teams was more complicated and time-consuming.

Commune-level institutions were the ones directly responsible for actual land tax collections and state grain purchases; but since these institutions at the commune level were essentially branches of county organizations, the local commune authorities merely collaborated with them and did not have real control over them. In the collection of the land tax, the key bodies were the Grain Management Office (*liang shih kuan li so*, or *liang kuan so*, for short) and five granaries run by it in the commune, one near the commune headquarters and four scattered throughout the commune. All the production teams throughout the commune delivered their quotas of tax grain directly to these granaries twice a year, once in the summer and once in the late fall, after the main harvests. The brigades, therefore, were not directly responsible for deliveries; they did, however, inform all their teams not only of their land tax liability but also of the schedule for deliveries and the granaries to which tax grain should be sent. Once delivered, most of the grain, apart from the small amount imposed by the commune as a local surtax, came under the control of the county-run Grain Management Office. Some of it was later moved to the larger county granaries, but a part was kept in storage in the commune-level granaries.

Similarly, each production team delivered to these same granaries its minimum quota of grain which had to be sold to the state. This delivery was usually made at the same time that the tax grain was sent. However, the teams received special receipts for such grain and then could redeem them for cash at the Grain Management Office, depositing the cash either in the commune-level bank or the brigades' Credit Cooperative. The prices which the state paid for this grain were considerably lower, however, than a free market price would have been. It was estimated in Commune C that the combined value of the land tax and the presumed loss to the producers due to the low state price for compulsory grain sales amounted to close to 20 percent of the value of the commune's total grain output.

Although these grain levies were the most important taxes imposed on Commune C and its subordinate units, a variety of other commercial, industrial, and miscellaneous taxes were collected in the commune. The collection of most of these was the responsibility of the commune-level Tax Office (*shui wu so*), which, like the Grain Management Office, operated essentially as a branch of the county government. Most of the receipts from these taxes were channeled directly to the county government, although a small proportion was considered to be local tax, or surtax (*ti fang shui*, or *ti fang fu chia shui*) and was turned over to the commune.

One other commune-level body was also involved in collection of taxes in Commune C. The Market Management Committee (*shih ch'ang kuan li wei yüan hui*) was, as its name implied, responsible for general supervision and control of all the markets in the commune, that is, the free markets, which in this area were revived from 1960 onward, after the Great Leap Forward. Part of the committee's responsibility involved the collection of certain taxes on transactions in these markets.

In 1964 both of the two free markets existing in Commune C— which had first been called "basic-level agricultural trade markets" (*nung yeh mao yi ch'u chi shih ch'ang*, or *nung mao ch'u chi shih ch'ang*), then "higher markets" (*kao chi shih ch'ang*), and finally "free markets" (*tzu yu shih chang*)[15]—were revivals of important markets that had existed previously in this region. As in the period before Communist takeover, both operated on ten-day cycles, and like most adjoining rural markets in China they were on alternating schedules. One met on the first, fourth, and seventh days of each cycle, and the other on the second, fifth, and eighth days. These were the only two important markets that had existed in this area before 1949, and Commune C included most of the natural villages that had traditionally traded in these two markets. It is significant that the natural villages not included were nevertheless allowed to continue using these markets, an indication that traditional patterns of economic relations were hard to ignore completely. Tax receipts from the transactions of persons from these villages were not kept by Commune C, however, but were transferred to the communes to which the villages now belonged.

On all market days, representatives of Commune C's Market

[15] There may have been some overlapping in the use of these terms.

Management Committee were present at the markets to police and regulate them in a variety of ways. These representatives checked to see that existing price restrictions were observed. They were also expected to ensure that peasants did not sell certain commodities on the free market until after they had fulfilled their quotas for com- pulsory sale of these commodities to the state. The peasants had cards indicating their quotas, and their sales to the state were registered on them. The committee's representatives, as already stated, also collected certain taxes. For some commodities, a fixed ad valorem tax was imposed on all sales; for others, small transac- tions were tax-free, but larger ones had to be measured with official scales, and fees were collected for the use of those scales.

All tax receipts collected by commune-level agencies were de- posited in the branch bank in the commune, another agency which was county-run. The largest part of the receipts was forwarded to the county, but a smaller part was credited to the commune and kept for it in the bank. Apart from its limited share of these tax receipts, the commune relied financially, to a large extent, upon the profits of its own economic enterprises, plus miscellaneous income from certain irrigation fees and the like. Actually, even though the commune drew up its own annual budget, its financial autonomy was limited. County approval had to be obtained for its budget. Moreover, because so much of the tax revenue collected in the commune had to be turned over to the county, the commune nor- mally had only limited resources to do more than maintain its pay- roll and minimum services. For major construction and development purposes, it could, however, obtain some outside financial support. For projects which the county government was likely to consider particularly important from its own point of view, such as the con- struction of a needed local granary or certain major water conserv- ancy projects, the county on occasion gave outright subsidies to the commune. For other purposes, such as building or expanding a local factory, the commune could request loans from the bank, which sometimes, although not always, was able to provide the nec- essary credits.

All in all, it was clear that in the period after the Great Leap For- ward, though Commune C's economic functions were far less im- portant than those originally envisaged, the commune was still the key level of local authority for carrying out certain basic governmental functions in the economic field. These, as stated, tended to be fairly traditional responsibilities rather than the dramatically new ones conceived during the first flush of enthusiastic communization in 1958.

Production Brigade B

General Characteristics and Organization

ONE OF Commune C's sixteen production brigades (*sheng ch'an ta tui*)—which we will call Brigade B—consisted of three natural villages, with a total population of twenty-seven to twenty-eight hundred people, or five to six hundred families.[16] Located in a fairly typical south China rice-growing area, all three of these population clusters were simple farming villages. One had a population of somewhat over one thousand, another slightly under one thousand, and the third between seven and eight hundred. The brigade's headquarters, located in one of these villages, was four kilometers from the commune headquarters, which was about the average distance between each of the sixteen brigades and the commune headquarters (the farthest was eight kilometers from commune headquarters). The county seat, however, was more distant, twenty-two kilometers away. (Commune C's headquarters was also about twenty kilometers from the county seat.)

When first formed, Brigade B had twelve fairly large production teams (*sheng ch'an hsiao tui*, or *sheng ch'an tui*) each of which was comparable to one of the earlier lower APC's in this area and consisted of forty to sixty families, or roughly two to three hundred individuals. In 1961, however, these were split into twenty-four production teams, and the average size dropped to a little over twenty families, or about one hundred people. The largest of the three natural villages in the brigade had ten teams; the other two villages had eight and six teams, respectively. No team had membership extending beyond the natural village in which it was located.

[16] In some parts of China, production brigades tend to be coterminous with a single natural village.

The production teams were themselves divided into small production groups (*sheng ch'an hsiao tsu*), each consisting of six or seven families, or roughly thirty to thirty-five persons. These were not administrative units such as the communes, brigades, and teams; they were simply convenient groupings for work assignments. In this area the members of a particular family group—that is, of a nuclear family, consisting of parents and children—tended to be assigned to one work group, although this was not the case in all nearby areas. In size, the work groups were roughly comparable to some of the earliest mutual aid teams. In schematic terms, there were about three work groups per team and thus between seventy and eighty work groups in the entire brigade.

In Brigade B, as in all of Commune C's brigades, the highest leadership organ was theoretically the Brigade Congress (*tai piao ta hui*), elected every year and consisting of over fifty people. In practice it invariably included all cadres holding definite functionary posts in the Brigade Party Branch (*ta tui chih pu*) and the Brigade Management Committee (*ta tui kuan li wei yüan hui*), as well as a minimum of one representative, and sometimes two, from each of the twenty-four production teams.

Nominations for membership in the congress were drawn up by the Brigade Party Branch Committee. Normally a single slate of nominees was selected by the Party and was then sent to the teams, each of which convened a general meeting of all team members to discuss and vote on it. It was possible at this stage for a team to disapprove of particular candidates, particularly ones belonging to that team, and suggest the substitution of other names, but this was done only rarely. As in virtually all elections in China, the process tended to be a *pro forma* endorsement of Party decisions. Consequently, most ordinary peasants in the brigade were said to have relatively little interest in the elections and did not take them too seriously; they realized that the process of selecting leadership really took place within the Party hierarchy.

When drawing up its slate of candidates, the brigade Party leaders had to obtain approval from the Commune Party Committee for candidates who were slated to become functionaries at the brigade level, but it did not have to obtain such approval for nominees for team representatives. Usually such approval was almost automatic, but the commune could, if it wished to do so, sponsor certain brigade cadres for leadership posts, or veto others.

Once the congress was chosen it met and elected the brigade chief (*ta tui chang*) and the ten congress members who were to make up the Management Committee. This too tended to be a *pro forma* process, since the Management Committee in Brigade B consisted simply of the eight persons slated to fill brigade posts, plus two other top Party leaders, the branch secretary and his deputy; everyone knew before the Management Committee was formally elected, therefore, who was to make up the group. After the committee was selected, the chief, acting on the basis of decisions already made by the Party Branch, then formally decided which of its members would fill each of the functionary posts in the brigade's table of organization.

The Brigade Congress met occasionally, when the Party Branch wished to involve a fairly large number of people in meetings to deal with important policy questions. The congress was useful mainly because it had representatives from all the teams. Its meetings were not very frequent, however. It was supposed to meet at least twice a year. Reportedly, in some places brigade congresses are supposed to meet four times a year; but in Brigade B once or twice a year was normal. Between congresses, team representatives were involved in many other sorts of meetings convened by the brigade.

The day-to-day work of Brigade B was handled by the Management Committee, which did meet frequently. Brigade B's committee had nine functionary posts filled by eight men: the brigade chief (*ta tui chang*); the deputy chief (*fu tui chang*, or *ta tui fu*); the economic management cadre (*ching chi kuan li kan pu*, or *ching kuan kan pu*); the deputy economic management cadre (*fu ching kuan kan pu*); the public security officer (*chih pao wei yüan*), who in Brigade B was also the militia chief (*min ping tui chang*); the cashier (*ch'u na*); the accountant (*k'uai chi*); and the secretarial clerk (*wen shu*). Even the Management Committee's power and importance were restricted, however, since all major policy decisions were actually made in meetings of the Brigade Party Branch.

Many brigades in China also have a so-called Supervision Committee, elected by the congress to serve as a watchdog agency; but in Brigade B, there was no such body.

The headquarters of Brigade B was located in one large house which formerly had been the home of a leading local landlord. It contained the key leadership organizations in the brigade, including the Party Branch (*tang chih pu*), the Brigade Office (*ta tui pan kung shih*), the Militia Office (*min ping pan kung shih*), and the headquarters of both the YCL (*ch'ing nien t'uan*) and the Women's Association (*fu nü hui*). Several other organizations operated by or located in the brigade were housed separately; these included the granary (*ts'ang k'u*), the Supply and Marketing Cooperative (*kung hsiao ho tso she*), and the Credit Cooperative (*hsin yung ho tso she*).

There was one telephone in the brigade, as well as one radio receiving set. Since both were located at the brigade headquarters, this was naturally the communications center for the entire area. While the facilities for modern communications were obviously still very limited, they were much better than they had been before 1949, when there was not a single telephone or radio in the area. Brigade B was now able to maintain close and continuous contact both with the headquarters of Commune C and with all its own twenty-four team offices.

Close contacts with the commune were also ensured by the fact that brigade cadres made frequent visits to the Commune Office. At least every two months all brigade Party secretaries and brigade chiefs attended important meetings which were convened by the commune's leaders and which normally lasted two or three days. Other brigade cadres, sometimes including even team cadres, were also called to attend periodic conferences convened by the commune authorities. To cite one example, in Commune C there was an annual conference, lasting two to three days, of all brigade and team accountants. Similar meetings were held for other specialized cadres.

All the brigades in Commune C submitted a fairly large number of regular written reports to the commune; the majority of these were based on comparable reports which the brigades required their teams to submit to them. Brigade B, for example, sent to the commune monthly reports on production and economic conditions; semiannual census reports; detailed reports on output after each harvest; several important annual economic reports on plans, targets, and output; and periodic reports on water conservancy matters, the public security situation, and other questions. Special progress and summary reports were also made, during and after every campaign.

In addition, close liaison was maintained between Commune C and all its brigades by telephone, and the brigades did a good deal of regular oral reporting through this channel. The commune-wide telephone link enabled the commune to call all its brigades at any time, either to give instructions or to request information.

The Party

The structure of authority in Brigade B, as at higher levels, consisted of two separate but interlocking hierarchies: that of the Party and that of the brigade itself. If Party primacy was striking at higher levels, it was even more so in the brigade. In fact, the Party's dominance in Brigade B was total.

Altogether there were roughly fifty Party members in the entire brigade, and almost all of them held leadership posts. Collectively, they ran the lives of the more than twenty-seven hundred members of the brigade. Organized into a single Party branch (*tang chih pu* or *ta tui chih pu*), the fifty local Party members formed a well-defined elite. Of the fifty, thirty-eight were brigade or team functionaries who worked in the Party or brigade and team offices; and roughly a dozen more were cadres or members connected with various other brigade-level organizations, such as the commercial and credit cooperatives and the factories. Forty of the fifty worked at the brigade level, while only ten worked in the teams. And of the total of fifty, forty-six were classified as local cadres; the only four who were not were workers in the brigade's "factories."

The Party Branch Committee (*chih pu wei yüan hui*), elected by the entire membership, was the top decision-making body in the brigade. It consisted of nine persons: eight who held defined posts as Party functionaries, plus the brigade chief. The Party secretary (*shu chi*) outranked everyone else in the brigade and was universally recognized as the top local leader. He had under him a deputy secretary (*fu shu chi*), a political committeeman (*cheng chih wei yüan*), an organization committeeman (*tsu chih wei yüan*), a study committeeman (*hsüeh hsi wei yüan*), a youth [work] committeeman (*ch'ing nien wei yüan*), a women's [work] committeewoman (*fu nü wei yüan*), and a propaganda committeeman (*hsüan ch'üan wei yüan*), who concurrently served as Party secretarial clerk (*wen shu*). The brigade chief (*ta tui chang*), who held no special Party post as such, was the ninth member of the committee. Only one of the nine members of the committee in Brigade B was a woman.

Two members of this group—the secretary and the deputy secretary—were engaged wholly and exclusively in Party work, while the other seven held concurrent jobs either in the brigade or in the Party-directed mass organizations. This high degree of overlapping ensured total Party control of the brigades. It meant that in terms of leadership there was virtually a merger of the Party and brigade organizational structures. As already indicated, one member of the Party Committee, who held no other Party post, was brigade chief. The Party youth committeeman was deputy brigade chief (*fu tui chang*, or *ta tui fu*), as well as secretary (*shu chi*) of the local YCL Branch. The political committeeman was both brigade public security officer (*chih pao wei yüan*) and militia chief (*min ping tui chang*). The organization committeman was the brigade's economic management cadre (*ching chi kuan li kan pu* or *ching kuan kan pu*). The women's committeewoman was chairwoman of the Women's Association (*fu nü hui chu hsi*). The study committeeman was brigade cashier (*ch'u na*). And the propaganda committeeman was secretarial clerk (*wen shu*) of the brigade as well as of the Party Branch. Only two men holding posts under the Brigade Management Committee—the deputy economic management cadre (*fu ching kuan kan pu*) and the accountant (*k'uai chi*)—were not members of the Party Branch Committee; and the former was a regular Party member, while the latter was a member of the local YCL Branch Committee.

In Brigade B, despite official policies to the contrary, all members of both the Party Branch Committee and the Brigade Management Committee were reportedly full-time functionaries; that is, they were exempt from ordinary agricultural labor (*t'o ch'an*). Although they helped out in the fields during busy periods, and also cultivated private plots, they did not participate in productive labor on the same basis as ordinary team members.

Because of the virtual merger—at least in the late 1950s and early 1960s—of Party and brigade leadership, all except two members of the Brigade Management Committee were present when the Party Branch Committee met, as it did frequently. It is not surprising, therefore, in view of the emphasis placed upon the primacy of the Party in China, that it was in these branch committee meetings that key policy decisions were made. When the Party leaders met as members of the Brigade Management Committee they simply wore different hats and dealt with more routine, day-to-day operational problems.

In addition to the positions already enumerated, a good many of the remaining cadre posts in the brigade were occupied by Party members. For example, a Party man headed the Supply and Marketing Cooperative, another was secretarial clerk of the militia, and twelve were cadres in the brigade's factories. Only a very few non-Party cadres occupied any important posts at all; these included the leading cadres in the Credit Cooperative and in the schools, as well as subordinate cadres in the Supply and Marketing Cooperative.

Branch "Party life" meetings in Brigade B, which normally took place on Friday afternoons, could not be held as regularly as in urban Party branches, and the ten Party members who were members of the teams and worked at locations other than the brigade headquarters could not always attend. Nevertheless, Party meetings were held with reasonable regularity, except during the busiest farming periods.

The YCL operated here as elsewhere as a Party-controlled subsidiary for youth, and, as already stated, was headed by a member of the Party Branch Committee. It had over thirty members scattered throughout the brigade, organized into one YCL Branch. Its meetings were quite frequent, but were more irregular than those of the Party. The YCL, in turn, led the local Young Pioneers organization, which had close to one hundred members, who were pupils in brigade primary schools. A YCL member who taught in one of the three primary schools in the brigade directed the Pioneers.

The local Women's Association, whose chairwoman was the only woman on the brigade's Party Branch Committee, was a very loosely organized body in Brigade B. It met only infrequently, and was not impressively active. It did, however, promote certain programs, such as home sanitation and birth control, which were especially relevant to women and home management.

Top Leadership

In the area of Brigade B, as throughout rural China, there was a total turnover of local leadership in the years immediately after Communist takeover, and the new elite which emerged—as exemplified above by the members of the local Party Branch Committee—was very different indeed from the rural elite which had dominated the area in the pre-1949 period.

In 1964 the Party Branch secretary in Brigade B was a local poor peasant who had not had any formal education. A man in his forties, he had been active in land reform and had joined the Party when a Party committee was first formed at the district level in this area in 1952 and began active recruitment of new Party members. Not long thereafter, he became a chief of an administrative village. Subsequently, he became branch secretary of the Party in the administrative village, then a member of the Management Committee of the newly formed commune, and later was "transferred downward" by the Party from Commune C to become branch secretary in Brigade B.

The deputy secretary was close to forty. Of poor peasant origin, he had nevertheless had some primary school education. He had joined the Party during the land reform period, had headed a militia unit organized under his peasant association, had then served in the PLA, and had subsequently become a functionary in a higher APC. When the commune was established, he was secretary of the Brigade Party Branch for a brief period, but he was later replaced in that post by a cadre "transferred downward," and became deputy secretary.

The brigade chief, a local poor peasant in his late thirties, was also a primary school graduate. He too had joined the Party during land reform. Thereafter he became the secretarial clerk in the local peasant association, and then moved on to a leadership post in the administrative village. His deputy, who was concurrently youth committeeman, was likewise in his thirties. Also a local poor peasant, he was a lower middle school graduate. In school he had joined the YCL. After later holding posts as production team leader in an APC and head of the commune granary, he joined the Party and became youth committeeman in the Brigade Party Branch.

The organization committeeman, in his thirties, was also a demobilized army man. A local person of poor peasant background, he had completed two years of lower middle school. He had joined the YCL while in school, and subsequently served in the army, became a Party member, and was sent back to engage in Party work in his home area.

The political committeeman was a man in his forties and came from a poor peasant family. Although he had not had any formal education, he was literate, since he had received substantial training while serving in the army. Thereafter, he was first assigned to work on an irrigation project in this area, before being selected as political committeeman of the Brigade Party Branch Committee.

The study committeeman, about thirty years old, was the youngest of the top leaders. A local poor peasant who had graduated from primary school, he had joined the Party during the cooperativization period, in 1956.

The women's committeewoman, in her fifties, was also a local person of poor peasant background. She had had no formal education and was only semiliterate. She had once married, but her husband had gone overseas, to southeast Asia.

The propaganda committeeman was a local poor peasant. He was in his thirties and had received some middle school training. After joining the YCL in middle school, he entered the PLA and joined the Party at that time. On his return from the army he became propaganda committeeman in his APC Party Branch and continued in this post in the brigade branch.

All these top brigade leaders were local persons.[17] A sizable number had either emerged as leaders during the class struggle of

[17] For a period, one "outsider"—from a nearby area—was assigned to be political committeeman in the brigade's Party Committee. Some ex-cadres report that there was a tendency to appoint outsiders to local public security posts in many situations where single-surname villages reinforced localism.

the land reform period or were demobilized soldiers who rose to leadership posts because of their army experience; every one of them, without a single exception, was classified as coming from a poor peasant background. Most members of this leadership group were in their thirties and forties. Their average educational level was very low. While the majority had had primary education and a few had started lower middle school, some had had no formal schooling at all. The brigade accountant, a YCL member, was the only person among the entire top group of cadres who had graduated from middle school.

There was not very much to distinguish the members of this group from the ordinary peasants in the brigade in terms of education or specialized technical skills. Their success and power rested on the fact that they had proven themselves as effective organization men and had therefore been accepted into the organized Party elite that monopolized all leadership posts in the area.

Economic Functions

The functions of production brigades in China have not been constant since communes were first established in 1958, but rather have changed as the regime has altered its policies toward the communes in general. After the organizational decentralization (*t'i chih hsia fang*) which took place in this area in 1961–1962, Brigade B in many respects became less important, in terms of economic functions, than either the commune to which it belonged or the production teams into which its members were divided. After this decentralization, agencies at the commune level continued to have primary responsibility, as indicated already, for certain crucial government functions of an economic sort, such as collection of the land tax and supervision of compulsory grain sales to the state, and still managed certain large-scale economic enterprises. And the production teams, as the basic "accounting units," now had primary responsibility—within the framework of over-all plans passed down from above through the commune and brigade—for managing production and distributing output. As a result, the roles assigned to the brigade were substantially reduced. Nevertheless, Brigade B continued to perform some important economic functions. Not only did it still act as intermediary between the commune and teams in the establishment of production targets and quotas for taxes and compulsory grain sales, it also continued to manage a few economic enterprises which were too large for the teams to handle and not sufficiently important for the commune to run directly, and it was an important level for the operation of both supply and marketing cooperatives and credit cooperatives.

Four members of the brigade staff dealt primarily with economic and financial matters, although, of course, the brigade chief and his deputy also concerned themselves with these matters continually. Most important were the economic management cadre and his deputy, who were responsible for over-all economic planning, budgeting, reporting, and management of the brigade's enterprises. Although their plans had to be based to a considerable extent either on instructions from the commune above or on information from their teams below, and also had to have the approval of the Brigade Management Committee, they nevertheless had important tasks of economic planning and management. Consequently, these economic posts required reliable Party men of some experience.

The brigade also had an accountant, who kept all records and prepared statistical reports, and a cashier, who handled all brigade funds. In Brigade B the cashier was concurrently deputy head (*fu chu jen*) of the local Credit Cooperative (*hsin yung ho tso she*).

The Credit Cooperative in Brigade B operated under the multiple leadership of two commune-level organizations (the Credit Cooperative and the People's Bank) and the brigade's Management Committee. Located in a building separate from the brigade headquarters, it performed several important functions. It provided loans both to production teams and to individual peasants, mainly, though not exclusively, for production purposes. It served as custodian of brigade funds; above a certain limit set by the commune, the brigades could not keep cash in their own offices but had to deposit it in a credit cooperative or bank. There was a limit, also, on the cash funds which the Credit Cooperative itself could keep, and everything above that had to be deposited in the commune's branch bank. Both production teams and individuals could also open accounts and make deposits in the cooperative, although this was a voluntary matter in

Brigade B. In addition, remittances from overseas Chinese were channeled from the commune's branch bank via the brigade's Credit Cooperative to the recipients. The credit cooperative also served as the local post office in Brigade B, receiving and sending mail and selling stamps.

In the general planning process as it affected Brigade B, the commune determined over-all quotas which established minimum output figures and other targets for the brigade as a whole, but the brigade then established, after discussion with its team chiefs, specific targets for each team.

As indicated earlier, the brigade's role in the actual collection of the land tax and grain sales to the state was minimal, since the teams made deliveries directly to granaries at the commune level. However, Brigade B was authorized by the commune to collect a small amount of additional grain directly from its teams for its own use. This was limited to a maximum of 1 percent of the total grain output of the brigade. To store this grain the brigade maintained a small granary (*ts'ang k'u*) of its own, which was located at the Brigade Office and was guarded when necessary by local militiamen. Brigade-level granaries were less important than either the commune-level granaries, where much state grain was stored, or the teams' granaries, where both seed grain and grain for distribution to team members were kept.

Earlier, the brigades in this area had played a considerably larger role in grain management. For example, from 1958 to 1960, all peasants in Commune C ate in public mess halls (*kung kung ch'ih t'ang* or *shih t'ang*). These were established on the basis of one mess hall for one to three production teams, that is, a mess hall for roughly one to three hundred people, but it was the brigade which had over-all responsibility for managing them. Management of these mess halls was one of Brigade B's major responsibilities—and headaches—at that time. Reportedly, the messes were highly successful and popular for a very brief initial period. The slogan of "communism" and the prospect of unlimited "free food," distributed on the basis of appetite rather than work, were very attractive, and at first the food provided in the mess halls was in fact plentiful and good. As a consequence the mess halls were viewed initially with considerable enthusiasm despite the revolution in personal living which they involved. But apparently this lasted for only two to three months in Brigade B; thereafter, the food in the mess halls was slowly but steadily restricted in quantity, and rapidly deteriorated in quality. When the 1959 harvest proved to be a failure, conditions became progressively worse. Finally, in 1960, the mess halls in Brigade B, as throughout its general area, were closed down, and thereafter the peasants again prepared and ate their meals in their own homes. Since by this time the mess halls had become very unpopular and the deepening food crisis made it extremely difficult to run them, the brigade was not reluctant to abandon this unsuccessful experiment in advanced "communism."

Despite its diminished role in food control and grain management, the brigade did attempt, even after the closing of the mess halls and the subsequent decentralization of powers in the commune, to maintain an over-all balance sheet on grain production and use, since this was perhaps the most crucial index of its general economic situation and performance. Reportedly, this balance sheet indicated that total grain production in Brigade B in 1963 amounted to over 900 long tons, of which 163 tons went to the state, 86.5 tons in the form of land tax (*kung liang*) and 76.5 tons in the form of compulsory grain sales (which were usually referred to locally as *yü liang*). The brigade itself collected what, in effect, was an additional surtax (*ti fang liang*, literally "local grain"), but the amount, 2.5 tons in 1963, was very small, less even than the maximum allowed. A total of 735 tons was kept, therefore, by the brigade's twenty-four production teams; this amounted, on the average, to slightly over 30 tons per team. The larger part, a total of over 480 tons, was distributed to team members as regular food grain (*k'ou liang*). Roughly 60 tons were used for labor bonuses and rewards (*lao tung liang*, literally "labor grain"); and 36 tons of so-called collective grain (*chi tung liang*, literally "free-use grain") were used by the teams for a variety of special purposes such as allocations to families whose breadwinners had died, emergency relief, and so on. About 18 tons were saved as seed grain (*chung tzu liang*). The rest, 141 tons, was used for other production expenses (*sheng ch'an fei yung*), for public accumulation funds to be used for capital construction (*kung chi chin*), and for the public welfare fund (*kung yi chin*).

The above figures indicate that close to 20 percent, by value, of the grain output of Brigade B went to the state in the form of either direct or indirect taxation—if one adds to the value of land-tax grain an estimate of the value lost in compulsory sales to the state due to the difference between the low state purchase price (Yo.08 per catty) and the rice price on the limited open market (Yo.30 per catty).[18]

Although deliveries of both land tax grain and compulsory grain sales to the state were made directly by the teams to commune-run granaries, Brigade B's Supply and Marketing Cooperative (*kung hsiao ho tso she*), operating under the over-all direction of the commune cooperative, purchased on behalf of the state a variety of other items, including eggs and fowl. A few commodities had to be sold by team members directly to the commune's Supply and Marketing Cooperative, and pigs had to be sold to the commune pig farm; but the brigade's Supply and Marketing Cooperative handled the purchase of many other items. The brigade cooperative also played a very important role of another sort in the life of all brigade members, since its small general store was the only commercial establishment directly serving the three villages within the brigade. This store stocked and sold a variety of goods, the most important of which were daily necessities and miscellaneous consumer goods—sugar, salt, matches, fish, cigarettes, wine, and the like. It did not sell cloth, which was in very short supply and strictly rationed; peasants from Brigade B had to go to the commune's Supply and Marketing Cooperative to purchase cloth.

To meet its administrative and operating expenses, the brigade relied heavily upon the profits of three enterprises which it owned and operated. (The small grain surtax which it levied was used in large part to provide allowances to team cadres when they attended meetings, as they frequently did, at the brigade headquarters; the

[18] One ex-cadre with experience in the field of finance believes that this estimate—and the figure for the land tax—may be too low, or at least that it is lower than in many areas. He believes that in much of south China the land tax, including local surtaxes, has amounted to 18 or 20 percent of output (not counting the loss involved in compulsory sales to the state). Some reports from ex-cadres indicate that in the years following 1958 the national average rate of the land tax was 15.5 percent of total normal annual output.

daily allowance given to a cadre attending such meetings was slightly above what he normally could expect to earn for an equivalent amount of time spent in agricultural work in his team.) Three enterprises produced the bulk of these profits. The most important of these was an agricultural products processing factory (*nung ch'an p'in chia kung ch'ang*),[19] a multipurpose plant which not only milled some rice but also processed some other agricultural commodities including sugar cane and melons. This factory possessed the brigade's only motor, a 24-horsepower gasoline engine. Among the brigade's leaders there had been some talk of plans to tap a little electricity from this engine for lighting purposes, but up to 1964 this had not been done and there were no electric lights anywhere in the brigade. Headed by a manager (*ch'ang chang*), the factory's staff included four other leading cadres, one of whom was a technical worker (*chi kung*) who maintained and repaired the motor. The labor force varied seasonally; at its peak it totaled fifty to sixty persons.

A second brigade enterprise was a brick and tile factory (*chuan wa ch'ang*). Staffed by a manager and three other cadres, it had a fairly stable work force of close to thirty, eight of whom were skilled workers with special knowledge relating to brick-and-tile-making, while the rest were unskilled helpers. Wages were paid on a piece rate: Yo.80 for 120 tiles, and Yo.04 to Yo.45 for 120 bricks.

The third brigade enterprise was a commercial establishment which purchased used goods (*fei p'in shou kou chan*). This "station" collected many kinds of used goods, and then processed and resold them, mainly for use elsewhere as raw materials. It was a small establishment with only three cadres and three other workers.

Of these three enterprises, two had existed before Communist takeover; only the agricultural products factory was new. The Great Leap had brought no permanent expansion in the number of local industries in Brigade B. As everywhere, small backyard steel furnaces were built here but were later abandoned. Commune C had mobilized many workers from all its brigades during that period and had employed them in a variety of new economic activities. Some were even sent out of the commune. But subse-

---

[19] At the village level, most enterprises labeled "factories" were really small workshops.

quently almost all those from Brigade B had returned to agricultural work in the brigade, and the commune was now severely limited in the number of men it could take from the brigade to use in commune-directed activities.

Apart from being used to meet brigade administrative expenses, profits from brigade enterprises could be distributed to members of the brigade through the teams, invested in the improvement of the existing brigade enterprises, or, theoretically, used to finance the construction of new factories. The Brigade Management Committee had the authority to decide how such funds were to be used, but it did so only after consultation with the team heads. In practice, however, the resources which the brigade could use for new construction purposes were extremely limited. For certain types of water conservancy projects it could obtain occasional subsidies from Commune C. It could not expect significant financial help from the commune to build a new brigade factory, however, since the commune was more likely to invest in enterprises of its own, and it was not easy for the brigade to obtain a large loan from the commune bank, even to finance new construction.

The brigade was responsible for routine repair and maintenance of all small irrigation works and ponds in its own area and was also encouraged to undertake new construction. Here again, it was less able than the commune to build new projects; and unlike the commune, it did not have any cadre specially responsible for water conservancy. The brigade's economic management cadre had general responsibility for this field. Sometimes he used militiamen to work on water conservancy projects. At other times laborers from the teams were requisitioned for this purpose.

In the field of general agricultural improvement, there were no trained experts in Brigade B. All its "agricultural specialists" were local farmers. Personnel sent by the county and the commune did visit Brigade B on occasion, however, and sometimes went to the team level as well. Furthermore, information or instructions from higher levels regarding new agricultural methods also reached the brigade, and through it, the teams.

Many of the agricultural innovations introduced in Brigade B were relatively simple ones, implemented "organizationally" without direct advice or supervision from qualified technical specialists. Some of these were successful; but here as elsewhere, the extreme forms of deep plowing and close planting promoted during the Great Leap, had had fairly disastrous results. When instructions to apply these methods were received by Brigade B's cadres, knowledgeable local peasants warned that they were unwise, but the cadres insisted that they be tried. The result was that much of one crop was totally lost, and many of the local peasants acquired a certain skepticism about technical changes promoted by higher Party authorities. Nevertheless, agricultural innovation and experimentation continued even after 1959, and they were apparently much more widespread and successful than similar efforts had been before Communist takeover. This was undoubtedly due in part to the fact that the entire Party-directed apparatus of political control, plus the apparatus of economic collectivization, provided an organizational mechanism which made it possible to ensure the implementation of directives from above in a way that had not been possible previously. It was also due to the fact that the regime placed great stress on the value of innovation and clearly had had some success in altering the basic attitudes of many cadres toward social and economic change.

Mass Communication and Mass Persuasion

In some respects, rural China is still fairly remote from the country's urban centers of power. Nevertheless, the Chinese Communists have successfully built up an organizational apparatus through which they are able to communicate effectively and continuously with the mass of the population at the grassroots level. The Party's instruments of ideological control do not operate as efficiently, by any means, in China's villages as in its cities; but organized efforts at mass persuasion have a much greater impact, and exert much more intense pressures, on China's peasant population now than has ever been the case before.

In the villages, as in the cities, coercive political control is an extremely important ingredient in the regime's over-all pattern of rule, yet at the same time the Communists rely to a striking degree on propaganda, agitation, and positive mass mobilization to carry out their programs. With self-righteous dedication and fervor they relentlessly pursue the goal of indoctrinating the entire population with a new Party-approved ideology which requires everyone to accept new values, new attitudes, and new patterns of behavior.

The extent to which systematic knowledge of Marxism-Leninism and the "thought of Mao Tse-tung" have reached the village level, however, is clearly limited.[20] In Brigade B, for example, the impact of organized political study (*cheng chih hsüeh hsi*) was restricted primarily to members of the elite, most particularly the cadres but also to a lesser extent the students. Members of the Party and the YCL engaged in some regular study in their "organizational life" meetings, and study was greatly intensified during political campaigns. Moreover, local students were exposed to periodic political lectures. However, not surprisingly in view of their relatively low average level education, even the local Party leaders did not have a very sophisticated understanding of the theoretical aspects of Marxism-Leninism.

Apart from the cadres and students, few people in Brigade B knew very much about the theory of Marxism-Leninism. All those with some formal education obtained a minimum exposure to it, it is true, but most adult peasants, the majority of whom were still illiterate, were said to have almost no understanding of it at all.

The regime was far from indifferent to the task of providing ideological training for ordinary peasants, however. On the contrary, the Party conducted an intensive and continual program to propagandize the entire adult population in the brigade as well as to educate the young, not so much in the theoretical aspects of Marxism-Leninism but rather in the general values, policies, and goals approved by the regime. While the written word played a significant role in this effort, the Communists inevitably placed major reliance on oral propaganda to reach the population, especially the majority who were illiterate. Consequently, while most peasants in Brigade B did not really understand Marxism-Leninism as such, they were constantly drilled in slogans and bombarded with general propaganda, designed to indoctrinate them in basic concepts of what was right and what was wrong, who was friend and who was foe, which sorts of activities were mandatory or permissible, and which,

[20] Since 1964, however, village-level efforts at indoctrination in the "thought of Mao Tse-tung" have been intensified.

discouraged or forbidden, what kinds of attitudes were praiseworthy and what kinds condemned, and which types of behavior brought rewards and which resulted in criticism or punishment.

In the regime's effort to propagandize and indoctrinate the peasant masses, virtually all members of the local elite, in the broadest sense —Party members, YCL members, non-Party cadres, and activists— were expected to play an active part. However, in the field of propaganda, as in every identifiable field of major activity, one member of the brigade's Party hierarchy was assigned special responsibility. The propaganda committeeman (*hsüan ch'üan wei yüan*), who was in charge of activities in this field, received written instructions and propaganda materials from Party personnel at both the commune and county levels. He also relied heavily for propaganda material on national, provincial, and local Party newspapers and journals. From time to time he also received special instructions by telephone from higher levels of the Party, outlining what to stress in current propaganda and how to promote a particular campaign. In addition, the brigade's one radio receiver, which was regularly monitored, was a constant source of grist for the propaganda mill.

In normal times (that is, between political campaigns) the propaganda committeeman in Brigade B could call on sixty to seventy persons to work under his direction, on a part-time basis. These men and women, or boys and girls, belonged to the two propaganda and indoctrination groups which had been organized in the brigade. Almost all were relatively young YCL members or ambitious activists. Since they were ordinary peasants, who participated in the regular work of the brigade's production teams to which all belonged, their propaganda work was normally carried out in their spare time, especially in the evenings. During slack agricultural seasons, or when major political campaigns were underway, however, they devoted a substantial proportion of their time to this work. Most had a somewhat higher level of education than did the general peasant population.

Roughly ten of these part-time propagandists were organized into a unit called, simply, the Propaganda Group (*hsüan ch'üan tsu*). The other fifty or sixty were involved in activities sponsored by a more loosely organized unit called the Culture, Recreation, and Drama Group (*wen hua yü lo hsi chü tsu* or *wen yü hsi chü tsu*).

This brigade propaganda force organized or participated in a variety of activities and programs. In every team in Brigade B, as well as at the brigade headquarters, there were small reading rooms which they helped to maintain. These rooms contained Party newspapers and journals, for the most part, but each had a few books as well. The brigade reading room carried six major papers, including the Peking *People's Daily* as well as provincial, special district, and county papers. The reading rooms at the team level generally received only three papers: the county and special district papers, plus a special supplement for peasants which was put out by the main provincial paper. At the brigade office, also, the organized propagandists maintained a special "blackboard newspaper" (*hei pan pao*). This was, as its name implied, a "newspaper" written by hand on a large blackboard, and it carried a selection of news and other material culled from newspapers, journals, and the radio, plus local brigade news. Its contents were changed every three to five days.

One of the most important media for systematic propaganda in Brigade B was the local, wired, radio-rediffusion broadcasting system (*yu hsien tien*). Not only was this system linked to "broadcasting stations" at higher levels, in both the commune and the county, but in Brigade B local Party leaders could themselves initiate "broadcasts" from a microphone located in the brigade office (this may have been rather unusual). The main outlets of the system were loudspeakers located at each of the twenty-four team offices, usually just outside the offices' front entrances, where sizable numbers of team members could gather and listen. Most of the programs consisted of rebroadcasts of news, features, and popular music carried by radio stations; these were simply piped into the system. But the brigade's leaders could, and occasionally did, use the rediffusion network themselves to communicate instructions to all the teams. Regular broadcasts from the county were scheduled in the evenings, the exact time varying according to the season. They always included an important national news program broadcast by Radio Peking, but most other programs originated from the provincial radio station. Chinese opera music was the most popular type of broadcast among the local peasants. This rediffusion network clearly provided a key propaganda link between higher-level authorities—national and provincial as well as county—and the masses in the villages. It was also one of the very few sources of regular entertainment locally available.

Motion pictures played a role in the propaganda system in Brigade B, but even though they were very popular they were less important in the system as a whole than some other media were. Neither Brigade B nor Commune C owned a motion-picture projector. When the brigade wished to show films, it had to rely, therefore, on the county's one roving Movie Team. It had to pay a remarkably high fee for each showing (Y60 each), and each team had to contribute its share to pay the bill. Consequently, Brigade B was able to arrange only occasional showings, perhaps two to four times a year. When films were shown, attendance was good, and reportedly the local peasants thoroughly enjoyed most of them, viewing them as major entertainment despite their high political content.

Perhaps most important form of all in the propaganda system as it operated in Brigade B was direct, face-to-face, oral propaganda conducted by the young volunteers working in the two groups under the direction of the brigade propaganda committeemen. This oral propaganda was generally more important than the modern media because it had a greater, more direct, and more continuous impact on a far larger number of people. Members of the Propaganda Group, or the Culture, Entertainment, and Drama Group, normally visited at least one of the brigade's three villages almost every evening, and this meant that each village was visited by them on an average of twice a week. When making such visits the youthful propagandists regularly conducted what was simply called "oral propaganda" (*k'ou t'ou hsüan ch'üan*), using megaphones and passing out news, information, directives, and exhortations of a variety of sorts. They also regularly convened informal propaganda meetings (*hsüan ch'üan hui*), usually out of doors, at which they made enthusiastic speeches on every imaginable topic.

Attendance by villagers at either the megaphone broadcasts or the propaganda meetings was usually "voluntary," but as in the case of so many "volunteer" activities in Communist China today, many pressures were exerted on them to attend, and those who were persistently indifferent risked criticism for their "reactionary" attitudes. The size of audiences varied, but it was not uncommon for the visiting group to have an audience of one hundred or more at each of their stopping places. Reportedly, men attended more regularly than women, and young people more frequently than their elders.

This sort of face-to-face oral propaganda obviously reached a very large proportion of the brigade's members at fairly regular intervals. The propagandists were urged, moreover, to translate propaganda into earthy, nonabstract terms that would be meaningful to villagers. Often, they spent much of their time discussing not vague generalities but specific good and bad people or activities, dealing with them in very concrete terms, praising particular local peasants for model behavior and criticizing others for substandard performance, comparing one team with another or the brigade as a whole with a neighboring brigade, and exhorting everyone to rectify specific faults and shortcomings.

Besides assisting in this regular oral propaganda work, the members of the Culture, Entertainment, and Drama Group also prepared and periodically performed a variety of operas, plays, dances, and musical shows, which invariably combined political education with entertainment. Two to four times a year, always including the Chinese New Year (or the "spring festival," as it is now called) and National Day, they put on special shows at the playground next to the brigade's largest school. During mass campaigns, they generally formed a number of *ad hoc* small groups (*hsiao tsu*), which put on frequent performances designed to promote the current campaign in all three villages in the brigade.

During every mass campaign, whether a political movement or a production drive, special instructions were sent down to the brigades from the county and commune authorities, and the propagandists in Brigade B went into high gear to help the local Party leaders mobilize everyone to take an active part. Such campaigns constituted one of the most important, if not the most important, means by which the authorities went about the task of implementing most of its major policies and programs at the village level. In each campaign, a few simple, concrete goals were specified, and then every available organizational and propaganda technique was used to mobilize the peasants to work hard to achieve the defined goals. In Brigade B, as elsewhere, campaigns occurred at very frequent intervals, and at times they overlapped, with the result that more than one campaign was being promoted simultaneously. During the most important campaigns, particularly the political ones, special work teams or other personnel were dispatched by the county to Commune C to brief both commune and brigade cadres on how to implement them, and sometimes one or more cadres from Brigade B were sent to either the commune or the county level to obtain special training relating to the campaign.

In Brigade B, during the most important campaigns, regular propaganda activities were greatly intensified. In addition innumerable mass meetings involving most of the brigade members were held, at which the top local Party leaders explained, harangued, and exhorted. One special feature of big campaigns in Brigade B was the establishment at brigade headquarters of special exhibitions (*chan lan hui*), consisting usually of posters, photographs, and statistical charts, which the mass of local villagers were systematically organized to see.

As already stated, at times several campaigns overlapped. In early 1964, for example, three movements were conducted simultaneously in Brigade B. The most important of these was a new "three-anti campaign" (*san fan yün tung*)—not to be confused with another "three-anti campaign" held in the early 1950s—which was a local variation of the national socialist education campaign (*she hui chu yi chiao yü yün tung*) then underway. In Brigade B this campaign attempted to reemphasize class consciousness, and involved intense efforts to renew hostility· and abuse directed against former landlords and rich peasants. Simultaneously, the brigade leaders also promoted one of their periodic campaigns to "increase production and reduce waste" (*tseng ch'an chieh yüeh yün tung*) and a new birth-control campaign (*chieh yü yün tung*).

Campaigns of this sort were clearly "effective" in Brigade B, in the sense that they did, in fact as well as theory, enable the local authorities to implement current policies, as defined by higher levels of authority, through mass mobilization of virtually the entire population of the brigade. However, it is equally clear that they involved significant costs. Much time and effort were "wasted" in endless meetings and "organizational activity" of many sorts. Priority goals constantly shifted, and important activities, including agricultural work, were sometimes neglected because other goals were the focus of the current campaign. Here as elsewhere, moreover, there were notable examples (including the backyard steel furnaces, deep plowing, and close planting) of successful local implementation of "policy mistakes" made at a higher level.

Education and Health

Mass propaganda and political campaigns are by no means the only methods by which the Communist regime in China attempts to "socialize" the population. The formal educational system also plays a vital role, of course, in the Communist Party's efforts to create a new value system in society, as well as in its programs to train the population with new skills required for modernization and development. In the long run, in fact, formal education will doubtlessly be even more important in its impact on society than most mass propaganda and agitational activities because it focuses on the tasks of indoctrinating and raising the level of general knowledge of the new generation, not the old one. In Brigade B, the growth of education and the expansion of literacy had their ups and downs in the decade and a half following Communist takeover, but over the years there was clearly a steady quantitative expansion of educational opportunities. This was one of the most notable achievements of the regime, in fact, and was so regarded by both the cadres and the masses.

In Commune C, the commune's Culture, Education, and Health Department was the local body responsible for education, and in each brigade one designated person, usually the Party propaganda committeeman, had similar responsibilities. However, prior to 1958, all schools were actually financed and run by the county, acting through the district government. This was true not only of the one lower middle school in Commune C, which was most closely supervised by the county authorities, but also, in this area at least, of the primary schools at both commune and brigade levels. There were three such primary schools at the commune level; in addition, every brigade had at least one, and sometimes several, primary schools.

Before 1958, in the administrative village that was later to become Brigade B, there had been three primary schools, one in each natural village; organizationally, however, two of these were considered branch schools (*fen hsiao*) of the largest school, situated in the village where the brigade's headquarters were located. Altogether the three schools had three administrative cadres—a principal (*hsiao chang*), a director of instruction (*chiao tao chu jen*), and a person in charge of general affairs (*tsung wu jen yüan*)—and eleven (at times twelve) teachers, most of whom were graduates of lower middle schools. All the schools taught primary grades one through six. Before 1958 they had roughly four hundred pupils, two hundred in the largest school and one hundred in each of the others. All three schools occupied former clan buildings that had been taken over by the regime. The district government, with money received from the county, allocated (through the central school) the funds necessary for running the three schools, and the administrative village itself had little real responsibility for or control over them.

Then, during communization and the Great Leap Forward, an attempt was made both to expand the school system and to decentralize responsibility for education, partly in order to reduce the financial burden on the county government. Developments during this period varied greatly from place to place in China. While the county retained full responsibility for both Commune C's lower middle school and the commune-level primary schools, and continued to subsidize the brigade's primary schools, including the three in Brigade B, these state supported primary schools at the brigade level were now restricted to the higher primary grades, and responsibility for financing lower primary education was shifted to the brigades themselves. In Brigade B, the three primary schools which already existed were continued but were now restricted to the upper primary grades, and the brigade established three new primary schools to handle the lower grades. An energetic effort was made at this time to promote universal primary education, and school enrollment rose greatly; for a brief period something close to complete enrollment of children of primary school age was achieved. At first, the brigade itself fully financed the three new schools. Soon, however, it found that it could not carry this large financial burden alone, and it started charging significant tuition fees in its schools. Instead of collecting these fees directly, though, the brigade had its production teams deduct a certain number of work points from the team accounts of peasants who sent children to school, and then funds equal to these work points were transferred from the teams to the brigade.

This caused school attendance to drop somewhat. But it nevertheless remained high; in 1964 it was estimated that perhaps close to 80 percent of children of primary school age were actually enrolled in the local schools.

A few, but not many, of the children who completed their primary education in Brigade B were then able to enroll in the lower middle school operated at the commune level. This school, serving all sixteen of Commune C's brigades, had a student body of roughly one thousand, which meant that on the average it could take only twenty students or so from each brigade every year. Only a very limited number of students were able to go still further and attend the higher middle school located at county headquarters.[21]

In addition to expanding primary school education, Brigade B also did its best to eradicate adult illiteracy. For this purpose it operated a so-called People's School for the Elimination of Illiteracy (*sao mang min hsiao*), which held evening classes for adults in the building of the largest local primary school. Some of the instruction in this literacy training program was given by regular teachers from the primary schools; in addition, other literate local people were mobilized to help out. As a result, illiteracy definitely declined. As of 1964, however, it was still substantial. Exact estimates were difficult to make, in part because of the difficulty of defining literacy precisely, as well as because of the lack of reliable statistics. According to one estimate, literacy among brigade members who were over thirty was higher than previously but was still only 30 to 40 percent. But among those of younger ages, literacy of at least a minimum sort was estimated to be close to 90 percent.

Paralleling the quantitative improvement in education, there had been some expansion of health and sanitation facilities in Brigade B in the years since Communist takeover. As of 1964 there was one Health Station (locally called *wei sheng chan*) in the brigade, staffed by a semitrained doctor and a male nurse. The brigade also had a trained midwife (*chieh sheng yüan*), who gave simple training to

[21] In many areas in China, numerous commune-supported, part-work, part-study agricultural middle schools were established during 1963–1964, which significantly expanded opportunities for middle school education, but this development had not yet taken place in Commune C in 1964.

other village women. The establishment of the station unquestionably resulted in some improvement of local health conditions compared with the period before 1949, when no such institution had existed. But the improvement was limited, since the station was capable only of dealing with outpatients and promoting sanitation and health campaigns. It could not deal with major medical cases requiring hospitalization. If cases were not too serious, they might be accommodated in the commune hospital; however, since this institution had only ten beds and was also rather primitive, the most serious cases had to be sent to the county hospital. Limited as all these local facilities were, they nevertheless had resulted in some improvement in health and sanitation conditions.

Political Control:
The Apparatus for Coercion

If the degree to which the Chinese Communists have extended their apparatus of mass persuasion and ideological control to the villages is remarkable, their success in establishing tight political control at the grassroots level is equally impressive. They have created, in fact as well as theory, a system of control which effectively enmeshes the mass of the population throughout the country, even in remote rural areas. Villagers who once looked upon the principal institutions of political power as fairly remote agencies, whose outreach one should and sometimes could try to evade, now live in the knowledge that the Communists' instruments of political power are an ever-present and inescapable reality.

In Commune C and Brigade B, as everywhere in China, at the heart of the system of political control was the Party itself, whose members were embedded in every important social group and grasped every important lever of power. The effectiveness of Party "leadership," however, was ensured by many specialized techniques and instruments of coercion that functioned under Party control.

Of particular importance, at least in this area, was the organized system of public security. The public security apparatus, led by the County Public Security Bureau but reaching down to the lowest levels of society, played an important role even in the villages. At the local level, as at higher levels, public security personnel had a very special status in the regime. The chiefs of public security units were generally regarded by other cadres and ordinary peasants alike as being coequal with the heads of the over-all organizations to which their units belonged. Ordinary people were constantly aware of the presence of these representatives and symbols of the police power of the regime, and a great many felt that they were under continual police scrutiny. Clearly there was widespread fear of arbitrary police power even when it was sparingly used. Moreover, since vertical lines of command were of overriding importance in public security work, most local people, including the cadres, were said to view public security men primarily as agents of higher police authority.

In Commune C, over-all control of the public security system was in the hands of the three-man Political and Legal Department, which has already been described. (In many communes in this general area, the top public security officers, called *kung an yüan*, were directly assigned to the communes by the County Public Security Bureau.) This department maintained one Public Security Substation (*p'ai ch'u so*), with a staff of seven armed policemen, at the commune level. Much of the public security work in the area was done, however, by public security committees, or committeemen, at the brigade and team levels, with the aid and support of local militia units. The militia was closely related to the public security apparatus, and at both commune and brigade levels, the top public security man concurrently headed the local militia unit.

In theory, each brigade in Commune C was supposed to have a public security committee (*chih an pao wei wei yüan hui*, often called *chih pao*, for short; the term literally means "committee for the protection of public order"), operating under the over-all direction of the Commune Political and Legal Department. In Brigade B, however, there was no committee, and one man, locally called the public security chief (*chih pao chu jen*) was responsible for work in this field. This man was concurrently political committeeman (*cheng chih wei yüan*) of the Brigade Party Branch Committee and local militia chief (*min ping tui chang*). In his capacity as militia chief, he was assisted by one secretarial clerk (*wen shu*).

Each of Brigade B's twenty-four production teams also had one man designated as public security officer (*chih pao wei yüan*), who worked under the close direction of the brigade. And all these security cadres belonged to a clear chain of command which ran from the county to the commune to the brigade to the team, a chain of command in which there was a large and continual flow of instructions downward and reports upward.

The basic responsibilities of all these security men were to register the population; check on and control all travel; exercise surveillance over all ostracized, undesirable, or suspicious persons; survey social conditions and public attitudes; take quick and strong action to suppress any political dissidence; and generally ensure the maintenance of law and order. In Brigade B, as in Commune C, the public security chief was also the principal mediator of interpersonal disputes, since Brigade B did not have any formal mediation committee as many other brigades in the area did. For the most part, the security cadres were able to perform their functions successfully without the frequent use of open or crude force. When armed support was needed, however, the public security chief of Brigade B was able to call upon his militia forces to provide it.

Brigade B, like all the other brigades in Commune C, had its own militia unit (*min ping tui*), which, as stated earlier, was under the over-all command of the chief of the Commune Political and Legal Department. In theory, most able-bodied members of the brigade were supposed to be organized into one huge unit of "Ordinary Militia." In the Great Leap period and immediately thereafter, the theory had some relationship to reality, and for a brief period almost everyone was drilled and given at least minimum training. Later, however, this effort was abandoned, at least in Brigade B, and by 1964 only the "Basic Militia" really existed; the register of the Ordinary Militia was simply a list of persons of militia age.[22]

In Brigade B, as of 1964, there were between twenty and thirty fairly well-trained men in the Basic Militia at the brigade level, many of them ex-soldiers, and the others mainly young unmarried local men, usually YCL members or at least activists, who were persons of reliable class background. There were also a number of similar militiamen in every production team. All the militiamen were "part-time

[22] Since 1964, the militia in Brigade B, as elsewhere in China, may well have been expanded, and the ordinary militia may have become more important again.

soldiers." They normally participated in regular agricultural production, and had to carry out their militia activities, including their training, in their spare time. The militiamen were not constantly armed, but arms were available. The brigade had a number of rifles and bayonets kept for the use of its unit; these were generally stored in the Brigade Office and were issued to the militiamen as needed, sometimes for training. The brigade public security chief, an ex-soldier, himself directed most of the training.

Apart from generally helping to maintain law and order in the brigade's area, the militia unit in Brigade B had special responsibility for protecting communications and irrigation works, and for crop watching during harvest periods. Its members were also expected to play leading roles in every campaign, including production campaigns, and to be model activists.

The entire strength of the militia in Brigade B—several dozen persons in 1964—was not remarkably large. Nevertheless, it apparently was large enough to give effective backing to the public security cadres whenever they required it. In the rare instances when it appeared that the brigade's militia forces (or the commune's, which were simply the sum of the brigade units) were not adequate to cope with specific problems—for example, a threat of serious local disorder—the commune could request assistance from the County Public Security Bureau. The universal realization that armed police forces from the county, or even regular troops from the PLA, could be brought in if necessary, helped to ensure that tight control would be successfully maintained at the local level, even during difficult periods, with relatively small numbers of armed men. Actually, the possibility that any open opposition to the regime might take violent forms, even if dissidence were to grow to serious proportions, had been minimized by the Communists, soon after takeover, when they had collected all privately owned weapons and had effectively disarmed the population.

In the area of Commune C, only once in the fifteen years following Communist takeover had there been any sort of situation requiring intervention by forces from the county level. Even this was not really a direct challenge to the authority of the regime but rather was a bitter dispute between two villages, over water rights, in which local militiamen had become involved. When this incident occurred, the County Public Security Bureau immediately sent a unit of People's Armed Police to the area, and it quickly reestablished order and arrested the leaders of both sides of the dispute.

To the members of Brigade B, the PLA, which of course was capable of providing the strongest sanction in the political control system and was recognized as being the ultimate prop of the regime, was a fairly remote force which infringed very little on their lives. This apparently was true despite the fact that Commune C was located near the south China coast, in an area important to national defense, and regular PLA troops were therefore frequently stationed in the general region and their numbers increased during every crisis period. During the first Taiwan Strait crisis in the mid-1950s, for example, "several thousand" PLA troops moved into the area that was later to become Commune C; about one hundred or more of them were sent to the area that eventually became Brigade B and were billeted in the villages, in peasants' homes, for about a year. Again, in 1958, during the second Taiwan Strait crisis, an even larger number of troops, perhaps as many as ten thousand, moved into the area of Commune C and stayed for a longer period, many of them until 1963; this time they built special barracks in hilly areas. Reportedly, in both instances the PLA troops generally were quite aloof but were carefully correct in their relations with local people, paying for all materials requisitioned and occasionally assigning soldiers to help in local projects. Apparently their discipline and good behavior made a relatively good impression on most local people. One burden was placed upon the members of Commune C by their presence, however. On both occasions, all brigades and teams were required to collect and store a certain amount of hay in their local granaries or storehouses for possible use by the PLA, either as fodder for animals or as straw bedding for transient soldiers.

In sum, the regular PLA's presence was felt to some extent at all times in Commune C, and during certain periods sizable numbers of troops were stationed in the area; but even in this coastal defense area the local people regarded the PLA as a fairly remote force, and it played no direct role in the local political system. There is little doubt that, as a force in the background, it served in a subtle way as the ultimate guarantee of the regime's power and legitimacy. But at the local level, the combination of public security personnel and militia alone provided the Party authorities with what appeared to be sufficient backing to maintain effective, unchallenged political control.

Control of Travel and Food

Under the political system which now exists in China, there are many different mechanisms for political control. Among them are systematic registry of the population and control over travel and movement, reinforced by food control through rationing. The Chinese Communists have not always insisted on universal identity cards for the population, as some other totalitarian regimes have done, and the tightness of controls over travel has varied from time to time and place to place. However, the authorities possess the capacity to impose strict controls whenever and wherever they so desire, and even when complicated travel documents have not been required, travelers arriving at their destinations in Communist China have had to register with local public security authorities, and in order to purchase basic rationed foodstuffs, especially grain and vegetable oil, they have had to possess valid ration tickets.

Because Commune C and Brigade B were located in coastal south China, their procedures governing travel in 1964 may have been somewhat more complicated than those in some other areas, but they were certainly not completely atypical. Different procedures governed ordinary travel (*lü hsing*) and permanent transfer of residence (*ch'ien yi*). Some ordinary travel within the county was fairly unrestricted, but when a member of Commune C wished to make any trip outside the county that would involve staying for a few days, even if it was only to a fairly nearby area, he had to obtain special permission to do so. To obtain such permission in Commune C and Brigade B, the prospective traveler first had to write, or have written for him, a "report" (*pao kao*), or request, to his production team's chief, stating where he wished to go and why, and his team chief's approval was required. If he obtained this approval, which the chief indicated by "chopping" the "report" and which the team accountant duly recorded, the applicant then took his request to the brigade's secretarial clerk (*wen shu*). If the case was routine—as most were—the clerk simply added his chop of approval, and recorded it. If any unusual questions or special problems were involved, however, the approval of the brigade's public security chief (*chih pao chu jen*) also had to be obtained; and on the most questionable cases the brigade branch Party secretary's endorsement was required. Approval by these key brigade leaders was mandatory when any member of the so-called "five [bad] elements" requested permission to travel. They were also required for any member of the overseas Chinese community requesting permission to visit relatives in Hong Kong. And they might be considered necessary for anyone if questions were raised about his recent work performance, political attitudes, or motives for traveling.

Once brigade approval was given, a certificate (*cheng ming*) was issued in duplicate to the applicant. Since the man who issued this served as secretarial clerk for both the brigade and the Brigade Party Branch, and since the public security chief, whose approval was sometimes required, was concurrently Party political and legal committeeman, it was not wholly clear, at least in the minds of some people, whether the certificate was issued on the authority of the brigade or the Brigade Party Branch. In any case, the fact that the Party secretary's endorsement was required on the most questionable cases indicated that in the final analysis the Party's view was what counted.

After an applicant had obtained his certificate, he then went to the commune's Grain Management Office (*liang kuan so*), where he exchanged one copy of his certificate for grain ration tickets (*liang p'iao*) that would enable him to purchase food supplies from state stores during his trip. These tickets were issued in several different denominations—one catty, three catties, and so on. The applicant kept the second copy of his certificate, which served, when necessary, as a kind of identity card during his trip. Sometimes he never had to use it at all, but if ticket sellers at bus or rail stations raised any questions about his credentials, the certificate could be produced on demand. The necessity to have authorization to purchase grain during a trip was a principal reason why the procedures described above had to be followed even in routine cases. Without special grain tickets a traveler could not purchase any rationed grain at state stores.

Theoretically, he might try to rely instead on the rations of the friends or relatives he visited, but in most cases this obviously imposed an unreasonable burden on them.

Many of the trips made by ordinary peasants in Commune C were visits to relatives living in nearby cities. When the travelers arrived in these cities on such trips they had to go through the following procedures. If the visitor was planning to stay over three days he had to go to the nearest public security substation and fill out a temporary population registration card, which was kept on file there until he left the city. If he was planning to stay for less than three days, and was an ordinary person, registration was not mandatory but was considered desirable. If he was a member of the "five [bad] elements," however, he had to register with a public security substation within twenty-four hours. Whoever he might be, the police registering him entered basic information about him in the household population registry book (*hu k'ou teng chi pu*) of the family being visited, and then validated this with the substation's chop, although if he were staying at a hotel, the hotel registry book served the same purpose. Once registered with the public security authorities, the visitor could then use his grain ration tickets to make purchases at the nearest state grain store. When the visitor left, he did not always have to report personally to the public security substation, but if he did not report, then the family with whom he had visited had to take their household population registry book to the substation to have the visitor's temporary registration canceled.

When peasants in Brigade B wished to visit nearby communes the procedures were less complicated, but permission still had to be obtained. For trips of less than five days, a team chief could grant permission; longer trips required approval by the Brigade Office. When travelers arrived at their destination, they had to follow procedures similar to those applied to all persons visiting Brigade B. All such visitors had to report on arrival to the brigade public security chief and then take their grain ration tickets to the commune's Grain Management Office to obtain authorization to purchase food. Overseas Chinese coming from abroad also had to produce a "letter of introduction" (*hui hsiang chieh shao hsin*), received at the time of their return to the country, which authorized them to visit their home village.

In practice, while control over travel by members of the "five [bad] elements" was very strict at all times, travel was generally not very restricted for ordinary peasants in Commune C. Personal travel was certainly inhibited, however, not only by the procedures described, but also by many other factors, such as the peasants' reluctance to forgo earning work points during absences from their communes. The actual volume of personal travel varied over the years in this area. Reportedly, it was fairly high in the first years after 1949, dropped during and immediately after cooperativization, rose sharply soon after communization (for special reasons that will be mentioned below), then declined again after reimposition of tighter controls from 1962 on.

Transfers of residence involved more complicated procedures than ordinary travel. Although enormous state-directed movements of people have taken place in China since 1949, the regime has generally attempted to control and restrict voluntary moves motivated solely by personal considerations. If a young man in Commune C wished for his own reasons to move to a nearby city to find employment, it was extremely difficult for him to obtain permission to do so. However, when requests from official agencies for labor in these cities were passed down the line from the special district to the county to the commune, they invariably produced the requested number of "volunteers." Male members of the commune who moved elsewhere to work found it difficult, however, even if they were going at the request of higher authorities, to obtain permission for their families to join them.

In Commune C, any individual peasant who on his own initiative requested permission to move elsewhere, first had to go through the preliminary stages of the procedures for ordinary travel already described, and at the brigade level had to obtain the Party secretary's approval. Then he also had to obtain permission from the commune authorities. If permission to move was granted—and often it was turned down—the secretarial clerk of the commune issued him a change of residence certificate (*hu k'ou ch'ien yi cheng*) and authorized him to obtain whatever grain ration tickets were required for the period of travel to his destination. On arrival at his destination, the person involved not only had to register immediately at a public security substation but also had to take his grain transfer certificate to a rationing station (*liang shih kung ying chan*) in order to exchange it for a regular grain ration book (*liang shih kung ying cheng* or *liang shih kung ying pu*). (When students moved to a school elsewhere, the school administration normally handled all of this for them.)

The existing combination of police registration and food control has created a mechanism for very effective control of population movement in Communist China. But to regulate one fifth of the human race is a complex matter, and there has been, and continues to be, some illegal movement of persons who travel or try to change residence without valid permission or grain certificates. In the region where Commune C was located such persons were often referred to as "black people" (*hei jen hei hu*, literally "black people and black households"). In "normal" times their number was relatively small, but during the food crisis of 1959–1961, when all controls loosened, there was a sizable amount of illegal movement. In some places, where grain shortages were critical, quite a few peasants simply ignored the existing controls established by the Party and public security authorities and struck out in search of employment and food. Not being able to assure them of either work or sustenance, cadres frequently looked the other way and let them go.

Illegal migrants of this sort "made do" in various ways. Some were able to move in with relatives or friends in the cities, and shared their food rations, limited as they were. Local public security authorities generally learned of the presence of these people, but on occasion they were willing to overlook them. In the confused 1959–1961 period, there were some who were able to engage in black market trading, and supported themselves that way, although this was not easy to do in normal times. Others in that confused period were able to join large labor groups working on construction projects in both urban and rural areas; the cadres managing these groups were sometimes willing to overlook the fact that they were "black people," partly because their labor was needed and partly because, in the prevailing situation of economic distress, the cadres themselves tended to sympathize with them. It was only during a relatively brief period, however, that controls were allowed to loosen to this extent. From 1962 onward, the control system was tightened again.

Sanctions in the Control System

The political system as it operates at the local level in China today is backed by a variety of legal and administrative sanctions, and the Party and government authorities show little hesitation about punishing those who show any signs of dissidence or even of obvious nonconformity. The existence of these sanctions, and the knowledge that local Party leaders have ultimate control over their use, plus the evidence accumulated over the years that anyone who challenges the Party's will is likely eventually to be severely punished, obviously help to explain the great authority and effective "leadership" which Party cadres have been able to exercise at the local level. The testimony of numerous emigrees indicates that there is a fairly pervasive sense of anxiety—and on the part of many it is active fear—about punishment that might result from any actions or words that can be interpreted by the Party leaders as opposition to their will. This anxiety, which reinforces the tendency to be submissive and responsive to the authority of the cadres, is a very important element which helps to explain the way in which the political system as a whole operates.

At present, formal law and organized courts play only a subsidiary role in the system of sanctions operating at the local level, as has been the case traditionally in China. Political and administrative measures rather than legal action are what most affect average people. The Party controlled state legal system is brought into operation whenever necessary, of course, in particular when serious criminal cases, either political or nonpolitical, are involved.

In Commune C and Brigade B, it was only on fairly rare occasions that the local Party leaders had to invoke the authority of either the People's Court or the People's Procuracy, both of which were located in the county seat. However, in the most serious criminal cases, the Court and Procuracy were involved. When such a case occurred, Brigade B's leaders, working through Commune C, could, if they so wished, request the county agencies to send personnel directly to the brigade to initiate an investigation or make an arrest even before any action was taken locally. But this was not what normally happened.

Usually, when a serious case occurred, the brigade public security chief first had his local militia unit take the offender into custody; then he might request the County Public Security Bureau to send policemen to arrest the man formally and transfer him to the County Detention Center, after which the county bureau, and if necessary the Court and Procuracy, handled the case. Sometimes, if there was little danger of the culprit's attempting to escape, the brigade public security chief would simply keep the man under surveillance, rather than taking him into custody, until the county authorities arrived. If a person was put in custody locally, however, he could be held only temporarily at either the commune or brigade level, since the only regular jail in the entire county was the one in the county seat.

The only regular People's Court in the county (*fa yüan*) was also at the county level. Periodically, however, the Court would set up temporary, *ad hoc* people's tribunals (*lin shih fa t'ing*) in Commune C, or in other communes, and conduct trials locally. During the early period of land reform and the initial campaign to suppress counterrevolutionaries in the early 1950s, these tribunals were extremely important, and conducted many local mass trials climaxed by public executions. In the area of Brigade B, which of course was then an administrative village, the tribunals tried over thirty landlords in those early years, of whom eight were shot and the rest sentenced to forced labor. This controlled use of extreme violence in the years immediately after Communist takeover clearly had a lasting effect on local people's attitudes. It starkly illustrated the almost unlimited coercive power which the Party could use when it so desired. Subsequently, local trials by people's tribunals became less important, but they continued to be held occasionally. In the early 1960s, show trials were held by *ad hoc* tribunals within Commune C perhaps twice a year, on the average. Apparently these generally involved cases which the authorities believed would be particularly "educational" to the ordinary peasants attending them, and it was felt that holding the trials where local people could attend would maximize their effectiveness in serving as a deterrent to the particular type of offenses involved. In theory, whether ordinary members of Commune C attended these trials was a matter of individual choice; but, in practice, large numbers of people from every brigade went because they felt that they had to; it was widely felt that nonattendance might be viewed as a sign of political indifference, at the least, and possibly of sympathy for the offenders.

Relatively few persons in Commune C, even serious political offenders, had been shot since the early Communist kangaroo trials in the period immediately after takeover. The majority of those given severe punishment in later years were sentenced to forced labor or to various sorts of political "control."

In this area, as elsewhere, there were several different types of forced labor. "Reform through labor" (*lao tung kai tsao*), which involved unpaid penal labor combined with some political indoctrination, was meted out only by a formal judicial process, by the People's Court or a tribunal. "Labor reeducation" (*lao tung chiao yang*), by contrast, could be and was imposed administratively by Party and public security authorities, and a person undergoing labor reeducation continued receiving—or at least accumulated to his credit—his regular salary. It involved more intensive political indoctrination than labor reform, and sometimes the physical labor was equally onerous. In theory, sentences involving labor reeducation were shorter than those of labor reform, but in practice they could be extended and sometimes lasted for years.[23]

In Commune C, however, sentences to labor reeducation were reportedly limited, in practice, to a maximum of ten months. Decisions to send persons to perform such labor were generally made by brigade Party branches. Sentences could be and were given not only for relatively minor infractions of the law, such as black-market trading, but also for many ill-defined political offenses, including persistent clinging to "bourgeois" or "feudalistic" attitudes, labels which were used very loosely.

The majority of sentences both to labor reform and labor reeducation in this area were meted out during major campaigns. The two kinds of offenders were handled separately. The commune's Political and Legal Department organized and managed those sen-

[23] To cite one example, an emigree ex-cadre reported in 1964 that a close relative of his had been undergoing labor reeducation—not labor reform—for seven years, and that the end was not yet in sight. This same refugee had himself served a briefer period of labor reeducation as a result of a decision made by the Party Committee under which he worked.

tenced to labor reeducation. They were placed in the commune-controlled Labor Reeducation Group (*lao tung chiao yang tui*) and assigned to various public works or other projects requiring manual labor. Over the years a very sizable number of persons in Commune C had undergone labor reeducation. In 1963 alone, for example, roughly one hundred persons reportedly worked in the commune's Labor Reeducation Group at one time or another, some for relatively short periods of time.

Persons sentenced to labor reform were handled at the county level. The County Public Security Bureau ran the special Labor Reform Farm (*lao kai ch'ang*) to which almost all persons in the county sentenced to labor reform were assigned, although a few were sent elsewhere. Altogether close to forty persons from Brigade B, most of them members of the "four [bad] elements," had served sentences of labor reform on this county farm. Some of these were landlords originally punished during land reform, but others had been sentenced during major campaigns in subsequent years. Roughly half of these had completed sentences and had returned to the brigade, where most were maintained under various forms of political "control"; the others were still working on the county farm in 1964.

The number of persons from Commune C and Brigade B who had been sentenced over the years to forced labor, while not enormous, had been sufficiently large to help create a deep respect on the part of ordinary commune members for the power of those in authority. It had reinforced the prevailing inclination to follow closely the instructions of local Party leaders, if for no other reason than to avoid the risk of being sent to forced labor. On the basis of testimony from emigrees who have served in either labor reform or labor reeducation groups, it seems probable that although forced labor may have had a genuine ideological impact on some of its victims, it probably alienated as many or more than it converted. It obviously created a deep and lasting resentment against the regime on the part of many who underwent it. Nevertheless, it clearly resulted in submission to authority on the part of those punished, and by demonstrating the penalties of getting into trouble, it reinforced the general tendency to be submissive.

Political control was, of course, only one of the concerns of the public security officers and others directing the control system. They were also responsible for handling a wide variety of mundane conflicts and disputes between individuals and social groups. Traditionally, most minor disputes in China have been handled through local mediation. The Communists have carried on this tradition. In many places, formal mediation committees (*t'iao chieh wei yüan hui*) have been established. Though mediation continued to be important in Brigade B and Commune C, no formal committee for mediation existed in 1964, and the top Party and public security authorities tended to monopolize this role as they did all others relating to basic law and order. In Brigade B, all the brigade's cadres were, in a sense, regarded as potential mediators, and at one time or another most of them had actually mediated disputes. The principal person among the cadres to whom minor property and family disputes and the like were taken was the brigade public security chief. Needless to say, because of his great power and prestige, his recommendations were extremely authoritative. He did not handle all types of disputes in Commune C, however; some, including divorce cases, were automatically referred to the Commune Political and Legal Department.

It was symptomatic and symbolic of the pervasive way in which the Party and public security authorities had intruded into people's lives in Commune C that they had come to dominate even the function of mediation, a function which traditionally in China had been fairly informal and autonomous and was generally independent from the more powerful formal instruments of state power.

Manipulation of Social Tensions and Conflicts

Both the process of revolutionary change and the maintenance of totalitarian control require, in the Chinese Communist view, a deliberate manipulation of social conflicts—especially those between classes—and the conscious maintenance of a state of dynamic social tension. Some observers have argued that orthodox, traditional Marxist concepts of class and class struggle have been distorted or underplayed, or at times even ignored, by the Chinese Communists. It has been pointed out by some, for example, that the Chinese Communists seem to have manipulated class concepts in an unusually pragmatic rather than dogmatic way, that they have attempted to bring a large number of nonproletarians into their movement at certain periods, under the slogan of a "united front," and that they have frequently put unusual stress in their propaganda on appeals to broad "nationalist" and "populist" sentiments rather than simply to concepts of class struggle. It has also been pointed out that the Chinese Communists have often tended to equate class status with attitudes and outlook, rather than economic and social factors alone, and have accepted the notion that people can "change their class" by endorsing the principal values and programs promoted by the Communist Party.

Even though these observations are valid in many respects, and even though the Chinese Communists' attitudes toward class are different in many ways from those held by Marx and other orthodox classical Marxists, nevertheless the importance of analyzing class conflicts, arousing class consciousness, and deliberately manipulating class struggle has been one of the fundamental tenets emphasized at all times by Mao and other Chinese Communist leaders. In practical, operational terms, the deliberate promotion and manipulation of class conflict has been, and continues to be, of very great significance in the functioning of the political system in Communist China.

One of the distinctive features of Chinese Communist rule at the village level, in fact, has been the policy of deliberately manipulating social tensions by the continued maintenance—more than a decade after the initial period of violent class struggle which eliminated landlordism—of sizable groups of clearly defined class enemies in the villages. These people, referred to at different times as either the "four [bad] elements" or the "five [bad] elements" are treated by the Communists as political outcasts and are discriminated against in a great many ways. They are regarded as social pariahs and provide concrete targets for class hostility and abuse by all other villagers. They are held up as "negative examples" and as living symbols of what happens to enemies of the regime.

In the area that is now Brigade B, as throughout rural China, one of the most important processes that occurred as a result of the land reform program in the early days of Communist rule, between 1950 and 1952, was the process of "class demarcation," which placed class labels on all inhabitants of the area. Each individual was labeled as belonging to one of the following categories: landless peasant, poor peasant, middle peasant, rich peasant, or landlord—or as belonging to some subcategory of these major class divisions. At the start the groups singled out as major enemies included not only the landlords (*ti chu*) but also other groups which, while not class groups in any strict, traditional sense, were nevertheless identifiable opponents of the regime or were considered by the Communists to be undesirable elements for a variety of reasons. In the area of Brigade B these included persons labeled as bandits (*t'u fei*), rascals or bullies (*e pa*), and secret society elements (*hei she hui fen tzu*, literally "black society elements"). In theory, rich peasants (*fu nung*)—that is, persons who rented out land as well as cultivating some themselves—were not to be regarded as class enemies in the early years. In practice, however, at least some rich peasants in this area were lumped together with the other four groups, and together they were popularly referred to as the five kinds of enemies (*wu fang mien ti ti jen*). Positions of political power were denied to them and were concentrated instead in the hands of those who had backgrounds as landless, poor, or middle peasants. Only persons belonging to these categories could join the new peasant associations, while the new village leaders were recruited almost entirely from the poor peasant group. Violent class warfare was directed in the early years against those belonging to all these enemy groups except the rich peasants, but it was the landlords who bore the brunt of the struggle. In the area of Brigade B, as stated earlier, over thirty landlords were the prime focus of attack, and of these, eight were shot and the rest sentenced to forced labor.

Those who were classified as belonging to any of these enemy groups were referred to as being "capped" (*tai mao tsu*). In theory, any person so classified could, by working hard and giving convincing evidence that he had changed his class outlook and fully supported the regime, in due time be "uncapped" (*chai tiao mao tsu*) and have his class status changed either to that of an enemy group of lower status, or to that of a middle peasant, thereby escaping entirely from the ranks of the enemy.

In the period from the end of land reform in late 1952 up to the peak of the cooperativization drive of 1955–1956, a few people in this area were able to have their class status changed.[24] Almost all of them were landlords who were able to be reclassified as peasants. The number was not great, however, even in those years. Then, during 1956, there was a general review of the class status (*chieh chi fu ch'a*) of everyone in the area, and a new term came into use at that time: the "four [bad] elements" (*szu lei fen tzu*). The ostracized groups now bore different labels from those used in the early years. Now the four key enemy groups were defined as counterrevolutionaries (*fan ko ming fen tzu*), landlords, rich peasants, and a miscellaneous group simply labeled "bad elements" (*huai fen tzu*). This last-named group consisted mainly of troublesome petty criminals whose offenses were essentially nonpolitical. At about the same time, the landlords in this area were divided into three separate categories which were, listed in order of culpability: rascal landlords (*e pa ti chu*), who were sometimes referred to as bureaucratic landlords (*kuan liao ti chu*), many of whom had worked for the Nationalist regime; ordinary landlords (*yi pan ti chu*); and overseas Chinese landlords (*hua ch'iao ti chu*). Overseas Chinese landlords were differentiated from the others because all overseas Chinese, as well as their relatives and dependents, benefited from certain special privileges, and even overseas Chinese landlords' families shared some of these benefits.

Shortly after this new classification of bad elements was introduced, two landlords in the area of Brigade B were able to alter their status. One overseas Chinese landlord was reclassified as a middle peasant (a big improvement in status), and one ordinary landlord was recognized as being an overseas Chinese landlord. But the others classified as bad elements found it impossible to improve their status.

It was during the nationwide "antirightist campaign" of 1957–1958 that still another new category of enemies, the rightists (*yu p'ai fen tzu*), was introduced. Thereafter, the term "five [bad] ele-

[24] The previously mentioned "Forty Article Charter for Agricultural Development" (see p. 334) specified that cooperatives could admit landlords, rich peasants, and even counterrevolutionaries as "uncapped" full members, provisional members, or members under "production control" (or in the case of counterrevolutionaries, as persons undergoing "reform through labor"). In some parts of China, many were admitted, although the number in this area was not large. During 1957 the class line hardened, and some were expelled.

ments" was adopted and widely used throughout the country. For the most part, however, the "antirightist campaign" affected people in urban rather than in rural areas. In some rural districts, it is true, a few "intellectuals"—for example, some teachers—were attacked; but in the area of Brigade B this particular campaign had no real impact, and not a single person in the brigade was "capped" as a rightist. Consequently the term "four [bad] elements" continued to be generally used by people in the brigade, even though they were aware of the broader term encompassing five enemy groups.

In Brigade B, it was not only possible to improve one's class status; there was also a possibility of being demoted in the scale of class enemies. The latter was actually the trend in Brigade B, in fact, in the years after 1960. In 1960, for example, five persons of rich peasant status in the brigade were reclassified as landlords.[25] And then in 1963, when the regime began to make renewed efforts to intensify class consciousness on a nationwide scale and stimulate intensified class struggle in the villages, several upper middle peasants in Brigade B were "capped" for the first time (they were labeled rich peasants), and one rich peasant was reclassified as a landlord.

It seems clear that at the present time, in the context of the revolutionized society existing in rural China, class categorizations such as these are basically artificial. For example, there have not been any landlords, at least in the literal sense of that word, in the area of Brigade B since late 1952, when land reform was completed. The present class status of most people, therefore, is generally an indication of the person's class origin, although it may be modified on the basis of attitudes and behavior. However, because the Chinese Communists assume that class origin is a fundamental factor influencing, or even predetermining, political attitudes and behavior, they still tend to believe that only those of landless and poor peasant origin are wholly reliable and truly "revolutionary."

Changes in class status have been based primarily on the Party's judgments about the person's attitudes, outlook, ideology, and behavior—to which economic factors, such as how much wealth one accumulates, have been relevant in some cases. Thus the Party has

[25] It seems strange (and difficult to explain in ideological terms) that these rich peasants were reclassified as landlords rather than as counterrevolutionaries, but apparently such cases did occur in this area.

not been entirely consistent in its own views as to whether the most important thing is a person's background, his current attitudes, or his present economic situation.

Those in Brigade B who were reclassified by the Party from middle to rich peasants, or from rich peasants to landlord, were simply persons whom the Party felt were opposed to the regime's policies. If a peasant devoted most of his attention to cultivation of his own private plot or to the development of a family-owned handicraft enterprise rather than to the collective work of his production team, and if as a result he became relatively affluent, this in itself might be presumed to be evidence of undesirable attitudes on his part, and could lead the Party to consider changing his class status.

As of 1964 there were altogether thirty-two persons in Brigade B who were formally (*cheng shih*) designated as members of the "four [bad] elements." Of these, three were classified as counterrevolutionaries, twelve as landlords, thirteen as rich peasants, and four as bad elements. Of the twelve landlords, six—all former members of the pre-1949 administrative village government—were classified as rascal landlords, two as ordinary landlords, and four as overseas Chinese landlords. The majority of the thirty-two had served forced labor sentences and subsequently returned to the brigade.

The names of all persons classified as "four [bad] elements" were posted in Brigade B's office, and special dossiers were maintained on them by Commune C's Political and Legal Department. Earlier, during cooperativization—and especially from 1957 on—many had been excluded from the APC's; but now, following communization, they were members of the commune, in the sense that they had to participate in production teams and were remunerated like everyone else on the basis of work points. They were not full-fledged members, however, since they were disenfranchised and were denied both the right to vote and the right to hold office. All of them, moreover, were kept under some sort of "control." Those who returned from the County Labor Reform Farm were placed under strict political control for one to three years, after which they might be placed under one of the looser forms of supervision. The three counterrevolutionaries were under the strictest form, called political control (*cheng chih kuan chih*), which was legally imposed. But many of the others were under either what was called production control (*sheng ch'an kuan chih*), which was less onerous, or supervised labor (*chien tu lao tung*), the lightest form of all. No member of the "four [bad] elements" could leave his production team, even to visit brigade headquarters, without obtaining permission from both his team chief and the local public security officer. In addition, all those under formal control had to report periodically to their local public security man. Members of the "four [bad] elements" were also victims of various forms of discrimination, including economic discrimination, which was sometimes subtle and sometimes not so subtle. For example, in 1963 in Brigade B, some individuals were pressured to make partial payment for the "free food" they had received in 1958. And it was not uncommon, apparently, for them to be treated unfairly in the calculation of work points, on the basis of which they, like all ordinary team members, were paid.

These political and economic measures may have been less painful to members of the "four [bad] elements," however, than the social discrimination which they experienced. They tended to be isolated from other villagers, many of whom avoided having close relations with them for fear of guilt by association. During political campaigns, they were often subjected to concentrated, intense abuse, and their lives were made miserable in many ways; among other things they were expected in public situations to humble themselves before the rest of the villagers and even to bow their heads when passing them.

Many of these persons, especially those classified as counterrevolutionaries or rascal landlords, felt that they had no real prospect of changing their class status. All decisions concerning changes of status were made by the top local Party leaders, and in Brigade B these leaders were not generally in favor of leniency toward those labeled as bad elements.

In theory, the classification of people as members of the "four [bad] elements" was supposed to affect only the individuals so classified and not their children or other relatives. In practice, this was true in some respects—for example, in the application of legal and other sanctions—but in subtle ways the members of the immediate family often suffered too. As has been noted already, class background was considered one of the fundamental criteria for selection and promotion of persons slated to hold leadership positions, and not surprisingly the relatives of ostracized people had a black mark against them which was often difficult to overcome. Moreover, the social discrimination against the "four [bad] elements" often affected their relatives as well, since ordinary villagers feared that close contacts even with the relatives might be contaminating. Some peasants opposed marriages between their children and the children of members of the "bad elements," because they were considered to have poor prospects for future advancement or success.

The total number of ostracized class enemies in Brigade B was comparatively small—thirty-two persons out of a population of roughly twenty-eight hundred, or only a little over 1 percent of the population. Ex-cadres from some other areas in the same general region have reported figures as high as 3 percent. Some assert, in fact, that instructions came down from higher Party authorities specifying that a definite percentage of the population be classified as "four [bad] elements," or "five [bad] elements." But the symbolic importance of these living class enemies could not be measured by numbers alone.

During 1963–1964, the Party leaders in Commune C took concrete steps—in line with new national policies that had emerged after the Tenth Party Central Committee Plenum in late 1962—to raise the level of class-consciousness and heighten the sense of social tension among all members of the commune. In each brigade, including Brigade B, a Poor and Lower Middle Peasants Association was established at that time. In Brigade B, the association had over three hundred members, organized fairly loosely under a chairman, deputy chairman, and a small committee consisting of six members. One of the Party's aims in setting up this new association was clearly to organize a special-interest group, consisting of the most "revolutionary" members of the brigade, to back Party-sponsored policies which might be unpopular with other members.[26] In concrete terms this association in Brigade B was expected actively to propagandize and mobilize the poorest peasants to struggle against all bourgeois, capitalist tendencies on the part of any members of the brigade. The

[26] Higher Party leaders apparently felt that in some areas these associations could also be effectively used to check up on local cadres who had been contaminated by "bourgeois" influences; but this did not seem to be the case in Brigade B, at least up until late 1964.

association attempted to reemphasize the class distinctions separating poor and lower middle peasants from others with higher class status, including the upper middle peasants, many of whom had benefited economically from the liberalized economic policies of the period after the Great Leap and therefore were showing increasing signs of being contaminated with "bourgeois" ideas. Almost by definition, the poor and lower middle peasants included in the association were persons who could be expected to resent the success of those who had profited most from private plots, individual handicrafts, and the like, and who would therefore be inclined to support Party policies which reemphasized "collective" interests and activities.

To what degree these measures have actually developed a heightened sense of genuine class consciousness in Brigade B or elsewhere would be difficult to determine with any accuracy. Some emigrees assert that a sense of class struggle was very real in the early days after Communist takeover, when there was unquestionably a fairly widespread feeling of grievance among the poorest peasants toward many of the old landlords who were then the main focus of attack; but some also assert that over time these feelings of bitterness steadily declined. Many factors may have operated to reduce the kind of class antagonisms which existed in the early years. When the communes were initially established, for example, ex-landlords and former rich peasants, who had previously been barred from membership in cooperatives, were now brought into the new organizations— albeit without full rights. They ate with others in the public mess halls and, for at least a brief period, had closer contacts with other villagers than previously. According to some emigrees, this tended to narrow the gap that had existed in earlier years between these class groups and others. It is very possible that the Communists' recent efforts to renew class struggle at the village level are partially in response to the fact that genuine class antagonism has declined.

It is by no means clear, therefore, to what extent ordinary peasants have participated in the persecution of members of the "four [bad] elements" because of real hostility toward them or because of a feeling that they had to do so in order to avoid criticism themselves. There is evidence to suggest that in some cases the latter motive has undoubtedly been predominant. There are reports, for example, of cases in which poor and middle peasants have publicly condemned and abused ex-landlords but have then privately apologized to them for doing so.

Even though the class antagonisms now being promoted by the Chinese Communists seem in many respects to be artificial and contrived, the class groupings which they have promoted are by no means wholly artificial. To an extent they do reflect real differences in group interests, which the Communists attempt to manipulate to mobilize maximum support for their policies and to minimize the possibility of effective village-level opposition.

In discussing the utility of retaining, in the villages, living symbols of the main class enemies of the regime, one ex-cadre quoted an old Chinese proverb to the effect that it is often useful to "kill a chicken to scare a monkey." He then went on to explain that the treatment of the "four [bad] elements" provided an instructive example which intimidated the mass of ordinary villagers and encouraged them to be submissive to the Party's will. He also pointed out that maintaining these living targets of class struggle has been a useful device for reemphasizing class struggle and reinjecting tension into society whenever the regime's leaders have felt that the dynamism of their revolutionary program was slackening or its momentum declining.

The Family and Other Social Institutions

In pre-Communist China, centralized political power, when effective, reached down to the county level, but management of village-level affairs was in large part left in the hands of local, nongovernmental social institutions which operated with a fairly high degree of autonomy.

One of the Chinese Communists' aims, and accomplishments, has been the destruction of almost all such social institutions inherited from the past, and the restructuring of rural society by the creation of new mass organizations under close Communist Party control. In pursuing this aim in the area of Brigade B, the Party not only shattered the political and social base of the old local elite, but also fractionalized society by creating new class groupings on the basis of the new criteria which it imposed on society. It abolished or undermined the most important of the traditional large-scale social institutions such as the clans and old-style religious bodies; and it regrouped the majority of the population into newly created mass organizations. In addition to the Party itself, these included the Peasant Association, the Young Communist League (at first called the New Democratic Youth League), the Women's Association, the militia, and the Poor and Lower Middle Peasants Association, as well as the new economic collectives.

Apart from families and clans, a variety of traditional social institutions had existed in the area of Brigade B before 1949. Among the most influential of these was a "secret" Buddhist society, called *hui tao men*, which maintained its own temple.[27] This organization was totally suppressed, and its temple was taken over by the Party, in the mid-1950s. There were also four other Buddhist temples of one sort or another in the area. The Party made a direct attack on them during a campaign against superstition in 1956, and then took over two of their buildings in 1958, one for use as a residence and the other as an office. The other two temples continued in existence but were stripped of most idols and other religious objects, and by the early 1960s few people—even old people—visited them any more, even though many older peasants did continue to conduct traditional religious ceremonies in their homes.

All clan temples in the area were also taken over by the Communists for use as offices, schools, or granaries. Consequently by 1964, none of the major traditional social institutions that had formerly operated in this area existed any longer, and all the important, large-scale, institutionalized, social groupings now were new creations of the Party, directly controlled by it. The most important of these have already been described, but one more deserves mention: the local Overseas Chinese Association.

The area of Brigade B, like many rural areas of coastal south China, was one from which there had been a good deal of migration to southeast Asia. As of 1964, over thirty families in the brigade— between 5 and 10 percent of the total population—were classified as overseas Chinese families, and the Overseas Chinese Association contained representatives from all of them. The brigade's Party organi-

[27] The term *hui tao men* can be used to refer not only to secret or Buddhist societies but to virtually all organizations, societies, and associations considered by the Communists to be reactionary.

zation committeeman directed this association, but its titular leader was a local non-Communist member of the overseas Chinese community who was regarded as relatively "progressive" (*chin pu*) by the local Party leaders. Although the association was not notably active in Brigade B, it was called together periodically, either by the Party's organization committeeman or by its titular head, for indoctrination sessions and for special meetings in which all overseas Chinese families were urged to maintain close contacts with their relatives abroad and solicit increased remittances from them.

One of the most difficult questions to answer about the impact of Chinese Communist policies on rural areas such as that of Brigade B is, To what extent has the Party been able to change the traditional family basis of Chinese society? There is no doubt that, as a result of the Communists' revolutionary policies, the role of the family has been weakened and changed; but the persistence of familial ties and influences may be greater in some respects than it appears on the surface.

All three of the natural villages in Brigade B were, like many other south China villages, composed essentially of people of one surname, who were related, even if only remotely. (In pre-Communist times, the custom of exogamous marriage was strictly observed in this area. In recent years there have been a few marriages of people with the same surname—not close relatives, however—but this is still the exception.) Where kinship groups and natural villages have been so closely identified, it is perhaps not surprising that though the Communists have done their best to establish new social institutions that cut across old kinship lines, it has not been possible for them to do so in any complete sense.

The Communists have been fundamentally opposed to basing new forms of social and economic organization on old familial lines because they have regarded the family, quite rightly, as a conservative element in society, one which tends to perpetuate loyalties competitive with those the Communists are attempting to introduce. Therefore, the Communists' aim has been to eliminate the influence of the extended family, reduce the role of the nuclear family, and build a society composed of various new kinds of small nuclear groups based on political, social, economic, and geographical factors which transcend or ignore family ties.

They have clearly had some success in doing this, but there have been limits to their ability to ignore traditional familial groupings. In the area of Brigade B, for example, it was not possible to escape totally from the influence of traditional family groups, even when cooperativization and communization were carried out. The first small mutual aid teams formed in this area often consisted of people who were closely related. When these teams were later merged to become lower APC's, most of the APC's consisted of people living in close proximity, in one natural village, and were therefore made up of persons with the same surname. Under the APC's, moreover, were small work groups which were often based on the original mutual aid teams, and although the Party made an effort to break up groups consisting of close relatives, many work groups still were composed of people with strong familial ties. In this area, it was only when higher APC's were formed that the collective organizations extended considerably beyond traditional groupings of people linked by significant kinship ties. Even then the subunits of the higher APC's tended to be units comparable to the earlier groups, and like them often were composed of people who were related. When communes were formed, there was still a degree of continuity, since the cooperatives and their subunits tended to be incorporated almost intact as subunits of the new communes.

In Brigade B, none of the twenty-four production teams operated in territory beyond the boundaries of a single natural village. Consequently, nearly every team was made up of people of the same surname, and frequently the teams consisted of people who were fairly close relatives.

At the brigade level, from time to time issues arose—particularly practical issues such as those involving water rights—in which the members of each of the three villages tended to act as a separate lobby group arguing for their own special interests. This probably would have been the case even if the villagers had not been composed of relatives, but the familial basis of the village social structure undoubtedly reinforced the existing sense of village solidarity and distinctiveness.

All three village surnames—Ts'ai, Yen, and Wu—were well represented among the brigade's cadres. Not surprisingly, however, the representation was unequal, and cadres named Ts'ai and Wu outnumbered those named Yen. Reportedly, the villagers in Yen village resented this, but the cadres named Yen did not. The cadres were expected to act as disciplined servants of the Party and the collective interest rather than as representatives of particular village or family interests, and apparently they generally did, in practice as well as in theory. Therefore, even when disputes or differences arose that tended to divide the brigades' membership along village or familial lines, the cadres usually worked together to promote what they, as Party members, believed to be the collective interests of the entire brigade—or of the Party itself.

Thus, while ordinary brigade members were still significantly affected by kinship ties, this was much less true of the cadres, who tended to identify with, and operate principally in the context of, the new social units created by the Party. Most cadres, in short, had transferred their prime loyalty to the political authorities whom they served. Nevertheless, familial ties were said to affect the cadres in at least one significant way in Brigade B, as at higher levels in the Chinese Communist bureaucracy. Reportedly, cadres often tended to give preferential treatment of various kinds to their own close relatives; and ordinary brigade members were said to be inclined to pay some deference to all the close relatives of cadres, as well as to the cadres themselves. It was generally felt, and may well have been at least partially true, that close relatives of cadres were in a preferred situation to "get ahead" in the brigade and were in less danger of being punished for minor misdemeanors than others were.

The continuing importance of certain familial ties, even beyond those of the nuclear family, does not mean, however, that there have not been profound changes in the role of the family in the area of Brigade B as throughout rural China. Party members and activists— i.e. all members of and aspirants to the new ruling elite group—are expected in most situations to place loyalty to higher political leadership above loyalty to family, and they generally do. The deliberate fostering of class consciousness and class tensions has cut across and weakened kinship ties. The collectivization of economic functions has fundamentally altered the family's economic role in society. The clans no longer have any important functions, and the nuclear family has lost many of the economic responsibilities that it had before and is no longer the crucial unit for the division of labor and the distribution of income that it once was.[28]

In Brigade B, as in much of China, perhaps the most dramatic and traumatic developments affecting the family were those which occurred during the first stage of communization, when it appeared briefly that even the nuclear family would suddenly be submerged by collectivism. This was the period when women were drawn out of their homes to work, children were put in nurseries, the aged were sent off to old people's homes, and families did not even eat their meals at home. But this period did not last for long. Interestingly, some emigrees report that after the first extreme period of communization, which posed many threats to the family, conditions in the following period tended, if anything, to strengthen familial ties and kinship solidarity. It was a period of hunger and hardship; and faced with the basic problem of how to eat and survive, relatives apparently closed ranks, doing the best they could to help each other out in the time-honored tradition of Chinese in times of adversity.

In short, the nuclear family continues to be a social institution of basic importance even under communization, and familial ties still operate and influence the regime in many different ways. But there can be no doubt that the role of the family has changed, and its social and economic importance has clearly been reduced by the Communists' restructuring of the economy and of society as a whole.

[28] One might say that in traditional rural China society was collectivized on the basis of the family, and that the Communists have recollectivized on the basis of new nuclear social units.

Production Teams

AS OF 1964, the real basis of collective farming in Commune C, as in most agricultural areas of China, was neither the commune nor its brigades, but the production teams (called *sheng ch'an hsiao tui* here, although reportedly in some places they are called simply *sheng ch'an tui*). In Brigade B, these teams operated under the close direction of the brigade, but ever since the decentralization after the Great Leap they had been the units which were actually responsible for managing production and distributing net income. The average size of the twenty-four teams under Brigade B was somewhat over twenty households, or more than one hundred people, although a few had as many as thirty households. This made them roughly the size of the small lower APC's that had existed in this area in the mid-1950s. Their powers and functions, however, were generally similar to those of the higher APC's that had existed just prior to communization.

Somewhat surprisingly, Party membership was extremely small at the level of the teams in this area. In fact, there were only ten Party members in all twenty-four teams, and every one of them was a team chief (*hsiao tui chang*). This meant that in fourteen teams there were no Party members at all. In each of these fourteen, however, there were at least some activists who were closely linked to the Party, and some of these activists were likely to be taken into the Party eventually. Local team cadres (*hsiao tui kan pu* or *ti fang kan pu*) who were not Party members were usually labeled activists. Since there were so few Party members and no Party organizations (not even *hsiao tsu*, or "cells") at the team level, the Brigade Party Branch itself provided political leadership for all the teams. The few Party members actually located in the teams belonged to the brigade branch and participated in its "Party life" whenever they could.

Each team was run by a team committee (*hsiao tui wei yüan hui*), which normally consisted of about nine members, including six team cadres and the heads of the subordinate production groups (*sheng sh'an hsiao tsu*) to which all team members were assigned. Generally there were three production groups per team, each having six or seven households. The Team Staff Office (*pan kung shih*) was normally located in one room in a peasant's home—generally that of the team chief, although if he did not have sufficient space, the office could be in the home of a leading local activist.

The annual elections of the Team Committee were comparable to elections at higher levels that have already been described. A slate of candidates was drawn up on the initiative of the brigade branch and was then presented to a general meeting of all team members, except those belonging to the "four [bad] elements," who were disenfranchised. The list almost always consisted of those persons slated to be team cadres and production group leaders, and since the Brigade Party Branch in effect selected these people, the vote usually was simply a formal endorsement of the branch's choices. Frequently a cadre from the brigade branch sat in at both the election meeting and the initial team committee organization meeting held soon thereafter, when cadre job assignments were formally decided on. When there was a Party member in a team, he was almost automatically elected as team chief. The others selected to be team cadres generally included, in addition to the outstanding local activists, some persons who had received simple training courses given by either the brigade or the commune to qualify them for essential team tasks such as accounting, which required at least minimum skills. Frequently, also, one or more respected farmers were selected, primarily because of their practical knowledge rather than their politics; but even they had to be persons who had demonstrated a willingness to cooperate with the Party and had acceptable class backgrounds.

The six team cadres included the chief (*tui chang*), the deputy chief (*fu tui chang*), the public security officer (*chih pao wei yüan*), the accountant (*k'uai chi*), the cashier (*ch'u na*), and the custodian (*pao kuan*). The three production group chiefs (*tsu chang*) were appointed to their posts, although they had to be elected to the Team Committee. Each production group also had an appointed work-point recorder (*chi fen yüan*)—in some places these apparently were team rather than production group cadres—but they were not considered to be members of the Team Committee.

With one exception, all these local cadres, like ordinary team members, were fully engaged in regular agricultural labor; but they received a small amount of extra remuneration, in the form of work points, for their administrative duties. (The chief was credited with five work days monthly, his deputy four, the custodian three, and the cashier two.) They were expected not only to take part in agricultural labor but to work harder than anyone else, in order to set good examples.[29] This meant in practice that many of their leadership and administrative functions had to be performed in their "spare time"; thus they carried a very heavy work load. The team cadres met frequently as a committee, at times almost daily, to discuss a wide variety of production and management problems.

Many of the teams' plans and programs were, in effect, determined by instructions from above. The brigade, for example, laid down specifications concerning the crops they should grow, and outlined general production targets, although it did consult with the teams before doing so. Many of the teams' basic obligations were defined, in fact, in contracts which they signed with the brigade. The brigade also informed all teams of their obligations regarding both the land tax and the compulsory sale of grain and a sizable range of other commodities which had to be sold to the state.

Within this general framework, however, the teams had both the authority and the responsibility to plan and manage their own production. They owned most of their own capital goods, including farm tools and draft animals. And as basic accounting and budgeting units, they determined the allocation of their net income, after taxes and compulsory sales. Traditionally, of course, individual peasant households had performed these functions in China—even tenant farmers in China before 1949 had largely managed their farms —but the task of managing groups of twenty to thirty families and sizable amounts of land was more complex and difficult than that

[29] The one exception, noted above, was the accountant, who also acted as team statistician, *t'ung chi*. Perhaps because he had so many time-consuming office chores, he was half exempt from agricultural labor, *pan t'o ch'an*.

which had formerly faced individual peasant households. The decentralization of managerial responsibilities from the communes, first to the brigades and finally to the teams, had to some extent reduced the complexities of the managerial tasks in the agricultural economy by reducing the size of the units to be managed, but it had also imposed heavy burdens on the teams and on the largely uneducated and often illiterate low-level cadres who ran them. While many of these cadres were experts in farming, very few had had special training to prepare them for new responsibilities such as keeping accounts, maintaining statistics, and reporting to higher authorities. In short, making the teams responsible for production management did place qualified farmers in charge of farming—even though they tended to use traditional methods, team cadres generally understood local conditions much better than higher-level cadres did and were able to avoid many of the mistakes that had been made by cadres at higher levels in the past—but it also created many new problems, which the teams are still attempting to solve.

Probably the most compelling motive for the decentralization of authority to the teams was the desire to spur production by reemphasizing economic incentives and by returning responsibility for the distribution of output to a level where the peasants could again see a direct relationship between their labor and the rewards they received. As the system operated in 1964, the Team Committee—sometimes after discussions involving all the team members—decided how its remaining grain (the amount left after the team had fulfilled its quotas for the land tax and compulsory sales to the state), as well as other crops and income, was to be used. Sometimes the communes and brigades laid down certain guidelines, specifying, for example, what percentage of net output should be used for reserves; but the teams were given real authority to decide what to do with their profits.

In one of Brigade B's teams which had 141 members, net output in 1963 was distributed roughly as follows: Total grain (rice) production amounted to 77,741 catties (over 38 tons). Of this, 14,490 catties were deducted for the land tax and compulsory sales, and 26,749 catties were reserved by the team itself for a variety of purposes (9,124 catties of this 26,749 ultimately went to team members —see below). The remaining 36,402 catties were distributed directly to team members. Of the 26,749 catties reserved for team use, 10,000 catties were used to pay off a grain loan received from the state during a period of local grain shortage, 6,125 catties were added to the team's reserves, 1,500 catties were set aside as seed grain for the following year, and 9,124 catties were used for a variety of purposes including allowances for cadres and militiamen on special duty, subsidies to pay the expenses of childbirth and funerals in poor households, special allowances for extra heavy labor, miscellaneous bonuses, and special relief. The team also received some cash for its compulsory sales to the state. Not only rice, but most of the team's important subsidiary crops, including soy beans, peanuts, hemp, and sugar cane, were sold at least in part to the state. The cash received, plus income from the sale of crop output that exceeded the team's quotas and some income from collectively run handicrafts, was used by the team largely for reinvestment purposes, including the purchase of draft animals, farm implements, and fertilizers.

Each team maintained its own granary (*ts'ang k'u*), which was supervised by the team custodian. The team accountant kept detailed accounts, records, and statistics relating to all the team's operations; these included records on all members' earned work points, which were based on daily reports submitted to him by the production group work-point recorders. The cashier was in charge of all team receipts and disbursements. The team public security officer served as the local representative of the county-wide public security network and, among other things, had primary responsibility for checking on all members of the "four [bad] elements."

Some of the most troublesome managerial problems faced by the teams arose in connection with distribution of their income. On the one hand, the team cadres were usually under pressure from higher authorities to devote as large a share as possible of their net produce to reinvestment and other collective purposes, but they were also under pressure from their team members to increase the amount distributed to them. Moreover, the decisions regarding distribution to team members involved many complexities. Distribution was based primarily on accumulated work points (*kung fen*), ten work points equaling one work day (*kung jih*). Every type of work had to be graded according to its difficulty and the skill it required, so that a standard number of work points could be assigned to it; then persons had to be judged as to how well they had performed the tasks assigned to them. There was no "free supply," as in the early days of communization.

When net income was distributed to team members each year, the accumulated work points of the team as a whole, as well as those of each team member, were totaled. A definite value was assigned to each work point by dividing the net income to be distributed by the total number of accumulated work points. Then each individual was remunerated on the basis of the number of work points he had earned. The team also paid its members for the human manure which they had delivered for use on the team's collective fields. It was difficult for the team cadres to obtain this manure for the collective fields, however, since many peasants preferred to use it on their own private plots.

Throughout Commune C, all peasants were assigned small private plots (*tzu liu ti*), for cultivation in their spare time. These had existed earlier, during the period of the APC's, and had subsequently been abolished at the time of communization, but they were reestablished in the period immediately after the Great Leap. In the teams under Brigade B, the plots were tiny patches of land, reportedly average three to five *li*, depending on the quality of the land (in this area one *li* equaled one one-hundredth of a *mou*). Moreover, they were not given as private property, but were simply assigned temporarily for use by individual peasants. In Brigade B the plot assignments were changed each year to discourage peasants from investing too much of their time and resources, including human manure, on them. But, in fact, here as elsewhere in China, the private plots were of enormous economic importance. Because the output of these plots was owned totally by the peasants cultivating them, and could be consumed, or sold on the free market, as they wished, the plots were cultivated with great care and skill, and their per acre output was far above that of the team's collective land. The crops produced on these plots did not enter at all into the accounts of the teams, brigades, or communes, but because of their success the plots were a major factor in the over-all agricultural economy and contributed largely to the general improvement of conditions from 1962 on, following the economic crisis of 1959–1961.

Clearly, the top leaders in Communist China disliked the necessity of making these and other concessions to the stubborn peasants' "bourgeois," "capitalist" tendencies; but even during the nation-wide "socialist education" movement of 1963–1964, when they again reemphasized the desirability of checking such tendencies and stressed the need to give priority to collective enterprises, they left the private plots in Commune C, as throughout almost all the country, untouched.

As of 1964, therefore, the production teams in Commune C operated as the basic agricultural collectives, under the supervision of the brigades and communes as well as higher levels of government authority, and the degree of individual enterprise allowed at the team level was greater, at least temporarily, than it had been at any time since the mid-1950s, prior to the regime's utopian initial experiments with communization.

How long this situation would last, however, was problematical. The lessons of agricultural failure learned during 1959–1961 seemed to have made many of China's top leaders cautious about "great leaps" and wary about attempts to move too rapidly toward their ultimate goals, but there seemed to be little doubt that if and when they thought it feasible, they would feel under strong pressure to move once again toward a higher level of collectivization and toward restoration of at least some of the features which had been characteristic of the communes in the initial period of their existence. As of 1964, the communes of 1958 were in one sense an unpleasant memory; but to many of Communist China's leaders they also remained a persistent dream.

Part IV
CONCLUSIONS

Some Generalizations
and Hypotheses

THE CHINESE Communist regime represents a revolutionary and totalitarian movement, operating in a tradition-rooted but changing
society, that has attempted not only to create a new polity but also
to use political power to achieve rapid modernization and to transform China's social structure and system of values. As such, it has
evolved organizational structures and modes of operation that blend,
in a unique fashion, elements from a variety of sources: the theoretical Leninist model of "democratic centralism," the post-Leninist
model of Soviet society, the Chinese Communists' own pre-1949 experience in conducting revolutionary struggle and administering
"liberated areas," and—not least important—China's centuries-old
traditions of authoritarianism, elitism, ideological orthodoxy, and
bureaucratic administration.

Case studies such as those included in this volume, which involve
microsocietal analysis of the structure and operation of Party and
government organizations in a few selected areas, obviously cannot
answer all the myriad questions one can raise about the nature of the
over-all political system that has evolved—and continues to evolve—
in this complex setting. But, examined in conjunction with information available from written sources, they do throw light on some
of the characteristics of the system, especially as it operates at the
local level. By studying the organization and operation of particular
institutions, one can gain insights into important aspects of the system as a whole, including the characteristics of the new elite who
provide leadership in the system (the cadres), the organization and
modes of operation of the institutional structures in which they work

(the bureaucracy), and the actual locus of decision-making and patterns of authority as they operate both within the bureaucratic elite and in relations between them and the mass of the population (political power).

What are some of the broad generalizations that emerge—at least as reasonable hypotheses—from a detailed examination of how the system works in concrete situations? First, and most obvious, perhaps, is the conclusion that despite innumerable problems the Communist leaders in China have been remarkably successful in establishing a political system that has extended the outreach and impact of central decisions and central power to an unprecedented degree. This does not mean that they have been able to forge political instruments that in practice enable them actually to achieve all their ambitious goals; the apparatus of power in Communist China today is plagued by many dilemmas, weaknesses, and inefficiencies, and it faces enormous problems. Yet in a basic sense, the Communists have been able to create a disciplined elite and new structures of Party and government organization which enable a handful of Party leaders at the top to make their will felt upon China's enormous population as never before. Policy impulses from the center must filter through complex bureaucratic structures of power before they reach and affect the masses, and the results do not always fulfill the leaders' hopes and expectations, by any means. But the political apparatus does transmit policy impulses from the center to the grassroots of society, where they actually affect people's lives—whether in the exact fashion intended or not—in a way that has never been the case in China before.

Traditionally in China, central power, transmitted through a well-established bureaucracy, reached the county (*hsien*) level with some degree of effectiveness—at least during periods when the country was unified under a strong regime—but at subcounty levels "informal government," run by traditional elite groups such as the "gentry" and by a variety of nongovernmental social institutions tended to dominate the scene. The Communists have basically altered this situation. They have largely destroyed both the old elite groups and most of the traditional social institutions, substituting for them a new Communist Party elite and new Communist-established and -dominated mass organizations, and have extended the formal bureaucratic instruments of Party and government rule down to the village level.

Perhaps even more important, the functions of government have been greatly expanded. Whereas in pre-Communist China—especially in imperial days but to a considerable extent even in the republican period—the government generally was content if social order could be maintained and taxes and conscriptees collected, the new centrally directed apparatus of political power is designed to change society, not simply to preserve it. Determined to alter the country's basic class structure, reindoctrinate the entire population in a new ideological orthodoxy, change fundamental patterns of behavior, and reorganize the economy to spur rapid development, the Communists have had to devise new political organizations and patterns of political action to achieve these ends. It is really no exaggeration to state that now the Party and government consider everything to be of political concern, and virtually nothing in the field of thought or action, whether involving groups or individuals, is viewed by the present regime as being outside the sphere of responsibility of political leaders. As a result, society has been politicized to an unprecedented degree. This has involved not only basic changes in the attitudes of both the leaders and the led, but also— not surprisingly—a great expansion of the organizational apparatus of political power at all levels. Dedicated to the aim of controlling and changing the totality of society, the regime has had to build new institutions to enable the nation's leaders not only to police the entire society but also to manage the economy as a whole and indoctrinate the mass of the population in Marxism-Leninism and the "thought of Mao Tse-tung"—in short, to achieve the basis for an effective totalitarian political and social system.

As in other Communist-ruled societies, the Communist Party dominates the political system and plays the key role in operating it. But in China the role of the Party is, if anything, even greater than in the Soviet Union and the other Communist countries in Eastern Europe. The Party constitutes the elite of the elite, and monopolizes ultimate policy- and decision-making authority. It maintains its own disciplined chain of command from the top to the bottom of society, parallel to the other hierarchies of power—the government, the mass organizations, and the military establishment—and through

Party units imbedded in these other hierarchies, exercises tight control over them. One of the striking characteristics of the system in China is the degree to which interlocking directorates link these hierarchies, as a result of the fact that key Party leaders hold concurrent posts in other organizational apparatuses.

The crucial role of the Party in China, even by contrast with other Communist-ruled countries, is reinforced by the fact that the Party has tended to go far beyond acting as director and supervisor of other political organizations and has constantly encroached upon government administration as such. In short, on many occasions and in many fields the Party has not simply supervised the running of things but has tended to step in and run them itself. This was most dramatically the case in the period of the Great Leap Forward and immediately thereafter, but it has been a recurring tendency at other times as well.

At the lowest levels of the political system, Party dominance has been such that there has sometimes been, in practical terms, a virtual merger of the Party and the government. The theory continues to be that the Party should avoid getting bogged down in administrative tasks and should instead maintain itself as a distinct elite of dedicated generalists directing those who are responsible for carrying out government administration, many of whom must, of necessity, be specialists. But repeatedly, in practice, the Party has been unable to resist the impulse to intervene in government administration and in effect has often taken over the responsibility of running things itself.

One result of the Party's insistence on unchallengeable political predominance in China has been that, to date at least, it appears to have been more successful than the Communists have been in some other countries, in resisting trends toward the development of parallel bureaucratic structures—in the government, the military establishment, collectives, commercial and industrial enterprises, and so on—possessing tendencies to see their own organizational interests in terms different from, and sometimes in opposition to, those of the Party apparatus as such. The Party's effective monopoly of policy-making on major issues, its frequent incursions into direct administration, and the prevalence of interlocking directorates have all contributed to this end.

Nevertheless, the problem of generalists versus specialists (which the Chinese Communists, with their penchant for slogans, label the "red and expert" problem) is a basic one and is likely, in fact, to become increasingly important as time goes on. The Chinese Communists' aim is to create a new leadership group that is both "red and expert," i.e. an elite group of individuals who not only possess the requisite specialized skills to handle the complex problems of running both the political system and society as a whole, but who, as dedicated Communists, are also effective generalists, able to perform multiple tasks and willing to put loyalty to the Party and overall system ahead of parochial interests associated with specialized skills and activities. In reality, however, the "red and expert" problem remains a fundamental one, and in fact is becoming increasingly important. In part it is a problem of relations between those key Party leaders at each level who tend to be political generalists and those intellectuals, technicians, and the like—many of them, especially at higher levels, non-Party cadres working for government agencies, and not a few of them persons educated and trained before Communist takeover—who tend to have the outlook of specialists and often, in the regime's view, are tainted with "bourgeois" or "revisionist" ideas.

The problem is broader and deeper than this, however. There has been a steady trend over the past seventeen years, within the Party itself as well as in the government and other organizations, toward functional specialization, at all levels. Most Party as well as government work in Communist China now tends to be grouped into one of several identifiable functional "systems" (*hsi t'ung*), and there is a tendency, at least to some extent, for persons working within a particular functional "system" to develop distinctive preoccupations, outlooks, and priorities. Since these "systems" include Party as well as government and other institutions operating in particular fields, they have not necessarily divided Party and government agencies into separate, competing Party and government hierarchies. They have, however, contributed significantly to the "red and expert" dichotomy, since in a subtle but important way tendencies have developed even within the Party for personnel to become associated with—and to associate themselves with—particular functional "systems." This important trend has doubtless been unavoidable, and it can be expected to continue, even under a regime that believes its key leaders should be dedicated generalists above all else. Many of the tasks of modernization require specialization, and it would be surprising if specialization did not affect the attitude of the specialists in ways the Party dislikes. The "red and expert" problem can be expected to grow, therefore; and even though the Party will doubtless continue in its dominating role, trends toward specialization within the Party itself are likely to challenge those Party generalists who are preoccupied chiefly with general problems of ideology and organization and who have tended to monopolize the top leadership posts at every level to date.

The new elite which has emerged in China since 1949, and which possesses both the power to control the political system and the prestige to dominate society as a whole, is very different from comparable groups in China's past. While many top Chinese Communist leaders came from nonproletarian and even "bourgeois" backgrounds, and while the Communists have had to use many persons from the "old society" whose specialized skills and experience have been scarce and therefore indispensable, the new leadership in China is currently dominated—even at higher levels, but particularly at "basic" levels in rural society—by a new breed of men and women who have emerged from the process of revolutionary upheaval. A high proportion of these leaders came from the poorest strata of society and had relatively little education. They emerged as members of the elite by proving that they had leadership and organizational skills during the guerrilla and other military operations leading to Communist victory, or by distinguishing themselves in the intense class struggles immediately after Communist takeover, or by playing "activist" roles in subsequent Communist-directed programs. Service in militia or army units, participation in mass organizations, and leadership in the earliest collective units organized by the Communists were common routes to acceptance into the new elite; and positive demonstrations of loyalty to the new ideological orthodoxy, as well as disciplined submission to Party leadership, have been essential requirements for admission to the ruling group.

The new elite, while dominated by trusted "old Party cadres," is not as homogeneous as it sometimes appears on the surface, however. In the broadest sense, it includes all those who hold functionary posts in any of the organizational structures of power in the country. All such persons are labeled "cadres" (*kan pu*), and they all enjoy power, prestige, and perquisites which set them apart from the "masses." Within the elite, though, there is a significant gap between Party cadres and non-Party cadres. It is the Party cadres who monopolize policy-making and the top leadership posts, while many of the non-Party cadres belong to various categories of specialists. Although the Party has increasingly attempted to absorb "intellectuals," especially new "proletarian intellectuals," into its own fold, and the graduates of educational institutions in China have flowed increasingly into the ranks of the Party as well as becoming non-Party cadres, a dichotomy between "nonintellectuals" and "intellectuals" (the "reds" and the "experts") has persisted, not only in relations between Party and non-Party cadres but even within the Party itself.

One of the most significant trends in recent years, moreover, has been the seemingly irresistible growth of complex bureaucratic patterns of social stratification even within the ranks of the Party cadres in Communist China. The Party has tried in many ways to resist these trends—for example, by promoting physical labor by cadres, sending personnel to work in rural areas, and taking such drastic steps as abolishing ranks within the army—but as the egalitarian heritage of active revolutionary struggle has tended to recede into the background, deep-rooted authoritarian and bureaucratic predispositions, especially the tendency to differentiate people by rank, have reasserted themselves. Consequently, virtually all cadres in Communist China today can be labeled and placed fairly accurately in the hierarchy of power and prestige on the basis of seniority in the Party, salary grade, and job rank. Significantly, while formal salary and job ratings are very important, informal ratings based on length of service in the Party appear to be just as important, and in fact the former tend to be equated with the latter. The growth of these patterns of social stratification has been a major factor contributing to the steady bureaucratization of the regime and the erosion of the elite's revolutionary character.

Another basic characteristic of the new elite—and one that creates a fundamental problem for the regime—has been the striking lack of upward mobility within the top ranks of the ruling group in recent years and the tendency of leaders at every level to cling to power and age in office. Throughout China, from the national capital to the rural counties, a surprisingly high percentage of the leaders who assumed top positions of authority in the early period, during and immediately after Communist takeover, still monopolize such positions. The fact that this has been the case at the national and provincial levels is known from detailed biographical studies of key personnel at these levels; data has not been available to make comparable studies of leadership at the county level and below, but case studies of particular areas, such as those included in this volume, suggest that it is true at these lower levels as well.

In short, even though the Communists were able to engineer a dramatic change in leadership at all levels of society during their early years in power, they have not been notably successful since then in building into their political system accepted practices and procedures for superannuating members of the takeover generation of leaders and infusing new and younger talent into top leadership positions. Consequently, as the revolution has aged, its top leaders at all levels have aged with it. The relative stability and cohesiveness of this leadership group, which for many years clearly constituted a major source of strength to the regime, has increasingly become a significant problem and potential source of weakness. This situation has already created some tensions and frustrations in the system, especially among lower-ranking members of the expanding elite, who have found the ladder of success leading to top leadership posts clogged by old Party leaders who continue to cling to power. Even more important, it poses many sorts of unanswerable questions about the future, since the mortality of the takeover leaders will result, before very long, in a fairly rapid and widespread turnover of leaders, with consequences that are not easy to foresee. This transition will begin at the top, where the leaders are the oldest, but once underway it is likely to have repercussions affecting leadership at every level throughout the country.

Despite problems of these sorts, however, the Communists have been generally successful to date in demanding the prime loyalty of, and imposing effective discipline upon, the very large numbers of cadres who compose the new elite in China and who staff the Party, government, and other bureaucracies which run the country. Many traditional patterns of behavior associated with bureaucrats in China, including endemic corruption, nepotism, and factionalism, appear to have been kept under effective control. In part, the Communists' success in this respect has been due to their ability to elicit positive commitment from the cadres to the primary goals of the regime, commitment based either upon acceptance of the ideological propositions which undergird the Communists' programs or upon responsiveness to the appeals of nationalism and patriotism. In part, however, it has also been due to the effectiveness of the personnel management techniques which the Communists have evolved to enforce discipline as well as elicit commitment.

In many respects the regime's totalitarian controls impose stricter discipline and tighter checks on the cadres who make up the bureaucratic elite than on most ordinary people in the society, with the notable exception of ostracized groups treated as public enemies. Detailed dossiers are maintained on all cadres. They are subjected to regular fitness reports which probe their activities and attitudes in great detail. They must participate in regular "study" sessions, where collective group pressures help to enforce conformity and discipline. Any shortcomings or failures on their part expose them to the risk of severe administrative punishments or to the possibility of political attacks in "struggle meetings" during periodic "rectification" campaigns. They live in a general atmosphere of restrictive security-consciousness; and to a substantial extent their lives have been "collectivized" in a fashion which bestows on them the benefits of the regime's paternalistic concern for their welfare, but also subjects them to close and continuous surveillance. They are subjected to frequent transfers—more often lateral than upward, and in recent years often downward, to rural areas—and most of them must participate in some sort of physical work, which the regime promotes to combat bureaucratism. And if they are Party or Young Communist League (YCL) cadres they must, in addition, participate actively in "Party life" or "League life," which involves regular and frequent group meetings as well as many other demands on their time and energies. As a result of all of these factors, the cadres in China today have relatively little personal life, they feel that they are under continual close scrutiny by higher authorities, and they are subjected to intense social pressures to submit and conform, pressures organized by higher Party authorities, but most often exerted by their colleagues. They must give continuous evidence of their loyalty and obedience to the regime, or they expose themselves to dangerous risks.

Organizationally, the Communists' success in building bureaucratic structures of power which are based in fact as well as in theory on the concept of "democratic centralism"—i.e. which combine mass participation with extreme concentration of decision-making power —creates a basic contrast between political organizations in China today and those in the pre-1949 period. The Chinese Nationalists, like the Communists, borrowed the concept of "democratic centralism" from the Soviet Union, but in practice they were never able either to achieve a broad base of political participation in their political institutions or to develop effective procedures for policy-making at the center.

If one simply examines tables of organization or organizational charts, it is evident that many of the political institutions in China today—particularly governmental institutions, but even Party organizations as well—are similar in numerous respects to ones that existed in the period before 1949. Moreover, despite the regime's success in disciplining its cadres and minimizing traditional practices such as corruption, nepotism, and factionalism, many bureaucratic patterns of behavior inherited from the past persist in the highly stratified bureaucracies that have developed over the past seventeen years. But there are also profound differences between the political institutions of the present and those of the past. Not only has there been a great proliferation of new institutions, created to perform new functions and carry out new responsibilities which the regime has undertaken for the first time, but even those institutions which bear most resemblance to previous ones operate in a fashion that is very different in many respects from the operation of comparable institutions in the past.

Communications within the entire apparatus of political power, and between this apparatus and the population, are far superior to what they were before. Despite some continuing imperfections, and the fact that communication downward is clearly more effective than communication upward in the system, there is no doubt that China's present leaders are able to transmit decisions far more effectively, and to gather information somewhat more efficiently, than leaders in the past.

One of the most striking and distinctive aspects of the operation of the regime in China today is its continued reliance, seventeen years after coming to power, upon mass campaigns, rather than on more routinized administrative methods, to carry out its major policies and programs. This revolutionary mode of operation was clearly a product of the techniques for mass mobilization developed by the Chinese Communists during their struggle for power and during the early years of class struggle when they consolidated their power. In essence, the campaign approach to policy implementation, which grows out of their commitment to what is called the "mass line," involves the setting of a few clearly defined immediate aims, the concentration of efforts and attention on these aims above all others, the mobilization and training of large numbers of cadres drawn from many segments of the political system to carry out a campaign, and finally the mass mobilization of the population as a whole to take action to achieve the defined goals. Such campaigns rest on the premise that the masses, if they are properly organized and infused with ideological fervor, can be activated to achieve most of the society's fundamental goals, even in a modernizing society. Human will and labor, rather than technical skills, are seen as the key ingredients of social progress. And it is the Party itself, rather than governmental or other institutions, which generally assumes prime responsibilities for directing these campaigns.

While the effectiveness of mass campaigns during the early years of revolutionary struggle in China was indisputable, their suitability and effectiveness now as a basic instrument to create a modernized and developed society is less clear. They do have some definite advantages. They enable Communist China's leaders to concentrate their efforts at any particular time on defined objectives and to mobilize tremendous numbers of people to work toward them. However, there is little doubt that in many respects they are costly and wasteful of time and effort; they often result in the neglect of nonpriority tasks; they frequently result in the misuse of the limited reservoir of specialized talent that the country possesses; they appear to have a built-in tendency toward political excess; and they are often extremely disruptive of more regularized and routinized governmental functions. This last effect is doubtless seen by Communist China's present leaders as an asset rather than a liability, however. In fact, their persistence in using revolutionary techniques of mass mobilization is obviously motivated in part by a conscious determination to combat routinization of government, which they fear will reinforce tendencies toward increased bureaucratization, a loss of revolutionary fervor on the part of China's cadres, the re-emergence of "bourgeois" values, the growth of "revisionism," and a general erosion of revolutionary momentum. In actual fact, these tendencies have steadily developed in Communist China, and as a consequence it has become increasingly difficult for Peking's leaders to mobilize the population in mass campaigns as it did in earlier years. But this appears to have reinforced their determination to try. It remains to be seen, however, how long this revolutionary method of resisting routinization and bureaucratization can be effectively pursued—particularly after a generational change in leadership occurs—and in fact one can question whether the regime will be able, over the long run, really to advance toward many of its goals of modernization without a higher degree of routinization that at present, even if the cost of routinization is increased bureaucratization and a slackening of revolutionary fervor. One can expect, therefore, a continuing dialectical interaction in Communist China between the efforts of many of the regime's leaders to promote the "mass line" and the steady growth of tendencies toward routinization and bureaucratization.

The problem of how to promote uninterrupted revolution in the face of existing trends is only one of many fundamental organizational issues that have confronted, and continue to confront, Communist China's leaders. Another is the problem of how best to distribute power and responsibility between various levels in the system. This long-standing question continues to be a fundamental issue and is by no means fully and finally resolved. The Communists have, however, attempted to find formulas that could somehow combine central control over basic policy-making with local responsibility for policy adaptation and implementation, and they have had some success. Traditional Chinese predispositions toward political centralization, combined with Communist propensities toward "centralism," have resulted in a high degree of effective central control over basic policy formulation, as well as effective suppression of the kind of regional, local, and other centrifugal forces that fractionalized China in the period before 1949. But at the same time the Communists have placed greater real responsibility for policy implementation upon local leaders than has been the case in the past and have demanded initiative and even innovation on the part of low-level cadres, within the limits set by centrally defined policies. In short, despite many rigidities that exist in China's present totalitarian system, where ultimate decisions are made by a handful of Party leaders, the Communists have consciously attempted to build some elements of flexibility into the system.

In practice, however, the proper balance between centralization and decentralization has not been easily achieved, and Peking has been forced to shift the balance repeatedly, making some serious errors in the process. Despite their mistakes, however, and despite the continued existence of many unresolved—and perhaps insoluble —problems, it is probably correct to say that the Communists have to date been able to achieve a higher degree both of effective central control over policy and of local responsibility for policy implementation than past rulers in China were able to achieve. It remains to be seen what success their formulas for coping with the centralization-decentralization problem will have in the future.

The search for suitable and stable administrative units has involved a range of other problems which, like those already mentioned, have by no means been fully resolved. During the past seventeen years there has been constant experimentation, and many changes have occurred affecting both the size and character of regional and local units. It seems clear, moreover, that the process has not yet ended, and that administrative stability has yet to be achieved. Despite all the changes, however, there have also been important elements of administrative continuity with the past. For example, the two most important levels of regional and local administration, the provinces and the counties, are not now radically different in size or configuration from what they were before Communist takeover.

At the lowest levels of local government, though, the regime's attempts to innovate have been greater. Particularly in the latter 1950s they moved steadily toward an enlargement of basic areas of local administration, and toward the merger of institutions responsible for government administration with those responsible for collectivized economic activities. The culmination of these trends took place when the communes were established. For a short period the communes represented not only an attempt to achieve a radical change in the organization of politics and economics at the lowest levels, but also a revolutionary collectivization of all aspects of people's lives. Subsequently, the most extreme collectivist features of the communes were abandoned. Despite the fact that the administrative institutions of government and collective economic organizations continue to be merged, the decentralization of authority from the communes to their subunits has involved a return, in a basic sense, to the situation that had existed before communization. Today the search for workable administrative forms at the local level continues, but the Chinese Communist leaders appear to be more cautious about introducing radical new experiments.

In many respects, a totalitarian system such as that which has evolved in Communist China over the past seventeen years appears to involve relatively little "politics," in the sense of open political competition between various groups to achieve power or influence policy. Elections are clearly ritualistic occasions for endorsing decisions already made by Party leaders, and representative bodies at all levels appear to be little more than symbolic devices to reinforce the Communists' claims to legitimacy. Despite the Chinese Communists' continued claim that they are supported by a united front, and their continued toleration of "minor parties" at least at the national level, the Communist Party obviously monopolizes real power, and authority seems to flow from top to bottom in the system without the kind of open political competition that constitutes the heart of politics in more pluralistic systems.

While all of this is true, however, the surface appearance of monolithism and political homogeneity is misleading in some respects. Under the surface, within the organizational structures of power, a very real and important process of bureaucratic politics takes place, focusing more, perhaps, on the allocation of resources and methods of implementing policies than on issues of basic policy or the question of who will occupy the key positions of authority—although even the latter are sometimes involved. There is constant competition of a sort, and there are many problems of adjusting interests between different agencies, between higher and lower levels of authority, between organizations belonging to different functional "systems," between institutions in different localities, and so on. There are also tensions and competition between different groupings of cadres, between old and new cadres, between local cadres and outsiders, and the like. To some extent, even at the lowest levels, various identifiable class or other social groupings appear to function, to some degree at least, as interest groups which, to the extent that they may be able to exert some influence on policy implementation are likely to do so more by showing "passive resistance" than by exerting active pressures, but which nevertheless have varying attitudes which must at least be taken into account by the local cadres responsible for implementing Party-defined policies. "Politics" of these various sorts is very different from the kind of overt political competition that takes place in multiparty, nontotalitarian systems, but it is of some importance and seems likely to grow in importance over time.

However, even recognizing that the system is less monolithic than it appears to be on the surface, the key issues concerning the political process in Communist China still relate more to the question of how the ruling elite attempts to implement Party-defined programs and impose its will on the population than to the question of how persons outside of the elite may try to exert some minor influence on public policy.

Many analysts of the political system in Communist China have been impressed, quite rightly, by the stress that is placed in China upon mass persuasion through intensive propaganda and indoctrination. Some have emphasized the pressures involved in the Chinese Communists' methods of "coercive persuasion"; others have highlighted the techniques by which the regime insists upon and generally achieves at least the appearance of "voluntarism." In some respects, the Chinese Communists—perhaps in part because of deep-rooted Chinese cultural traditions stressing the desirability and possibility of achieving ideological consensus throughout society—appear to devote more attention than other totalitarian leaders to the task of propagandizing and indoctrinating the mass of the population. Case studies of particular institutions and areas indicate that while the cadres are the ones subjected to the most intensive forms of systematized political persuasion, and while ordinary persons in rural China may not be greatly influenced by the abstract theories of the new ideological orthodoxy, nevertheless the regime has developed effective techniques and mechanisms even at the village level for continuous efforts at mass persuasion of the population as a whole.

Case studies also indicate, however, that in dealing with the population the regime uses a complex mixture of persuasion and coercion, and the instruments of police rule—the public security apparatus and other elements in the "political and legal system"—play an extremely important role. The police apparatus of the regime in China has been little known, because it is rarely described or even mentioned in available publications, and its importance has often been underestimated because the Chinese Communists have consciously avoided, except perhaps for brief periods as during the early land reform, reliance on the kind of crude police state terror that was characteristic of the Stalinist period in the Soviet Union. It is clear from the testimony of ex-cadres, however, that at the local level the public security apparatus is extremely powerful and pervasive in its influence, at least in some areas of Communist China, and that police controls of a variety of sorts, as well as ideological, economic, and other controls, play a very significant role in the over-all political system. It seems clear, in fact, that police and ideological controls are mutually reinforcing in a fundamental sense. The major forms of both legal and administrative punishment, such as "reform through labor" and "labor reeducation," demand ideological reform, while the effectiveness of the regime's propaganda and indoctrination efforts is clearly reinforced by the population's realization that non-conformity may be interpreted as a sign of political dissidence, and any signs of the latter are likely to invoke suppression by the apparatus of police control.

In a basic sense, the military traditions of the Chinese Communists, dating to their guerrilla warfare days, appear to have had a continuing and significant influence on the way in which the regime approaches the problems of dealing with the population. This is evident not only in the continued maintenance throughout the country of paramilitary organizations such as the militia but more generally, even though more subtly, in the ideals of disciplined labor and regimented conformity which have influenced numerous Chinese Communist programs and activities. These ideals, like many of the most extreme utopian concepts motivating Communist China's leaders, were most evident during the Great Leap Forward, when the communes at first tried to handle their work groups as if they were simply units of a huge labor army, and the slogan of "militarizing life" was openly and enthusiastically proclaimed; but they have had a significant influence on the Party's operational methods even at other periods.

As has been stressed earlier, the idea of the "mass line," demanding a close interaction between the cadres and the masses and constant efforts to implement policies by mobilization of the masses, is fundamental to the Chinese Communists' concepts of how power should be exercised to engineer continuing revolution. And despite trends over time toward bureaucratization, and the existence of a real and important gap between the cadres and the masses, the regime has in fact developed institutions and evolved techniques which make possible unprecedented mass mobilization, especially through mass campaigns.

In a basic sense, such mobilizational efforts reflect certain fundamental assumptions about society and the relationships of state and society (or, more precisely, Party and state and society) that are inherent in the Communists' concepts of "contradictions" and "class struggle." To a substantial degree, local cadres, like the Party's top leaders, view society in terms of "class" groupings defined by the Party. To some extent, these groupings are arbitrary—in the sense that they do not really represent with any accuracy the conceptions of class divisions prevailing among the general population prior to Communist takeover—and in addition they are often based on the social and economic backgrounds of individuals more than on current realities. Nevertheless, the cadres tend to view and treat people differently on the basis of "class" status, and to assume, not wholly erroneously, that there can be significant differences and conflicts of interest (i.e. "contradictions") between various groups. In many of their mass mobilization activities they consciously attempt to manipulate real or latent tensions between groups and to mobilize certain groups to struggle against others. This manipulative approach to social forces—i.e. the management of "contradictions" and the self-conscious utilization of class conflicts—is clearly viewed as necessary to maintain a fairly high level of tension in society (which is in marked contrast to the traditional Chinese view that every effort should be made to harmonize interests and minimize conflicts); and a significant degree of social tension achieved through "struggle" is believed to be essential for continuing revolution. Some of the concrete manifestations of this approach at the local level are highlighted much more clearly by ex-cadres describing particular local situations than they generally are in the available published sources. One remarkable fact that emerges from local cases studies, for example, is that at the village level the Chinese Communists still continue to maintain, seventeen years after takeover and a decade after collectivization, important groups of ostracized, politically disenfranchised class enemies, the "five [bad] elements," who play an important role in the system as living "negative examples" and targets for recurring efforts to promote class struggle.

One of the most difficult questions to answer about the character of the present political system in Communist China is the degree to which the regime has been able to achieve consensus and positive support among the population as a whole, or the extent to which it faces active dissent and opposition of various sorts. The testimony of a limited number of ex-cadres who have cut their ties with the regime obviously cannot be used alone to form a judgment on this question, but in general ex-cadres do not present a picture very different from that which one can infer from published materials from Communist China. The general picture that emerges from all available sources is a very mixed one in which the regime seems to have been able to create a strong base of organized support but must deal with numerous and fairly widespread sources of dissatisfaction and tension. The support comes not only from the ranks of the cadres, the majority of whom seem to identify strongly with the system even if they may dislike many aspects of it, but also from substantial segments of the population who have benefited in one way or another from the regime's policies, or who have recognized, even when conditions have been worst, that they have been treated preferentially by comparison with other groups in society. Dissatisfactions, of varying sorts and of varying intensity, are widespread, however, and are shared not only by members of those groups which have been the principal victimized targets of the regime's policies, but also by significant numbers of others who object to coercive regimentation and to the forced pace of disruptive social change, or who simply have been disillusioned by the regime's failures to achieve economic improvements as rapidly as promised. There is little evidence, however, that dissatisfaction has been translated into organized opposition capable of challenging the regime, and as long as the Party's apparatus and the institutions of political control remain intact, as they have to date, there seems to be little prospect that really, effective organized opposition will develop.

To a very large degree, the Communists were able to establish a strong claim to political legitimacy soon after achieving power, in part because all potential major competitors were so badly discredited. Since 1949 this claim has faced no strong challengers on the China mainland despite the continued existence of the Nationalist regime on Taiwan. Even though for a brief period during the economic crisis that followed the Great Leap Forward the Communist regime's legitimacy may have been somewhat shaken, ex-cadres who have defected from mainland China since that time assert that at present few people, including even those most hostile to the regime, can conceive of the emergence in the near future of any really effective challenger to the Communist Party's monopoly of power and authority.

The key question for the years immediately ahead, therefore, is not whether the regime is likely soon to be ousted or fundamentally altered but rather how it will evolve and change. It is entering a transitional period in which a new generation of leaders will emerge and will have to attempt to cope not only with the immense unsolved problems of economic development and modernization but also with some of their persistent and growing organizational problems. It remains to be seen how they will deal with the challenge of increased routinization and bureaucratization to their ideals of revolutionary "mass line" politics, the steady growth of functional specialization and the growing "red and expert" problem, the delicate problems involved in determining the correct balance between centralization and decentralization, the search for a higher degree of administrative stability, the problem of managing bureaucratic politics within a system that idealizes monolithic unity, and the question of what mixture of persuasion and coercion should be employed in dealing with the population.

As the revolution ages, changes in the characteristics of the elite, in the organization and operation of political institutions, and in the distribution and exercise of political power are bound to take place. In fact, a process of evolutionary change appears to have been underway for some time. However, we can only wait to see whether really major changes will occur in the transitional period which Communist China is now entering, and if so, what impact such changes may have on the political system as a whole.

APPENDIX

FIGURE 1

Ministry M and Its Subordinate Bodies in Relation
to Party and Government Hierarchies

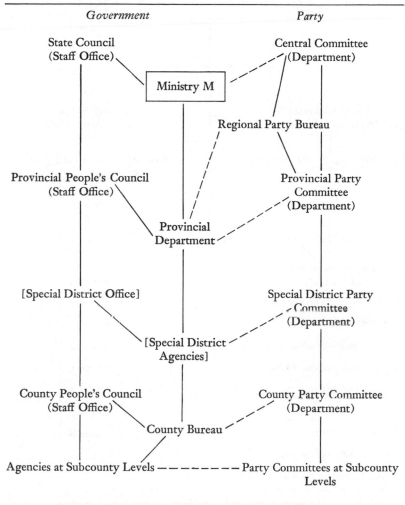

Government   *Party*

State Council (Staff Office)

Central Committee (Department)

Ministry M

Regional Party Bureau

Provincial People's Council (Staff Office)

Provincial Party Committee (Department)

Provincial Department

[Special District Office]

Special District Party Committee (Department)

[Special District Agencies]

County People's Council (Staff Office)

County Party Committee (Department)

County Bureau

Agencies at Subcounty Levels — — — — — — Party Committees at Subcounty Levels

———— channels of command within government and Party
— — — channels of command from Party to government

449

FIGURE 2

Organization of Ministry M

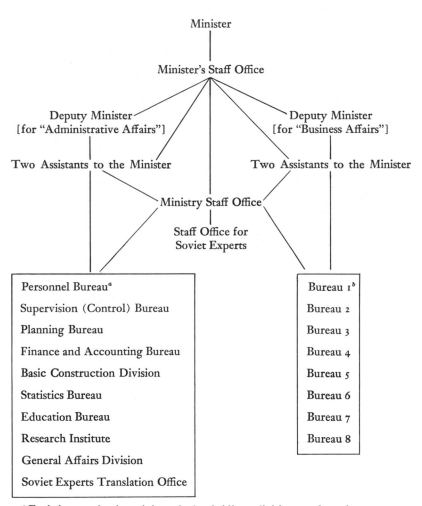

^a Each bureau in the ministry had subsidiary divisions and sections.
^b For reasons explained in the text (see p. 95), these bureaus are not referred to here by name.

FIGURE 3

Party Organization in Ministry M

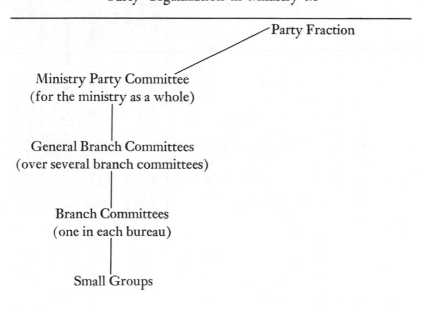

FIGURE 4

Major Administrative Divisions to the County Level

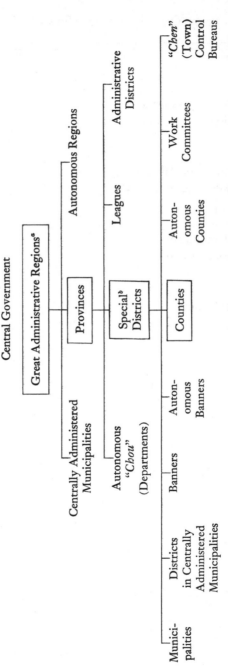

General Note: The most numerous major units are those whose titles are given at the same level on the figure.

[a] Large regions now have Party organizations but no government units. The Party organizations at this level are bureaus of the Central Committee and are therefore "dispatched organs" with a supervisory role, not a part of the regular Party hierarchy.

[b] Special district offices and other equivalent units are "dispatched organs" which, on behalf of the provinces (or equivalent units) supervise lower-level organizations. They are not, in theory at least, basic elements in the regular hierarchy. "Autonomous *chou*" (departments) are, at least in some places, regular units rather than "dispatched organs," and therefore differ from special districts in this respect.

FIGURE 5

Major Administrative and Collective Subunits under County A

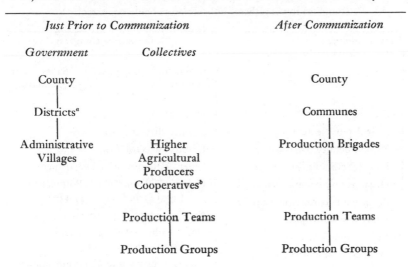

Just Prior to Communization		*After Communization*
Government	*Collectives*	
County		County
Districts[a]		Communes
Administrative Villages	Higher Agricultural Producers Cooperatives[b]	Production Brigades
	Production Teams	Production Teams
	Production Groups	Production Groups

General Note: In theory, the communes took over the governmental powers of the administrative villages; but in this area they were generally units equivalent in size to the former districts.

[a] Districts were in theory "dispatched organs," operating on behalf of the county to supervise the administrative villages, but at times they tended to operate as an additional level of regular government.

[b] In this area the tendency just prior to communization was for higher agricultural producers cooperatives to be coterminous with administrative villages.

FIGURE 6

Structure of Leadership Organizations in Commune C
(numbers in parentheses indicate posts held concurrently)

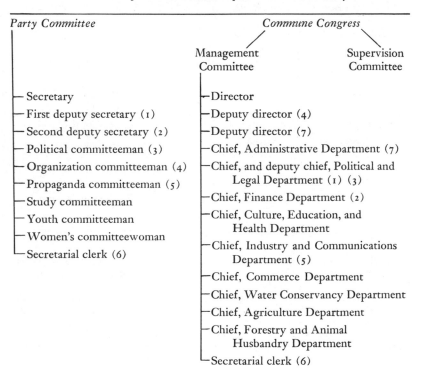

Party Committee

— Secretary
— First deputy secretary (1)
— Second deputy secretary (2)
— Political committeeman (3)
— Organization committeeman (4)
— Propaganda committeeman (5)
— Study committeeman
— Youth committeeman
— Women's committeewoman
— Secretarial clerk (6)

Commune Congress

Management Committee

Supervision Committee

— Director
— Deputy director (4)
— Deputy director (7)
— Chief, Administrative Department (7)
— Chief, and deputy chief, Political and Legal Department (1) (3)
— Chief, Finance Department (2)
— Chief, Culture, Education, and Health Department
— Chief, Industry and Communications Department (5)
— Chief, Commerce Department
— Chief, Water Conservancy Department
— Chief, Agriculture Department
— Chief, Forestry and Animal Husbandry Department
— Secretarial clerk (6)

FIGURE 7

Structure of Leadership Organizations in Brigade B
(numbers in parentheses indicate posts held concurrently)

Party Branch Committee

— Secretary
— Deputy secretary
— Political committeeman (1)
— Organization committeeman (2)
— Youth committeeman (3)
— Study committeeman (4)
— Women's committeewoman (5)
— Propaganda committeeman (6)
— Secretarial clerk (6)

Brigade Management Committee

— Chief[a]
— Deputy chief (3)
— Economic management cadre (2)
— Deputy economic management cadre
— Public security officer (1)
— Militia chief (1)
— Cashier (4)
— Accountant
— Secretarial clerk (6)

Young Communist League Branch
— Secretary (3)

Women's Association
— Chairwoman (5)

[a] The brigade chief was also a member of the Party Branch Committee but without any titled functionary post.

TABLE I

Functional "Systems" and Their Central Supervisory Bodies in Party and Government

Party Central Committee Departments and Committees	Functional "Systems"	Government State Council Staff Offices
Organization Department[a]	Organization and Personnel	None[a]
[Political and Legal Department] [b]	Political and Legal Affairs,[c] or Internal Affairs	Internal Affairs Staff Office[d]
Propaganda Department[e] Higher Education Department[f]	Propaganda and Education, or Culture and Education	Culture and Education Staff Office
United Front Work Department	United Front Work or Party-Mass Work[g]	None[g]
Agriculture and Forestry Political Department[h]	Agriculture and Forestry	Agriculture and Forestry Staff Office
Industry and Communications Political Department[i]	Industry and Communications	Industry and Communications Staff Office
Finance and Trade Political Department[j]	Finance and Trade	Finance and Trade Staff Office
Military Affairs Committee	Military Affairs[k]	None[l]
International Liaison Department	Foreign Affairs	Foreign Affairs Staff Office
Women's Work Committee	Women's Work	None
None[m]	Youth Work	None

[a] "Organization" (Party work including personnel matters) and "personnel" (in the government) are not generally called a "system" by cadres in China, but in many respects they have the characteristics of one. There is no personnel staff office in the government coordinating personnel matters, however. Formerly the State Council's Personnel Bureau handled personnel matters; now they are handled by the Ministry of Internal Affairs. Conceivably the Internal Affairs Staff Office may now operate in this field as well as in political and legal affairs. Over-all supervision of personnel matters in both Party and government is, in any case, exercised by the Organization Department.

[b] No Central Committee political and legal department has ever been publicly mentioned, but departments with this title are known to exist at lower levels, and some ex-cadres believe that such a body also exists at the Central

456

Committee level. Formerly the Central Committee had a Social Affairs Department, engaged in political security work, but it is believed to have gone out of existence.

c When two titles are listed for a "system," the first is the one generally used in reference to government and the second is the one generally used in reference to the Party.

d This was formerly called the Political and Legal Staff Office.

e At lower levels there are sometimes culture and education departments or education departments.

f The Higher Education Department's existence was first revealed in 1965. Its personnel is not yet known.

g The terms "united front system" and "Party-mass system" are believed to refer to similar united front activities, although the latter term may cover a broader range of activities. Formerly a staff office dealt with state capitalism, a facet of united front work, but no such office exists now.

h Formerly Rural Work Department.

i Formerly Industrial Work Department and Communications Work Department.

j Formerly Finance and Trade Department.

k At lower levels the term "armed forces work" is often used for Party bodies.

l The government's National Defense Council plays a supervisory role but is not comparable to State Council staff offices.

m The Young Communist League supervises work in this field. No Party youth department exists at the national level. However, at lower levels, Party committees often have youth work committees, which lead the League's activities.

TABLE II

Organization of County X

Party		Government

Party Congress
Party Committee
Standing Committee
  First Secretary
  Secretary
  Deputy Secretaries
Party Committee Staff
  Office
  Secretary General
  Work Group
  Campaign Staff Office
Control Committee
	Leading bodies in Party
	and government
		People's Congress
		People's Council
		Standing Committee
		  Magistrate
		  Deputy Magistrates
		People's Council Staff
		  Office
		  Secretary General

Young Communist League Young Pioneers	Party affiliates	
(*See below:* United Front Department)	Leading united front body in government	People's Political Consult- ative Conference

Women's Association[a]
Labor Union
Association of Commerce
  and Industry
Overseas Chinese Associ-
  ation
	Party-directed mass or-
	ganizations under Unit-
	ed Front "System"	

	Government bodies di-
	rectly under People's
	Council, and not clearly
	under any "system"
		Civil Affairs Section
		Planning and Statistics
		  Committee
		Labor Bureau
		Market Management
		  Committee[b]

	Major "Systems" Indicating Government Bodies Supervised by Par- ticular Party Departments	
Organization Department	Organization or Person- nel	Personnel Section
Political and Legal De- partment	Political and Legal Affairs	Political and Legal Staff Office Public Security Bureau People's Court People's Procuracy
[Armed Forces Depart- ment] [c] Seacoast Department	Armed Forces Work	Military Service Bureau

[a] These mass organizations are not Party units, as such, but are closely directed by the Party.

[b] The Market Management Committee's work is closely coordinated with the work of agencies in both the Finance and Trade "System" and the Political and Legal "System."

[c] This department exists only on paper.

TABLE II (*Continued*)

Party	Major "Systems"	Government
United Front Department	United Front Work	Overseas Chinese Affairs Section Office for the Reform of Private Entrepreneurs
Propaganda and Education Department	Propaganda and Education or Culture and Education	Education Bureau Office for the Elimination of Illiteracy (Association for the Dissemination of Science)[a] Culture Bureau Cultural Hall and Library New China Bookstore Broadcasting Station Health Bureau Physical Education and Sports Committee
Rural Work Department	Rural Work or Agriculture, Forestry, and Water Conservancy	Agriculture, Forestry, and Water Conservancy Staff Office Agriculture Bureau Agricultural Exhibition Agricultural Extension Station Water Conservancy Bureau Agriculture and Land Reclamation Bureau Forestry Bureau Meteorological Station Veterinary Station
Finance and Trade Department	Finance and Trade	Finance and Trade Staff Office Finance and Tax Bureau Grain Bureau Commerce Bureau People's Bank Supply and Marketing Cooperative[a]
Industry and Communications Department	Industry and Communications	Industry Bureau Construction Bureau Handicraft Cooperative[a] Communications Bureau Transportation Management Station Navigation Management Station Postal and Telecommunications Bureau

[a] These bodies are not, strictly speaking, government bodies but in many respects they operate as such.

459

Glossary

ch'a hsien　查線

　　Lineman (telephone repairman—*short form*).

ch'a hsien yüan　查線員

　　Lineman (telephone repairman).

chai tiao mao tzu　摘掉帽子

　　To "uncap."

chan　站

　　Station.

chan chang　站長

　　Station director, or station master.

chan hsien　站線

　　"Front," a term sometimes used to describe organizational sectors or "systems" (see *hsi t'ung*).

chan lan hui　展覽會

　　Exhibition.

ch'ang chang　廠長

　　Factory manager.

ch'ang cheng kan pu　長征幹部

　　Long March cadre.

ch'ang wei 常委

Standing committee (*short form*).

ch'ang wu wei yüan 常務委員

Standing committeeman.

ch'ang wu wei yüan hui 常務委員會

Standing committee.

chao tai so 招待所

Guest house.

ch'ao ling t'uan yüan 超齡團員

Overage members of Young Communist League.

ch'ao o wan ch'eng chi hua 超額完成計劃

To overfulfill plans.

ch'ao sung 抄送

To send copy (information copy) of a document.

ch'e chan 車站

Vehicle (Bus, Railway, etc.) Station.

chen 鎮

Town (market town).

chen so 診所

Clinic.

cheng chih chiao yüan 政治教員

Political instructor.

cheng chih chih tao yüan 政治指導員

Political director or instructor.

cheng chih chü 政治局

Politburo (Political Bureau).

cheng chih ch'u   政治處

Political Division.

cheng chih fan   政治犯

Political criminal.

cheng chih hsieh shang hui yi   政治協商會議

Political Consultative Conference.

cheng chih hsüeh hsi   政治學習

Political study.

cheng chih k'o   政治課

Political class.

cheng chih kuan chih   政治管制

Political control.

cheng chih kung tso tsu   政治工作組

Political Work Group.

cheng chih li shih   政治歷史

Political history (one's personal political background).

cheng chih mou sha   政治謀殺

Political murder.

cheng chih mou sha an chien pao kao   政治謀殺案件報告

Report on a case of political murder.

cheng chih pao wei k'o   政治保衞科

Political Security Section.

cheng chih ti wei   政治地位

Political status, or political standing.

cheng chih wei yüan   政治委員

Political commissar, political committeeman.

cheng chih wen t'i　政治問題

Political problem.

cheng fa chih pu　政法支部

Political and Legal [Party Organization] Branch.

cheng fa lien ho pan kung shih　政法聯合辦公室

Joint Political and Legal Staff Office.

cheng fa pan kung shih　政法辦公室

Political and Legal Staff Office.

cheng fa pu　政法部

Political and Legal Department in the Party or in a commune.

cheng feng　整風

Rectification.

cheng fu pan ti [ta] shui li　政府辦的(大)水利

Government-Run [Large] Water Conservancy Works.

cheng hsieh　政協

Political Consultative Conference (*short form*).

cheng kung tui　政工隊

Political Work Team.

cheng ming　證明

Certificate.

cheng pao　政保

Political security (*short form*).

cheng pao k'o　政保科

Political Security Section in Public Security Bureau (*short form*).

cheng pien yün tung　整編運動

Reorganization campaign (*short form*).

cheng she cheng tang   整社整黨

Rectification of commune and Party.

cheng she chien she yün tung   整社建社運動

Campaign for rectification and construction of communes.

cheng shih   正式

Formally, or formal (as in formal appointment).

cheng shih tai piao   正式代表

Regular representative.

cheng shih wei yüan   正式委員

Regular [Party] committeeman.

cheng shou ku   征收股

Tax Collection Section.

cheng ts'e   政策

Policy (used for short-term policy, as contrasted with *fang chen*, long-term policy).

cheng tun pien chih yün tung   整頓編制運動

Reorganization campaign.

cheng wei   政委

Political commissar (*short form*).

ch'eng kuan kung she   城關公社

City commune.

chi chi fen tzu   積極份子

Activist.

chi ch'i hsiu p'ei ch'ang   機器修配廠

Machine repair and assembly factory.

chi chien ch'u   基建處

Division of Capital Construction.

chi ch'uan   機船

Motorboat, or motorized boat.

chi fen yüan   記分員

Work-point recorder.

chi hua   計劃

Plan (generally used for short-term plan, as contrasted with *kuei hua*, long-term plan).

chi hua chü   計劃局

Planning Bureau.

chi hua ch'u   計劃處

Planning Division (*short form*).

chi hua ts'ao an   計劃草案

Draft plan.

chi hua t'ung chi wei yüan hui   計劃統計委員會

Committee on Planning and Statistics.

chi kan min ping   基幹民兵

Basic Militia.

chi kan ta hui   積幹大會

Congress of Cadres and Activists.

chi kuan chih pu   機關支部

"Organization Branch" (a Party branch in a government or Party organization).

chi kuan min ping   機關民兵

"Organization Militia" (e.g. militia in government organizations).

chi kuan pao   機關報

Organization paper (official organ).

chi kuan pao wei k'o　機關保衛科

　　Organizational Security Section.

chi kuan tsung chih pu　機關總支部

　　"Organization General Branch."

chi kung　技工

　　Technical (specialist) worker (*short form*).

chi kung yüan　記工員

　　Work-point recorder.

chi kuo　記過

　　To record errors.

chi lu　記録

　　Record (record book).

chi lü　紀律

　　Discipline.

chi mi　機密

　　Very secret (a security classification of documents, higher than *mi chien* but lower than *chüeh mi*).

chi pao　機保

　　Organizational security (*short form*).

chi pao k'o　機保科

　　Organizational Security Section (*short form*).

chi pen chien she　基本建設

　　Capital construction.

chi pen chung tien　基本重點

　　Basic keypoint area.

chi pieh　級別

　　Rank (used for salary rank, as contrasted with *chih pieh*, job rank).

chi sheng　級昇

Promotion.

chi shih　集市

Rural trade fair.

chi shu jen　技術人

Specialist, or technician.

chi shu jen yüan　技術人員

Specialist, or technician; technical personnel.

chi shu kung jen　技術工人

Technical (specialist) worker.

chi tu　季度

Season (quarter of the year).

chi t'uan　集團

Clique.

chi tung hsiao tui　機動小隊

Mobile team.

chi tung liang　機動糧

Collective grain; literally, mobile grain reserves.

chi t'ung ch'u　計統處

Statistics Division.

chi t'ung ku　計統股

Statistics Section.

chi yao tsu　機要組

Secret and Important [Materials] Group (unit in a Postal and Tele-communications Bureau that handles classified materials).

ch'i　旗

Banner.

ch'i hsiang chan   氣象站

Meteorological Station.

ch'i hsiang yüan   氣象員

Weather (meteorological) personnel (cadres).

ch'i yi chiang ling   起義將領

"Uprising general."

ch'i yi jen shih   起義人士

"Uprising personage."

ch'i yi kan pu   起義幹部

"Uprising cadre."

chia   甲

A unit of approximately ten families, under the *pao-chia system* prior to 1949 (under Nationalist rule).

chia ch'iang chi ts'eng ling tao   加強基層領導

Strengthen basic-level leadership.

chia lo   家落

A grouping of one to two hundred households within a natural village (a temporary administrative grouping used by the Communists in some areas for a brief period after takeover).

chia shu wei yüan hui   家屬委員會

Family Dependents' Committee (a dormitory or apartment committee).

chia t'ing chiu fen   家庭糾紛

Family dispute.

chia t'ing ch'u shen   家庭出身

Family (class) background.

chiang chih   降職

Job demotion.

chiao ch'a ling tao 交叉領導

Multiple leadership.

chiao chih yüan 教職員

School administrators and teachers.

chiao kuan chih pu 交管支部

Communications Management [Party Organization] Branch.

chiao tai 交代

To give an explanation, or statement (e.g. about one's past).

chiao tao chu jen 教導主任

Director of instruction, or curriculum director.

chiao tao ch'u 教導處

Curriculum (literally, Education Guidance) Division, or Office.

chiao t'i chi 交替級

Overlapping of rank levels and jobs.

chiao ts'ai pien yi ch'u 教材編譯處

Educational Materials Division.

chiao t'ung chü 交通局

Communications Bureau, or Communications and Transportation Bureau.

chiao t'ung ch'u 交通處

Communications and Transport Division.

chiao t'ung kuan li 交通管理

Traffic management.

chiao yü chü 教育局

Education Bureau.

chiao yü ch'u 教育處

Education Division.

chiao yüan hui yi   教員會議

Conference, or meeting, of teaching personnel.

ch'iao chüan   僑眷

Families of overseas Chinese (i.e. immediate families of overseas Chinese themselves, not other relatives in China).

ch'iao lien   僑聯

Overseas Chinese Association (*short form*).

ch'iao lien hui   僑聯會

Overseas Chinese Association (*short form*).

ch'iao shu   僑屬

Dependents of overseas Chinese (i.e. dependents in China).

ch'iao wu k'o   僑務科

Overseas Chinese Affairs Section (*short form*).

chieh chi fu ch'a   階級覆查

Review of classes (i.e. of class status).

chieh fang chan cheng kan pu   解放戰爭幹部

Liberation war cadre.

chieh fang chün   解放軍

Liberation Army.

chieh shao hsin   介紹信

Letter of introduction.

chieh sheng yüan   接生員

Midwife.

chieh shou kung tso   接收工作

Receiving [new members] work.

chieh tai shih   接待室

Reception Office.

chieh yü yün tung 節育運動

Birth-control campaign.

chien ch'a 監察

Supervision.

chien ch'a chü 監察局

Bureau of Supervision.

chien ch'a kung tso 檢查工作

Investigation work.

chien ch'a wei yüan hui 監察委員會

Control Committee (in the Party); also Supervision Committee (in a commune).

chien ch'a wei yüan hui shu chi 監察委員會書記

Secretary of [Party] Control Committee.

chien ch'a yüan 檢察員

Procurator; staff member of Procuracy.

chien ch'a yüan 檢察院

Procurator-general's Office.

chien ch'a yüan chang 檢察院長

Procurator-general, or chief Procurator.

chien chih chien chi 減職減級

Job and/or salary demotion.

chien chu kung ch'eng kung szu 建築工程公司

Building Construction Company.

chien chu kung szu 建築公司

Construction Company.

chien pao 簡報

Brief report.

chien she chü 建設局

 Construction Bureau.

chien t'ao 檢討

 Self-criticism (*short form*).

chien ting 鑑定

 Assessment, or audit (e.g. annual personnel assessments).

chien tu lao tung 監督勞動

 Supervised labor.

chien wei hui 監委員

 [Party] Control Committee (*short form*).

chien yin k'o 監印科

 Printing Section.

ch'ien yi 遷移

 To move one's residence.

ch'ien yi cheng 遷移證

 Moving certificate (certificate to move one's residence).

chih an 治安

 Social order, or public security (*short form*).

chih an chü liu 治安拘留

 Detained for social order.

chih an chü liu fan 治安拘留犯

 Detained social order criminals.

chih an chü liu pao kao 治安拘留報告

 Report on social order detentions.

chih an k'o 治安科

 Social Order Section (in Public Security Bureau) (*short form*).

chih an pao wei wei yüan hui 治安保衞委員會

Public Security Committee. Literally, Protection of Social Order Committee; however, *chih an* is virtually identical in meaning to *kung an* and in some instances is best translated simply as public security.

chih an t'iao chieh wei yüan hui 治安調解委員會

Social Order (or Public Security) and Mediation Committee.

chih hang 支行

Subbranch bank.

chih hsia shih 直轄市

Centrally administered municipality.

chih hui pu 指揮部

Command, headquarters.

chih kung hsüeh hsi hsiao tsu 職工學習小組

Staff and Workers Study Group.

chih li chou 直隸州

Independent department (in the Imperial period).

chih li t'ing 直隸廳

Independent subprefecture (in the Imperial period).

chih pao 治保

Public Security Committee or public security committeeman (*short form*).

chih pao chu jen 治保主任

Public security chief.

chih pao wei yüan 治保委員

Public security officer; literally, officer for protection of social order.

chih pu 支部

[Party] Branch.

chih pu wei yüan hui 支部委員會

[Party] Branch Committee.

chih shih 指示

Instruction or directive (e.g. from one government or Party organ to another).

chih shih fen tzu 智識份子

Intellectual.

chih tu ch'u 制度處

Systems Division.

chih yüan ping 志願兵

Volunteer soldier.

ch'ih t'ang 吃堂

Mess hall, dining hall (see also *shih t'ang* and *fan t'ing*).

chin chi tien hua hui yi 緊急電話會議

Urgent, or emergency, telephonic conference.

chin pu 進步

Progressive.

chin pu jen yüan 進步人員

Progressive people.

ch'in tsa jen yüan 勤雜人員

General service personnel (messengers, cleaning personnel, etc.).

ching ch'a chü 警察局

Police Bureau (under Nationalist rule).

ching chi kuan li kan pu 經濟管理幹部

Economic management cadre (in a brigade).

ching chi tu li 經濟獨立

Economically independent (i.e. an independent accounting unit).

ching kao 警告

Warning.

ching kuan kan pu 經管幹部

Economic management cadre (*short form*).

ching li 經理

Manager.

ching wei pan 警衛班

Guard Unit.

ch'ing hsi k'ai ch'u 清洗開除

Dismissal (of a cadre).

ch'ing nien 青年

Youth.

ch'ing nien t'u chi tui 青年突擊隊

Youth Shock Squad (a production unit).

ch'ing nien t'uan 青年團

Young Communist League (YCL), or Communist Youth League.

ch'ing nien wei yüan 青年委員

Youth [work] committeeman.

ch'ing shih 請示

To ask for instructions from, or submit for approval to, a higher level in the bureaucracy.

chiu ch'ang 酒廠

Wine factory, brewery.

chiu chi kung tso 救濟工作

Relief work.

chiu fen 糾紛

Dispute.

chiu san 九三

September 3d [society].

ch'iu sha 仇殺

Deliberate, or planned, murder.

ch'iu shou tung chung yün tung 秋收冬種運動

Fall harvest and winter planting campaign.

chou 州

Department (in the Imperial period).

ch'ou tiao 抽調

Temporarily assign or transfer.

ch'ou yün ku 籌運股

Transportation [Planning] Section.

chu ch'i shou kung ch'ang 竹器手工廠

Handicraft factory manufacturing bambooware.

chu hsi 主席

Chairman.

chu hsi t'uan 主席團

Presidium.

chu jen 主任

Head, director.

chu li yen chiu yüan 助理研究員

Assistant researcher.

chu pan kan shih 主辦幹事

Special staff member; literally, staff member for important work.

chu sung 主送

Send document (original of document).

chü 局

Bureau.

chü chang 局長

Bureau chief.

chü chang chi kan pu 局長級幹部

Bureau-chief level cadre.

chü chang hui yi 局長會議

Conference, or meeting, of bureau chiefs.

chü chang k'uo ta hui yi 局長擴大會議

Enlarged conference, or meeting, of bureau chiefs.

chü k'o chang 區科長

Bureau and section chiefs.

chü lo pu 俱樂部

[Recreation] club.

chü min wei yüan hui 居民委員會

Residents' Committee.

chü wu hui yi 局務會議

Bureau affairs meeting (i.e. bureau staff meeting).

ch'u 處

Division. This term might also be translated in other ways but it is translated as division in this book to differentiate it from *chü* (bureau), *shih* (office), *k'o* (section), etc.

ch'u ch'ai 出差

To make an official trip (i.e. any trip on official business).

ch'u chang 處長

Division chief.

ch'u chang chi kan pu　處長級幹部

Division-chief level cadre.

ch'u chi ho tso she　初級合作社

Lower [Agricultural Producers] Cooperative.

ch'u chi hsiao hsüeh　初級小學

Lower primary school.

ch'u fen　處分

Punish, punishment.

ch'u hsü ku　儲蓄股

Deposits Section.

ch'u li　處理

Mete out punishment.

ch'u na　出納

Cashier.

ch'ü　區

District.

ch'ü chang　區長

District chief.

ch'ü chi kan pu　區級幹部

District-level cadre.

ch'ü kan tui　區幹隊

District Cadre Team.

ch'ü wei hui　區委會

District Party Committee (*short form*).

ch'ü wei shu chi　區委書記

Secretary of District Party Committee.

chuan ch'ü　專區

Special district, or special commissioner's district.

chuan wa ch'ang　磚瓦廠

Brick and tile factory.

chuan yeh　轉業

Demobilized (transferred).

chuan yeh chün jen　轉業軍人

Demobilized (transferred) army man, or soldier. These are demobilized soldiers assigned to particular jobs at the time of demobilization. (Contrast with *fu yüan chün jen*.)

chuan yüan　專員

Special commissioner (of a special district).

ch'uan ta pao kao hui yi　傳達報告會議

Report meeting (for reporting instructions or information from above).

ch'üan hsien chih shih　全縣指示

Instruction to the entire county.

ch'üan hsien szu chi k'uo kan hui　全縣四級擴幹會

All-county four-level enlarged cadre conference.

ch'üan kuo t'ing chang hui yi　全國廳長會議

National conference of [Provincial] department chiefs.

ch'üan min chieh ping　全民皆兵

Everyone a soldier (campaign).

ch'üan tang ch'üan min ta kao chi fei yün tung　全黨全民大搞積肥運動

Campaign for the entire Party and all the people to collect fertilizer.

chüeh mi　絕密

Top secret (the highest security classification of documents; see also *chi mi* and *mi chien*).

chüeh yi　決議

Resolution.

ch'ui shih　炊事

Cook (*short form*).

ch'ui shih yüan　炊事員

　　Cook.

chün hsien　軍線

　　Military [telephone] line, or system.

chün hsün k'o　軍訓科

　　Military Training Section.

chün hsün t'i yü yün tung　軍訓體育運動

　　Military-training physical-education movement.

chün kuan　軍官

　　Officer (in the army).

chün shih chiao yüan　軍事教員

　　Military instructor.

chün shih hua　軍事化

　　Militarize.

chün tui kan pu　軍隊幹部

　　Army (military) cadre.

chün yu　軍郵

　　"Military post" (postal service for secret material).

chün yung liang　軍用糧

　　Military grain; literally, grain for military use.

ch'ün chung　群衆

　　The masses.

ch'ün keng sheng ch'an yün tung　春耕生産運動

　　Spring sowing and production campaign.

chung chi kan pu　中級幹部

　　Middle-rank cadre.

chung chi ling tao kan pu　中級領導幹部

　　Middle-rank leadership cadre.

chung hsin   中心

Nucleus, center, major focus of work, keypoint.

chung hsin hsüeh hsiao   中心學校

Central (primary) school.

chung hsin kung tso   中心工作

Central work (i.e. priority or major work).

chung hsüeh wen hua ch'eng tu   中學文化程度

Middle school cultural level.

chung tien   重點

Keypoint area (see also *tien hsin*, which is more commonly used in writing).

chung tien hsiang   重點鄉

Keypoint administrative village.

chung tzu liang   種籽糧

Seed grain.

chung wei (yü)   中尉

First lieutenant.

chung yang kan pu   中央幹部

Central cadre [in government or Party].

chung yang kuan yü mu ch'ien nung ts'un kung tso chung jo kan wen t'i ti chüeh ting   中央關于目前農村工作中若干問題的決定

Decisions of the Central Committee Concerning Certain Problems of Current Rural Work.

chung yang kuan yü nung ts'un she hui chu i chiao yü yün tung chung yi hsieh chü t'i cheng ts'e ti kuei ting (ts'ao an)   中央關于農村社會主義教育運動中一些具體政策的規定草案

Central Committee Regulations on Several Specific Policies Concerning the Rural Socialist Education Campaign (Draft).

chung yang ts'ai cheng fa kuei hui pien 中央財政法規彙編

Central government financial laws and regulations.

e pa 惡霸

Rascal, bully.

e pa ti chu 惡霸地主

Rascal or bully landlord.

fa ching 法警

Court policeman.

fa ling 法令

Law or decree.

fa t'ing 法庭

Tribunal.

fa t'ing yüan 法庭員

Tribunal staff member.

fa yüan 法院

Court.

fan ko ming chi t'uan tsu chih pao kao 反革命集團組織報告

Report on counterrevolutionary cliques and organizations.

fan ko ming fen tzu 反革命份子

Counterrevolutionary element (i.e. person).

fan kung yu chi tui t'u chi fu chien lien chiang hsien lu huo fei fang wen chien hui pien 反共游擊隊突擊福建連江縣鹵獲匪方文件彙編

Documents Captured by Anti-Communist Guerrillas in Lienchiang Hsien, Fukien.

fan ti fang chu yi yün tung 反地方主義運動

Antilocalism campaign.

fan t'ing   飯廳

Dining hall, or mess hall.

fan tung piao yü pao kao   反動標語報告

Report on reactionary propaganda activities (such as posters or slogans).

fan yu ch'ing yün tung   反右傾運動

Campaign against rightist tendencies.

fang chen   方針

Policy (used for long-term policy, as contrasted with *cheng ts'e*, short-term policy).

fang chih p'in kung szu   紡織品公司

Textile Products Company.

fang wu kuan li k'o   房務管理科

Housing Management Section.

fei cheng ch'ang szu wang pao kao   非正常死亡報告

Report on unnatural deaths.

fei liao ch'ang   肥料廠

Fertilizer factory.

fei p'in shou kou chan   廢品収購站

Rejects (or Used Goods) Purchasing Station.

fei tang kan pu   非黨幹部

Non-Party cadre.

fen chan   分站

Substation (branch store run by cooperative).

fen ch'ü   分區

Subdistrict.

fen hang   分行

  Branch bank.

fen hsiao   分校

  Branch school.

feng chien tsu chih   封建組織

  Feudal organization.

fu   府

  Prefecture (in the Imperial period).

fu cheng wei   副政委

  Deputy political commissar.

fu ching kuan kan pu   副經管幹部

  Deputy economic management cadre (in a brigade).

fu chu hsi   副主席

  Deputy chairman.

fu chu jen   副主任

  Deputy head, deputy director.

fu chü chang   副局長

  Deputy bureau chief.

fu ch'u chang   副處長

  Deputy division chief.

fu hsien chang   副縣長

  Deputy magistrate.

fu k'o chang   副科長

  Deputy section head.

fu li   福利

  Welfare.

fu li kan pu   福利幹部

Welfare cadre.

fu li wen t'i   福利問題

Welfare problems.

fu lien   婦聯

Women's Association, or Women's Federation (*short form*).

fu lien chu hsi   婦聯主席

Chairwoman of Women's Association, or Federation.

fu lien hui   婦聯會

Women's Association, or Women's Federation (*short form*).

fu mi shu   副秘書

Deputy staff secretary.

fu nü   婦女

Women.

fu nü hui   婦女會

Women's Association, or Women's Federation (*short form*).

fu nü hui chu hsi   婦女會主席

Chairman of Women's Association, or Federation.

fu nü kan pu   婦女幹部

Women's [work] cadre.

fu nü lien ho hui   婦女聯合會

Women's Association, or Federation.

fu nü wei yüan   婦女委員

Women's [work] committeeman, or committeewoman.

fu nung   富農

Rich peasant.

fu pu chang   副部長

Deputy minister, or deputy department head (in Party or commune).

fu she chang   副社長

Deputy commune director.

fu shih p'in kung szu   副食品公司

Subsidiary Food Products Company, or Foodstuffs Company.

fu shu chi   副書記

Deputy [Party or YCL] secretary.

fu so chang   副所長

Deputy head of office, of substation, etc.

fu tsu chang   副組長

Deputy chief of Production Group, or other group.

fu tsung li   副總理

Deputy premier.

fu tui chang (see also *ta tui fu*)   副隊長

Deputy chief (e.g. of brigade, group, etc.).

fu tze jen   負責人

Responsible person, head.

fu yen chiu yüan   副研究員

Associate researcher.

fu yüan   復員

Demobilized (see also *chuan yeh*).

fu yüan chang   副院長

Deputy hospital director.

fu yüan chün jen   復員軍人

Demobilized army man [who is returned to his home village or town]; contrast with *chuan yeh chün jen*.

hang chang　行長

　　Bank manager.

hang ching　行警

　　Bank policeman.

hang hai kuan li chan　航海管理站

　　Navigation Management Station.

hang kuan chan　航管站

　　Navigation Management Station (*short form*).

hei jen hei hu　黑人黑戶

　　"Black people," or "black households" (people who move or travel illegally).

hei pan pao　黑板報

　　Blackboard newspaper.

hei she hui fen tzu　黑社會份子

　　Secret society elements; literally, "black society" elements.

hei shih　黑市

　　Black market.

ho she ping hsiang yün tung　合社併鄉運動

　　Campaign to incorporate cooperatives and integrate administrative villages.

ho t'ung　合同

　　Contract.

hou pu ch'u　後補處

　　Rear Services Division.

hou pu tang yüan　後補黨員

　　Alternate Party member (in former usage); see also *yü pei tang yüan*.

hou pu wei yüan　後補委員

　　Alternate [Party] committeeman.

hsi chü hsüeh hsiao　戲劇學校

　　Opera School.

hsi t'uan　劇團

　　Opera Troupe.

hsi t'ung　系統

　　System, organizational sector, or network.

hsia chi kan pu　下級幹部

　　Lower-ranking cadre.

hsia fang　下放

　　Transfer downward.

hsia fang kan pu　下放幹部

　　Transfer downward of cadres.

hsia fang lao tung　下放勞動

　　Transfer downward for labor.

hsia hai t'ou ti pao kao　下海投敵報告

　　Report on defectors.

hsia shou hsia chung yün tung　夏收夏種運動

　　Summer harvest and planting campaign.

hsiang　鄉

　　Administrative village; this term has also been translated as township.

hsiang chang　鄉長

　　Chief of administrative village.

hsiang chih pu　鄉支部

　　Party branch in administrative village.

hsiang ch'ün chung ta hui 鄉群眾大會

Congress of village masses (in an administrative village).

hsiao chang 校長

School principal.

hsiao chang hui yi 校長會議

Conference, or meeting, of school principals.

hsiao cheng tang yün tung 小整黨運動

Small Party rectification campaign.

hsiao fan 小販

Peddler.

hsiao kuo 小過

Small error.

hsiao ling tao kan pu 小領導幹部

Small leadership cadre (a leadership cadre of relatively low rank).

hsiao tsu 小組

Cell, small group.

hsiao tui chang 小隊長

[Production] team chief.

hsiao tui kan pu 小隊幹部

[Production] team cadre.

hsiao tui wei yüan hui 小隊委員會

[Production] team committee.

hsieh li shih 恊理室

Aide's (or Assistant's, or Assistant Manager's) Office.

hsieh li yüan 恊理員

Aide, or assistant.

hsien   縣

County (can also be translated as district, but in this book that term is reserved for *ch'ü*).

hsien chang   縣長

County magistrate.

hsien ch'ang hui yi   現場會議

On-the-spot conference (e.g. meeting of representatives of experimental farms).

hsien ch'eng   縣城

County seat.

hsien chi kan pu   縣級幹部

County-level cadre.

hsien jen min cheng fu   縣人民政府

County People's Government (prior to 1954).

hsien jen min tai piao ta hui   縣人民代表大會

County People's Congress.

hsien jen min wei yüan hui   縣人民委員會

County People's Council.

hsien tang wei yüan hui   縣黨委員會

County Party Committee.

hsien t'u kai t'uan   縣土改團

County Land Reform "Regiment," or Group.

hsien wei   縣委

County Party Committee (*short form*).

hsien wei chih pu   縣委支部

Party Committee Branch (Party branch for persons connected with Party Committee itself).

hsien wei pan kung shih   縣委辦公室

> County Party Committee Staff Office.

hsin hua shu tien   新華書店

> New China Bookstore.

hsin kan pu   新幹部

> New cadre.

hsin yung ho tso she   信用合作社

> Credit Cooperative.

hsin yung she   信用社

> Credit Cooperative (*short form*).

hsing cheng   行政

> Administration.

hsing cheng chieh shao hsin   行政介紹信

> Administrative letter of introduction.

hsing cheng chü liu   行政拘留

> Administrative detention.

hsing cheng ch'ü   行政區

> Administrative district.

hsing cheng hui yi   行政會議

> Administrative conference, or meeting.

hsing cheng kan pu   行政幹部

> Administrative cadre.

hsing cheng kuan li   行政管理

> Administrative management.

hsing cheng kung tso hui   行政工作會

> Administrative work meeting.

hsing cheng pu　行政部

    Administrative Department (in a commune).

hsing cheng shih wu　行政事務

    Administrative affairs (i.e. administration).

hsing cheng ti wei　行政地位

    Administrative status, or standing.

hsing cheng ts'un　行政村

    Administrative village.

hsing shih　刑事

    Criminal.

hsing shih an chien pao kao　刑事案件報告

    Report on criminal cases.

hsing shih chen ch'a yüan　刑事偵察員

    Investigator of crime (i.e. detective).

hsing shih fan　刑事犯

    Criminal [who has committed a nonpolitical crime].

hsing ying chu jen　行營主任

    This term is loosely translated as "personal representative" (of the Office of the President, an institution under the Nationalist regime).

hsiu chien hsiu li shui li yün tung　修建修理水利運動

    Campaign for the repair and building of water conservancy projects.

hsiu chien yün tung　修建運動

    Campaign for the repair and building of water conservancy works (*short form*).

hsiung sha　凶殺

    Manslaughter (accidental killing).

hsüan chiao   宣教

> Propaganda and education (*short form*).

hsüan chiao pu   宣教部

> Propaganda and Education Department.

hsüan ch'uan   宣傳

> Propaganda.

hsüan ch'uan chiao yü (also *hsüan chiao*)   宣傳教育

> Propaganda and education.

hsüan ch'uan hui   宣傳會

> Propaganda meeting.

hsüan ch'uan tsu   宣傳組

> Propaganda Group.

hsüan ch'uan wei yüan   宣傳委員

> Propaganda committeeman.

hsüeh ch'ü   學區

> School district.

hsüeh hsi   學習

> Study.

hsüeh hsi hsiao tsu   學習小組

> Small Study Group.

hsüeh hsi wei yüan   學習委員

> Study committeeman.

hsüeh hsiao chih pu   學校支部

> School Branch (of Party or YCL).

hsüeh hsiao kung tso pu   學校工作部

> School Work Department (e.g. in a YCL committee).

hsüeh sheng hui   學生會

Student Association (same as *hsüeh sheng wei yüan hui*).

hsün fu   巡撫

Provincial governor (in the Imperial period).

hsün pao kao   旬報告

Ten-day report.

hu   戶

Household.

hu chi min ching   戶籍民警

Census People's Police (*short form*).

hu chu tsu   互助組

Mutual Aid Team.

hu k'ou ch'ien yi cheng   戶口遷移證

Change of residence certificate.

hu k'ou teng chi pu   戶口登記部

Household population registry (census) book.

hu k'ou tiao ch'a   戶口調查

Census survey (or registration, or investigation).

hu shih   護士

Nurse.

hua ch'iao   華僑

Overseas Chinese.

hua ch'iao ch'u ju kuan li kan pu   華僑出入管理幹部

Management cadre for exit and entry into the country of overseas Chinese.

hua ch'iao ch'u ju kuo pao kao   華僑出入國報告

Report form on arrivals to and departures from the country of overseas Chinese.

hua ch'iao hsin ts'un   華僑新村

Overseas Chinese new village.

hua ch'iao lien ho hui   華僑聯合會

Overseas Chinese Association.

hua ch'iao shih wu k'o   華僑事務科

Overseas Chinese Affairs Section.

hua ch'iao tai piao ta hui   華僑代表大會

Congress, or meeting, of overseas Chinese.

hua ch'iao ti chu   華僑地主

Overseas Chinese landlord.

huai fen tzu   壞份子

Bad element[s] (one category of the so-called "five [bad] elements," *wu lei fen tzu*).

huai hai chan yi kan pu   淮海戰役幹部

Huai Lake Battle cadre.

hui hsiang chieh shao hsin   回鄉介紹信

Letter of introduction authorizing return to one's village.

hui k'o shih   會客室

Guest room.

hui pao   會報

Report (often means oral report).

hui tao men   會道門

Religious sect.

hui yi   會議

    Conference, meeting.

hun yin chiu fen   婚姻糾紛

    Marriage dispute (e.g. divorce).

jen k'ou t'ung chi   人口統計

    Population statistics, or census data.

jen mi ku   人秘股

    Personnel and Secretariat Section (short for *jen shih mi shu ku*).

jen min cheng chih hsieh shang hui yi   人民政治協商會議

    People's Political Consultative Conference.

jen min chien ch'a yüan   人民檢察院

    People's Procuracy.

jen min fa t'ing   人民法庭

    People's Tribunal.

jen min fa yüan   人民法院

    People's Court.

jen min lai fang chieh tai shih   人民來訪接待室

    Reception Office for People's Visits.

jen min lai hsin   人民來信

    People's letters.

jen min lai hsin lai fang chieh tai shih   人民來信來訪接待室

    People's Letters and Visits Reception Office.

jen min p'ei shen yüan   人民陪審員

    People's assessor, or juror.

jen min shou ts'e   人民手冊

    People's handbook.

jen min t'ung hsün 人民通訊

People's letters or bulletins (see also *jen min lai hsin*).

jen min yi yüan 人民醫院

People's Hospital.

jen min yin hang 人民銀行

People's Bank.

jen shih 人事

Personnel.

jen shih chü 人事局

Personnel Bureau.

jen shih kan pu 人事幹部

Personnel cadre.

jen shih kan shih 人事幹事

Personnel staff member.

jen shih k'o 人事科

Personnel Section.

jen shih ku 人事股

Personnel Section.

jen wei 人委

People's Council (*short form*).

jen wei chih pu 人委支部

People's Council [Party Organization] Branch.

jen wei chü k'o chang hui yi 人委局科長會議

People's Council meeting of bureau and section chiefs.

jen wei pan kung shih 人委辦公室

People's Council Staff Office.

jen yüan tiao p'ei   人員調配

Assignment (transfer) of cadres.

jih pao   日報

Daily newspaper.

ju tang   入黨

Join the Party.

ju tang shen ch'ing shu   入黨申請書

Application for Party membership.

juan chi   軟級

Soft class.

kai pien chieh chi ch'eng fen   改變階級成份

To change or redefine class status.

k'ai ch'u kan pu   開除幹部

To expel or fire a cadre and deprive him of cadre status.

k'ai ch'u tang chi   開除黨籍

Expulsion from the Party.

kan pu   幹部

Cadre.

kan pu hsüeh hsiao   幹部學校

Cadre school.

kan pu k'uo ta hui yi   幹部擴大會議

Enlarged cadre meeting, or conference.

kan pu shen ch'a pao kao   幹部審查報告

Report on investigations of cadres.

kan shih   幹事

Staff member.

k'an ping cheng 看病證

Card for a medical visit (e.g. to a hospital).

k'an shou so 看守所

Detention Center.

kang t'ieh chih hui pu 鋼鐵指揮部

Iron and Steel Headquarters, or Command.

k'ang jih chan cheng kan pu 抗日戰爭幹部

Anti-Japanese war cadre.

kao 告

Warning.

kao chi 高級

High, higher.

kao chi chung hsüeh 高級中學

Upper middle school (senior or higher middle school).

kao chi ho tso she 高級合作社

Higher [Agricultural Producers] Cooperative.

kao chi hsiao hsüeh 高級小學

Higher primary school.

kao chi kan pu 高級幹部

High-ranking cadre.

kao chi ling tao kan pu 高級領導幹部

High-ranking leadership cadre.

kao chi shih ch'ang 高級市塲

Higher market, an early name for free market.

kao chung 高中

Upper middle [school] (*short form*).

kao teng kan pu hsüeh hsiao   高等幹部學校

> Higher cadre school.

ko hang ko yeh tsu chih   各行各業組織

> Organizations of all trades.

ko jen ch'eng fen   個人成份

> Individual [class] status.

ko jen li shih   個人歷史

> Personal history.

k'o   科

> Section. (*Ku* also means section, but one of lower rank or smaller size.)

k'o chang   科長

> Section chief.

k'o chang chi kan pu   科長級幹部

> Section-chief level cadre.

k'o hsüeh lun wen t'ao lun hui   科學論文討論會

> Meeting to discuss research papers.

k'o hsüeh p'u chi hsieh shang hui yi   科學普及協商會議

> Association for the Dissemination of Science.

k'o p'u hsieh hui   科普協會

> Association for the Dissemination of Science (*short form*).

k'o yüan   科員

> Section member.

k'ou liang   口糧

> Grain ration, food grain.

k'ou t'ou hsüan ch'uan   口頭宣傳

> Oral propaganda.

ku　股

　Section or subsection (in some government organizations); also department (in some communes).

ku chang　股長

　Section (or subsection, or department) head.

ku kan kan pu　骨幹幹部

　Backbone cadre.

ku yüan　股員

　Section member.

kua hao fei　掛號費

　Registration fee.

k'uai chi　會計

　Accountant (*short form*), accounts.

k'uai chi ch'u　會計處

　Accounting Division.

k'uai chi ku　會計股

　Accounting Section.

k'uai chi yüan　會計員

　Accountant.

k'uai k'uai ling tao　块块領導

　Regional geographical leadership (as contrasted with *t'iao t'iao ling tao*, vertical leadership).

kuan chang　館長

　Director of the Hall (e.g. the Cultural Hall).

kuan li　管理

　Management.

kuan li chü   管理局

　　Management Bureau, or Administrative Bureau.

kuan li kan pu   管理幹部

　　Management cadre.

kuan li wei yüan hui   管理委員會

　　Management Committee (of a commune or brigade).

kuan li yüan   管理員

　　Management worker (cadre).

kuan liao chu yi   官僚主義

　　Bureaucratism.

kuan liao ti chu   官僚地主

　　Bureaucratic landlord.

kuang po ta hui   廣播大會

　　Broadcast meeting (i.e. organized listening group).

kuang po tien t'ai   廣播電臺

　　Broadcasting Station.

kuang po yüan   廣播員

　　Broadcaster, or announcer.

kuei ch'iao   歸僑

　　Returned overseas Chinese.

kuei hua   規劃

　　Plan (long-term), or programs.

kuei hua ch'u   規劃處

　　Planning Division (for long-term plans).

kuei ting   規定

　　Regulation.

kung an chü 公安局

Public Security Bureau.

kung an hsüeh yüan 公安學院

Public Security College.

kung an tui 公安隊

Public security company, or forces, or group.

kung an tui chang 公安隊長

Chief of public security.

kung an yüan 公安員

Public security officer.

kung ch'ang chih pu 工廠支部

Factory [Party Organization] Branch.

kung ch'ang ho chi kuan shih ku an chien pao kao 工廠和機關事故案件報告

Report on cases of incidents in factories and organizations.

kung chi chin 公積金

Public accumulation fund (in a commune).

kung chi yüan 供給員

General affairs supply cadre.

kung chiao 工交

Industry and communications.

kung chiao pu 工交部

Industry and Communications Department (in the Party or in a commune).

kung ch'ü 工區

Work district.

kung fei chih liao cheng 公費治療證

Free medical treatment card.

kung fen　工分

    Work point.

kung han　公函

    Official letter.

kung hsiao ho tso she　供銷合作社

    Supply and Marketing Cooperative.

kung hui　工會

    Labor Union, or Trade Union.

kung jih　工日

    Workday.

kung kung shih t'ang　公共食堂

    Public mess hall.

kung liang　公糧

    Land (grain) tax; literally, public grain.

kung p'an ta hui　公判大會

    Public trial meeting.

kung shang lien　工商聯

    Federation, or Association, of Industry and Commerce (*short form*).

kung she　公社

    Commune.

kung she pan ti shui li　公社辦的水利

    Commune-Run Water Conservancy Works.

kung szu ho ying ch'i yeh　公私合營企業

    Joint state-private enterprise.

kung tso cheng　工作證

    Work card (i.e. identification card).

kung tso hui yi   工作會議

> Work conference, or meeting.

kung tso tsu   工作組

> Work group.

kung tso tsung chieh   工作總結

> Summary report of work.

kung tso wei yüan hui   工作委員會

> Work committee.

kung tzu   工資

> Salary, wages.

kung yeh chü   工業局

> Industry Bureau.

kung yeh hsüeh hsiao   工業學校

> Industrial school.

kung yeh shang yeh lien ho hui   工業商業聯合會

> Federation, or Association, of Industry and Commerce.

kung yi chin   公益金

> Public welfare fund (in a commune).

kung ying ku   供應股

> Rationing Section.

k'ung chih shu tzu   控制數字

> Control figure, target.

kuo chia ch'u pei liang   國家儲偹糧

> National reserve grain.

kuo chia kan pu   國家幹部

> State cadre.

kuo min ching chi t'ung chi tzu liao 國民經濟統計資料

Statistical materials on the national economy.

kuo wu yüan 國務院

State Council.

kuo ying ch'i yeh 國營企業

State enterprise.

k'uo kan hui yi 擴幹會議

Enlarged cadre conference, or meeting (*short form*).

k'uo ta 擴大

Enlarged.

k'uo ta kan pu hui yi 擴大幹部會議

Enlarged cadre conference, or meeting.

k'uo yin chi 擴音機

Loudspeaker.

lao kai 勞改

Labor reform (*short form*).

lao kai ch'ang 勞改場

Labor Reform Farm.

lao kai tui 勞改隊

Labor Reform Unit, or Team.

lao kan pu 老幹部

"Old cadre."

lao pai hsing 老百姓

Common people; literally, old hundred names.

lao tung chiao yang 勞動教養

Labor reeducation, or rehabilitation through labor.

lao tung chiao yang tui 勞動教養隊

Labor Reeducation Group.

lao tung chü 勞動局

Labor Bureau.

lao tung kai tsao 勞動改造

Labor reform, or reform through labor.

lao tung liang 勞動糧

Grain for bonuses and rewards; literally, labor grain.

lao tung pao wei (t'i ts'ao) chih tu 勞動保衛(體操)制度

Labor defense system (a physical exercise program).

lao tung sheng ch'an ti yi hsien 勞動生產第一綫

Make productive labor the first (i.e. priority) task.

lao tung shou ts'e 勞動手冊

Work book.

lao tung yü tu shu hsiang chieh ho 勞動與讀書相結合

Combine labor and study.

li ch'ang 立場

Standpoint.

li lun hsüeh hsi 理論學習

Theoretical study.

li shih wen t'i 歷史問題

Historical problems (e.g. in one's personal background or record).

li t'ang 禮堂

Meeting hall.

liang kuan so 糧管所

Grain Management Office (*short form*).

liang p'iao　糧票

　　Grain [ration] ticket.

liang shih chia kung ch'ang　　糧食加工廠

　　Rice mill; literally, grain processing factory.

liang shih chih pu　糧食支部

　　Grain [Party Organization] Branch.

liang shih chü　糧食局

　　Grain Bureau, or Food Bureau.

liang shih kan pu　糧食幹部

　　Grain cadre.

liang shih kuan li chan　糧食管理站

　　Grain Management Station.

liang shih kuan li so　糧食管理所

　　Grain Management Office.

liang shih kung ying chan　糧食供應站

　　Grain Rationing Station.

liang shih kung ying cheng　糧食供應證

　　Grain ration card, or book.

liang shih kung ying pu　糧食供應簿

　　Grain ration book.

lieh hsi tai piao　列席代表

　　Observer-representative.

lien　連

　　Company (military).

lien chang　連長

　　Company commander.

lien ho chen so 聯合診所

Joint clinic (composed of former private practitioners).

lien hsiang 聯鄉

Joint, or united, administrative village.

lin mu pu 林牧部

Forestry and Animal Husbandry Department (in a commune).

lin shih chieh shao hsin 臨時介紹信

Temporary (provisional) letter of introduction.

lin shih fa t'ing 臨時法庭

Temporary (*ad hoc*) tribunal.

lin shih kan pu 臨時幹部

Temporary (provisional) cadre.

lin shih yün tung hsiao tsu 臨時運動小組

Temporary campaign small group.

lin shih yün tung pan kung shih 臨時運動辦公室

Temporary campaign staff office.

lin yeh chü 林業局

Forestry Bureau.

ling tao chi kou 領導機構

Leadership organization.

ling tao kan pu 領導幹部

Leadership cadre.

liu lei cheng chih an chien pao kao 六類政治案件報告

Reports on six types of political cases.

liu shih t'iao 六十條

Sixty Articles.

liu tang ch'a k'an   留黨察看

Probation [and investigation] within the Party.

liu tung tsu   流動組

Mobile group, or team.

liu yung kan pu   留用幹部

"Retained cadre."

lü hsing   旅行

Travel.

lü hua yün tung   綠化運動

Tree-planting campaign.

mao chu shih yen ch'ang   毛猪試驗塲

Experimental Pig Farm.

men shih pu   門市部

Business department or sales outlet.

meng   盟

League.

mi chien   密件

Secret (the lowest of three security classifications of documents).

mi chih   密植

Close planting.

mi mi   秘密

Secret.

mi mi hsüan p'an   秘密宣判

Secret trial.

mi mi ju tang   秘密入黨

Secret admission to the Party.

mi mi tiao ch'a　秘密調查

Secret investigation.

mi pu　密捕

Secret arrest.

mi shu　秘書

Staff secretary (as contrasted with *shu chi*, Party secretary; *wen shu*, clerical secretary; and *wen yin*, secretary typist).

mi shu chang　秘書長

Staff secretary-general.

mi shu kan shih　秘書幹事

Staff member of Staff Secretariat.

mi shu k'o　秘書科

Staff Secretariat Section.

mi shu ku　秘書股

Staff Secretariat Section.

miao p'u　苗圃

Nursery (for trees or plants).

mieh huo　滅火

Fire extinguishing.

min cheng kan pu　民政幹部

Civil affairs cadre.

min cheng t'iao chieh　民政調解

Civil affairs mediation.

min ching　民警

People's policeman.

min ching hsiao tui　民警小隊

People's Police Small Group, or Team.

min ching tui　民警隊

> People's Police Unit (or group).

min ching tui chang　民警隊長

> Chief of People's Police Unit, or Group.

min chu jen shih　民主人士

> Democratic personage.

min chu tang p'ai　民主黨派

> Democratic parties and groups.

min pan hsüeh hsiao　民辦學校

> "People-operated" schools.

min pan ti　民辦的

> "People-operated" (e.g. schools).

min ping chuan yeh tui　民兵專業隊

> Military Specialists Group.

min ping kan pu　民兵幹部

> Militia cadre.

min ping k'o　民兵科

> Militia Section.

min ping pan kung shih　民兵辦公室

> Militia Staff Office.

min ping t'uan　民兵團

> Militia Regiment.

min ping tui　民兵隊

> Militia Unit, or Group, or Team.

min ping tui chang　民兵隊長

> Chief of Militia Unit, or Group, or Team; militia chief.

min shih   民事

Civil (i.e. in law, as in civil case).

ming ling   命令

Order.

mo fan   模範

Model.

mou (or *mu*)   畝

One sixth of an acre.

mu ch'i ch'ang   木器廠

Furniture factory.

mu ch'uan yün shu tui   木船運輸隊

[Wooden] Boat Transportation Group.

mu pan ch'uan   木板船

Wooden boat.

mu ts'ai kung szu   木材公司

Lumber Company.

nan hsia kan pu   南下幹部

Southbound cadre.

nei ch'in   內勤

Clerk (who works in an office on internal affairs).

nien chung chien ting piao   年終鑑定表

Year-end [personnel] assessment [Report] Form.

nung chan hui   農展會

Agricultural Exhibition (*short form*).

nung chan kuan   農展館

Agricultural Exhibition Hall.

nung ch'an p'in chia kung ch'ang   農産品加工廠

Agricultural products processing factory.

nung hsieh ch'ang   農械廠

Agricultural implements, or machinery, factory.

nung hui   農會

Peasant Association (*short form*).

nung hui chu hsi   農會主席

Chairman of Peasant Association.

nung k'en chü   農墾局

Bureau of Agriculture and Land Reclamation.

nung lin shui   農林水

Agriculture, forestry, and water conservancy.

nung lin shui pan kung shih   農林水辦公室

Agriculture, Forestry, and Water Conservancy Staff Office.

nung mao ch'u chi shih ch'ang   農貿初級市塲

Basic-level agricultural (rural) market (*short form*).

nung min hsieh hui   農民協會

Peasant Association.

nung tai ku   農貸股

Agricultural Loans Section.

nung ts'un fu tao yüan   農村輔導員

Agricultural extension worker, or rural instructor or counselor.

nung ts'un jen min kung she t'iao li hsiu cheng ts'ao an
農村人民公社條例修正草案
Revised Draft Regulations on the Work of the Rural People's Communes.

nung ts'un jen min kung she t'iao li ts'ao an   農村人民公社條例草案

Draft Regulations (Rules) on the Work of the Rural People's Communes.

nung ts'un kung tso pu   農村工作部

Rural Work Department.

nung yeh chan lan hui   農業展覽會

Agricultural Exhibition.

nung yeh chi shu chih tao chan   農業技術指導站

Agricultural Technology Extension Station, or Agrotechnical Station.

nung yeh chi shu chih tao yüan   農業技術指導員

Agricultural technology extension worker, or agrotechnical instructor.

nung yeh chü   農業局

Agriculture Bureau.

nung yeh chung hsüeh   農業中學

Agricultural middle school.

nung yeh hsüeh hsiao   農業學校

Agricultural school.

nung yeh kan pu   農業幹部

Agricultural cadre.

nung yeh kang yao szu shih t'iao   農業綱要四十條

Forty-Article Charter for Agricultural Development.

nung yeh mao yi ch'u chi shih ch'ang   農業貿易初級市塲

Basic-level agricultural (rural) markets (one of the early names for free markets).

nung yeh pu   農業部

Agriculture Department (in a commune).

nung yeh sheng ch'an ho tso pu   農業生產合作部

Agricultural Production Cooperative Department (a Party department that was the predecessor, at least in some areas, of the Rural Work Department).

nung yeh sheng ch'an ho tso she　農業生產合作社

　　Agricultural Producers Cooperative (APC).

nung yeh shih yen chan　農業實驗站

　　Agricultural Experimental Station.

nung yeh yen chiu so　農業研究所

　　Agricultural Research Institute.

pa ta piao chun　八大標準

　　Eight Great Standards.

pai huo kung szu　百貨公司

　　Department store, General Goods Company.

pai huo p'u　百貨舖

　　General goods store.

p'ai　排

　　Platoon.

p'ai chang　排長

　　Platoon leader.

p'ai ch'u chi kou　派出機構

　　Dispatched organization, organization with delegated powers.

p'ai ch'u so　派出所

　　Public Security Substation.

p'ai tzu　牌子

　　Plaque, or tablet (e.g. in clan temples).

pan　班

　　Squad.

pan kung fei　辦公費

　　Funds for office operation.

pan kung shih　辦公室

Staff office (or simply office).

pan kung shih chu jen　辦公室主任

Head (director) of a staff office.

pan kung t'ing　辦公廳

Staff office (e.g. in a ministry).

pan she kung tso tsu　辦社工作組

Work teams, or groups, to run cooperatives or communes.

pan shih yüan　辦事員

Lowest-ranking cadres in a ministry section.

pan t'o ch'an　半脱產

Half-exempt from [agricultural] labor.

p'an chüeh　判決

Court decision.

p'an hsing pao kao　判刑報告

Report on court sentences.

pao　保

A unit of approximately ten *chia*, or roughly one hundred families, under the *pao-chia* system prior to 1949 (under Nationalist rule).

pao chia chih tu　保甲制度

Pao-chia system.

pao chien yüan　保健員

Health worker.

pao kao　報告

Report.

pao kuan　保管

Custodian (e.g. in a brigade) (*short form*).

pao kuan yüan　保管員

    Custodian.

pao mi chih tu　保密制度

    Security system.

pao mi kan pu　保密幹部

    Security cadre; literally, protection of secrecy cadre.

pao wei　保衞

    Security; literally, protection (often used in a sense similar to *kung an*, public security).

pao wei ch'u　保衞處

    Security Division.

pao wei hsiao tsu　保衞小組

    Security Small Group.

pao wei k'o　保衞科

    Security Section (i.e. Guard Section).

pao wei yüan　保衞員

    Security officer.

pei an　備案

    Information copy (of a document); to keep on file.

pei chan liang　俻戰糧

    National defense grain; literally, grain for preparation for war.

pei ching kan pu　北京幹部

    Peking cadre.

p'ei pei　配備

    To assign (personnel).

p'ei yang　培養

    To nurture or cultivate (e.g. cultivate a new Party member).

p'ei yang kung lu tui   培養公路隊

Road Repair Group.

pen wei chu yi   本位主義

"Departmentalism," or "vested-interestism."

p'eng t'ou hui yi   碰頭會議

Face-to-face meeting, *ad hoc* meeting.

p'i fa pu   批發部

Wholesale outlet; literally, wholesale department.

p'i p'ing   批評

Criticism.

p'i p'ing chiao yü   批評教育

Education through criticism.

pien chih   編制

Table of organization.

pien lun hui   辯論會

Debate, meeting for argument.

ping yi chü   兵役局

Military Service Bureau.

ping yi chü chih pu   兵役局支部

Military Service Bureau [Party Organization] Branch.

ping yi k'o   兵役科

Military Service Section.

ping yi kung tso tsu   兵役工作組

Military Service Work Group.

p'ing hsing yün tung   平行運動

Adjustment movement.

p'o huai chün kung yao ti ho chiao lien pao kao 破壞軍工要地和教練報告

Report on sabotage of important military installations.

pu 部

A central government ministry, a Party department, a commune department (in some communes).

pu chang 部長

Minister, head of a department, etc.

pu chang chi kan pu 部長級幹部

Minister-level cadre.

pu chang chu li 部長助理

Assistant to the minister.

pu chang pan kung shih 部長辦公室

Minister's Staff Office.

pu jen pao kao 捕人報告

Report on arrests.

pu wu hui yi 部務會議

Ministry affairs meeting (i.e. ministry staff meeting).

p'u ch'a 普查

General survey (*short form*).

p'u pien tiao ch'a 普遍調查

General survey.

p'u t'ung kan pu 普通幹部

Ordinary cadre.

p'u t'ung kung jen 普通工人

Ordinary worker.

p'u t'ung min ping 普通民兵

Ordinary Militia.

p'u t'ung ping   普通兵

Ordinary soldier.

p'u t'ung ts'ang k'u   普通倉庫

Ordinary granary.

p'u tzu   舖子

Store.

san chi so yu   三級所有

Three-level ownership.

san fan yün tung   三反運動

Three-anti campaign.

san pa hsien kan pu   三八綫幹部

1938-line cadre (a cadre who joined the Party before 1938).

san pa kan pu   三八幹部

1938 cadre (a cadre who joined the Party before 1938).

sao mang min hsiao   掃盲民校

People's School for the Elimination of Illiteracy.

sao mang pan kung shih   掃盲辦公室

Staff Office for the Elimination of Illiteracy.

shang chung hsia   上.中.下.

"Top-middle-bottom" (a method of surveying).

shang yeh chih pu   商業支部

Commerce [Party Organization] Branch.

shang yeh pu   商業部

Commerce Department (in a commune).

shao hsien tui   少先隊

Young Pioneers (*short form*).

shao nien hsien feng tui   少年先鋒隊

Young Pioneers.

shao pu shao sha to kuan   少捕少殺多管

Reduce arrests, reduce capital punishment, and increase [political] control.

shao wei   少尉

Second lieutenant.

she chang   社長

Commune director (also cooperative head).

she chih chü   設治局

Preparatory county; literally, preparatory bureau.

she ch'ing pao kao   社情報告

Report on social conditions.

she hui chih an k'o   社會治安科

Social Order Section.

she hui chu yi chiao yü yün tung   社會主義教育運動

Socialist education movement.

she hui chu yi yün tung   社會主義運動

Socialization movement.

she hui kuan hsi   社會關係

Social relations (friends, etc.).

she hui tiao ch'a   社會調查

Social survey.

she tang wei   社黨委

Commune Party Committee (*short form*).

she tang wei yüan hui   社黨委員會

Commune Party Committee.

she yüan tai piao ta hui   社員代表大會

> Commune Congress.

shen ch'ing ju tang chih yüan shu   申請入黨志願書

> Application for Party membership.

shen fen cheng   身份證

> Identity card, or certificate.

shen kan pan kung shih   審幹辦公室

> Staff Office for the Investigation of Cadres.

shen keng   深耕

> Deep plowing.

shen kuan hui   神館會

> Religious sects or societies (including secret societies).

shen p'an yüan   審判員

> Judge.

sheng   省

> Province.

sheng ch'an chiao yüan   生産教員

> Production instructor.

sheng ch'an fei yung   生産費用

> Production expenses.

sheng ch'an hsiao tsu   生産小組

> Production Group (under Production Team in a commune).

sheng ch'an hsiao tui   生産小隊

> Production Team (see also *sheng ch'an tui*).

sheng ch'an kuan chih   生産管制

> Production control.

sheng ch'an kuan li ch'ü　生產管理區

Production management district (a unit established in some areas at the level of old administrative villages when enlarged higher APC's were established; also in some areas after communization, between a commune and its brigades).

sheng ch'an kuan li kan pu　生產管理幹部

Production management cadre.

sheng ch'an pao kao　生產報告

Production report.

sheng ch'an ta tui　生產大隊

Production Brigade.

sheng ch'an tui　生產隊

Production Team.

sheng chi　昇級

Promotion.

sheng chih　昇職

Job rank promotion.

sheng huo　生活

Livelihood.

sheng huo chien t'ao hui　生活檢討會

Livelihood criticism meeting.

sheng kuo chia kung ch'ang　生菓加工廠

Fruit processing plant.

sheng tang wei yüan hui　省黨委員會

Provincial Party Committee.

sheng wei　省委

Provincial Party Committee (*short form*).

shih 室

Office.

shih 市

Municipality.

shih ch'ang kuan li wei yüan hui 市場管理委員會

Market Management Committee.

shih erh t'iao 十二條

Twelve Articles.

shih fan hsüeh hsiao 師範學校

Normal school.

shih hsi yen chiu yüan 實習研究員

Research trainee.

shih kuan hui 市管會

Market Management Committee (*short form*).

shih t'ang 食堂

Mess hall, dining hall.

shih t'ang chao tai k'o 食堂招待科

Mess Hall and Guest House Section.

shih wu 事務

Affairs (meaning administration); also general affairs cadre (*short form*).

shih wu chi kan pu 十五級幹部

Grade fifteen cadre.

shih wu kan pu 事務幹部

General affairs cadre.

shih yen ch'ang 試驗塲

Experimental Farm.

shih yen shih   試驗室

Laboratory.

shih yen tien hsing   試驗典型

Keypoint experiment, sample.

shih yen t'ien   試驗田

Experimental field, or plot.

shou fa   收發

Receiving and sending clerk (*short form*).

shou fa shih   收發室

Communications Reception Center; literally, Receiving and Sending Office.

shou fa yüan   收發員

Receiving and sending clerk.

shou ju k'o   收入科

Revenue Section.

shou kou chan   收購站

Purchasing Station.

shou kung yeh ho tso she   手工業合作社

Handicraft Cooperative.

shu chi   書記

[Party] secretary.

shu chi yüan   書記員

Court clerk.

shu mien t'ung chi pao kao   書面統計報告

Written statistical report.

shu mu shou yi chan   畜牧獸醫站

Veterinary Station.

shuang ch'ung ling tao   雙重領導

   Dual leadership.

shui ch'an chih pu   水產支部

   Aquatic Products [Party Organization] Branch.

shui ch'an kung szu   水產公司

   Aquatic Products Company.

shui li chü   水利局

   Water Conservancy Bureau.

shui li kan pu   水利幹部

   Water conservancy cadre.

shui li kan pu hui yi   水利幹部會議

   Conference of water conservancy cadres.

shui li pu   水利部

   Water Conservancy Department (in a commune).

shui ni ch'ang   水泥廠

   Cement factory.

shui wu chü   稅務局

   Tax Bureau.

shui wu k'o   稅務科

   Tax Section.

shui wu ku   稅務股

   Tax Section.

shui wu so   稅務所

   Tax Office.

so chang   所長

   Head of institute, or center, or office.

so wu hui yi   所務會議

Institute affairs meeting.

su ch'ing fan ko ming yün tung   肅清反革命運動

Campaign to liquidate, or purge, counterrevolutionaries.

su fan pan kung shih   肅反辦公室

Staff Office for the Liquidation, or Purging [of Counterrevolutionaries].

su fan yün tung   肅反運動

Campaign to Liquidate, or Purge, counterrevolutionaries (*short form*).

su lien chuan chia fan yi shih   蘇聯專家翻譯室

Translation Office for Soviet Experts.

su lien chuan chia pan kung shih   蘇聯專家辦公室

Staff Office for Soviet Experts.

su she   宿舍

Apartment, dormitory.

szu   司

Bureau.

szu chi pan   司機班

Car pool; literally, drivers' group.

szu hsiang   思想

Thought.

szu hsiang hui pao   思想彙報

Verbal (oral) report on one's thoughts.

szu jen kai tsao pan kung shih   私人改造辦公室

Staff Office for the Reform of Private Entrepreneurs.

szu kai pan kung shih   私改辦公室

　　Staff Office for the Reform or Private Entrepreneurs (*short form*).

szu lei fen tzu   四類份子

　　Four [bad] elements.

szu t'ang   祠堂

　　Clan temple.

ta chia   打架

　　Fight, conflict.

ta hsing cheng ch'ü   大行政區

　　Great administrative region.

ta hui   大會

　　Congress, large meeting.

ta kuo   大過

　　Large error.

ta tui   大隊

　　Brigade (i.e. a production brigade); also a large group (as in *min ching ta tui*, People's Police Group).

ta tui chang   大隊長

　　Brigade chief, or director.

ta tui chih pu   大隊支部

　　[Production] Brigade [Party] Branch.

ta tui fu   大隊副

　　Deputy brigade chief.

ta tui kuan li wei yüan hui   大隊管理委員會

　　Brigade Management Committee.

ta tui pan kung shih   大隊辦公室

　　[Production] Brigade Office.

ta tzu 打字

    Typist (*short form*).

ta tzu pao 大字報

    Large character newspaper, or bulletin.

ta tzu yüan 打字員

    Typist.

ta yüeh chin 大躍進

    Great Leap Forward.

tai hsiao tien 代銷店

    Sales agent or agency.

tai li 代理

    Act for.

tai mao tzu 带帽子

    To be "capped."

tai piao ta hui 代表大會

    Congress.

t'ai 臺

    Station.

t'ai chang 臺長

    Station director (e.g. of Broadcasting Station).

t'an pai 坦白

    Confess.

tang an 檔案

    File, dossier (e.g. personnel dossier).

tang an kuan 檔案館

    File room, archives.

tang an kuan li 檔案管理

Manager of files, or archives (*short form*).

tang an kuan li yüan 檔案管理員

Manager of files, or archives.

tang chih pu 黨支部

Party Branch.

tang ch'ün 黨群

Party-masses.

tang ch'ün chi kuan chih pu 黨群機關支部

Party Mass Organization [Organization] Branch.

tang fei 黨費

Party dues.

tang hsiao 黨校

Party school.

tang hsiao tsu 黨小組

Party Small Group, or Cell.

tang hsün pan 黨訓班

Party training class.

tang kan pu 黨幹部

Party cadre (term used for Party members who are cadres in Party organizations).

tang k'o 黨課

"Party class" (lecture sessions given by Party).

tang nei chi kuo 黨內記過

Record of errors or transgressions (internal Party errors).

tang tai piao ta hui 黨代表大會

Party Congress.

tang ti fang wei yüan hui 黨地方委員會

Special District Party Committee.

tang ti kan pu 黨的幹部

Party cadre. This term can also be translated as "Party's cadre"; it has variable usage, and can mean Party members who are cadres in Party organizations, or Party members who are cadres in any organizations, or, on occasion, "state cadres"; at times it is used in a special and restricted sense to mean all Party and non-Party persons who are cadres in Party organizations.

tang ti sheng huo 黨的生活

"Party life."

tang ti wen chien 黨的文件

Party document.

tang tsu 黨組

Party Fraction, leading Party members' group.

tang t'uan pan kung shih 黨團辦公室

Party and Young Communist League Staff Office.

tang wei 黨委

Party Committee (*short form*).

tang wei hui 黨委會

Party Committee.

tang wei wei yüan 黨委委員

Party Committee member.

tang yüan 黨員

Party member.

tang yüan kan pu 黨員幹部

Party cadre. This term can also be translated as "Party member cadre"; it is applied to all Party members who hold any cadre positions, whether in the Party, government, mass organizations, or other institutions.

t'ang ch'ang   糖廠

    Sugar factory.

tao   道

    Circuit (in the Imperial period).

t'e ch'ing an chüan pao kao   特情案卷報告

    Report from public security secret agents.

t'e ch'ing pao kao   特情報告

    Report on activities of enemy agents.

t'e ch'ing yüan   特情員

    Public security secret agents.

t'e k'uai   特快

    Urgent, fast, express.

t'e p'ai yüan   特派員

    Special agents.

t'e yüeh pao kao   特月報告

    Monthly report on enemy secret agents.

teng chi pu   登記簿

    Registration book, or registry.

teng chi shu   登記書

    Registration book, or registry.

ti chu   地主

    Landlord.

ti erh fu shu chi   第二副書記

    Second deputy [Party] secretary.

ti fang chu yi   地方主義

    Localism.

ti fang fu chia shui   地方附加稅

 Local surtax.

ti fang kan pu   地方幹部

 Local cadre.

ti fang kuo ying kung ch'ang   地方國營工廠

 Local state-run factory.

ti fang liang   地方糧

 Local grain, or local surtax on the land tax.

ti fang shui   地方稅

 Local tax.

ti fang wei yüan hui   地方委員會

 Special District [Party] Committee.

ti wei   地位

 Status, standing.

ti wei   地委

 Special District Party Committee (*short form*).

ti wei hui   地委會

 Special District Party Committee (*short form*).

ti yi fu shu chi   第一副書記

 First Deputy [Party] Secretary.

ti yi kan pu ch'u   第一幹部處

 First Cadre Division.

ti yi shu chi   第一書記

 First Party Secretary.

t'i chi pu t'i hsin   提級不提薪

 Rank promotion without automatic salary raise.

t'i chih hsia fang　體制下放

Organizational decentralization.

t'i ts'ao　體操

Calisthenics, physical exercise.

t'i wei hui　體委會

Physical Education (or Physical Culture) and Sports Committee (*short form*).

ti yü yün tung wei yüan hui　體育運動委員會

Physical Education and Sports Committee.

tiao ch'a yen chiu ch'u　調查研究處

Investigation (or Survey) and Research Division.

tiao tung　調動

Transfer assignment.

t'iao chieh wei yüan hui　調解委員會

Mediation Committee.

t'iao li　條例

Regulations, rules.

t'iao p'ei　條配

Transfer.

t'iao p'ei ku　條配股

Transfer Section.

t'iao t'iao ling tao　條條領導

Vertical leadership.

tien ch'ang　電廠

Electric plant.

tien hsing　典型

Keypoint area.

tien hsing tiao ch'a   典型調查

Keypoint investigation, or survey.

tien hsün tsu   電訊組

Telegraph/Telephone Group (in Postal and Telecommunications Bureau).

tien hua hui pao   電話彙報

Telephonic report, or meeting.

tien hua hui yi   電話會議

Telephone conference.

tien ying tui   電影隊

Movie Team.

t'ien tsai jen huo   天災人禍

Floods and droughts.

ting an   定案

Final form of a document; final decision in a case.

t'ing   廳

Department (in provincial government); also Subprefecture (in the Imperial period).

t'ing ta pao kao hui yi   聽大報告會議

Report meeting; literally, meeting to hear major reports.

to ch'ung ling tao   多重領導

Multiple leadership.

t'o ch'an   脫產

Exempt from [agricultural] labor.

tou cheng hui   鬥爭會

Struggle meeting.

ts'ai ch'an chiu fen 財產糾紛

Property dispute.

ts'ai cheng chü 財政局

Finance Bureau.

ts'ai cheng k'o 財政科

Finance Section.

ts'ai cheng ku 財政股

Finance Section.

ts'ai cheng pu 財政部

Finance Department (in a commune); also Ministry of Finance.

ts'ai kou k'o 採購科

Purchasing Section for [Agricultural] Products.

ts'ai k'uai chü 財會局

Bureau of Finance and Accounting.

ts'ai k'uai kan pu 財會幹部

Finance and accounting cadre.

ts'ai k'uai k'o 財會科

Finance and Accounting Section.

ts'ai k'uai ku 財會股

Finance and Accounting Section.

ts'ai liao tsu 材料組

Materials Group.

ts'ai mao 財貿

Finance and trade.

ts'ai mao pan kung shih 財貿辦公室

Finance and Trade Staff Office.

ts'ai mao pu   財貿部

> Finance and Trade Department.

ts'ai shui chih pu   財稅支部

> Finance and Tax [Party Organization] Branch.

ts'ai shui chü   財稅局

> Finance and Tax Bureau.

ts'ai wu   財務

> Financial personnel (cadres).

ts'ai wu ch'u   財務處

> Finance (Financial Affairs) Division.

ts'ai wu yüan   財務員

> Financial personnel (cadres).

ts'an chia ko ming   參加革命

> "Join the revolution."

ts'an chia tang   參加黨

> Join the Party (see also *ju tang*).

ts'an chün yün tung   參軍運動

> Movement to join the army (conscription campaign).

ts'an k'ao hsiao hsi   參考消息

> Reference News.

ts'an k'ao tzu liao   參考資料

> Reference Materials.

ts'an mou ch'u   參謀處

> Staff Division.

ts'ang k'u   倉庫

> Granary, warehouse.

ts'ang kuan k'o 倉管科

Section for Management of Granaries, or Warehouses.

ts'ang kuan ku 倉管股

Granary (or Warehouse) Section.

ts'ang kuan yüan 倉管員

Personnel (cadres) for the management of granaries, or warehouses.

ts'ao an 草案

Draft.

ts'e chih 撤職

To fire, to dismiss (e.g. a cadre); see also *k'ai ch'u kan pu.*

tseng ch'an chieh yüeh yün tung 增産節約運動

Campaign to increase production and reduce waste.

tso chan chü 作戰局

War Bureau.

tso t'an hui 座談會

Forum, discussion meeting, symposium.

tsu 組

Group, small group.

tsu chang 組長

Group chief (e.g. of Production Group).

tsu chih 組織

Organization.

tsu chih pao tung pao kao 組織暴動報告

Report on organized riots.

tsu chih pu　組織部

　Organization Department.

tsu chih sheng huo　組織生活

　"Organizational life."

tsu chih wei yüan　組織委員

　Organization committeeman.

ts'un chang　村長

　Village chief.

tsung chieh　總結

　Summary, résumé.

tsung chih pu　總支部

　General [Party] Branch.

tsung ho chi hua k'o　綜合計劃科

　Comprehensive Planning Section.

tsung ho ch'u　綜合處

　Comprehensive [Statistics] Division.

tsung ho tso she　總合作社

　General cooperative.

tsung kung hui　總工會

　General Labor Union.

tsung pien chi　總編輯

　Editor-in-chief.

tsung tu　總督

　Governor-general, viceroy (in the Imperial period).

tsung tui   縱隊

   Column (a military unit); also general group, large group.

tsung t'ung fu   總統府

   Office of the President (under the Nationalist regime).

tsung wu   總務

   General affairs.

tsung wu ch'u   總務處

   General Affairs Division.

tsung wu jen yüan   總務人員

   Person in charge of general affairs.

tu chiang (nan hsia) kan pu   渡江南下幹部

   Yangtze crossing (southbound) cadre.

tu li ying   獨立營

   Independent Battalion.

tu li ying chang   獨立營長

   Commander of Independent Battalion.

tu pao tsu   讀報組

   Newspaper Reading Group.

t'u fei   土匪

   Bandit.

t'u kai tui   土改隊

   Land Reform Team (*short form*).

t'u shu kuan   圖書館

   Library.

t'u shu kuan li yüan 圖書管理員

> Library management personnel (cadres).

t'u shu shih 圖書室

> Library Office (i.e. a small library).

t'u shu tzu liao shih 圖書資料室

> Library and Materials Office.

t'u ti kai ko kan pu 土地改革幹部

> Land reform cadre.

t'u ti ko ming kan pu 土地革命幹部

> Land revolution cadre.

t'uan 團

> Regiment; League (YCL).

t'uan chang 團長

> Regimental commander.

t'uan chih pu 團支部

> Young Communist League Branch.

t'uan k'o 團課

> League (YCL) class.

t'uan ti sheng huo 團的生活

> "League (YCL) life."

t'uan wei 團委

> League (YCL) Committee (*short form*).

t'uan wei hui 團委會

> League (YCL) Committee.

t'uan wei shu chi　團委書記

 Secretary of League (YCL) Committee.

tui chang　隊長

 Group chief, team head.

tui hua hsüan ch'uan　對話宣傳

 Face-to-face oral propaganda.

t'ung chan　統戰

 United front.

t'ung chan pu　統戰部

 United Front Department.

t'ung chi　統計

 Statistics; also statistician (*short form*).

t'ung chi chü　統計局

 Statistics Bureau.

t'ung chi ch'u　統計處

 Statistics Division.

t'ung chi ku　統計股

 Statistics Section.

t'ung chi yüan　統計員

 Statistician.

t'ung chih　通知

 [Circular] notice.

t'ung hsün tsu　通訊組

 Mail Group (in Postal and Telecommunications Bureau).

t'ung hsün yüan　通訊員

 Messenger, correspondent.

t'ung kou t'ung hsiao 統購統銷

Unified (state) purchase and supply; planned purchase and supply.

t'ung pao 通報

Circular notice or instruction.

tzu chih ch'i 自治旗

Autonomous banner.

tzu chih chou 自治州

Autonomous department, or simply autonomous *chou* (under an autonomous region).

tzu chih ch'ü 自治區

Autonomous region.

tzu chih hsiang 自治鄉

Autonomous administrative village.

tzu chih hsien 自治縣

Autonomous county.

tzu chuan 自傳

Personal history.

tzu jan ts'un 自然村

Natural village.

tzu liao shih 資料室

[Reference] Materials Office.

tzu liu ti 自留地

Private plot.

tzu wo chien t'ao 自我檢討

Self-criticism.

tzu yu shih ch'ang 自由市塲

Free market.

wai tiao tsu   外調組

External (Outside) Investigation (Survey) Group; also Office in Charge of Personnel Transfer to Other Units.

wan chin yu kan pu   萬金油幹部

"Tiger Balm cadres"; literally, 10,000 Gold Balm (the name of "Tiger Balm") cadres; meaning cadres constantly shifted in jobs, cadres shifted to meet all needs.

wei ping pan   衞兵班

Guard Unit, or Company.

wei sheng chan   衞生站

Health Station.

wei sheng chü   衞生局

Health Bureau.

wei sheng kan pu   衞生幹部

Health cadre.

wei sheng so   衛生所

Hŏspital, or Health Center, in a commune.

wei sheng yüan   衛生院

Hospital, or Health Center.

wei sheng yüan   衛生員

Health officer, or cadre.

wei sheng yün tung   衛生運動

Health or sanitation campaign.

wei yüan   委員

Committee member, committeeman.

wen chiao   文教

Culture and education (*short form*); also cultural instructor.

wen chiao hsi t'ung   文教系統

Culture and education system.

wen chiao kan pu   文教幹部

Culture and education cadre.

wen chiao wei sheng   文教衛生

Culture, education, and health.

wen chiao wei sheng pu   文教衛生部

Culture, Education, and Health Department, in a commune.

wen chien chih shih   文件指示

Written instruction.

wen chü k'o   文具科

Supplies (Stationery) Section.

wen chü kung szu   文具公司

Stationery Goods Company.

wen hua ch'eng tu   文化程度

Cultural (i.e. educational) standard.

wen hua chiao yüan   文化教員

Cultural instructor.

wen hua chü   文化局

Bureau of Culture.

wen hua hsüeh hsi hsiao tsu   文化學習小組

Cultural Study Small Group.

wen hua kan pu   文化幹部

Cultural cadre.

wen hua kuan   文化館

Cultural Hall.

wen hua kung   文化宮

Cultural Palace.

wen hua yü lo hsi chü tsu   文化娛樂戲劇組

Culture, Recreation, and Drama Group.

wen hua yüan   文化員

Cultural worker.

wen shu   文書

Clerical secretary, or secretarial clerk.

wen t'i   文體

Culture and sports, or physical education.

wen yin   文印

Secretary-typist (also can mean person in charge of printing).

wen yü hsi chü tsu   文娛戲劇組

Culture, Recreation, and Drama Group (*short form*).

wu ch'an chieh chi   無産階級

Proletariat.

wu chia k'o   物價科

Price Section.

wu chuang ching ch'a   武裝警察

Armed Forces Police.

wu chuang pu   武裝部

Armed Forces Department.

wu chuang pu chang   武裝部長

Head of Armed Forces Department.

wu chuang tui   武裝隊

Armed Forces Group (an armed police unit).

wu fang mien ti ti jen   五方面的敵人

Five kinds of enemies, or enemies in five respects.

wu jen hsiao tsu   五人小組

Five-Man Small Group.

wu lei fen tzu   五類份子

Five [bad] elements.

wu lei fen tzu pien hua pao kao   五類份子變化報告

Report on [class] changes of the five [bad] elements.

wu ta kan pu   五大幹部

Five Big Cadres.

yang lu tui   養路隊

Road Repair Group (*short form*).

yao fei   藥費

Medicine fee (charges for prescriptions, etc.).

yao ts'ai kung szu   藥材公司

Medicine Company.

yeh wu   業務

"Business affairs," or "business work" (i.e. substantive work).

yeh wu chih tao   業務指導

"Business" (substantive) guidance, work guidance.

yeh wu hsüeh hsi hsiao tsu   業務學習小組

"Business study" (i.e. study related to one's substantive work, rather than political study).

yen an kan pu   延安幹部

Yenan cadre.

yen chiu so   研究所

Research Institute, or Research Office.

yen chiu tsu 研究組

　　Research Group.

yen chiu yüan 研究員

　　Researcher.

yen hai min ching 沿海民警

　　Seacoast People's Police, or Coastal People's Police.

yen hai pu 沿海部

　　Seacoast Department, or Coastal Department.

yi liao chan 醫療站

　　Health Station.

yi pan kan pu 一般幹部

　　Ordinary cadre.

yi pan ti chu 一般地主

　　Ordinary landlord.

yi sheng 醫生

　　Doctor.

yi shih jen yüan 醫士人員

　　Medical personnel or workers.

yi wu jen yüan 醫務人員

　　Medical personnel or workers.

yi wu lao tung 義務勞動

　　Labor service.

yi wu ping 義務兵

　　Compulsory service soldier, conscriptee.

yi yao chih pu 醫藥支部

　　Medicine [Party Organization] Branch.

yi yao kung szu   醫藥公司

Medicine Company, or Medical Supplies Company.

yin chang   印章

Seal, chop.

yin hang chih pu   銀行支部

Bank [Party Organization] Branch.

yin hang kan pu   銀行幹部

Bank cadre.

yin shua ch'ang   印刷廠

Printing plant.

yin ti chih yi ling huo yün yung   因地制宜靈活運用

Apply policy flexibly to suit local conditions.

ying   營

Battalion.

ying chang   營長

Battalion commander.

ying yeh so   營業所

[Small] Bank Office; literally, Business Department.

ying yeh yüan   營業員

Commercial employee (c.g. a salesman).

yu ch'ang   油廠

[Vegetable] Oil Factory.

yu chih ku   油脂股

Oils and Fats Section.

yu chih kung szu   油脂公司

Oils and Fats Company.

yu hsien tien　有綫電

Rediffusion broadcasting (i.e. wired system).

yu hung yu chuan　又紅又專

Red and expert.

yu p'ai fen tzu　右派份子

Rightist element.

yu shang erh hsia yu hsia erh shang　由上而下　由下而上

From top to bottom and from bottom to top.

yu tien chü　郵電局

Postal and Telecommunications Bureau.

yu wen t'i　有問題

To have problems.

yü liang　餘糧

"Surplus grain" (term used for compulsory sales of grain to the state).

yü pei shen p'an k'o　預備審判科

Section for the Preliminary Examination of Cases.

yü pei tang yüan　預備黨員

Alternate Party member (candidate Party member).

yü shen　預審

Preliminary examination of a court case, or case preparation (*short form*).

yü shen k'o　預審科

Section for the Preliminary Examination of Cases (*short form*).

yü suan　預算

Budget.

yüan chang　院長

Court president, or chief judge; also hospital director, or superintendent.

yüeh chi　越級

Skipping levels (e.g. in communication within the bureaucracy).

yüeh pao　月報

Monthly report.

yüeh pao kao　月報告

Monthly report.

yüeh tui kuan li yüan　樂隊管理員

Manager of Music Group.

yün shu chan　運輸站

Transportation Station.

yün shu kuan li chan　運輸管理站

Transportation Management Station.

yün tung　運動

Campaign, or movement; also sports.

yün tung hui　運動會

Sports meet.

yün tung pan kung shih　運動辦公室

Campaign Staff Office.

Index

Administration, local: counties as most important unit, 117–20; recent administrative changes below county level, 313–38; evolution of, from pre-1949 period, 318–21; districts as units of rural administration, 319–20; innovations at lowest levels, 439–40; *see also* Government, and names of units

Administrative villages, 110, 121; *see also under* County A

Agricultural Experiment Station, Commune C, 355–56

Agricultural producers cooperatives (APC's), 314, 317, 336, 337; development of, 323–24; in Administrative Village I, 333–35; in area of Brigade B, 415, 418

Agriculture: production planning in Commune C, 317, 327–28, 342, 355; forty-article charter for development, 334–35, 406; Brigade B, 378–79 County X: Bureau, 159, 202, 276–80; Agricultural Technology Extension Station, 203, 278–79; Veterinary Station, 203, 280; Bureau of Agriculture and Land Reclamation, 203, 283

Agriculture and Forestry Political Department (Central Committee), 4

Association for the Dissemination of Science, County X, 202, 259, 267–68

Association of Industry and Commerce, County X, 199, 256

Autonomous areas, 113–14

Bank, People's, *see* People's Bank

Banners, 117

Bourgeois elements, 33, 431, 432, 438

Brigades, *see* Production brigades, Production Brigade B

Bureaucracy: position of ministries, 3–10; Party dominance, 35–37, 55, 188–89, 429–36; as structure of authority, 38–39, 118, 436; stratification of status, 38–47; salary and job grades, 41–43, 55; personnel management, 48–63; guest houses for, 100, 138; "rectification" campaigns, 167–68, 169–72; mobility in, 177–79; *see also* Administration, local; Cadres; Government; and individual units

Bureaucratism, 438; Party hostility toward, 38–39, 58, 172

Business, socialization of, County X, 254–56

Cadres: "study" (indoctrination) system, 20, 26, 30–32, 164–65, 213–14, 435, 441–42; "struggle" meetings, 33, 34, 171, 330, 435; and political campaigns, 33, 384; as members of the elite, 35–36, 39, 47; definition of, 39; state, 39–40, 187–88; types of, 39–41, 188–89; local, 40–41; military, 40, 47, 53–54, 132, 243; salary and job grades, 41–43, 190–93, 433; "old" and "new," 43–45; seniority, 43–45, 188–89, 433; "anti-Japanese war," 44; "long march," 44; "Yenan," 44, 130, 131, 132, 188; "liberation war," 45; "1938," 45; "uprising," 45; ranking systems other than seniority, 45–47, 189–90; groupings, 46–47; personnel dossiers, 49, 146–47, 165–66, 170, 435; "assessments" (evaluations), 50–52, 166–68; "transfer-downward" policy, 51, 60–61, 134, 174–76, 337; advancement opportunities, 54–56;

Cadres (*Continued*)
  factors in advancement, 56–57; raises, promotions, and transfers, 57–58, 177, 181–83, 435; mobility of, 58–60, 176–79; dissemination of directives, 75; visits to and from the ministry, 75–78; personal life, 102–3, 435–36; in county organizations, 118*n*–19*n*; punishments in County X, 144–47, 152; "rectification" campaigns, 167–68, 169–72, 435; manual labor by, 172–74; in Brigade B, 365, 366, 378, 379, 381, 399, 415–16, 418, 419–20; in China today, summary, 434–36; *see also* Personnel
  non-Party cadres, 13, 18–19, 20, 35–36, 46, 53, 433; definition of, 39; as "intellectuals," 46; in Ministry M, 25, 26, 28, 29, 31, 34, 36, 50, 55, 67–68, 76, 91, 93, 101, 103; in County X, 136, 138, 140, 146, 151, 152, 164, 165–66, 167, 181–83, 186, 187, 190, 207, 211, 213, 239, 253
  Party cadres, 7, 18; in Ministry M, 24, 26, 28–29, 35, 44–45, 46, 50, 52, 53, 67–68, 91, 93, 101, 103; definition, 39, 43*n*–44*n*; in County X, 136, 138, 140, 143, 145, 146, 151, 159–60, 162–68 *passim*, 181–83, 186, 187, 190, 207, 211, 213, 239, 253
Campaigns: County X, 140–43; Production Brigade B, 384–85; in implementing Party policies and programs, 437–38; *see also* Political campaigns
Central Committee, *see under* Communist Party
Civil Affairs Section, County X, 159, 216–17, 240
"Class demarcation," 404–6
Class status, 330, 406–8, 443–44; "five [bad] elements," 231–33, 395, 404, 406–7, 410; "four [bad] elements," 402, 404, 406, 407, 408–10
Class struggle, 330–31, 410–12, 437, 443–44
Collective living: Ministry M, 99–103; County X, 138
Collectivization, 95, 102, 125, 314–15; in County A, 323, 332–36; in Administrative Village I, 332–35
Commerce, County X, *see* Finance and trade "system"
Commune C, 339–62; general description and evolution, 339–43; produc-

tion brigades, 339, 341, 342, 358; production teams, 342, 358, 418–24 *passim;* factories, 354; economic functions, 357–62, 377–78; taxation, 359–61; relations with Brigade B, 363, 364, 366–67, 373, 377–78, 386–87, 388, 390; travel restrictions, 394–99; use of sanctions in control system, 399–403; labor reform and re-education, 401–2; structure of leadership organizations, 454 (*figure*); *see also* Brigade B
  departments, 352–57; Finance, 345, 346, 351, 353; Industry and Communications, 345, 351, 354–55; Political and Legal, 345, 346, 351, 352, 390, 391, 403, 408; Administration, 351, 353; Culture, Education, and Health, 351, 353–54, 386; Water Conservancy, 351, 355; Agriculture, 351, 355–56; Commerce, 351, 356; Forestry and Animal Husbandry, 351, 356–57
  organization, 349–52; Commune Management Committee, 344, 345, 349, 350–52, 357; Commune Congress, 349–50; Commune Supervision Committee, 349, 350
  Party in, 343–49; leaders in higher posts (elite), 343; branches, 343, 344; members, 343–44; Commune Committee, 343, 344, 345, 346, 350, 353; County Committee, 344; dominance of, 344–45; top leadership, 346–49, 454 (*figure*)
  subordinate units: Commune Credit Cooperative, 351, 353, 359, 373; Grain Management Office, 351, 353, 359–60, 395, 396; Tax Office, 351, 353, 360; Market Management Committee, 351, 353, 360–61; Agricultural Experiment Station, 351, 355–56; People's Bank, 352, 353, 373; Supply and Marketing Cooperative, 352, 356
Communes, 121; Management Committee, 168; conscription, 244; introduction, 314–15, 320; militia, 315, 316; large units and merger of government and collectives, 316–18; number, 322, 339; establishment in County A, 336–38
Communications, County X, *see* Industry and communications "system"

Communications Political Department, Industry and (Central Committee), 4

Communist Party: as central and ultimate authority, 3, 123, 428–29; "general systems" of command, 8–9, 431–32; leadership and control, 18–37, 177–78, 432–35; "Party life," 19–20, 25–27, 157, 161–64, 369; "study" (indoctrination) system and sessions, 20, 26, 30–32, 164–65, 213–14, 435, 441–42; monopoly of leadership posts, 23–25, 126–33, 177–78, 433–34; political campaigns, 25, 32–35, 50, 69–70, 384–85, 409; recruitment and selection of members, 27–29, 179–81; as elite in the bureaucracy, 35–37, 188–89, 429–36; "red and expert" concept, 54, 431–32, 433; membership in County X, 124–25, 153–57; takeover and reorganization of County A, 325–38; role in modern China, 427–46; centralized power, 428–29; expansion of government functions, 429–31; present status of support, 444–45
    branches, 19–20; Ministry M, 24–25, 27; County X, 125, 153, 157, 158–61, 206; Commune C, 343, 344; Brigade B, 364, 365, 366, 367, 368, 370, 418, 419
    Central Committee: as major Party power, 3, 80, 336, 342n; departments and committees, 4, 6, 18, 49, 80, 86 (see also individual names); relation to Ministry M, 21–23, 64, 71; regional bureaus, 110, 111–13
    committees: provincial, 5n, 73, 242, 336; in Ministry M, 11, 24–25, 26, 27, 31, 32, 33, 48; special districts, 115, 126, 149; County X, 123–29 passim, 132, 133, 137, 138, 140–44 passim, 148, 150, 152, 154, 158, 162, 164, 168, 170–71, 173–74, 183, 189, 195, 196, 199, 206, 208, 216–20 passim, 234, 249, 281, 282, 301, 307; Commune C, 343–46 passim, 350, 353; Brigade B, 364, 367–68, 369, 390
    Control Committee, 4n, 62
    Fractions, 19; Ministry M, 24, 64; County X, 159, 219
    Politburo, 3, 21, 23, 80
    political departments, 4, 5n
    Secretariat, 3, 4, 23n

Standing Committee, 23
    see also subhead "Party in" under Commune C, County X, Ministry M, Production Brigade B

Cooperatives and cooperativization: County X, 296–98, 303, 304; agricultural producers (APC's), 314, 317, 323–24, 336, 337; County A, 332, 334; Credit Cooperative, Commune C, 351, 353, 359, 373; Supply and Marketing, Commune C, 352, 356

Counties: and planning, 82–83; units during Nationalist period, 108–9; changes in system of, 117–18; as most important local administrative unit, 117–20; for analysis of specific topics see also County X

County A, 325–38; development of agricultural producers cooperatives, 323–24; changes and developments in initial Communist takeover and reorganization, 325–28; Party Committee, 326, 331, 336, 337; districts, 327, 332, 334, 335; establishment of communes, 336–38; major administrative and collective subunits (before and after communization), 453 (figure)
    administrative villages, 327, 328–29, 331, 332, 334, 335, 337; Administrative Village I, collectivization of, case study, 332–35

County X, 120–308; general description, 120–22; administrative divisions, 121; local vs. outside leaders, 133–34; mess hall and housing of cadres, 137–38; campaigns and policies, 140–43; work schedules, 193–94; government institutions and activities, 205–309, 458–59 (table); magistrate and deputies, 210–11; system of political control, 219–31; control over "five [bad] elements," 231–33; united front work, 250–51; school system, 260–65
    cadres: Party, 136, 138, 140, 143, 145, 146, 151, 159–68 passim, 181–83, 186, 187, 190, 207, 211, 213, 239, 253; non-Party, 136, 138, 140, 146, 151, 152, 164–67 passim, 181–83, 186, 187, 190, 207, 211, 213, 239, 253; punishments, 145–47, 152, 171; personnel management and control, 161; manual labor by, 172–74; "transfer downward" campaign, 175–76; mo-

County X, cadres (*Continued*)
bility of, 176–79; prospect for advancement, 177, 181–83; seniority, 188–89; other ranking systems, 189–90; salaries, 190–93

departments, 127, 143, 147–51; Seacoast, 122*n*, 127, 128, 158, 194, 197–98; Political and Legal, 127, 128, 129, 131, 158, 159, 194–97, 220, 241; Organization, 127, 128, 131, 136, 141, 144, 145, 146, 151–53, 154, 157, 158, 162–70 *passim*, 173–74, 179–80, 182, 199, 213, 214, 227, 243, 246, 248, 278; Rural Work, 127, 128, 131, 139, 158, 194, 202–3, 276; Propaganda and Education, 127, 128, 143, 158, 164, 194, 199, 200–2, 213, 217, 259, 270, 274, 302; Industry and Communications, 127, 128, 158, 170, 203–4, 247, 270, 299; Finance and Trade, 127, 128, 158, 170, 203–4, 276; United Front, 127, 128, 158, 194, 198–200, 207, 209, 251, 253, 254; Armed Forces, 127, 132 (*see also* Military Service Bureau); heads and deputy heads, 128–29

government organization, 458–59 (*table*); *see also* appropriate subheads

major subordinate units (bureaus, divisions, sections, etc.): Overseas Chinese Affairs Section, 12*n*, 158, 198, 199, 250–54; People's Council, 123, 142, 159, 206, 207–8, 210, 216, 217, 302, 307; People's Political Consultative Conference (PPCC), 128, 198, 208–9, 251, 257; Grain Bureau, 129, 131, 132, 160, 189, 203, 285–90; Special Work Group, 136, 139–40; Personnel Section, 145, 146, 152, 159, 160, 164, 166, 167, 170, 213–14, 220, 226; Finance and Tax Bureau, 145, 156, 160, 203, 227, 290–93; Labor Bureau, 158, 217–18; Education Bureau, 159, 202, 217, 226, 259, 260; Office for Elimination of Illiteracy, 159, 202, 259, 265–67; Bureau of Culture, 159, 202, 259, 268–69; Physical Education and Sports Committee, 159, 202, 259, 274–75; Bureau of Health, 159, 202, 271–74; Bureau of Agriculture, 159, 202, 277–80; Bureau of Agriculture and Land Reclamation, 159, 203, 283; Forestry Bureau, 159, 203, 283–84; Bureau of Industry, 159, 203, 299–300, 302; Construction Bureau, 159, 203, 304–5; Committee on Planning and Statistics, 159, 214–16; Civil Affairs Section, 159, 216–17, 240; Transportation Bureau, 160; Aquatic Products Company, 160, 197, 296; New China Bookstore, 160, 202, 226, 259, 270; Postal and Telecommunications Bureau, 160, 203, 226, 305–6; Communications Bureau, 160, 203, 306–7; Bureau of Commerce, 160, 218, 227, 294–95; Office for the Reform of Private Entrepreneurs, 198, 254–56; Water Conservancy Bureau, 202, 203, 227, 280–83; Cultural Hall and Library, 202, 259, 268–69; Opera Troupe and Movie Team, 202, 259, 268–69; Broadcasting Station, 202, 259, 270–71; People's Bank, 203, 212, 227, 293–94; Agricultural Technology Extension Station, 203, 278; County Veterinary Station, 203, 280; Transportation Management Station, 203, 307–8; Navigation Management Station, 204, 227, 308; People's Congress, 205–7, 209, 210; People's Council Staff Office, 211–13; Market Management Committee, 218, 298; Meteorological Station, 284; *see also* subheads Military Service Bureau, Public Security Bureau

Military Service Bureau, 127, 128, 132, 159, 189, 228, 241–49; conscription, 242–44; militia forces, 244–49

Party: organization and operation, 123–204, 458–59 (*table*); Committee, 123–29 *passim*, 132, 133, 137, 138, 140–44 *passim*, 148, 150, 152, 158, 162, 164, 168, 170–71, 173–74, 183, 189, 195, 196, 199, 206, 208, 216–20 *passim*, 234, 249, 281, 282, 301, 307; growth of, 124–25; Congress, 125–27, 144, 206; branches, 125, 153, 157, 158–61, 206; leaders in higher posts (elite), 126–33, 188–89; Standing Committee, 126, 127–29, 132, 133, 140; key posts, 127, 130–32, 188–89; Control Committee, 128, 143, 144–45, 158, 182, 189; social characteristics of leaders, 129–32; secretaries and deputies, 130–32, 134–35; Committee Staff Office, 131, 135–39, 141, 154; staff secretary-general, 135–36;

cadres in, *see under* subhead "cadres"; total staff, 143; School, 143, 153, 158, 163, 168–69; membership, 153–57; committees and branches, 157; "Party life," 157, 161–64; Fraction, 159, 219; School Branch, 160, 261; classes, 163; "study" (indoctrination) system and sessions, 164–65, 213–14; "rectification" campaigns, 167–68, 169–72; recruitment of members, 179–81; organization, 458–59 (*table*); *see also* subhead "departments"

Public Security Bureau, 128, 144–45, 159, 170, 189, 195, 196, 197, 218, 220–37 *passim*, 238–39, 243, 249, 257, 261, 280, 303–4; control over "five [bad] elements," 222, 231–33, 236; security system, 224–37; policemen, 224–27; weapons control, 228; use of violence, 228–29; control over population movement, 233–34; "social surveys," 234–35; public security reports, 235–37

County Y, 120, 131, 132
County Z, 120, 131, 132
Court, *see* People's Court
Culture, Bureau of, County X, 159, 202, 259, 268–69

Democratic centralism, 3, 436

East China Bureau, 112*n*
Economic functions: Commune C, 357–62; Brigade B, 372–79
Economic "systems," County X, 275–84
Education: Higher Education Department, Central Committee, 4, 5*n*; of cadres and their dependents, Ministry M, 88–90; County X, 260–65; Commune C, 354; Brigade B, 386–88

Factories, County X, 300–4
Finance and Trade Political Department (Central Committee), 4
Finance and trade "system," County X, 284–98
"Five [bad] elements," 231–33, 395, 404, 406–7, 410
Five Year Plan, 111
Forced labor, 401, 402, 405
Forestry: Bureau, County X, 159, 203, 283–84; and Animal Husbandry, Commune C, 351, 356–57

Forestry Political Department, Agriculture and (Central Committee), 4
"Four [bad] elements," 402, 404, 406, 407, 408–10

General Labor Union, County X, *see under* Labor Union
General Political Department, Party, 4*n*
Government: functional "systems," 6–7; "general systems," 6–7, 8–9, 150, 431–32; central control, 35–37, 428–29, 438–39; administrative divisions from central government to county level, 107–16, 452 (*figure*); basic levels defined, 109–10; autonomous regions, 109; autonomous counties, 109, 113; municipalities, 109, 113; centrally administered municipalities, 109, 113, 114–15, 117, 119; great administrative regions, 110–13; districts, 110, 117; provinces, 113–15; autonomous departments, 113, 116; special districts, 115–16; leagues, 116; banners and autonomous banners, 117; central supervisory bodies in Party and government, 456–57 (*table*); *see also* Administration, local; Communist Party
Government, county, *see* Counties; County X
Government, provincial, *see* Provincial governments
Grain: Bureau, County X, 7, 129, 131, 132, 160, 189, 203, 285–90; production, Commune C, 358–60; production, Brigade B, 374, 375–76; production by team, Brigade B, 421–22
Great Leap Forward, 86*n*, 112, 123, 138, 194, 245, 248, 253, 287, 301, 315, 316, 360, 361, 377, 379, 387, 411, 418, 423, 430, 443, 445

Health activities: Bureau of Health, County X, 159, 202, 271–74; Commune C, 354; Brigade B, 388–89
Housing, collective: Ministry M, 99–103; County X, 137–38

Illiteracy: Office for Elimination of, County X, 159, 202, 259, 265–67; People's School for Elimination of, Brigade B, 388

Industry and Communications Political Department (Central Committee), 4

Industry and communications "system," County X, 298–308

Inner Mongolia, 113, 116, 117n

Intellectuals: 155–56, 157; cadre terminology for, 46

International Liaison Department (Central Committee), 4

Kao Kang, 111

Kiangsi, 44, 117n

Labor: Bureau, County X, 158, 217–18; rural mobilization of, 315, 341; reeducation and reform by, 401–2

Labor Union, 20: in Ministry M, 11, 29–30, 69; General, in County X, 143, 159, 164–65, 185–86, 199, 257, 275

Landlords, 33, 229, 330, 404, 405–6, 407–8

Land reform, 124, 228–29, 319, 321, 327–28, 331

Leagues, 116

Liaoning, 116

Local administration, see Administration, local

Lo Jui-ch'ing, 196

Mandarin language, 133–34

Mao Tse-tung, 380, 404

Marxism-Leninism, 31, 380

Masses: lowest social status of, 39; "people's letters" from, 77–78, 139, 201

Mass persuasion, 441–42; County X, 258–59

Mess halls: Ministry M, 99–100; County X, 137–38; communes, 315, 316; Commune C, 341, 342, 374; Brigade B, 374–75

Meteorological Station, County X, 284

Military Affairs Committee (Central Committee), 4

Military Service Bureau, County X, see under County X

Militia, 442; County X, 244–49; County A, 326; Brigade B, 391–94; Commune C, 392–93

Ministries: position in bureaucracy, 3–10, 71; "general systems," 6–7, 8–9; development and functions, 9–10;

chop, or seal, of authority, 13; Party Fractions in, 19; personnel management, 48–63 passim (see also Personnel); patterns of work, 64–70; security system, 65–66; channels of authority and communication, 71–94 passim; downward flow of authority, 72–74; central authority, 74–75; planning activities, 78–84; in-service training and education, 88; publishing, 93; for analysis of specific topics see also Ministry M

Ministry M, 11–103; categories of work, 15–6, relation to Central Committee and State Council, 21–23; salaries and job grades, 41–43; "transfer downward" policy, 51, 60–61; patterns of work, 64–70; meetings, 64–65; secrecy and security-consciousness, 65–68, 102; Staff Office, 65, 96; work schedules, 68–69; channels of authority and communication, 71–94; downward flow of authority, 73–74; central authority and local flexibility, 74–75; official visits to and from, 75–78; role in planning, 82–83, 84; in-service training and education, 88–90; publishing, 93–94; collective living, 99–103; transportation, 99; relation to Party and government hierarchies, 449 (figure)

major subordinate units (bureaus, divisions, sections, etc.), 14–17, 95; Personnel Bureau, 13, 25, 28, 31, 33, 48–49, 52, 56, 87; Bureau of Supervision, 61–63, 77, 87; Planning Bureau, 78–79; Investigation and Research Division, 79; long- and short-range plans divisions, 79, 82; Bureau of Statistics, 85–86; Accounting Division, 87; Finance Division, 87; Systems Division, 87; General Affairs Division, 87, 95–103; Bureau of Finance and Accounting, 87–88; Division of Capital Construction, 87–88; Education Bureau, 88–90; Research Institute, 91–93; Printing Section, 95, 97; Supplies Section, 95, 97; Security Section, 95, 98–99; Mess Hall and Guest House Section, 95, 99–100; Library, 97–98; Housing Management Section, 97, 101–2; Guard Unit, 98

organization, 11–17, 450 (figure);

top leaders and offices, 11–12; minister and deputy ministers, 12; Ministry Staff Office, 13–14; Staff Office and Translation Office for Soviet Experts, 14
  Party in: Party Committee, 11, 24–25, 26, 27, 31, 32, 48; Party organization, 23–25, 451 (figure); Party Branch, 24–25, 27; Party cadres, 24, 26, 28–29, 35, 44–45, 46, 50, 52, 53, 67–68, 91, 93, 101, 103; Party Fraction, 24, 64; "Party life," 25–27; "study" (indoctrination) system and sessions, 26, 30–32; recruitment and selection of members, 27–29; political campaigns, 33, 69–70; political meetings, 68–69
Ministry of Finance, 72, 80, 81, 82, 84, 87
Ministry Staff Office, in Ministry M, 13–14
Minorities, County X, 256–58
Motion pictures: Movie Team, County X, 202, 259, 268–69; in Brigade B, 383
Municipalities, centrally administered, 108, 109, 113, 114–15, 117
Mutual aid teams: County A, 323, 324, 331; Administrative Village I, 333–34

Nationalist period, administrative system, 108–9
National People's Congress, 84; as highest state power, 3
New China Bookstore, 160, 202, 226, 259, 270
New Democratic Youth League, 323, 413; see also Young Communist League
Newspapers, Party, 26, 200–1, 382

Office for the Reform of Private Entrepreneurs, County X, 254–56
Organization Department (Central Committee), 4, 22–23, 49
Overseas Chinese, 395, 396, 406
Overseas Chinese Affairs Section, County X, 122n, 158, 198, 199, 250–54
Overseas Chinese Association, 199, 254, 261; in Brigade B, 413–14

"Party life," 19–20, 25–27, 157, 161–64, 369

Peasant associations, 321, 329, 330, 331, 405, 413; Poor and Lower Middle, Brigade B, 410–11, 413
Peking, 114, 119n
People's Bank, County X, 203, 212, 227, 293–94
People's Congress, 80, 110; County X, 205–7, 209, 210
People's Council: as principal organ of local state power, 110; County X, 123, 142, 159, 206, 207–8, 210, 216, 217, 302, 307
People's Court, 128, 159, 170, 189, 195–96, 206, 229, 237, 239–41, 399–400
People's Daily, 26, 201, 382
"People's letters": in Ministry M, 77–78; in County X, 139, 201
People's Liberation Army (PLA), 4n, 130, 132, 248, 249, 275, 306, 325, 326, 392, 393; conscription for, 241–44
People's Political Consultative Conference (PPCC), 128, 198, 208–9, 251, 257
People's Procuracy, 63, 129, 131, 145, 159, 170, 189, 195–96, 206, 228, 237–39, 399–400
Personnel: of Ministry M, 13, 16–17, 23–25, 27–29, 30–32, 41, 50, 52–54, 55, 58, 61; Bureau, in Ministry M, 13, 25, 28, 31, 33, 48–49, 51, 52, 56, 61 (see also Ministry M above); Party monopoly of personnel units in Ministry M, 20; management, 48–63; "assessments" (evaluations), 50–52, 166–68; "transfer downward" policy, 51, 60–61, 134, 174–76, 337; sources of, 52–54; Section, County X, 145, 146, 152, 159, 160, 164, 166, 167, 170, 213–14, 220, 226; management and control, County X, 161; see also Cadres
Physical Education and Sports Committee, County X, 159, 202, 259, 274–75
Planning, 78–84; role of central authorities, 7; of work, Ministry M, 69–70; Bureau, Ministry M, 78–79; process, 79–81; State Planning Commission, 79, 80, 81; role of Ministry M and provincial departments, 82–83; draft and final plans, 83–84; County X, 159, 214–17, 304–5
Police, see Public Security
Political and Legal Department (Central Committee), 5n

Political campaigns, 25; Ministry M, 32–35, 50, 69–70; Brigade B, 384–85, 409; see also Campaigns

Political control: over "five [bad] elements," 231–33, 395, 404, 406–7, 410; over "four [bad] elements," 402, 404, 406, 407, 408–10

Brigade B, 389–94; public security, 389–91; militia, 391–94; control of travel and food, 394–98; sanctions in system, 399–403, 408

County X, 219–21; methods of control, 229–31

Political departments (Central Committee), in relation to Ministry M, 21–23

Procuracy, see People's Procuracy

Production Brigade B, 363–417; general characteristics and organization, 363–67; relations with Commune C, 363, 364, 366–67, 373, 377–78, 386–87, 388, 390; production teams, 363, 372, 375, 390–91, 415, 418–24; production groups, 364; economic functions, 372–79; factories, 377; mass propaganda and indoctrination, 379–86; campaigns, 384–86; education, 386–88; People's School for Elimination of Illiteracy, 388; Health Station, 388; health, 388–89; public security, 389–91; political control, 389–94; militia, 391–94; control of travel and food, 394–98; use of sanctions in control system, 399–403; social tensions and conflicts, 403–12; Poor and Lower Middle Peasants Association, 410–11; family and other social institutions, 412–17; structure of leadership organizations (Party Branch Committee and Brigade Management Committee), 455 (figure)

organization: Congress, 364, 365; Management Committee, 364, 365, 368, 369, 373, 378, 455 (figure); brigade chief, 365, 366, 367, 368, 370–71, 373, 392, 396; militia chief and office, 365, 366, 368; public security officer, 365, 368, 400; Credit Cooperative, 366, 369, 373–74; Supply and Marketing Cooperative, 366, 369, 376; Propaganda Group, 381, 383; Culture, Recreation, and Drama Group, 381, 383, 384

Party in: Party Branch, 364, 365, 366, 367, 368, 370, 418, 419; Party Branch Committee, 364, 367–68, 369, 390; Party Branch committeemen, 367–68, 370–71, 381; Party dominance, 367–70, 389; Party members in leadership posts, 367, 370–72, 381

Production brigades, 121, 317, 337, 338; number, 322; Commune C, 339, 341, 342, 355; see also Production Brigade B

Production teams, 317, 324, 334, 337, 338; number, 322; Commune C, 342, 358; Brigade B, 363, 372, 375, 390–91, 415, 418–24

Propaganda, 441–42; Department, County X, 127, 128, 143, 158, 164, 194, 199, 200–2, 213, 217, 259, 270, 274, 302; Brigade B, 379–86; Group, Brigade B, 381, 383; see also Education, Political control

Propaganda Department (Central Committee), 4, 26

Provinces: as key units in administrative system, 108, 109, 113–15; great administrative regions responsible for, 111–13

Provincial governments: Party Committee, 5n, 73, 126, 140, 149, 242, 336; "transfer downward" to, 60–61; investigations by Bureau of Supervision, 61–62; delegation of authority to from above, 72–73; visits to Ministry, 77; role in planning, 82–83; under Nationalists, 108–9

Provincial People's Congress, 206

Provincial People's Council, 73

Public security, 442; provincial department, 234; Bureau, County X, see under County X; see also Security

Radio broadcasting: County Broadcasting Station, County X, 202, 259, 270–71; Brigade B, 382

"Rectification" campaign, 167–68, 169–72, 435

"Red and expert" concept, 54, 431–32

Red Flag, 26

Religious groups, County X, 256–58

Rural Work Department, County X, 127, 128, 131, 139, 158, 194, 199, 202–3, 276

Schools, see Education

Seacoast Department, County X, 122n, 127, 128, 158, 194, 197–98

Security, 198; Ministry M, 66–68, 98–99; County X, 221–37, 303–4; Brigade B, 389–94; Commune C, 390–94, 400–1
Shanghai, 114, 119*n*
Shensi, 44
Sinkiang, 113
Social Affairs Department (Central Committee), 5*n*
Social tensions and conflicts, 403–12; *see also* Class struggle
Soviet Experts, Staff Office and Translation Office for, Ministry M, 14
Special districts, 115–16
State Council, 3–4, 64; staff offices, 4, 5, 6, 86; "general systems" of command, 8–9; relation to Ministry M, 21–23, 71; Personnel Bureau, 49; and planning, 80, 81, 82; *see also* Government, Ministries
State Economic Commission, 72, 80, 81, 82, 84
State Planning Commission, 72, 79, 80, 81
State Statistical Bureau, 85, 86
State stores and cooperatives, 295–98
Statistics: Division, provincial department, 82–83; Bureau, Ministry M, 85–86; State Statistical Bureau, 85, 86; Committee on Planning and, County X, 159, 214–16
"Struggle" meetings, 33, 34, 171, 330, 435
Supervision: Bureau of, Ministry M, 61–63, 77; Ministry of, 62, 63*n*

Taiwan, 113, 197, 209, 393, 445
Taxation: Finance and Tax Bureau, County X, 145, 156, 160, 203, 227, 290–93; Commune C, 351, 353, 359–61; Brigade B, 374, 375–76
Tibet, 108, 113

Trade Political Department, Finance and (Central Committee), 4
"Transfer downward" policy, 51, 60–61, 134, 174–76, 337
Transportation, County X, *see* Industry and communications "system"
Tsinghai, 117*n*

United front activities, County X, 250–51; overseas Chinese, 251–54; socialization of business, 254–56; minorities and religious groups, 256–58
United Front Department: Central Committee, 4; County X, 127, 128, 158, 194, 198, 200, 207, 209, 251, 253, 254

Water conservancy: County X, 202, 203, 227, 280–83; Commune C, 355
Wives of Party officials, 35*n*, 54*n*
Women's Association, 20, 323, 329, 336, 337; Ministry M, 11–12, 30; County X, 143, 154, 159, 186; Commune C, 345; Brigade B, 366, 368, 369–70, 413
Women's Work Committee (Central Committee), 4, 5*n*
Working hours, 68–69; 193–94

Yenan cadres, 44, 130, 131, 132, 188
Young Communist League (YCL), 5*n*, 20, 125, 435; Ministry M, 11, 27, 29, 31, 36, 51, 69, 91; County X, 136, 143, 154, 155, 156, 159, 162, 179–80, 183–84, 198, 199, 227, 243, 261, 263, 268; County A, 336, 337; Commune C, 345; Brigade B, 366, 368, 369, 381, 391, 413
Young Pioneers, 184–85
Yunnan, 117*n*

Studies of the East Asian Institute

The Ladder of Success in Imperial China by Ping-ti Ho. New York, Columbia University Press, 1962; reprint, John Wiley, 1964.

The Chinese Inflation, 1937–1949 by Shun-hsin Chou. New York, Columbia University Press, 1963.

Reformer in Modern China: Chang Chien, 1853–1926 by Samuel Chu. New York, Columbia University Press, 1965.

Research in Japanese Sources: A Guide by Herschel Webb with the assistance of Marleigh Ryan. New York, Columbia University Press, 1965.

Society and Education in Japan by Herbert Passin. New York, Bureau of Publications, Teachers College, Columbia University, 1965.

Agricultural Production and Economic Development in Japan, 1873–1922 by James I. Nakamura. Princeton, Princeton University Press, 1966.

The Korean Communist Movement and Kim Il-Song by Dae-Sook Suh. Princeton, Princeton University Press, 1967.

The First Vietnam Crisis by Melvin Gurtov. New York, Columbia University Press, 1967.

Japan's First Modern Novel: Ukigumo of Futabatei Shimei by Marleigh Grayer Ryan. New York, Columbia University Press, 1967.

Cadres, Bureaucracy, and Political Power in Communist China by A. Doak Barnett with a contribution by Ezra Vogel. New York, Columbia University Press, 1967.